GLOBALISATION, CRIMINAL LAW AND CRIMINAL JUSTICE

The book consists of the keynote papers delivered at the 2012 WG Hart Workshop on Globalisation, Criminal Law and Criminal Justice organised by the Queen Mary Criminal Justice Centre. The volume addresses, from a cross-disciplinary perspective, the multifarious relationship between globalisation on the one hand, and criminal law and justice on the other hand. At a time when economic, political and cultural systems across different jurisdictions are increasingly becoming, or are perceived to be, parts of a coherent global whole, it appears that the study of crime and criminal justice policies and practices can no longer be restricted within the boundaries of individual nation states or even particular transnational regions. But in which specific fields, to what extent, and in what ways does globalisation influence crime and criminal justice in disparate jurisdictions? Which are the factors that facilitate or prevent such influence at a domestic and/or regional level? And how does or should scholarly inquiry explore these themes? These are all key questions which are addressed by the contributors to the volume. In addition to contributions focusing on theoretical and comparative dimensions of globalisation in criminal law and justice, the volume includes sections focusing on the role of evidence in the development of criminal justice policy, the development of European criminal law and its relationship with national and transnational legal orders, and the influence of globalisation on the interplay between criminal and administrative law.

Globalisation, Criminal Law and Criminal Justice

Theoretical, Comparative and Transnational Perspectives

Edited by

Valsamis Mitsilegas
Peter Alldridge
and
Leonidas Cheliotis

·HART·
PUBLISHING
OXFORD AND PORTLAND, OREGON
2017

Hart Publishing
An imprint of Bloomsbury Publishing Plc

Hart Publishing Ltd
Kemp House
Chawley Park
Cumnor Hill
Oxford OX2 9PH
UK

Bloomsbury Publishing Plc
50 Bedford Square
London
WC1B 3DP
UK

www.hartpub.co.uk
www.bloomsbury.com

Published in North America (US and Canada) by
Hart Publishing
c/o International Specialized Book Services
920 NE 58th Avenue, Suite 300
Portland, OR 97213-3786
USA

www.isbs.com

**HART PUBLISHING, the Hart/Stag logo, BLOOMSBURY and the
Diana logo are trademarks of Bloomsbury Publishing Plc**

First published in hardback, 2015
Paperback edition, 2017

British Library Cataloguing-in-Publication Data
A catalogue record for this book is available from the British Library.

ISBN: HB: 978-1-84946-474-1
PB: 978-1-50991-381-7

Typeset by Compuscript Ltd, Shannon
Printed and bound in Great Britain by
Lightning Source UK Ltd

To find out more about our authors and books visit www.hartpublishing.co.uk. Here you will
find extracts, author information, details of forthcoming events and the option to sign up for our
newsletters.

TABLE OF CONTENTS

List of Contributors   vii

Introduction   1
Valsamis Mitsilegas, Leonidas K Cheliotis and Peter Alldridge

1. The Concept of Crime and Transnational Networks of Community   7
    Roger Cotterrell

2. The Changing Roles of Social Indicators: From Explanation to
    Governance   25
    David Nelken

3. Illicit Globalisation: Myths and Misconceptions   45
    Peter Andreas

4. Prologue: Political Economy and Policing: A Tale of Two Freudian Slips 65
    Robert Reiner

5. The Failures of Police Legitimacy: Attacks from Within   87
    Margaret E Beare

6. Seeing Like a Small State: Globalisation and the Politics of Immigration
    Detention in the Margins of Europe   113
    Leonidas K Cheliotis

7. The UK and EU Criminal Law: Should we be Leading, Following or
    Abstaining?   135
    John R Spencer

8. The European Union and the Global Governance of Crime   153
    Valsamis Mitsilegas

9. The Interplay of Criminal and Administrative Law in the Context of
    Market Regulation: The Case of Serious Competition Infringements   199
    Christopher Harding

10. Cartel Enforcement: A Product of Globalisation   219
    Michael O'Kane

Index   237

LIST OF CONTRIBUTORS

Peter Alldridge is Drapers' Professor of Law at the School of Law, Queen Mary University of London.

Peter Andreas is a Professor of Political Science and International Studies and the Associate Director of the Watson Institute for International Studies at Brown University.

Margaret E Beare is a Professor at the Osgoode Hall Law School, York University, Toronto.

Leonidas K Cheliotis is an Assistant Professor in Criminology at the Department of Social Policy, London School of Economics and Political Science.

Roger Cotterrell is Anniversary Professor of Legal Theory at the School of Law, Queen Mary University of London.

Christopher Harding is a Professor at the Department of Law and Criminology, Aberystwyth University.

Valsamis Mitsilegas is Head of the Department of Law and Professor of European Criminal Law at Queen Mary University of London.

David Nelken is Professor of Comparative and Transnational Law in Context at the Dickson Poon School of Law, King's College, London.

Michael O'Kane is a Partner and Head of Business Crime at Peters & Peters.

Robert Reiner is Emeritus Professor of Criminology in the Law Department, London School of Economics and Political Science.

John R Spencer is a Professor of Law and Co-director of Centre of European Legal Studies at the Faculty of Law, University of Cambridge.

Introduction

VALSAMIS MITSILEGAS, LEONIDAS K CHELIOTIS
and PETER ALLDRIDGE

Based on contributions from the 2012 WG Hart Legal Workshop at the Institute of Advanced Legal Studies (IALS) in London, this collection of essays addresses the multifarious relationship between globalisation, on the one hand, and criminal law and justice, on the other. The 2012 WG Hart Workshop was organised by the Queen Mary Criminal Justice Centre in collaboration with the IALS. We would like to thank the Institute for its support for the event and Aleksandra Jordanoska for her expert assistance in the preparation of this volume. At a time when economic, political and cultural systems across different jurisdictions are increasingly becoming, or are perceived to be, parts of a coherent global whole, it appears that the study of crime and criminal justice policies and practices can no longer be restricted within the boundaries of individual nation states or even particular international regions. But in which specific fields, to what extent and in what ways does globalisation influence crime and criminal justice in disparate jurisdictions? Which are the factors that facilitate or prevent such influence at a domestic and/or regional level? And how does or should scholarly inquiry explore these themes?

In the opening chapter, **Roger Cotterrell** considers the questions arising from local, national, transnational and international definitions of crime in light of the late Bill Stuntz' distinction between a core and a much wider concept of crime. Similar distinctions recur throughout the history of criminal law theory, back at least as far as Bentham's contempt for Blackstone's use of the distinction between *mala in se* (wrong by nature) and *mala prohibita* (wrong merely because prohibited).[1] On the one hand, crime consists of murder, robbery, assault, rape, theft and few other offences. On the other hand, it covers a much wider range of acts. Cotterrell suggests that, as the state grows more ambitious, and as its connections with international 'networks of community' become wider and stronger, the contours of crime as a category change: the process of politico-legal criminalisation potentially embraces more and more wrongs that are distant from the everyday popular conceptions of crime. Whilst an approach to the definition of crime

---

[1] J Bentham, 'A Comment on the Commentaries' (1776) reprinted in JH Burns and HLA Hart (eds), *Collected Works of Jeremy Bentham* (London, Athlone Press, 1977) 63.

grounded in a need to protect human rights and dignity has drawn support elsewhere, Cotterrell suggests a different approach.

David Nelken, a scholar who has long been at the forefront of the analysis of what can and cannot usefully be done by comparisons between legal systems, interrogates the significance of comparison in both the study and reality of globalisation as it relates to crime and criminal justice. Nelken's introduction of the notion of 'junk comparison', in the context of the increasing use of global quantitative indicators in various areas of criminal justice, is timely. While he disparages comparison by juxtaposition, he explains what the role of indicators can tell us about the changing connections between the local and the global levels of crime and criminal justice. He goes on to describe and contrast three situations or 'moments' in which indicators play a role in and through comparison. The first is where social scientists (or sometimes other actors) try to explain differences in aspects of crime or criminal justice amongst nation states or other units of interest. The second is where legal actors or others make proposals or otherwise act on the basis of their perceptions (right or wrong) of what they think is happening in criminal justice systems or organisations elsewhere. The third is where comparison forms part of efforts to impose general norms relevant to crime and criminal justice more widely and to bring practice elsewhere into line with such standards. He examines the strengths and limitations of each.

Peter Andreas argues that there is much to be learnt about the symbiotic relationship between those who commit crimes related to borders, and the enforcement of those borders. He challenges common myths and misconceptions about the illicit side of globalisation and emphasises the ways in which states shape and even exploit the illicit global economy. He argues that illicit globalisation is not new and its relationship to the state is not only antagonistic but also in some respects mutually profitable. Thus, paradoxically, illicit global market actors are pursued by the state but also kept in business by the state. He argues that this illicit sphere of the global economy is a serious concern, but that sweeping claims of unprecedented transnational crime threats are overstated and that a longer view gives a better perspective.

There follows a powerful argument by **Robert Reiner** for studying contemporary policing through a political economy perspective, necessitated in no small part by the international rise of neo-liberalism and its crucial implications for law and order. Reiner recognises with approval the vigorous resuscitation of political economy approaches to research on punishment since the turn of the millennium, yet his call for a political economy of policing grows out of the mainstream of sociology of the police. That is to say, far from dismissing the vast body of empirical sociological research on policing in a wholesale fashion, as some other critical policing scholars have done previously, Reiner draws on the various methodological and substantive lessons learnt or at least produced from empirical policing scholarship over the years to set the foundations of political economy of policing today.

In her chapter, **Margaret Beare** sheds light on key operations of the police in an increasingly globalised environment, including explicitly politico-economic operations such as the policing of G20 meetings, and examines the ways in which the police attempt to maintain legitimacy, not just in the eyes of the public but also in the eyes of police workers themselves, when new surveillance technologies, international media, national inquiries and commissions of investigation invade institutional secrecy and turn what might be normalised police work into scandal or controversy. Beare demonstrates that once such 'humiliations' are publicised, a 'prisoner's dilemma-type' response is likely to occur, where blame from within is publicly directed in all directions, although this risks further undermining the legitimacy of the force as members may turn on their organisation. Beare's focus is specifically on the police in Canada, yet her findings are relevant internationally as jurisdictions adopt or adapt the 'harmonised' language, policies, technologies and legal requirements of control to the realities of local policing tasks.

Leonidas Cheliotis reaches broadly similar conclusions in his account of the juncture between two phenomena that are both closely associated with globalisation: the rise of irregular international migration over recent decades and the contemporaneous increase in the prominence of international judicial, inspectorate and non-governmental bodies that work in their diverse capacities to ensure that international human rights legislation is observed inside the borders of individual nation states, including by taking steps to pre-empt, stop or redress policies and practices of immigration control that stand in violation of human rights treaties. Cheliotis problematises the effectiveness of such external interventions by focusing on the reactions of Greece, an EU Member State that has been repeatedly reprimanded and punished by international actors for the excessive use of, and inhuman and degrading conditions of, administrative detention of irregular migrants inside its national borders. One might expect states occupying a peripheral position in the international arena to respond positively to pressures from prominent or otherwise powerful actors abroad, but the case of Greece illustrates that being a small power may actually be associated with less effective foreign pressures.

Two contributions in this volume address the work of the European Union, an organisation which has emerged as a prominent global actor in the field of criminal law and justice in recent years. The contribution by **John Spencer** examines the relationship between the EU and its Member States in the field of criminal law by focusing on the impact of the Europeanisation of criminal law and justice on the legal and political system of the United Kingdom. Spencer's analysis of the growing scepticism in the UK towards the production of criminal law norms and institutions by the EU is of particular relevance in the light of the recent decision of the UK government not to accept the full powers of the EU institutions with regard to the so-called EU 'third pillar' measures upon the expiry of the five-year transitional period from the entry into force of the Lisbon Treaty on 30 November 2014. This reluctance to accept the supranational criminal law powers of the EU may come as a surprise in the light of the fact that, as Spencer notes, the UK has in the past promoted European integration in the field, most notably by leading calls for the application of the principle of mutual recognition in criminal matters whose most emblematic expression has been the adoption of the Framework Decision on the European Arrest Warrant. Spencer explains the UK stance on the grounds of the perceived 'moral superiority of the common law' and the misguided belief that Brussels has a master plan to impose a uniform system of criminal justice. The current debate and negotiations on the establishment of a European Public Prosecutor's Office under Article 86 of the Treaty on the Functioning of the European Union (TFEU) demonstrate that a top-down vision of a largely centralised EU criminal law does not necessarily sit easily with the legal and constitutional traditions of EU Member States.

While the contribution by Spencer focuses on the internal dimension of EU criminal law, namely on the relationship between EU law and national law, the chapter by **Valsamis Mitsilegas** considers the external dimension of EU criminal law and justice. The chapter focuses on the emergence of the EU as a global actor in the field of criminal law and justice by establishing a typology of the EU's involvement in and implementation of global measures in the field. Mitsilegas demonstrates that, notwithstanding its internal constitutional and substantive debates on the content and reach of EU criminal law, the EU has played a prominent role in the evolution of the main international initiatives adopted since the fall of the Berlin Wall to address newly prominent security threats including drug trafficking, organised crime, money laundering and, particularly post-9/11, terrorism. The structure of the chapter highlights the multi-level and multi-dimensional character of the globalisation of criminal law by focusing on the role of the EU in the development of 'hard law' international and regional treaties, of 'soft law' instruments including the 40 Recommendations of the Financial Action Task Force (FATF) and of 'global administrative law' measures including terrorist sanctions imposed by the United Nations Security Council. The chapter highlights the quest by EU institutions to achieve synergy between EU criminal law and global initiatives in the field and in doing so to preserve the autonomy of EU law, and demonstrates the EU's increased assertiveness when acting within the wider, pan-European framework of the Council of Europe. The analysis also brings forward the key challenge facing the EU in its emergence as a global actor in criminal matters, namely the extent to which it is feasible to promote the external dimension of EU criminal law without at the same time compromising internal EU substantive and constitutional law, and in particular the very values upon which the Union is based (such as the protection of fundamental rights and safeguarding the rule of law). Mitsilegas discusses these challenges in the context of the *Kadi* litigation, where the European judiciary has attempted to promote the autonomy of EU law and to uphold European values without questioning the authority of the Security Council sanctions system.

The closing chapters in this volume examine a subject which lies at the heart of the globalisation of criminal law, in particular the law of economic crime, namely the relationship between criminal and administrative law. **Christopher Harding** begins his chapter with the question 'what do criminal law and administrative law have in common?' and proceeds to offer a detailed, theoretically and empirically informed, overview of the distinction between criminal and administrative law. The chapter highlights the challenges in achieving a clear distinction between criminal and non-criminal (administrative) law. Harding argues that resort to a penal sanction does not imply that the conduct thereby dealt with is necessarily highly culpable from a moral point of view; and that a high quantum of resulting harm or damage does not imply that the acts leading to that outcome are highly culpable in a moral sense. The chapter then goes on to bring together this general analysis by focusing on the specific case of serious competition infringements, with the author claiming that the possible resort to administrative offences and sanctions may increasingly appear to be a viable option. The relationship between criminal and administrative law in the field of competition law is also analysed in the chapter by **Michael O'Kane.** His chapter contains a comparative analysis of cartel enforcement in a number of jurisdictions including the United States, the UK and the EU. The author highlights the emergence of common worldwide trends, in particular as regards the use of leniency programmes for the purposes of cartel enforcement. However, at the same time, the chapter highlights the limits of these new models of enforcement in a transnational context. O'Kane's analysis raises pertinent questions about the extent to which competition enforcement at the national level can be effective in the absence of a global level playing field.

1

The Concept of Crime and Transnational Networks of Community

Introduction: Politics, Culture and Crime

Is there a need for a concept of crime? Surely debates around this issue have now been played out? Louk Hulsman notes that 'there is no "ontological reality" of crime'.[1] That is, the term seems to refer to no irreducible, distinctive social phenomenon existing independently of legal definition. Crime is what the state (or some international agency authorised by states) declares it to be through law. By designating an offence as 'criminal', state law links it to pre-existing assumptions about the kinds of punishment appropriate for criminal behaviour and, it seems, *any* conduct might be so designated. Crime is what the criminal law in a given society at a given time states it to be. For criminal lawyers in general what matters is the procedure and substance of this law. Moreover, juristically rationalising it is not the same as conceptualising 'crime' as a social entity.

Yet the immense variety of kinds of conduct labelled as criminal sometimes attracts comment and even concern[2] because 'the sheer number of criminal offences has grown exponentially'.[3] In this situation, doubts about the coherence of 'crime' as a category have tended in practice to be pushed aside, so William Stuntz suggested, by making criminal law

> not one field but two. The first [field] consists of a few core crimes . . . The second consists of everything else. Criminal law courses, criminal law literature, and popular conversations about crime focus heavily on the first. The second dominates criminal codes.[4]

* I am grateful to Bill Gilmore, Leonidas Cheliotis, Philip Stenning, David Nelken and Robert Reiner for their comments.

[1] LHC Hulsman, 'Critical Criminology and the Concept of Crime' in J Muncie, E McLaughlin and M Langan (eds), *Criminological Perspectives: A Reader* (London, Sage, 1996) 300.

[2] WJ Stuntz, 'The Pathological Politics of Criminal Law' (2001) 100 *Michigan Law Review* 505.

[3] D Husak, 'Crimes Outside the Core' (2004) 39 *Tulsa Law Review* 755, 768.

[4] Stuntz, 'Pathological Politics', above n 2, 512.

In other words, crime as a basic social category is assumed to be well understood but that understanding may depend on generalisations from some seemingly prominent kinds of criminalisation, often leaving aside much else.

Whatever the truth of this as regards juristic and popular perspectives on crime, criminologists have been concerned with conceptualising crime and have generally divided into two broad camps in doing so. One camp expressly or tacitly adopts a broadly legal demarcation of crime as its practical focus: what the state, through its law, marks out as crime provides criminology with its basic subject matter and its scholarly field. However, for strong intellectual and moral–political reasons, many other criminologists have rejected the idea that the subject matter of their field is given to them by legal–political fiat. Fearing to be 'kings without a country',[5] they preferred to produce their own concept of crime, or to discard crime as a concept in favour of a more independent focus for their knowledge-field.[6] Alongside this, for moral and political reasons, efforts have been made to open up or replace the idea of crime, in order to cover types of behaviour typically not criminalised by state law, or thought to be treated insufficiently seriously by the state, or in which the state and its agents are themselves implicated.[7]

Until recently, such efforts to escape the state law focus have had limited effect. If the state is not to hold a monopoly in declaring what is to count as crime, where else can the authority to define crime be found? If critical criminologists, setting out to challenge state law definitions of crime, have sometimes found a hearing, it is surely because they have appealed to widespread concerns about serious wrong-doing. Their aim has been to link established popular notions about the seriousness of crime to other widely felt social concerns. Beyond popular assumptions that crime is what criminal law says it is, other popular ideas exist as to what are serious social wrongs, what *should* be treated as criminal, and what is 'really' criminal even if law does not declare it to be so. But what authoritative conceptualisations of crime could come from such diffuse popular understandings? Is it possible to speak of a *cultural* authority underpinning ideas of crime, as contrasted with the *political* authority of the state and its juristic servants – 'cultural' broadly referring here to bonds of shared tradition, interests, beliefs, values or emotions that may hold people together in conditions of relatively stable social co-existence? In some circumstances can this cultural authority be important? Studying its character would be an essentially sociological enterprise.

Where the state extends criminalisation beyond certain limits, cultural attitudes might not support this; popular ideas of crimes as *mala in se* (wrong by nature) might be significantly out of alignment with the scope and character of some state *mala prohibita* (acts that are wrong merely because prohibited). The

---

[5] *cf* JM Van Bemmelen, 'The "Criminologist": A King Without a Country?' (1951) 63 *Juridical Review* 24.

[6] See generally, S Henry and MM Lanier (eds), *What is Crime? Controversies over the Nature of Crime and What to Do about It* (Lanham, Rowman & Littlefield, 2001).

[7] See, eg DL Rothe and DO Friedrichs, 'The State of the Criminology of Crimes of the State' (2006) 33 *Social Justice* 147.

same position might arise where the state is seen to 'under-criminalise', to condone impunity or to provide inadequate punishments. More generally, it might arise where the state, in punishing or not punishing, is seen to serve special interests rather than a broad public interest – or where the very idea of public interest becomes confused. Cultural definitions of crime might matter when the state's general practice in criminalising begins to be questioned. Thus, when cultural authority *does* largely support the state's political authority in treating crime, this may depend on the state being seen as a secure, reliable regulator – as holding what Max Weber called a monopoly of legitimate violence in its territory[8] – together with a popular sense that the state and its law represent a relatively stable socio-political and economic order against which crime is easily seen as a serious threat which the state identifies and addresses.

This paper argues that the state monopoly of defining crime is being weakened, especially by the transnational spread of criminal jurisdiction – that is, the increasingly felt need to apply ideas of crime coherently across and irrespective of national boundaries. If this is so, the question of how and by whom the meaning of 'crime' is to be settled assumes renewed importance. What I have termed cultural authority (the authority of popular ideas arising in everyday social life) to shape the concept of crime may have new significance as the political authority to shape it becomes less clear. So, in what follows, suggestions are made of ways in which the state's independent power to determine what is criminal is becoming destabilised or restricted. The question then arises: where can the idea of crime in the transnational context find a supporting input of cultural authority? The answer suggested is in emerging transnational networks of community – networks that now extend beyond the various social networks from which national popular ideas about crime have arisen.

State and Crime: Perspectives from Social Theory

If the state's sole authority to criminalise has usually been popularly accepted this is surely partly because no other authority has seemed sufficiently focused to compete with it. But it may also be because popular assumptions about what the state criminalises have tended to conform to popular views about what crime is. In this respect Stuntz's idea of 'two fields' of criminal law, one known, the other unknown, seems important. What has been popularly seen as the state's management of the idea of crime – and as such accepted as legitimate – has actually been only part of its extensive practice of criminalisation.

---

[8] M Weber, 'Politics as a Vocation' in HH Gerth and CW Mills (eds and trans), *From Max Weber: Essays in Sociology* (London, Routledge & Kegan Paul, 1948) 78.

Some warrant for this view might be found in Weberian and Durkheimian socio-legal theories.[9] Weber has little to say directly about crime, presumably because in his perspective the state's power to criminalise is just one of many regulatory techniques it possesses and can deploy pragmatically. Central to these techniques is the relatively formal character of modern law which sustains the idea of both its autonomy as a rational system and its usefulness as an all-purpose regulatory device, available equally for private purposes and for the state to fulfil its administrative functions. If the modern state typically successfully claims a monopoly of legitimate violence,[10] much of its power, in Weber's view, is exercised through enunciated rules, and administration rather than politics typifies the everyday life of state and society.[11] His emphasis on rational administration easily morphs into more abstract contemporary social theories that envisage systems and networks as somehow taking on lives of their own, perhaps even ultimately unbounded by the jurisdictional reach of nation states.

One might imagine that as the administrative structures and tasks of the state extend and its law proliferates to frame them, the possibilities of criminalisation also expand, but into esoteric areas of regulation that reflect the sheer complexity of modern social and economic organisation – what can be called forms of 'administrative' criminalisation. 'Crime' does not appear at all in the index of the English edition of Weber's magnum opus *Economy and Society*,[12] but we might imagine that, in his typical modern state, categories of *mala prohibita* proliferate. So if criminal law is, indeed, actually two fields – one highly visible in popular consciousness, the other largely unseen – the growth of the unseen part may typify the progress of modernity and the flourishing of the state. Can we then speculate that, as the state grows more ambitious (Weber's theory suggests no strong reasons why it should not) – the process of politico-legal criminalisation potentially embraces more and more wrongs that are distant from everyday popular conceptions of crime – the contours of crime as a category change? Is it the case that no particular problems arise from this divorce from popular conceptions?

Émile Durkheim provides a striking contrast to such an outlook.[13] He too sees the modern state's regulatory capacities and ambitions as vastly expanding; there is surely more and more law. But, unlike Weber, he pays careful attention to assessing how much of it is properly to be seen as penal. Whereas Weber's mod-

---

[9] For a somewhat parallel comparison, see J Terpstra, 'Two Theories on the Police: The Relevance of Max Weber and Emile Durkheim to the Study of the Police' (2011) 39 *International Journal of Law, Crime and Justice* 1.

[10] Weber, 'Politics as a Vocation', above n 8, 78. See also M Weber, *Economy and Society: An Outline of Interpretive Sociology*, Vol I (Berkeley, University of California Press, 1978) 314 ('Today legal coercion by violence is the monopoly of the state').

[11] A striking illustration of this point is that a stable state may be able to continue administrative functions effectively even when political processes fail to produce a government: see, eg G Bouckaert and M Brans, 'Governing without Government: Lessons from Belgium's Caretaker Government' (2012) 25 *Governance* 173; C Devos and D Sinardet, 'Governing without a Government: The Belgian Experiment' (2012) 25 *Governance* 167.

[12] Weber, *Economy and Society*, above n 10.

[13] É Durkheim, *The Division of Labour in Society* (Basingstoke, Macmillan, 1984).

ern state seems to need no specific cultural authorisation for its criminalisation practices, Durkheim's does. Punishing crime has to be seen as a *special* focus of law, to be distinguished clearly from all the many other regulatory objectives which law and state must address. As modern regulation expands, most of this expansion is aimed not at defining and punishing crime but at peacefully and non-violently coordinating and repairing social relations, for example, by guaranteeing compensation, rectifying arrangements turned sour, providing useful administrative structures, and facilitating cooperation and interdependence. Despite all the many new regulatory demands on the state in modern conditions, the idea of crime remains something that 'society', not the state, determines. Thus the state operates through what I earlier called cultural authority in criminalising and punishing.

There is something both powerful and unreal in this Durkheimian picture – a paradox which has long produced deeply polarised views in the criminological literature. Crucially, as regards Stuntz's postulated 'two fields' of criminal law,[14] how does Durkheim analyse the 'unseen' field – the areas of *mala prohibita* largely unknown to most people; the realm of regulatory, technical, managerial, administrative, public health and other offences not necessarily seen as 'wrong in themselves'? Occasionally, Durkheim refers to examples of such offences but they are clearly not his concern and he generally ignores them. When he writes of crime he means something popularly condemned in society and which affronts the moral outlook of the average person. He therefore sees only part of what criminal law addresses. On the other hand, a strength of Durkheim's view is that his idea of crime is something powerful, enduring (despite all regulatory changes) and stable. The political authority of the state (acting on behalf of society) in punishing crime meshes with the cultural authority that makes crime a readily intelligible concept. Crime is a distinct moral phenomenon (however varied the forms it takes). It consists of wrongdoing generally regarded by citizens as constituting such a serious threat to the moral security of society (not just particular interests of individuals) that it is to be repressed by collective action through the agency of the state. Crime, as Durkheim puts it, offends the collective consciousness (or conscience) of society.

From a Weberian perspective, the main problem of transnational criminalisation must be to ensure adequate political authority to regulate appropriately. The key question will be: what happens to the state's monopoly of legitimate violence? Can it be extended transnationally, shared with other states, or somehow conferred on transnational political authorities? In a Durkheimian perspective, however, as ideas of crime become transnational, cultural authority must be found for them if they are to be coherent and meaningful.[15]

The implications can, however, be pushed well beyond anything in Durkheim's writings. If the idea of crime were somehow to be loosened from the state's

[14] Stuntz, above n 2.
[15] S Nimaga, *Émile Durkheim and International Criminal Law: A Sociological Exploration* (*Saarbrücken*, VDM Verlag Dr Müller, 2010).

modern monopoly of criminalisation could it become a focus for potentially unlimited *struggle and dispute*? Does the power to fix the meaning of crime potentially become a political prize to be fought over? If the idea of crime has been used to identify threats to a social order and to justify the use of penal violence to repress these threats, what if *competing* claims are made to harness the idea of crime for such purposes? What if the nature of the threats and their sources are viewed in competing ways? Finally, what if those who could once be securely labelled by the state as criminals now invoke the idea of crime to *condemn the state* and its agents as criminal? The ultimate scenario is that the idea of crime might become uncontrollably contested and unstable. In this way the issue of cultural authority returns to haunt insecure political authority in conceptualising crime and legitimising criminal punishment.

In the transnational development of criminal justice, debates around the meaning of crime surely assume increasing importance. For example, both extradition and extraterritorial law enforcement sometimes attract popular controversy as to whether 'crime' is being given the same meaning in all states involved, or whether one state is seeking to impose its own understanding of crime (and the way it should be dealt with) on another. As transnationalism advances, nationalistic views of crime find new prominence. 'Loose interpretation' of strict dual criminality requirements for transnational criminal justice cooperation,[16] or reliance on 'analogies' between offences in different jurisdictions, can be causes for concern.[17] Popular, nationalistic 'extradition fury' fanned by media reports suggests that the idea of crime is not something to be entrusted entirely to the state to negotiate with other states; cultural resonances are important. This may be the case particularly where extradition offences are outside Stuntz's field of popularly 'known' crimes and so their wrongfulness may depend on technical definition.[18]

Aspects of cyber crime provide other illustrations. Hacking and cyber attacks are not only perpetrated by individuals or organised crime groups targeting state or other public facilities or private bank accounts and databases. They may also be acts of state agencies trying to crush opposition or attack other states.[19] Thus, transnational crime can destabilise distinctions between the state and the criminal, and between cyber crime, cyber terrorism and cyber warfare. The idea of the

---

[16] Requirements that the act for which extradition is sought must amount to an offence in both the requested and requesting state. *cf* JG Kester, 'Some Myths of United States Extradition Law' (1988) 76 *Georgetown Law Journal* 1441, 1461 (claiming that in US practice 'the double criminality requirement often does not mean much'); AE Lardo, 'The 2003 Extradition Treaty Between the United States and United Kingdom: Towards a Solution to Transnational White Collar Crime Prosecution?' (2006) 20 *Emory International Law Review* 867, 890 (noting the 'liberal interpretation of dual criminality espoused by US prosecutors'). Under the European Arrest Warrant procedure the requirement has been either weakened or removed.

[17] Lardo, 'The 2003 Extradition Treaty', ibid, 889–92, 898–902.

[18] Kester, 'Some Myths of United States Extradition Law', above n 16, 1492 (stressing that 'social norms and business ethics and duties vary considerably, and not improperly, even among the Western democracies'); and on UK–US controversies, see Lardo, above n 16, 898–99.

[19] See, eg C Billo and W Chang, *Cyber Warfare: An Analysis of the Means and Motivations of Selected Nation States*, Institute for Security Technology Studies Research Paper, 2004 available at www.ists. dartmouth.edu/docs/cyberwarfare.pdf.

criminal state (or its agents) arises as an aspect of the broader relocation of the state from a position of overall supervisor and controller of criminal justice processes to that of a participant or subject in these processes – sometimes as victim, agent, offender, or promoter or obstructer of criminal justice.

The state is said to be 'losing control over the monopoly of coercion hitherto under its aegis'[20] but it is unwise to generalise so broadly. Certainly, in some cases the state is subject to attacks (from terrorism, corruption and organised crime) which it struggles to criminalise in the face of weakening resources and authority.[21] Instead of being above the criminal fray, some states find themselves in the midst of it, battling to enforce their view of criminality in the face of apathy or controversy – so that the crime label may seem to cease to matter (only the balance of coercive forces counts) or it is harnessed to the interests of those who wish to use it to condemn opposing interests. Otherwise, criminalisation in practice is partially taken from the control of the state through privatisation initiatives or by being entrusted to the care of transnational criminal justice agencies (such as international tribunals) or merely to stronger states with greater power to impose it.

The Concept of Crime and International Criminal Law

The emergence of so-called international criminal law (ICL), especially in the last half century, represents perhaps the most visible emergence of a transnational arena of criminalisation in which some states (or at least their agents) have potentially become subjects (rather than controllers) of criminal justice. It is necessary to say 'some' states because others surely dominate in practice in this transnational arena, lending their continuing monopolies of legitimate force within their territory to guarantee ICL in operation. Because this guarantee is limited, selective and uneven, so that it is currently hard to imagine some state authorities being subject to it, ICL is seen as both embryonic and insecure in its legitimacy.[22] And

---

[20] JH Mittelman and R Johnston, 'The Globalization of Organized Crime, the Courtesan State and the Corruption of Civil Society' (1999) 5 *Global Governance* 103, 123.

[21] See, eg D Garland, 'The Limits of the Sovereign State: Strategies of Crime Control in Contemporary Society' (1996) 36 *British Journal of Criminology* 445.

[22] The issues regularly feature in public debate: eg J Copnall, 'Bashir warrant: Chad accuses ICC of anti-African Bias' *BBC News Africa* (London, 22 July 2010) available at www.bbc.co.uk/news/world-africa-10723869; S Milne, 'If there were global justice, Nato would be in the dock over Libya' *The Guardian* (London, 16 May 2012) available at www.guardian.co.uk/commentisfree/2012/may/15/global-justice-nato-libya#start-of-comments ('there is of course no question of NATO leaders being held to legal account for the Libyan carnage, any more than they have been for more direct crimes carried out in Iraq and Afghanistan … [President Bush] boasted of authorising the international crime of torture and faced not so much as a caution'). For a valuable discussion of legitimacy problems, see R Henham, 'Some Reflections on the Legitimacy of International Trial Justice' (2007) 35 *International Journal of the Sociology of Law* 75, and on 'even-handedness', see E Heinze, 'Even-handedness and the Politics of Human Rights' (2008) 21 *Harvard Human Rights Journal* 7.

although it is called *international* law, it might be best described as transnational[23] because it addresses individuals rather than states, in some cases irrespective of nationality or citizenship.[24]

Like criminal law in national contexts, ICL can be rationalised juristically into a system of thought[25] but it displays no general idea of crime as a social phenomenon. Crime is primarily what the statute of the International Criminal Court and the Court's interpretations declare as offences. The statute lists specific crimes organised under headings of genocide, crimes against humanity, and war crimes; the headings themselves are not defined apart from the specific offences they encompass.[26] The assumption seems to be that – in the light of ICL's history – these offences need only be stated in order to be accepted as instances of crime: a reasonable assumption insofar as they include such matters as 'murder', 'extermination', 'enslavement', 'torture', 'rape', 'causing serious bodily or mental harm', 'enforced sterilization', wanton 'destruction and appropriation of property' and 'pillaging'. Central ideas of crime in ICL are clearly built out of categories of crime accepted in both juristic and popular understandings in all modern western societies – that is, as transnational extensions of ideas of crime in the first of Stuntz's two fields of criminal law; the 'known' field that most obviously defines crime in popular understandings. Beyond these ideas of crime in ICL is, however, much else which invokes, for example, established categories of illegality enshrined in the 1949 Geneva Conventions or in other principles of international law, and includes acts aimed at destroying specific victim groups, wanton destruction of natural environments or cultural heritage, and a range of outlawed weapons and tactics for waging war.

Looked at in terms of possibilities for cultural legitimation, the category of crime in ICL seems a strange compendium – a packaging of disparate elements. These include efforts to 'humanise' modern warfare (for example, outlawing the use of certain types of weapons or tactics) – that is, imposing rules about the way to conduct violence that surely find little or no presence in domestic (national) cultural understandings of crime. They also include concerns about protecting natural and cultural environments, which are present in many western legal systems but often as civil rather than criminal matters, and when criminal, perhaps popularly seen as *mala prohibita* as much as, if not more than, *mala in se*. Finally, they also include much that in popular perception is usually very obviously crime (for example, deliberately inflicting serious harm to a person's body or property

---

[23] EK Leonard, *The Onset of Global Governance: International Relations Theory and the International Criminal Court* (Aldershot, Ashgate, 2005) 6.

[24] G Werle, *Principles of International Criminal Law*, 2nd edn (The Hague, TMC Asser Press, 2009) paras 184–85, 234–35.

[25] See, eg K Ambos, 'Toward a Universal System of Crime: Comments on George Fletcher's *Grammar of Criminal Law*' (2007) 28 *Cardozo Law Review* 2647, 2667–71.

[26] ICC Statute 2187 UNTS 90/37 ILM 1002 (1998)/[2002] ATS 15, Arts 5–8. The statute does add requirements of context, eg that crimes against humanity occur as part of a widespread or systematic attack on a civilian population. A 2010 amendment to the statute now defines the crime of aggression, previously merely signalled in the text.

without lawful excuse). If some kind of popular legitimation is available for ICL it might be hard to spell it out in general terms. But could it be that this is not needed; that adequate politico-legal authority, relying on the combined monopolies of violence possessed by the treaty-supporting states, sustains the somewhat incoherent transnational concept of crime?

Politico-legal authority alone seems, however, an unstable basis for extending transnationally the concept of crime. The spectre of victors' justice that has hung over ICL since the Nuremburg trials is now transformed into a suspicion that ICL is a means by which some states try to impose a global criminal justice system on other (usually weaker) ones, so that the concept of crime is a mechanism of military-police control extended beyond the national arena to control foreign populations, perhaps by analogy with the 'dangerous classes' or 'under-classes' addressed by state criminal justice. It may be that the only way to avoid ICL being seen in this way is to identify clearly forms of cultural legitimation on which it can draw, but also to recognise that under current conditions there is no single global culture that can fully legitimise a transnational concept of crime. Instead, what may exist are important networks of community, existing not only within nations but also transnationally, that can support the extension of ideas of crime across national boundaries.

The serious violent acts that constitute crimes against humanity according to the legal definitions may seem to epitomise 'crime' so obviously that universal cultural authority for their recognition is undeniable – the cultural appeal is to a global idea of 'humanity'. But what one population sees as atrocities can sometimes be dismissed by another as justified retaliation; wanton destruction can appear as collateral damage; targeted killings as suppressing terrorism; and terrorist violence as action against injustice and to achieve freedom. Where killing, rape, enslavement, appropriation of property and so on are directed against people seen as enemies or as utterly alien, their criminal character is sometimes totally denied. A popular understanding of crime presupposes a degree of solidarity in a network of community, whether that network is national or transnational. It is doubtful whether 'humanity' designates such a communal network of solidarity today, except as an aspiration for the future.[27] However, something less may exist – an evolving transnational arena in which some ideas of human rights and human dignity are acquiring relatively stable meanings and can thus inform criminalisation.

Without stable cultural understandings of crime its politico-legal designation risks ongoing challenge, especially because, being ultimately guaranteed by the authority of states, it cannot escape controversy about the extent of this state authority. Attitudes to war as an instrument of the state reveal this starkly. During the twentieth century the idea became established that criminal liability could arise from the mere pursuit of war by states (as distinct from anything occurring

---

[27] *cf* CC Gould, 'Transnational Solidarities' (2007) 38 *Journal of Social Philosophy* 148.

in the course of that pursuit).[28] Therefore, to that extent, the rights of nation states in international law were scaled down. The military historian Martin van Crefeld writes: 'Once the legal monopoly of armed force, long claimed by the state, is wrested out of its hands, existing distinctions between war and crime will break down.'[29] One consequence could be that war (involving invasion, military intervention and imposed regime change), although distinguished legally in modern times from the idea of punishment, might come to be treated as a sanction against criminal activity by states. One writer has suggested that the idea of war as punishment 'remains alive and well in the moral imaginations of modern societies, even if diplomats and lawyers carefully scrub it from official justifications for armed conflict'.[30] While he rejects this view of war he sees no reason why states, like corporations, should not be capable of assuming criminal responsibility.

The idea of criminal acts by states has been debated juristically, but it has been suggested that such acts should not be called crimes 'as they do not provoke punishment in a way analogous to that of domestic law'.[31] Punishability is surely a key issue. However, various sanctions against states are possible including: economic sanctions (which might be analogised to fines in domestic law); isolation, boycott or exclusion as a 'pariah' from the international intercourse of states (which might be analogised to exclusion from 'the social' produced by imprisonment of an offender); or military action to effect regime change (which might even be imagined as 'capital punishment' of a state). These speculations remain unreal if acts against an 'offender' state are seen only as serving the special interests of another state (or a limited coalition of states). Such acts could only be legitimised as punishment if they were aimed at addressing not the 'private' interests of particular aggrieved states,[32] but serious threats to the 'international community' of states as a whole; that is, if they constituted action to protect the existence of a common transnational socio-political order which international criminal justice is seen to serve.

Generalising to current forms of transnational criminalisation, two basic requirements for a transnational concept of crime are highlighted by this discussion: first, the existence of *mechanisms to punish offenders*, and second, *transnational networks of community* on behalf of which criminalisation and punishment is undertaken. Efforts to address the first of these requirements are being made through transnational cooperation between states. The streamlining of extradition and European Arrest Warrant procedures, on the one hand, and the willingness of coalitions of states to engage in humanitarian intervention, on the other, represent strongly contrasting examples (whatever controversies may surround

---

[28] Werle, *Principles of International Criminal Law*, above n 24, part 6.
[29] Quoted in S Cohen, 'Crime and Politics: Spot the Difference' (1996) 47 *British Journal of Sociology* 1, 16.
[30] D Luban, 'War as Punishment' (2011) 39 *Philosophy & Public Affairs* 299, 300–301.
[31] Nimaga, *Émile Durkheim and International Criminal Law*, above n 15, 62.
[32] That war is usually a matter of such 'private' inter-state conflicts is a key reason why Luban in 'War as Punishment', above n 30, denies that it can be accepted as a form of punishment.

them). However, the nature of transnational social networks supporting crimi-nalisation needs much more analysis. References to an 'international community' or 'community of humanity'[33] served by ICL remain for the most part purely rhe-torical because they are ungrounded in any sociological inquiry about what 'com-munity' might mean and what kind of existence it might have.

Locating Ideas of Crime in Networks of Community

This paper has referred to cultural (as contrasted with politico-legal) authority to conceptualise crime. That cultural authority can best be seen as arising in many different networks of social relations of community.[34] Bonds of community of varying degrees of stability or fluidity, transience or permanence, can arise from: common or convergent interests; shared beliefs or ultimate values; co-existence in particular cultural or physical environments; or emotional allegiances. In social life, these four very different types of communal bonds are combined (often with some types dominating) in social networks of varying size, complexity and stabil-ity: examples would include: trading or financial networks; networks of religious believers; social or ideological movements; ethnic or kinship groups; and local or linguistic populations linked primarily by co-existence in the same territory or by sharing common history or traditions. Membership of such networks overlaps; people move in and out of and are usually involved simultaneously in many of them. Crucially today, such networks of community can be not merely national in extent but also intra-national or transnational – thus, not limited in their extent by the boundaries of nation states. Just as emerging forms of transnational law can be seen as finding (or needing) cultural bases of authority in such transna-tional networks,[35] so can transnational ideas of crime.

Can anything be said in general terms about ideas of crime that could emerge from such communal sources? It was noted earlier that, when scholars' efforts to replace politico-legal definitions of crime have gained a sympathetic hearing, this is likely to be because, in various ways, they have reflected widespread popular ideas about crime. Three such broad approaches in criminological and penologi-cal literature seem most prominent. The first is a *social harm conception* of crime, richly elaborated in various ways. On this view the essence of crime (or perhaps the fundamental problem that legal ideas of crime only partly address) is serious

---

[33] See, eg M Renzo, 'Crimes against Humanity and the Limits of International Criminal Law' (2012) 31 *Law and Philosophy* 443, 454, claiming that accountability for crimes against humanity is 'to the members of the international community (rather than just to their fellow citizens)'.

[34] On the idea of networks of community as the locus of law and as sources of legal authority, see R Cotterrell, *Living Law: Studies in Legal and Social Theory* (Aldershot, Ashgate, 2008) 17–28; and gen-erally, R Cotterrell, *Law, Culture and Society: Legal Ideas in the Mirror of Social Theory* (Aldershot, Ashgate, 2006).

[35] R Cotterrell, 'What is Transnational Law?' (2012) 37 *Law & Social Inquiry* 500.

social harm or injury,[36] or the creation of danger, significant risk or insecurity to individuals or society. The second approach views *crime as upsetting a 'moral balance'* in society, so that justice requires punishment of the offender to re-establish this – to proclaim society's condemnation, its recognition and its judgement of the gravity of the wrong done; in this perspective, law in practice might not always provide what criminal justice is thought to require.[37] The third approach is grounded in a *need to protect human rights and dignity* so that what the idea of crime recognises (or should recognise) are serious denials or attacks on basic conditions of life that humans are entitled to enjoy.[38]

In the context of discussion here, these approaches suggest possible broadenings of or amendments to politico-legal ideas of crime – ones that might reflect sentiments, interests, values or traditions not always seen as fully reflected in criminal law. Because these approaches tend to focus on what crime does, more than on the nature of the criminal, some criminologists extend them to embrace not only acts of individual offenders but also those of corporations, groups, states, state agents or international organisations[39] and even – at the extreme – to include wrongs (such as poverty, racism, sexism, imperialism, colonialism and exploitation) that are not necessarily seen as always having specific, identifiable agents. On the other hand, doubts among critical criminologists themselves about such ideas being 'too woolly and polemical'[40] may suggest that they go beyond what most popular ideas of crime will encompass. Jeffrey Reiman, criticising such expansive concepts of crime, claims: 'Individuals think about their actions, they respond to arguments and moral considerations, and their actions are subject to their choices. None of this applies easily to groups or structures.'[41] Thus, he argues, the idea of individual responsibility is basic to most contemporary ideas of crime. Extensions outside it will need special justification.

To go beyond these limited suggestions about conceptualising crime it is necessary to return to the notion of networks of community. No meaningful concept of crime could encompass *all* kinds of popularly recognised harms, injustices or infringements of rights. What could distinguish those that are covered? Crime surely involves some harm, injustice or dehumanising right-infringement produced by the acts of others in *a common social environment* (embracing both victim and offender) that presupposes basic conditions for co-existence in it. Absence of such a common environment can, as noted earlier, make ideas of crime so controversial as to be practically unworkable. Thus popular ideas of crime in fact presuppose the context of some network of community. Even if it is individuals

---

[36] See, eg K Lasslett, 'Crime or Social Harm? A Dialectical Perspective' (2010) 54 *Crime, Law and Social Change* 1.

[37] *cf* RL West, 'The Lawless Adjudicator' (2005) 26 *Cardozo Law Review* 2253 (on the 'criminal' judge).

[38] For discussion of these various orientations see, eg Henry and Lanier, *What is Crime?*, above n 6.

[39] DO Friedrichs and J Friedrichs, 'The World Bank and Crimes of Globalization: A Case Study' (2002) 29 *Social Justice* 13.

[40] Cohen, 'Crime and Politics', above n 29, 6.

[41] J Reiman, Book Review (2006) 46 *British Journal of Criminology* 362, 363.

who are victims of crime, the seriousness of the crime has to be judged ultimately by its consequences in that network as a whole. If criminal punishment rather than individual redress is required, it is because the wrong is viewed as sufficiently serious to threaten the order or security of the entire communal network, the general ideas of justice widely presumed within it, or the basic conditions of trust and interdependence (solidarity) that underpin it. People can be passionate about crime because they treat it as a threat to the way that social life – that is, the networks of community in which they see themselves as involved – must be organised.

This is a view of crime that is clearly much closer to Durkheimian than Weberian perspectives. Weber's image of powerful modern states extending their regulatory capacities suggests a growing scope of what I earlier called administrative criminalisation (focused on managing socio-economic complexity) and it allows us easily to imagine its expansion transnationally through the cooperation of states, but it does not address issues of cultural authorisation of ideas of crime. Thus it is necessary to see, through some examples, how ideas of crime might be shaped and stabilised by transnational networks of community and what the limits of any transnational cultural legitimation of ideas of crime may be.

The international crime of piracy provides an interesting illustration since it seems, both historically and today, the perfect example of a globally recognised crime, long established in international custom and supported by universal jurisdiction. The nationality or state allegiance of both offenders and victims is largely irrelevant, and the authorities of any state have authority in international law to prosecute piracy. The pirate is said to be the 'enemy of all humanity' (*hostis humani generis*) and criminally punishable on this basis.[42] Is this then a rare example of criminalisation supported by a genuinely universal (global) network of community – a true community of humanity? Perhaps unfortunately, the answer has to be negative. What supports this idea of crime is not a global community of belief or ultimate values (perhaps focused on universal human rights and dignity) but rather the existence of common or convergent interests in transnational trade. The relevant network of community is primarily economic in nature. States now address piracy to protect their nationals from physical harm, but more fundamental (certainly in establishing customary piracy jurisdiction) is the need to protect property and *economic interaction* via the high seas or air routes.[43] In this respect states act on behalf of transnational trading networks from whose welfare and success they benefit.

Much other transnational criminalisation is similarly grounded in the interests of transnational economic networks. Hence its cultural legitimacy comes from

---

[42] See, eg KC Randall (1988) 'Universal Jurisdiction under International Law' (1988) 66 *Texas Law Review* 785, 792–95.

[43] Piracy is defined as a crime committed for 'private' (ie typically economic rather than political) purposes and under old customary international law it covered robbery but not murder: see, eg E Kontorovich, '"A Guantanamo on the Sea": The Difficulty of Prosecuting Pirates and Terrorists' (2010) 98 *California Law Review* 243, 252–53.

those networks – not from any wider constituency of global authorisation. Much administrative criminalisation (the phrase, though not Weber's, surely reflects the outlook of his socio-legal theory) is concerned to facilitate effective instrumental relations on which the increasingly complex structures of productive economic interaction across national boundaries depend. Crimes of money-laundering, fraud, counterfeiting, insider-trading, corruption, price-fixing, racketeering, environmental pollution and so on, proliferate in this context. However, many of these crimes are poorly understood by most people; the exact nature of the criminality involved – the practical meaning of these crimes – is mainly given by understandings internal to the (primarily) economic networks of community (for example, business and financial networks, and networks of state and international enforcers policing them) that are involved. Hence what might be readily understood in these networks as crime – as *mala in se* – might well be seen outside them as criminality only in some vague sense: as offences because designated as such – *mala prohibita*.[44]

In this light Durkheimian approaches to understanding crime in transnational contexts surely need substantial modification to be convincing. Transnational crime in general cannot be seen as an affront to some all-embracing transnational collective consciousness.[45] The idea of such a global consciousness as a basis of universal cultural authority for criminalisation is a myth, just as the idea of a global 'international community' is a mythical foundation of a universal politico-legal authority. More plausible is the idea of limited transnational networks relying on different kinds of dominant relations of community. Many are networks of primarily instrumental (economic) community. Others are territorially-based – regional networks dominated by traditional relations of community based on co-existence in a single environment. Often there is overlap: so that the European Union's transnational criminal law can be seen as supported by the nature of the EU as both a region of geographically and historically determined co-existence (a matter of common fate and common tradition) and a relatively integrated economic network (a matter of increasing instrumental interaction in industry, commerce and finance). However, it might also be seen as based in a Europe-wide community of belief in 'European values' – lending it cultural authority, or even in an emotional allegiance to a presumed distinct European identity requiring protection.

Despite its difficulties, the Durkheimian understanding of crime as related to a collective consciousness – a set of beliefs and ultimate values held in common by people and uniting them in social relations of community – should not be discarded. Durkheim saw this collective consciousness as a reality in modern political societies, however limited the scope of universally shared beliefs and values might have become in complex, diverse modern life. He saw 'moral individual-

---

[44] By contrast, attacks on the person and property (homicide, theft etc) that threaten local environments of co-existence are easily and widely 'visible' as crime insofar as these environments are essential to life.

[45] Henham, 'Some Reflections on the Legitimacy of International Trial Justice', above n 22, 84–85.

ism' – the value system that defends the autonomy and dignity of every human being as of equal value – as not only possible but necessary as the overarching moral bond of complex modern societies. Only by treating every other person as of equal human worth with oneself would it be possible to relate constructively with people in conditions where their experiences, lifestyles, aspirations and understandings might differ radically. Durkheim thus saw moral individualism – which can be seen as the prototype of universal human rights discourse – as essential for basic solidarity in diverse, complex and fragmented modern societies.[46]

If the value system of moral individualism is very limited in scope (it leaves much to be filled in as to what dignity and autonomy entail) it is nevertheless powerful in its demands. As regards criminal law it mandates condemnation of fundamental human rights violations but also humane treatment of offenders and prisoners. It outlaws all cruel and unusual punishments, including capital punishment, and it marks out all serious physical and psychological harms deliberately inflicted on individuals (whether free citizens or prisoners in custody) as the most important crimes. Hence, one might think, this value system offers powerful moral authority to support international criminal law in many of its most central designations of offences.

Up to a point this is so. ICL can be seen as gaining cultural authority from a transnational network of community held together primarily by a common commitment to beliefs and ultimate values centred on human rights. Its authority not only derives politically from the acceptance by states of the Rome Statute and the jurisdiction of the International Criminal Court, but also comes from the fact that this law and its court reflect a widely-held popular aspiration to the realisation of humanitarian values. However, it seems important to accept that this network of community is not worldwide. It co-exists with other networks that may espouse different beliefs or values or may not be characterised by any public agreement on ultimate values or beliefs. It is sometimes said, indeed, that the human rights constituency reflects a specifically European experience, with which non-European states and populations may or may not find reasons to link themselves. The idea of networks of community emphasises always the *relativity* of cultural authority: the diversity and contingency of its locations.

Though human rights embodying the values of an international community are often said to underpin ICL it is important to note that Durkheim's value system of moral individualism is justified, not juristically or philosophically but *sociologically as appropriate to complex, secular, highly diverse modern societies*. This value system is necessary (even if often violated in practice) to unite and underpin networks of interdependence in such societies. One could speculate that, insofar as more and more of the world takes on the characteristics of these societies, moral individualism will spread, extending a transnational network of community emphasising human rights understood in a western European sense. But in a

---

[46] R Cotterrell, 'Justice, Dignity, Torture, Headscarves: Can Durkheim's Sociology Clarify Legal Values?' (2011) 20 *Social & Legal Studies* 3.

sociological view this extension might not be inevitable. Ideas of human rights remain the property of certain networks of community, not of a 'community of humanity'.

Conclusion: The Relativity of the Concept of Crime

As argued earlier, crime, treated as a cultural rather than a purely politico-legal idea, is best seen as action threatening the existence of a network of community – its basic conditions of order, underlying ideas of justice or fundamental supports of solidarity. Because there are innumerable networks of community reflecting different combinations of communal bonds – common interests, shared beliefs or ultimate values, emotional allegiances and rejections, or the mere fact of co-existence in a common environment – it follows that ideas about crime will vary. Crime is a relative idea, rooted in specific social settings. The idea of criminal responsibility presupposes not some irreducible characteristics of human beings, but a *social environment* that gives meaning to the concept of crime. Insofar as states retain the monopoly of legal violence in their territory, any cultural legitimacy comes from the national political society as a communal network. However, as criminalisation increasingly crosses state boundaries or even ignores them, this social environment to give cultural legitimacy must itself become transnational.

Thus criminalisation must reflect transnational ideas of order, justice and solidarity. If it does not do so the popular support it obtains for law enforcement may be inadequate. Like all transnational law, transnational criminal law has to find secure grounding in populations that can culturally 'own' this law. To ignore that requirement is to risk stretching the politico-legal authority of regulation beyond the point where its success can be assumed. The message is hardly new. It is one that the pioneer of sociology of law, Eugen Ehrlich, taught a century ago: official state-created and state-supervised law, if it is to be strong, has to take account of the 'living law' of popular experience: in this paper's terms – politico-legal authority has to be grounded in cultural authority.[47]

The relativity of the concept of crime as understood in networks of community is certainly troubling in important respects. Relations of community judged valuable by the members of a network may sometimes be condemned as pathological and evil when viewed from outside it. Moreover, what is seen as criminal in one such network may be the opposite in another. Within Nazi networks of community shaped by a common purpose of organising genocide, any form of brutality could be justified for the larger shared aims. Such networks were also based, for some members at least, on bonds of shared belief. Individuals challenging such

---

[47] E Ehrlich, *Fundamental Principles of the Sociology of Law* (New Brunswick, Transaction Publishers, 2002, reprint).

aims and beliefs in any way could be and often were judged as criminals.[48] Today, from the standpoint of some transnational networks of community united especially by shared beliefs, Western secular states can be condemned as criminal. At the same time, acts condemned in many networks of community as terrorist crimes can be hailed in others as heroic deeds. Again, economic networks of community may have different 'internal' conceptions of acceptable or expected behaviour, so that what might be seen in one communal context as corrupt or otherwise criminal could be seen in another as normal and necessary practice. In addition, transnational networks of community may exist specifically to pursue enterprises that are seen as obviously and seriously wrongful (transnational organised crime) beyond them.

As transnational processes of criminalisation accelerate, the problem of different understandings of the nature of crime may be addressed partly by forceful repression of some understandings by others – as in the destruction of the Nazi regime in war and the criminalisation of its leaders. In such circumstances, the old Weberian claimed monopoly of legal violence by the nation state is transformed into organised repression by coalitions of international states, or by international agencies supported by adequate military power supplied by states. In other cases, forms of coercion, influence or persuasion not involving the use of military force may be available. Broadly speaking, it is necessary to envisage the process of transnationalisation of crime on two planes. The first is that of the *political* relations between states, and the dynamics of international organisations supported by the politico-legal authority of states. The other is that of *intercultural* dialogue, involving the interaction, interpenetration and eventual coordination of networks of community.

Durkheimian theory gives some grounds for predicting the ongoing spread of ideas of human rights, though not necessarily their global universalisation or the removal of major differences of interpretation of their meaning. On both the politico-legal and the cultural planes, however, it seems clear that the ongoing transnationalisation of the idea of crime will be pursued most effectively and enduringly through negotiation and compromise. This, in turn, will depend on an ongoing effort to translate, transnationally, innumerable communal understandings of what can be assumed as universal aspirations for order, justice and solidarity. The possibilities and limits of that process indicate the extent to which the concept of crime can acquire stable transnational content.

---

[48] HW Koch, *In the Name of the Volk: Political Justice in Hitler's Germany* (London, IB Tauris, 1989).

2

The Changing Roles of Social Indicators: From Explanation to Governance

Does it still make sense to think about criminal justice systems in terms of separable national jurisdictions at a time of international and even global links between crime threats and criminal justice responses? More exactly, to what extent is a global 'gaze' on crime threats possible and desirable? Can such a perspective avoid the risk of taking as global what is in fact local? As these questions suggest, there is increasing recognition that the globalisation of the 'local' depends on the localisation of the (supposedly) global and that this is not just a matter of impersonal macro-social forces but also involves agents who bring this about[1]. But so far there is little agreement on how best to study these processes.

In this paper I shall try to take the current debate on such matters further by focusing in particular on the role played by (global) social indicators in constructing comparisons and making evaluations. Indicators are especially well established in discourses that aim to produce demographic, economic, financial, social data about world societies. They are a staple of quantitative social science explanations, especially, but not only, in comparative research across countries and cultures. At the same time, in showing how a given country, place, organisation or individual stands in relation to others, they are also essential to a wide range of policy science evaluations.[2] Whilst broadly supporting their use in the monitoring of human

---

* Contributors to the workshop 'Comparative Criminal Justice in a "Global" Age' on which this collection is based, were invited, inter alia, to 'examine the reasons why and the ways in which crime and criminal justice should be studied in a comparative and international context, especially against the background of globalisation. Areas to be covered included: How is globalisation to be defined in relation to such trends as the ascendancy of neoliberal capitalism, the advent of 'late modernity', or the emergence of 'risk society'? To the extent that global or globalising trends affect the various spheres of society and criminal justice within nation states, which should be our analytical foci, operations and tools?

[1] See J Savelsberg, 'Globalisation and States of Punishment' in D Nelken (ed), *Comparative Criminal Justice and Globalisation* (Farnham, Ashgate, 2011); and J Muncie, 'On Globalisation and Exceptionalism' in D Nelken (ed), *Comparative Criminal Justice and Globalisation* (Farnham, Ashgate, 2011).

[2] It would be interesting to know why (evidence-based) policy evaluation is now so much in vogue after being so out of favour in the 1980s. In our own field it is enough to think of disillusion over the value of studying 'what works', or the criticisms that followed attempts to predict dangerous offenders. It may just be fashion but the answer could also have something to do with the increasing need to operate at the international level.

rights violations, academics find the way that they are employed in ranking their own institutions or scientific contributions somewhat more controversial!

The concern here, however, is not with the merits of indicators in general, or given indicators in particular. Rather, it has to do with what the role of indicators can tell us about the changing connections between the local and the global levels of crime and criminal justice. Following a short survey of the difficulties posed by globalisation to traditional kinds of comparative research, I will go on to describe and contrast three situations or 'moments' in which indicators play a role in and through comparison. The first of these is the familiar one where social scientists (or sometimes other actors), try to explain differences in aspects of crime or criminal justice amongst nation states or other units of interest. The second 'moment' is where legal actors or others make proposals or otherwise act on the basis of their perceptions (right or wrong) of what they think is happening in criminal justice systems or organisations elsewhere. The third is where comparison forms part of efforts to impose general norms relevant to crime and criminal justice more widely and to bring practice elsewhere into line with such standards.

I shall use the important recent debate about the so-called 'punitive turn' in crime control, as measured by differences in incarceration rates, as an illustration of the need to give attention to all three of these 'moments'. However, I will be arguing that the implications of distinguishing these moments of comparison go well beyond this. I conclude by reflecting on the way such 'moments' are (increasingly) affecting each other. This will suggest that, increasingly, our job as comparativists is not only to offer our own comparisons but to understand how others compare, and even more, to appreciate how (some) comparisons become accredited facts – and standards – in the world.

The Challenge of Globalisation to Criminal Justice

Increasingly, worldwide interconnections of trade, information and other forms of exchanges and interdependence are coming to replace more local ones.[3] The consequences of what is commonly categorised as globalisation for the economic fortunes of countries, cities or parts of them, means that the causes of ordinary crime problems, and not only those perpetrated by transnational criminal organisations, often have little to do with the unit in which they are located.[4] As it blurs the differences between existing 'units', globalisation changes the meaning of place and the location and significance of boundaries In addition, different kinds

---

[3] See D Nelken, 'Afterword: Studying Criminal Justice in Globalising Times' in D Nelken (ed), *Comparative Criminal Justice and Globalisation* (Farnham, Ashgate, 2011) on which this section largely relies.

[4] D Nelken, 'The Globalisation of Crime and Criminal Justice: Prospects and Problems', in M Freeman (ed), *Law and Opinion at the End of the 20th Century*, Current Legal Problems (Oxford, Oxford University Press, 1997).

of units emerge both as objects and as agents of control. As one leading author puts it 'one can no longer study, for example, Italy by simply looking at what happens inside its territory, but rather need to acknowledge the effects that distant conflicts and developments have on national crime and security concerns and vice versa'.[5]

However, comparative criminal justice textbooks and readers still reveal considerable uncertainty about how best to integrate the effects of globalisation into traditional classificatory and descriptive schemes. Material that fits awkwardly into the normal comparative paradigm is sometimes relegated to a separate book,[6] to an early chapter,[7] or a closing one.[8] Titles such as Winterdyk and Cao's *Lessons from International/Comparative Criminology/Criminal Justice* signal that a variety of related topics are being dealt with – but do not say how, if at all, they may be connected.[9] Sheptycki and Wardak distinguish 'area studies', 'transnational crime issues' and 'transnational control responses'[10] although they admit that more needs to be said about whether the account of a country's criminal justice system should focus more on internal factors or on external influences.[11] Even Crawford, in his valuable introduction to a collection on *International and Comparative Criminal Justice and Urban Governance*, admits that the chapters themselves are only 'loosely connected parts'.[12]

In general, although there has undoubtedly been an increase in interest in global criminological issues, so far this has not displaced the older type of comparative enquiries which principally devote themselves to explaining differences in national laws, ideas and practices across different jurisdictions. Conversely, studies of the best ways to respond to supposed transnational threats or to defend human rights often pay too little attention to the difficulties of comparative enquiries, except perhaps to lament the obstacles created by differences between places. This can be explained, to some extent, by the fact these endeavours have different aims and audiences. Nevertheless, trying to keep comparative and

---

[5] K Aas, *Crime and Globalization* (London, Sage, 2007) 286. See also K Aas, 'Victimhood of the National? Denationalizing Sovereignty in Crime Control' in A Crawford (ed), *International and Comparative Criminal Justice and Urban Governance* (Cambridge, Cambridge University Press, 2011).

[6] PL Reichel, *Handbook of Transnational Crime and Justice*, 4th edn (London, Sage, 2007).

[7] PL Reichel, *Comparative Criminal Justice Systems*, 5th edn (Upper Saddle River, Prentice Hall, 2007).

[8] H Dammer, E Fairchild and JS Albanese, *Comparative Criminal Justice* (Belmont, Thomson, 2006).

[9] J Winterdyk and C Liqun (eds), *Lessons from International/Comparative Criminology/Criminal Justice* (Whitby, De Sitter, 2004).

[10] J Winterdyk and L Cao (eds), *Transnational and Comparative Criminology* (London, Glasshouse Press, 2005).

[11] ibid. It may be plausible that the account of criminal justice in Saudi Arabia in their book treats the country as autonomous (though more could have been said about its pan-Islamic mission.) However, it is less obvious why the chapter on South Africa focuses mainly on internal developments whereas the chapter on West Africa is all about its vulnerability to the outside world.

[12] Adam Crawford 'International and comparative criminal justice and urban governance' in A Crawford (ed), *International and Comparative Criminal Justice and Urban Governance* (Cambridge, Cambridge University Press, 2011) 1–38 at 17. But see J Muncie, D Talbot and R Walters (eds), *Crime, Local and Global* (Devon, Willan/Open University Press, 2009) for a more synthetic text.

globalisation issues strictly apart has little to recommend it other than to allow for the continuation of 'business as usual', and it risks, as will be shown, missing a variety of interesting interconnections.

For a wide range of questions regarding international relations, human rights, truth commissions, restitutive justice or transitional justice, for example, the proper role of international criminal institutions can only be fully grasped when compared to more local means of handling conflicts. International law and conventions that seek to spread or enforce human rights have obvious implications for matters such as corruption and terrorism – but they are also relevant to the length of ordinary criminal trials.[13] More generally, responding to transnational phenomena such as irregular migration has profound effects on the provisions, temper and everyday practices of local systems of criminal justice.

Some authors argue that it is the comparative perspective that must now be subordinated to a more synoptic gaze. Nick Larsen and Russell Smandych explain that the cross-cultural study of crime and justice has evolved from a 'comparative' or 'international' approach to what is now increasingly referred to as a 'transnational' or 'global' approach to crime and justice . . . the effects of rapid globalisation have changed social, political and legal realities in such a way that comparative and international approaches to crime and justice are inadequate to capture the full complexity of these issues on a global scale.

In particular, they draw attention to 'global trends in policing and security, convergence and divergence in criminal justice and penal policy, and international criminal justice, war crimes and the global protection of human rights'.[14] However, Piers Beirne, in the preface to their collection, warns against going too far down this road. He concedes that 'globalisation and transnational crime do indeed tend to blur the relatively distinct boundaries and mobilities that exist between nations and between sovereign territories'.[15] However, he insists that

> comparative criminology still has a vital role to play, both in its own terms and also adjacent to global criminology and as one of its key constituents . . . the question of how globalisation and transnational crime affect different societies – similarly or differently, both similarly or differently at the same time, or somewhere in between – is first and foremost a comparative one.[16]

On the other hand, Francis Pakes offers another solution. He suggests that the comparative approach could be seen as a matter of methodology, whereas globalisation is the 'object of study'. It concerns the 'what' not the 'how', describing something taking place in the world – such as the trafficking of illegal goods – or

---

[13] D Nelken, 'Normalising Time: European Integration and Court Delays in Italy' in H Petersen, H Krunke, A Kjær and MR Madsen (eds), *Paradoxes of European Integration* (Farnham, Ashgate, 2008).

[14] N Larsen and R Smandych (eds), *Global Criminology and Criminal Justice: Current Issues and Perspectives* (Buffalo, NY, Broadview Press, 2008) xi.

[15] P Beirne, 'Preface' in Larsen and Smandych (eds), *Global Criminology and Criminal Justice*, ibid, ix.

[16] ibid.

people. Hence there cannot really be any contradiction.[17] However, Pakes does concede that the term 'globalising criminology' can also be used as if it related to methodology. He therefore draws a further distinction between what he says are two senses of 'Global Criminology', that are 'subject to conceptual confusion'. He claims that:

> Strong 'global criminology' should probably take the world as its unit of analysis. It might address questions such as the relation between climate change and civil unrest, transgressions and control. Here, 'global' denotes the object. In contrast, globalised criminology frequently refers to relations: those who advocate it frequently argue that we need to take the interconnectedness of the world into account.[18]

The discussion of social indicators that follows may help to illustrate how object and method merge.[19]

Indicators for Comparison

Most comparisons of crime and criminal justice make some use of indicators in the form, for example, of statistics of crime and victimisation, or rates of arrests, prosecution, sentencing and imprisonment.[20] Comparison of prison rates has been particularly important in possibly the most important recent debate within comparative criminal justice, concerned with the alleged 'turn to punitiveness', initiated by Garland's influential account of the rise in late modernity of the 'culture of control'.[21] Garland drew his examples from the United States and the United Kingdom, but others have sought to demonstrate that there are, in fact, more varied patterns amongst different nation states. Cavadino and Dignan, for instance, argued that this depended on the levels of enthusiasm for neo-liberal social policies. As Table 1 shows, neo-liberal societies have the highest prison rates. This is because (oversimplifying somewhat) they follow social and economic policies that lead to what they describe as 'exclusionary cultural attitudes towards our deviant and marginalised fellow citizens'.[22] On the other hand, what they call Continental European corporatist societies are said to 'pursue more inclusive economic and social policies that give citizens more protection from unfettered market forces' and to 'see offenders as needing re-socialisation which is

---

[17] F Pakes, 'The Comparative Method in Globalised Criminology' (2010) 1 *Australian and New Zealand Journal of Criminology* 17, 30.

[18] ibid at 18–19.

[19] For what is in some ways a parallel approach (focused on criminologists), see the work of Mariana Valverde, eg M Valverde, 'The Question of Scale in Urban Criminology' in A Crawford (ed), *International and Comparative Criminal Justice and Urban Governance* (Cambridge, Cambridge University Press, 2011).

[20] J van Dijk, *The World of Crime* (London, Sage, 2008); G Newman, *Global Report on Crime and Justice* (Oxford, Oxford University Press, 1999).

[21] D Garland, *The Culture of Control* (Oxford, Oxford University Press, 2001).

[22] M Cavadino and J Dignan, *Penal Systems: A Comparative Approach* (London, Sage, 2006) 23; M Cavadino and J Dignan, 'Penal Policy and Political Economy' (2006) 4 *Criminology and Criminal Justice* 435, 447.

the responsibility of the community as a whole'.[23] This is even more true for Scandinavian social democratic types of society as well as for Japan.

Table 1 Imprisonment Rates per 100,000 in 12 countries, (2002 and 2008)[24]

NEO-LIBERAL COUNTRIES	
USA	701
South Africa	402
New Zealand	155
England and Wales	141
Australia	115
CONSERVATIVE CORPORATIST COUNTRIES	
Italy	100
Germany	98
Netherlands	100
France	93
SOCIAL DEMOCRACIES	
Sweden	73
Finland	70
ORIENTAL CORPORATIST COUNTRIES	
Japan	63

This is not the place to try and do justice to what is an ongoing debate.[25] Nevertheless, although neo-liberalism is certainly a plausible candidate for part of the explanation for the recent increase in prison rates, as well as an important factor in explaining differences between places, this may not apply outside the range of countries being compared here. There are countries, such as China, which make high use of prison without being neo-liberal, and others, such as Russia or South Africa, where moves towards neo-liberalism have coincided with a reduc-

[23] Cavadino and Dignan, *Penal Systems*, above n 23, 24; Cavadino and Dignan, 'Penal Policy and Political Economy', above n 23, 448.

[24] Adapted from Cavadino and Dignan, *Penal Systems*, above n 23. The figures in brackets are updated from those they relied on in that book. Source: www.kcl.ac.UK/depsta/law/research/icps/worldbrief/wpb_stats.php. Although there have been some recent changes in incarceration rates they have not been sufficient to put into question the rank order they are proposing.

[25] Cavadino and Dignan themselves are still developing their ideas about the exact causal connections between the social and political factors that best explain differences in prison rates. See M Cavadino and J Dignan, 'Penal Comparisons: Puzzling Relations' in A Crawford (ed), *International and Comparative Criminal Justice and Urban Governance* (Cambridge, Cambridge University Press, 2011).

tion in the use of prison. This suggests that a wider range of variables than those connected to political economy may also lead to greater or lesser punitiveness. And, even for the countries chosen for comparison, given the considerable difference in its level of imprisonment would it not be better to have an explanation that singled out and sought to explain the US case rather than take it simply as an illustration of the influence of neo-liberalism?

Does the use of prison numbers as indicators in such comparisons help us compare like with like? Or do they make this more difficult? Are the Netherlands and Italy really similarly punitive – and for similar reasons of political economy? It is difficult to be sure that we are comparing like with like once we accept the need to include forms of social control that apply 'outside' the criminal justice system. It is not for nothing that Cavadino and Dignan entitle their chapter on Japan 'Iron Fist in a Velvet Glove'. In Italy we need to think not only of the family and extended family – especially important with respect to the handling of juvenile delinquency – but also of family-like groups in maintaining social order in many sectors of public and private life. Some of those helping to maintain 'order' in the Southern regions (and hence keeping prison rates low) are actually criminal groups!

Using prison rates as a measure of relative levels of harsh 'punitiveness' would only seem to make sense if we assume that similar rates of crime and victimisation are being handled by each of the criminal justice systems being compared. But there are reasons to think that some of the places in Cavadino and Dignan's table with higher prison rates also tend to have higher crime rates. The USA certainly has more lethal violence than any of the other countries in the list and South Africa also suffers exceptional levels of homicide, violence and rape. One recent comparison of overall victimisation rates for ten crimes places England and Wales at the top with the Scandinavian countries and Japan being the lowest.[26] It is also important to see who is in prison, for what crimes, and how they arrived there. Many of the countries that have lower rates, Sweden for example, or Switzerland, (or the Netherlands in its glorious period as a 'beacon of tolerance'), use shorter prison terms – but actually send relatively *more* people to prison than those with higher overall rates. Does this show less punitiveness than sending fewer people for longer periods? It certainly complicates any argument we may want to make about punitiveness and inclusiveness.

However, the chief criticism of such use of official statistics (and indicators more generally) is that if we are to make proper sense of them, what needs to be understood is the social processes that produce them in the first place. Take Italy, for example. Here the quotidian practices shaped by its Byzantine criminal procedure seem to be a more proximate explanation of its relatively low rates than any desire for inclusiveness or the generosity of its welfare or work training systems (welfare payments mainly go to pay pensions). The typical procedural guarantees of the adversarial system (centring on the forensic contest of the trial), that were

---

[26] van Dijk, *The World of Crime*, above n 21, 158.

introduced in the 1989 reform of criminal procedure were simply added to the ones that belong to the inquisitorial tradition. Even quite minor cases go through a series of procedural hoops and are reviewed by a large number of judges, and there are two stages of appeal (the first stage being a retrial on the facts). Uniquely, the so-called 'prescription' statute of limitations period continues to run until the Cassation court has given its final verdict. Cases not completed before then become null and void.

Whatever difficulties there may be in correctly identifying the independent variables that can explain variations in punitiveness and tolerance, it can be even more important to think about the cross-national meaning of dependent variables such as punitiveness, leniency and tolerance. It is difficult to speak sensibly about punitiveness and tolerance in different cultures without specifying what the various actors in each of the societies concerned mean by these words. Are punishment and tolerance on the same continuum? Is tolerance the name we give to the outcome of intentional choices – for example, the willingness to organise welfare interventions? Or is it an alternative to such interventions – just the name we give to deliberate or even negligent non-enforcement of available sanctions? Can there be too little punishment? Is tolerance always good? What about tolerance of others committing crime as a result of a lack of civic responsibility and of minding one's own business? Can it be irrelevant that what external observers call tolerance, locals may call permissiveness, indulgence, favouritism, neglect, indifference, impunity, denial and collusion?[27]

Studying How Other Compare

The strength of Cavadino and Dignan's approach, however controversial the details of their thesis may be, is their demonstration that what happens in the criminal justice process is shaped by contrasting domestic choices in social and economic policy. Nevertheless, the increasing interdependence consequent on globalisation puts into question any explanation that presupposes that what happens in a specific context is independent of what happens elsewhere. This involves understanding the interplay of the global and local rather than seeking to explain contrasting patterns of locally rooted variables. Even they sometimes suggest that what they are really explaining are local differences in responses to crime that 'persist' despite the homogenising effects of globalisation.

Processes of mutual contacts and influence certainly did not begin with what is now called globalisation. Empire and colonialism has been fundamental in shaping criminal justice systems in much of the world, and ideas and practices of criminal justice have always circulated between countries and elites. It is questionable how far penal systems were ever 'embedded' in given nation state contexts[28] and

---

[27] D Nelken, 'Italian Juvenile Justice: Tolerance, Leniency or Indulgence?' (2006) 6 *Youth Justice* 107.
[28] D Nelken, 'Theorizing the Embeddings of Punishment' in D Melossi, M Sozzo and R Sparks (eds), *Travels of the Criminal Question: Cultural Embeddedness and Diffusion* (Oxford, Hart Publishing, 2011).

any given national system is, at least in part, a reworking of ideas coming from elsewhere. Italian criminal justice, for example, is currently moulded by scholarship that reflects, on the one hand, the importance of German penal doctrine among law professors of substantive criminal law, and, by contrast, the more recent revolution in criminal procedure owing to the import of Anglo-American ideas. Centuries ago, the ideas, first of Beccaria and then of Lombroso, spread from Italy to create the foundations for the classical and positivist schools of criminology in the USA and UK.

Arguably, however, greater access to international media means that local meanings are increasingly transformed, challenged and sometimes dislodged.[29] People in Continental European countries, fed on television episodes of Perry Mason, assumed that they too had an adversarial systems of criminal justice – those who encounter the police outside the USA may still expect to be read their *Miranda* rights. Concern over security merges fears of terrorism or transnational organised crime, or most insidiously, illegal immigration, with worries about domestic threats. Local debates make ever more reference to what is (said to be) going on in other places. Policy-makers and legal actors act on information and ideas about practices in other societies and sometimes make decisions in the light of where they stand in relation to others. The introduction of International Crime Victimisation surveys, for example, had an influence on policy-makers and (to a lesser extent) on public opinion in the Netherlands where it produced 'a wholesale change in the philosophy of criminal justice policy'.[30]

Comparison thus becomes a second-order task in which we need to grasp how others go about comparing, why given claims are made about what goes on elsewhere, and what consequences follow from this. In this light, tables such as those created by Cavadino and Dignan, in addition to their potential role in explanations, must also be seen as social artefacts that can be and are taken up by actors engaged in local struggles about the proprieties of penal practices. The decline in the prison rate in Finland, which post-World War II, had one of the highest prison rates in Europe but now has one of the lowest, was in large part a result of the successful efforts of the elite there to bring their incarceration rates into line with published evidence of the rates in other Scandinavian countries.[31] The Canadians also keep a watchful eye on their own rate so as to show how much lower it is than that of their powerful neighbour (but they are less concerned that their rate is higher than those in Europe.) Policy-makers in Scotland would like to be able to show that their criminal justice system is more enlightened than that of England and Wales – and sometimes it is.

---

[29] A Appadurai, *Modernity at Large: Cultural Dimensions of Globalization* (Minneapolis, University of Minnesota Press, 1996).

[30] D Downs, 'Comparative Criminology, Globalization and the "Punitive Turn"' in D Nelken (ed), *Comparative Criminal Justice and Globalization* (Farnham, Ashgate, 2011).

[31] HV Hofer, 'Prison Populations as Political Constructs: the Case of Finland, Holland and Sweden' (2003) 1 *Journal of Scandinavian Studies in Criminology and Crime Prevention* 21; T Lappi-Seppala, 'Penal Policy in Scandinavia' in M Tonry (ed), *Crime, Punishment and Politics in Comparative Perspective*, Crime and Justice, Vol 36 (Chicago, University of Chicago Press, 2007).

To analyse how others use comparisons we first need to examine who is involved. Who translates (sometimes literally) supposedly best practices into the vernacular – and in what ways, and for what reasons? What are the differences between, and amongst, judges, lawyers, police, probation officers and prison officers? What about the roles of representatives of businesses such as security providers or those who build and run private prisons? What part is played by politicians, non-governmental organisations and other pressure groups, regulatory bodies, journalists, advisers and even academics themselves? Attention also needs to be given to the role of institutions, singly, collectively or in competition. In Europe – but also beyond – European Union institutions and the European Human Rights Court are important players. The same crime threat – say trafficking of human beings – may involve a variety of non-governmental organisations and inter-governmental organisations such as the UN Commissioner for Rights, the International Labour Organization, or the International Organization for Migration, Human Rights Watch, Amnesty International and so on.[32]

We also need to study what is being borrowed or copied. In general, we may be dealing with scripts, norms, institutions, technologies, fears or ways of seeing. Other ways of defining problems and solutions may be relevant, involving conceptual legal innovations such as 'the law of the enemy', new forms of policing, mediation, or restitutive or therapeutic justice. Another set of questions concerns the means by which criminal justice ideas and practices are learned about and spread – and the way different kinds of initiatives can follow their own distinctive circuits. We can also ask when comparison becomes relevant at the national, subnational or super-national levels. It takes little skill to discover that what purports to be global frequently comes out of the USA but members of the EU, amongst others, are also quite actively involved, singly and collectively.

Some exchanges may involve groups of 'experts', others only concern 'virtual' conversations, as in the way judges read sentences in other jurisdictions as they seek to provide justifications of local practices such as the retention or abolition of the death penalty. Remarkably, but not exceptionally, systems, such as the accusatorial system of criminal procedure, become influential abroad at the same time as being highly criticised in their home countries. Indeed, success in 'selling' ideas abroad can be used as capital in arguments about the same systems back home. As important, however, is the need to research why some ideas do not travel, why, for example, day fines and conditional dismissals are used only in some places in Europe.[33]

There are already a number of case studies that illuminate such processes. Jones and Newburn examine the outcomes of efforts in England and Wales to introduce US practices regarding private prisons, 'three strikes and you're out' sentencing

---

[32] D Nelken, 'Human Trafficking and Legal Culture' (2011) 43 *Israel Law Review* 479, and D Nelken, 'Transnational Legal Processes and the (Re)Construction of the "Social": The Case of Human Trafficking' in D Feenan (ed), *The 'Socio' in Socio-Legal Studies* (Basingstoke, Palgrave Macmillan, 2013).

[33] See also W Twining, 'Have Concepts, Will Travel: Analytical Jurisprudence in a Global Context' (2005) 1 *International Journal of the Law in Context* 5.

reform, and zero tolerance policing. The authors see themselves as trying to rec-oncile 'insights coming from the broad global/convergence and local divergence vantage points'.[34] Although they show clear evidence that borrowing has taken place, they conclude that this has made relatively little difference in practice. By contrast, another recent description of transplanting US-style institutions (that unfortunately does not refer to Newburn and Jones) comes to rather different conclusions. In his excellent account of the introduction of US-type problem-solving courts to five other common law jurisdictions, Nolan stresses how much was in fact successfully taken over. His concern is that such borrowing will even-tually bring about some penetration of wider aspects of US culture in societies that are purportedly critical of it.[35]

These authors may also be using different criteria for judging success. Newburn and Jones are worried that borrowing from the USA could increase incarceration rates (and their negative finding helps explain the continuing gulf between the USA and England and Wales). Nolan has a more diffuse fear of cultural imperial-ism. He also recognises that any borrowing is inevitably affected by differences in the legal and general culture of the importing country, indeed he shows us how the actors involved explicitly seek to modify what they are importing. Both Nolan and Newburn and Jones restrict themselves to borrowing amongst jurisdictions within the common law world. By contrast, Loic Waquant insists that the American *doxa* has penetrated thinking in Continental European countries such as France.[36]

Jacqueline Ross has provided a series of richly detailed analyses that focus on the problem posed for cooperating in the battle against transnational crime by the fact that the US and European nations conceptualise, legitimate and control under-cover policing in substantially dissimilar ways.[37] In comparing US and Italian methods of regulating covert police operations, Ross tells us that whereas Americans primarily worry that covert agents may corrupt innocuous targets, Italians are more concerned that covert operations may slide into state-sanctioned lawlessness.[38] In America, effort is made to strengthen the rights of the potential object of entrapment, but in Italy it is left to the prosecutor to keep the police in line. There are considerable differences in the status given to informants and what they are allowed to do by way of breaking the law. Ross doubts that harmonisation

[34] T Jones and T Newburn, *Policy Transfer and Criminal Justice* (Buckingham, Open University Press, 2007) 8.

[35] JL Nolan, *Legal Accents, Legal Borrowing: The International Problem-Solving Court Movement* (Princeton, NJ, Princeton University Press, 2009).

[36] L Waquant, *Prisons of Poverty* (Minneapolis, University of Minnesota Press, 2009) and L Waquant, *Punishing the Poor: The Neo-liberal Government of Social Insecurity* (Durham, NC, Duke University Press, 2009). *cf* D Nelken 'Denouncing the Penal State' (2012) 4 *Criminology and Criminal Justice: Special Issue on Neo-Liberal Penality* 331.

[37] See, eg J Ross, 'Impediments to Transnational Cooperation in Undercover Policing: A Comparative Study of the United States and Italy' (2004) 3 *American Journal of Comparative Law* 569; and J Ross, 'The Place of Covert Surveillance in Democratic Societies: A Comparative Study of the United States and Germany' (2007) 55 *American Journal of Comparative Law* 493.

[38] Ross, 'Impediments to Transnational Cooperation', above n 38.

of these countries' legal regimes is feasible, even if this type of law enforcement is treated as exceptional with its own special rules. She concludes with a mental experiment that shows the need for major changes in the domestic roles of prosecutors for the two countries to be able to work properly together.[39]

Given that Italy is the Continental European country that has done most to try to move towards the adversarial system, the extent of remaining differences is all the more remarkable. Ross rightly notes that, in theory, giving Italian prosecutors' discretion not to prosecute justice collaborators would involve a major change in their system of criminal justice (in fact requiring a change in the constitutional requirement of obligatory prosecution). When it comes to actual practice, she concedes that it is hard for outsiders to understand or copy the Italian system of unofficial official discretion which allows them to work round rules where officially there is no discretion. As she rightly says, this puts a premium on being able to cover your back through political and personal networks (though she could also have said that this is true in Italy more generally).

Ross also tells us of a number of practical problems that obstruct cooperation, from the lack of legal status for US undercover agents in Italy to the lack of the language skills that would allow Italians to penetrate foreign crime rings. Yet – if we step back from her legal analysis – it is also important to understand why there are nonetheless so many examples of 'successful' collaboration between Italy and the USA, for example, in apprehending suspected terrorists. Some might argue that this is because Italy's secret service(s) quite often do not keep to their own laws, and even the national police sometimes respond to political dictates. Only later, sometimes much later, if at all, are they brought to book by the more proactive members of the judiciary.[40] But – in Italy – the question whether the government or the judges are more authorised to interpret the law is a subject of continuing controversy.

Indicators for Governance

The third 'moment' that concerns us here finds its place in efforts to construct a global perspective.[41] In particular, we shall focus on the role of comparison in

[39] ibid.

[40] The *La Repubblica* newspaper of 14 February 2013, 22–23 reported that Nicolò Pollari, the head of the Italian secret police organisation SISMI (and a general in the Italian financial police) was sentenced to ten years in prison by the Court of Appeal (reversing the lower court) for the kidnapping of Abu Omar, the Mullah of the Milan mosque and delivering him into the hands of the CIA and out of the country. His other police collaborators received slightly lower sentences. Pollari told the newspapers that he had obeyed the law. He claimed he would never have agreed to an illegal kidnapping (saying he would never have agreed to such illegal instructions even in the Fascist period). State secrecy prevents him, he complained, saying what really happened. Three different governments, of the centre right, centre left and technicians government had all stated the case was covered by state secrecy and asked the court not to hear it.

[41] Shifting to the global level raises the question of whether there really can be a view from everywhere (or nowhere). For some, this is a matter of arguing of universal standards deriving, for example, from natural law – or human rights. For others, it is a matter of fact testified to by an emerging or

exercises that use indicators to rank countries or other units in the course of developing and applying globalising standards and monitoring and evaluating compliance with such standards. This happens with standards and recommendations emanating from the UN, the Council of Europe and the Strasbourg Court of Human Rights, together with many other IGOs and NGOs and networks in areas relevant to crime and criminal justice concerning how criminal procedure should be organised, trial delays avoided, or prisons managed.

Although there is no consensus on how best to define these types of indicators, a recent attempt by Merry, Fisher and Davis has the potential to become widely accepted.[42] 'An indicator', they tell us

> is a named collection of rank-ordered data that purports to represent the past or projected performance of different units. The data are generated through a process that simplifies raw data about a complex social phenomenon. The data, in this simplified and processed form, are capable of being used to compare particular units of analysis (such as countries or institutions or corporations), synchronically or over time, and to evaluate their performance by reference to one or more standards.[43]

A range of questions can be asked about these processes. Why have such indicators emerged? Why are they attractive to decision makers? How far is this process similar and different from the making of the modern (welfare) state? According to students of governmentality, the concern with standardisation and normalisation can be traced to the rise of insurance and technical standardisation.[44] What is there in common in the role of indicators dealing with different (social) problems? What units are being monitored? How far does measuring itself help constitute them? How do indicators relate to other instruments in play? How should indicators be legitimated? Is scientific consensus or agreement by the parties involved more important for this purpose?[45]

Typically, social indicators collected for governmental purposes have, and are intended to have, practical consequences. They are aimed at providing cross-national comparisons, horizontal accountability between governments, or domestic criteria for applying international protocols. Through the use of this tool, individuals, organisations and countries are made responsible for their own

---

existing consensus. But are types of crime really equally disapproved of across the world? See Newman, *Global Report on Crime and Justice*, above n 21 and van Dijk, above n 21. For criticism, see D Nelken, 'Criminology: Crime's Changing Boundaries' in P Cane and M Tushnet (eds), *The Oxford Handbook of Legal Studies* (Oxford, Oxford University Press, 2003).

[42] K Davis, A Fisher, B Kingsbury and SE Merry (eds), *Governance by Indicators: Global Power through Classification and Rankings* (Oxford, Oxford University Press, 2012).

[43] ibid at 16.

[44] According to students of governmentality, the concern with standardisation and normalisation can be traced to the rise of insurance and technical standardisation. See especially, F Ewald, 'Norms, Discipline and the Law' (1990) 1 *Representations* 138.

[45] See D Nelken, 'Defining Global Indicators' in F Koenraadt, C Kelk, F Kristen and D Siegel (eds), *Liber Amicorum Chrisje Brants* (Den Haag, Boom Lemma, 2013) and D Nelken, 'Regulating Social Indicators' in F Calderoni and S Caneppele (eds), *Essays in Honour of Ernesto Savona* (New York, Springer, 2013).

behaviour as they seek to comply with the measures of performance articulated in an indicator. So there is much more is going on than comparison 'for its own sake' (whatever that might be). Sally Merry talks of indicators having 'knowledge' and 'governance' effects.[46] Numerical measures that submerge local particularities and idiosyncrasies into universal categories produce a world knowable without the detailed particulars of context and history. Such knowledge is presented as objective and often as scientific, but the interpretations that lurk behind the numbers are rarely presented explicitly.

'Indicators', Merry tells us, are 'performative', naming produces knowledge by announcing categories to be measured as if they were self-evident, open to public scrutiny, simple in conception and readily accessible, in a way that private opinions are not. But the labels thus chosen do not necessarily accurately reflect the data that produce the indicators. The problem for her (and for many other critics) is one of de-politicisation. Indicators replace judgements on the basis of values or politics with apparently more rational decision-making on the basis of statistical information but they do not eliminate the role of private knowledge and elite power in decision-making even as they represent it as technical, statistical expertise.[47] In general, indicators mobilise questionable categorisations of actors, actions, problems, diagnoses and solutions.[48]

When it comes to indicators of compliance, everything depends on the quality of the information provided. What if data purporting to be an objective assessment by World Bank officials or credit rating agencies about whether or not states are honest about repaying their debts, actually relies on subjective judgements? Many ranking exercises explicitly re-present the subjective perceptions of other people, as in public opinion barometers that seek to estimate levels of corruption or the quality of public services. The targets of indicators may certainly be tempted to try to 'game' the requirements and 'manufacture' compliance. However, it is also true that they often face arbitrary or equivocal standards. You may receive either more or less help, if you are identified as a 'fragile state' or as having a poorly functioning health system, depending on the political circumstances of the donors. There may be little that the targets of indicators themselves can do to affect those circumstances.

There are also problems with the information provided by those lower down in the hierarchy of the monitoring organisation such as those charged with showing how funds are being used in refugee relief. Refugee protection field officers, we are told, are asked to collect information on 154 detailed indicators. To consider just one of these indicators, can they really be expected to count the number of latrines per 40,000 refugees, given the lack of access and security inside the camps? Field

---

[46] SE Merry, 'Measuring the World: Indicators, Human Rights, and Global Governance' (2011) 52 *Current Anthropology* (Sup 3).

[47] ibid.

[48] See, eg B Sokhi-Bulley, 'Governing (through) Rights: Statistics as Technologies of Governmentality' (2011) 20 *Social & Legal Studies* 139.

officers often have to combine this task with their main responsibilities of resolving problems on the ground. Not surprisingly, they tend to give priority to the job of saving lives over that of monitoring compliance, especially where they consider it impossible to do both. Similarly, they may report on the distribution of water supplies but not the number of evictions of refugees, since this would risk alienating host states.

The risk of what we might call 'junk comparisons' arises because of the uneven quality of information available in different places. Many indicators are set up to measure what can most easily be measured, irrespective of whether or not this gets to the heart of the 'problem'. It is certainly implausible to give credence to the number of conventions a State has signed up to as evidence of its political will to deal with problems of discrimination in society. These questionable choices are made worse by the way information is later processed. Fundamental errors are introduced by working with false assumptions or confusing causes with consequences. Binary options are imposed on complex and contested materials. Questionable choices are made in adding or multiplying different sources of data that have been gathered using competing methodologies.

There is also the problem of translating meaning and significance. Of special relevance for our purposes, the plausibility of indicators becomes problematic where places or practices are in some respects incommensurable. Values such as the rule of law or judicial independence may be given different interpretations in different places – or at least be assessed differently because of different circumstances. Law itself also works differently in different cultures because there are likely to be a variety of other mechanisms that may substitute for law or conflict with it. But a common feature of many indicators is the assumption of what has been called 'legal universalism'. Studies of the 'better business' indicator provide ample evidence of this. Those who created this indicator appear to have missed the importance in many countries of criminal prosecution for debt collection. It takes local knowledge to understand that in countries where it is apparently more simple to set up a business it may also be more difficult to keep those businesses running without a tortuous process of obtaining licenses. By contrast, elsewhere, bribes, lawyers and personal connections may be the expeditious, if less than ideal, methods of getting round apparent bureaucratic impediments.

Moreover, the charge is made that many indicators often purport to describe only a constructed object, an artefact (such as IQ tests) of the very attempt at measurement. This is easily seen with notions such as 'state fragility'.[49] Do we really know how to determine the effects of political institutions across different realities so as to be able to predict the drivers of fragility? The very idea of 'state-ness' is no more than an assemblage that brings into connection ideas based on prototypes of influential Western states and Weberian notions of the monopoly

---

[49] N Bhuta, 'State Failure: The US Fund for Peace Failed States Index' in K Davis, A Fisher, B Kingsbury and SE Merry, *Governance by Indicators: Global Power through Classification and Rankings* (Oxford, Oxford University Press, 2012).

of violence or take the many popular indicators for measuring the 'rule of law'. Procedural, substantive or institutional definitions can all be used but each of these emphasises some political concerns over others. By ranking different places, indicators also construct the units they are comparing as if they existed independently, for example, making it seem that the post-Westphalian international state system had not been affected by globalisation. But, of course, the act of monitoring countries in relation to each other is itself evidence of growing interdependence and the whole point of ranking is to make places act on such awareness.

Significantly, as with the Cavadino and Dignan thesis seeking to explain different levels of imprisonment, there are links between governmental social indicators and the issue of neo-liberalism. But now the relationship is not just to do with one kind of independent political economy variable. It has to do more with the very reason for the growth of indicators, the forms they take, and the consequences of using them. Some see the obsession with indicators of Gross National Product (GNP), for example, as one of the main causes for the recent financial crash, as well as the growing levels of social inequality and the neglect of the environment. Global social indicators seek to shape individual behaviour through governance of the soul and self-management rather than command and control models. They often are expressly intended to shift responsibility to States and other targets.

These indicators, especially but not only, those employed by international financial organisations, are almost always created in the 'global North' which sets the agenda, names the indicator and assembles the criteria – while data collection typically takes place mostly in the 'global South'. They involve an allegedly doctrinaire approach to removing state control over economic action in poorer countries. Critics of the 'better business' indicator, for example, argue that this helps block land reform and is implicated in the 'land grabs' which lead to the displacement of populations, impoverishment, and the loss of livelihoods. Although promising to create work, what actually happens is that the best jobs go to foreigners and the dangerous, poorly paid, jobs go to local workers. What is more, much of this development involves producing food for others when there is not enough to support the local area so that dependence on foreign economic interests increases.[50]

The main competitor to the GNP indicator, Sen and Nussbaum's 'human capabilities' approach,[51] explicitly sets itself up against neo-liberal ideology by building into its ranking scheme a recognition of equality and its benefits. However, for some commentators, any and every use of indicators, however benign, represents

---

[50] KE Davis, B Kingsbury and SE Merry, 'Indicators as a Technology of Global Governance' (2012) 46 *Law and Society Review* 71.

[51] See MC Nussbaum, *Women and Human Development: The Capabilities Approach* (Cambridge, Cambridge University Press, 2005) and A Sen, 'Human Rights and Capabilities' (2005) 2 *Journal of Human Development* 151.

a vehicle of neo-liberalism. Even when what needs to be monitored has to do with matters such as human rights or the rule of law, the method being used is one taken from business models designed to provide for satisfactory auditing of how far goals have been met and whether money has been spent wisely.

Conclusion

This chapter has suggested that one way of seeing how comparison changes under the influence of globalisation is to study the (changing) role of social indicators. I have, for the purpose of analysis, distinguished three 'moments' in which indicators are used for purposes of comparison but the real point is to see how these different uses of indicators also interrelate and interact, for example, by exploring the overlap between indicators seen as pointers to data that needs explanation, and indicators as yardsticks for evaluation.

There is an interesting ambiguity in the passage from the second to the third sentence of the definition of indicators provided by Merry, Kingsbury and Davis. Being, as they put it, 'capable of being used' is not the same as actually being fashioned as a tool for this purpose. Should we perhaps envisage a continuum whereby indicators turn from 'facts' into 'standards' – and perform an increasingly 'performative' role as they move from the supposedly neutral task of providing explanation to that of providing local guidance or overarching standards? Are we talking only of temporal sequence or do indicators come in different species with predictably different consequences? It seems likely that the 'same' phenomena that count as 'facts' for one group at any one time – can serve as a 'standard' for another group or at another time.

Whether or not indicators play a role in governance, even where this is not why they have been developed, may in part be a question of definition.[52] But it may also be an empirical question capable of further investigation. Evidence from the world of criminal justice would seem to suggest that they can and do. It suggests that even without being formalised into what are officially labelled as indicators, facts can produce 'effects', as when technical language, documents and other objects function as 'actants'.[53] The adviser to the United Nations – whose figures were the source of Cavadino and Dignan's table – urged all countries to shape their criminal justice practices so as to aim at a rate of no more than 100 prisoners per 100,000 of the population.[54] Any higher prison rate was taken to be

---

[52] For example, in T Landman and E Carvalho, *Measuring Human Rights* (London, Routledge, 2010) the authors include the category of socio-economic and administrative statistics alongside the categories of events-based, standards-based and survey-based ways of evaluating the performance of human rights.

[53] B Latour, 'On Actor-Network Theory: A few Clarifications' (1996) 4 *Soziale Welt* 369.

[54] R Walmsley, *World Prison List* (2008) available at http://apcca.org.

a deviations from a standard. But where is that standard coming from? Could it be set too low?[55]

There is a variety of types of feedback between the different moments. Just as some indicators used by IGOs and NGOs are prepared with the help of academics, there are many efforts at academic explanations that use concepts such as fragile states which were originally created for practical purposes.[56] Many case studies show that practical and normative concerns shape the initial definition of good indicators. Some would argue that more harm is actually caused by 'strong states' than the 'fragile states' for whom indicators are readily available. We should not in any case assume that academic explanation is always disinterested or that knowledge and governance effects are restricted to indicators used in professional roles or created for specific practical tasks. Academics often choose for comparison places that serve as a 'foil' to their own societies, offering a model against which to assess local practices, either by providing evidence of what should be copied, or, sometimes, what needs to be avoided.

Do those who make indicators take issues of comparison seriously enough or would their efforts at explanation and standardisation become impossible if they were to do so?[57] What is clear is that if indicators are to play a prescriptive role in setting standards and distributing resources then issues of regulation arise. Can anything be done to improve the making and use of indicators? Must this always involve making other indicators? Some think that (some) indicators should be subjected to principles of administrative law, although there are obvious difficulties in achieving this in an international context. There may be good reasons to try to regulate some organisations which use indicators, such as credit rating agencies. Alternatively, we may prefer to grant those using or subject to indicators more rights to participation or contestation. Is the goal to thereby increase the accuracy of the result? Or is the aim to increase that legitimacy (and perhaps therefore also the effectiveness) of the exercise of power that is reflected in this use of indicators? If we want to identify poor standards, or failures to comply, we can hardly expect the targets of censure to give their agreement to a process that penalises them.

In some cases it could be more appropriate to leave indicators to be criticised according to the professional consensus of social scientists rather than try to 'legalise' them. But are social scientists' own methodological protocols sufficient to ensure robust means of constructing indicators for purposes of global ranking?[58]

---

[55] Care is also needed in spelling out any policy ideas that are assumed to help in reaching a given standard. Interestingly, the recommendations provided on how to reach the rate of no more than 100 prisoners per 100,000 of the population include the injunction to avoid short prison sentences but many of the countries with the lowest rates are, in fact, those that make most use of short sentences.

[56] S Karstedt, 'Exit: The State. Globalisation, State Failure and Crime' in D Nelken (ed), *Comparative Criminal Justice and Globalisation* (Farnham, Ashgate, 2011). Some would argue that more harm is actually caused by 'strong states' than the 'fragile states' for whom indicators are readily available.

[57] Because many standards are efforts to overcome rather than acknowledge diversity, this is sometimes used as an alibi for poor comparison.

[58] In the field of human rights, see EA Andersen and AN Feldt, *Human Rights Indicators at Programme and Project Level – Guidelines for Defining Indicators, Monitoring and Evaluation*

Alternatively, could we not simply eliminate indicators or at least try to reduce their influence?[59] Certainly, it is important to understand how different scientific disciplines, or positions within them, are implicated in the growth or contestation of indicators. Reliance on indicators is much less favoured, for example, by those who prefer qualitative approaches in social science or those who rely on ethnographic methodology. Such commentators insist that, in the end, indicators have less to do with facts or standards than they do with interpretations, interpretations of interpretations and so on. However, even interpretativists who try to compare places use limited information as a clue to the wider universe and even those who have reservations about comparisons based on indicators may still want to understand how such comparisons succeed in being accepted and how this feeds into the practice of making and using indicators as standards.

(Copenhagen, The Danish Institute for Human Rights, 2006); and Landman and Carvalho, *Measuring Human Rights*, above n 53.

[59] Curiously, what some see as advantages of indicators other see as drawbacks. Those who advocate indicators see them as making practice knowable and comparable, producing impartiality, simplicity, efficiency, consistency and transparency, overcoming relativism, and allowing learning from experience. Those who think they are dangerous argue that they oversimplify, are partial and misleading, involve false comparisons, homogenisation and false universalisation, and that they are ideological.

3

Illicit Globalisation Myths and Misconceptions

PETER ANDREAS*

Introduction

Illicit non-state transnational economic actors, ranging from drug traffickers to money launderers to black market arms dealers, are often depicted as increasingly agile, sophisticated, border-defying and technologically savvy. States, in sharp contrast, are typically described as increasingly besieged, outsmarted, poorly equipped, clumsy and even incompetent in dealing with the illicit side of globalisation. In this view, state power necessarily weakens as illicit markets strengthen. In short, illicit globalisation is the poster child for arguments that states are 'losing control'.

This standard account is articulated in various forms by scholars, policymakers, pundits and journalists. In bemoaning the retreat of the state, Susan Strange has called transnational organised crime 'perhaps *the* major threat to the world system'.[1] James Mittelman has warned of a growing 'nexus of organised crime and globalisation', arguing that global organised crime groups 'not only impair globalisation's licit channels but are also playing a key role in setting new rules'.[2] Phil Williams has described transnational organised crime as 'the HIV virus of the modern state, circumventing and breaking down the natural defenses of the body politic'.[3] Most states in the past, according to Williams, 'seemed to have the capacity' to keep this threat 'under control', but this is 'no longer so obviously the case'.[4] Claire Sterling has even popularised the notion of a post-Cold War 'pax mafiosa' – a 'planet-wide criminal consortium' that threatens

---

* This paper is partly adapted from P Andreas, 'Illicit Globalisation: Myths, Misconceptions, and Historical Lessons' (2011) 126 Political Science Quarterly 403.
[1] S Strange, *The Retreat of the State: The Diffusion of Power in the World Economy* (New York, Cambridge University Press, 1996) 121.
[2] J Mittelman, *The Globalization Syndrome* (Princeton, Princeton University Press, 2000) 210, 214.
[3] P Williams, 'Transnational Organised Crime and the State' in RB Hall and TJ Biersteker (eds), *The Emergence of Private Authority in Global Governance* (Cambridge, Cambridge University Press, 2003) 165, 161.
[4] ibid.

'the integrity and even the survival of democratic governments in America, Europe, everywhere'.[5]

These dire pronouncements have been echoed in policy circles, with US Senator John Kerry exclaiming: 'We are compelled by the globalisation of crime to globalise law and law enforcement.'[6] Jessica Mathews has pointed to organised crime and trafficking as the dark side of a fundamental 'power shift' away from states.[7] Moises Naim has boldly labelled the conflict between states and global crime as 'the new wars of globalisation', with states increasingly on the losing side.[8] Crime has gone global, he contends, 'transforming the international system, upending the rules, creating new players, and reconfiguring power in international politics and economics'.[9] Joining the loud chorus of warnings, Misha Glenny has recently dubbed this new global threat 'McMafia'.[10]

At first glance, this standard story of illicit globalisation seems depressingly accurate. Traffickers *are* routinely defying borders, mocking law enforcement and sometimes violently challenging the state. These concerns, which resonate with the popular imagination, are confirmed daily in media stories and policy publications. It is clear that the same global transformations in communication, transportation and finance that aid legitimate business also aid illicit business. Globalisation reduces transaction costs for both legitimate and illicit market actors. Moreover, some policies designed to encourage and facilitate licit commerce can unintentionally aid illicit commerce.[11]

However, while containing many truths, this prevailing picture of illicit globalisation obscures as much as it reveals. It distorts and distracts as much as it informs and ultimately generates more heat than light, with troubling policy implications. The temptation to simply blame globalisation is much too easy and convenient and can fuel calls to further escalate rather than re-evaluate flawed policies and policing strategies.

In this paper I question the conventional wisdom about illicit economic globalisation. I argue that popular claims of loss of state control are overly alarmist, misleading, suffer from historical amnesia, and are based on dubious data. Drawing from historical and contemporary empirical illustrations, I challenge

---

[5] C Sterling, *Thieves' World: The Threat of the New Global Network of Organised Crime* (New York, Simon and Schuster, 1994) 13–14.

[6] J Kerry, *The New War: The Web of Crime That Threatens America* (New York, Touchstone, 1997) 169.

[7] J Mathews, 'Power Shift' (1997) *Foreign Affairs* 50.

[8] M Naim, 'The Five Wars of Globalisation' (2003) *Foreign Policy* 5.

[9] M Naim, *Illicit: How Smugglers, Traffickers, and Copycats are Hijacking the Global Economy* (New York, Doubleday, 2005) 5.

[10] M Glenny, *McMafia: A Journey through the Global Criminal Underworld* (New York, Knopf, 2008). See also, KL Thachuck (ed), *Transnational Threats: Smuggling and Trafficking in Arms, Drugs and Human Life* (Westport, Praeger, 2007).

[11] In the case of drugs, see K Raustiala, 'Law, Liberalization, and International Narcotics Trafficking' (1999) 32 *New York University Journal of International Law and Politics* 1. More generally, see P Andreas, 'Transnational Crime and Economic Globalisation' in M Berdal and M Serrano (eds), *Transnational Organised Crime and International Security* (Boulder, Lynne Rienner, 2002).

common myths and misconceptions about illicit globalisation and emphasise the ways in which states shape and even exploit the illicit global economy. Contrary to conventional wisdom, illicit globalisation is not new, and its relationship to the state is not only antagonistic but also symbiotic.

In the next section I review the dimensions of illicit globalisation and then evaluate standard claims regarding the magnitude of illicit global flows. I then examine the contemporary and historical relationship between states and illicit markets, and the role of new technologies and violence in shaping this relationship. I also point to the many ways in which states promote or otherwise benefit from illicit flows. I conclude by suggesting that the standard story about illicit globalisation is not only overblown but can have counterproductive policy consequences, and I call for more scholarly attention to overcome the common tendency to either overlook or overstate illicit globalisation.

Dimensions of Illicit Globalisation

The dominant account of illicit globalisation often categorises illicit cross-border economic flows as 'transnational organised crime' – a broad term that can be difficult to define. This tends to focus attention on large criminal organisations (often mislabelled as 'cartels'[12]) and mafia-like leaders (often colourfully described as 'kingpins' and 'drug lords') rather than particular market sectors or activities. At root, much of what makes organised crime transnational involves some form of profit-driven smuggling across borders. Transnational organised crime is therefore simply a new term for an old economic practice that varies greatly across time, place and smuggling activity.

The illicit side of the global economy includes: the trade in prohibited commodities (such as heroin and cocaine); the smuggling of legal commodities to circumvent sanctions and embargoes or to evade taxes (including one third of all cigarette exports);[13] the black market in stolen commodities (most notably intellectual property theft); the clandestine movement of people (migrants, sex workers); the trafficking of endangered species and animal parts (such as ivory); and the laundering of money generated by these and other illicit activities. Some of these illicit flows are little more than a law enforcement nuisance (the cross-border trade in stolen vehicles), but others receive intense policy attention and media scrutiny (drug trafficking and migrant smuggling) and still others have clear security implications (sanctions busting, arms trafficking, nuclear smuggling and terrorist financing).

---

[12] Cartels, by definition, engage in price fixing. Criminal organisations, even the most powerful ones, have not shown this capacity.

[13] This is determined by the fact that official cigarette exports are about one-third higher in volume than official cigarette imports. The discrepancy is accounted for by diversion to the black market (ie cigarettes informally imported off-the-books to avoid taxes).

Despite their great diversity, illicit transnational economic flows share some basic characteristics: they are unauthorised by the sending and/or receiving country,[14] and they move across borders via mechanisms designed to evade detection and apprehension. They are also an increasingly prominent source of conflict and tension in international politics, most notably in United States and European Union relations. In an era of economic liberalisation and deregulation, there is a counter move of re-regulation through intensified policing of illicit flows within, along and across national borders.

Some countries, otherwise at the margins of the global economy, have market niches in the illicit sphere: exports of rare animals from Madagascar; heroin from Afghanistan and Myanmar (Burma); migrant workers from Ecuador; and cannabis from Morocco. Others have a niche in laundering and sheltering illicit financial flows (Cayman Islands). Many developing countries are becoming more economically integrated with wealthier countries, through both formal and informal processes. This is evident, for example, in the US–Mexico, Spain–Morocco and Montenegro–Italy economic relationships.

Illicit flows reflect broader power asymmetries in the international system, which are reinforced by borders and their enforcement. For instance, unable to access first world labour markets through the front door, many workers from developing countries attempt to gain clandestine access through the back door via the use of professional smugglers. Many citizens of developing countries cope economically either by facilitating illicit flows (such as drug crop cultivation) or by becoming an illicit flow (a smuggled migrant). Clandestine entrepreneurs produce, transport, sell, or otherwise enable illicit flows as an alternative ladder of upward social mobility where opportunities for advancement in the legal economy may be limited or blocked. Others attempt to challenge power asymmetries through organised violence – partly aided and sustained through illicit flows of money, arms and other supplies. Some of these armed conflicts prompt international intervention, including imposition of arms embargoes and provision of humanitarian aid – which in turn can become entangled in various illicit flow dynamics (such as embargo busting and diverting relief supplies to the black market).

The most powerful states in the international system typically determine which illicit flows are at the top of the policing agenda. Thus, policing the global antiquities trade, a concern for source countries such as Egypt, Iraq, Peru and Guatemala, is relatively weak, with wealthy collectors in advanced industrialised countries the primary source of demand.[15] Similarly, illicit toxic waste exports from rich to poor countries receive considerably less law enforcement scrutiny than the export of labour from poor to rich countries.[16] The US – a global policing superpower – has

[14] In some cases this is institutionalised at the international level in the form of global prohibition regimes. See E Nadelmann, 'Global Prohibition Regimes: The Evolution of Norms in International Society' (1990) 44 *International Organization* 479.

[15] See especially, SRM Mackenzie, *Going, Going, Gone: Regulating the Market in Illicit Antiquities* (Leicester, Institute of Art and Law, 2005).

[16] J Clapp, *Toxic Exports: The Transfer of Hazardous Wastes from Rich to Poor Countries* (Ithaca, Cornell University Press, 2001).

successfully exported its anti-drug agenda and police methods to the rest of the world[17] while simultaneously obstructing and weakening initiatives to more forcefully police illicit flows of small arms. Indeed, not just illicit flows but also the policing of such flows mirror broader power asymmetries in the international system.

(Mis)measuring Illicit Globalisation

The total amount of illicit transnational economic activity has no doubt grown substantially in recent decades – as the conventional account of illicit globalisation repeatedly tells us. However, as an overall percentage of global economic transactions, there is little evidence that illicit flows have actually increased, and they may indeed be no larger (and quite possibly much smaller) than in previous historical eras. Importantly, the significant liberalisation of trade in recent decades has greatly reduced the incentives to engage in smuggling practices based on evading tariffs and export/import duties, historically the main type of illicit trade. Instead, global smuggling is now increasingly about evading trade prohibitions and bans.

Unfortunately, standard accounts of the magnitude of illicit globalisation tend to provide little or no historical comparison and make bold numerical assertions based on dubious data. Illicit economic flows are, of course, inherently difficult to measure – the market actors, after all, are trying to avoid being counted – but while this presents profound measurement problems, it has not inhibited statistical claims. The official numbers (from government offices and agencies and international organisations such as the UN and INTERPOL) are highly problematic yet go largely unchallenged. All too often, little effort is made to try to explain where the numbers come from and why they are credible.[18]

This is illustrated in the case of illicit drugs. The US State Department produces the annual, 'International Narcotics Control Strategy Report', which estimates illicit drug production by other countries. Peter Reuter points out that:

> No detail has ever been published on the methodology of these estimates, beyond the fact that they are generated from estimates of growing area, crop per acre, and refining yield per ton of raw product; the information sources, even the technology used to produce them (for area estimates) are classified.[19]

He concludes that the estimates 'show inexplicable inconsistency over time and across sectors of the industry. Some numbers are simply implausible.'[20]

---

[17] Friman argues that this makes it possible for the US to export some of the costs of prohibition. See HR Friman, 'Externalizing the Costs of Prohibition' in HR Friman (ed), *Crime and the Global Political Economy* (Boulder, Lynne Rienner, 2009).

[18] For a more general discussion, see P Andreas and K Greenhill (eds), *Sex, Drugs, and Body Counts: The Politics of Numbers in Global Crime and Conflict* (Ithaca, Cornell University Press, 2010).

[19] P Reuter, 'The Mismeasurement of Illegal Drug Markets: The Implications of its Irrelevance' in S Pozo (ed), *Exploring the Underground Economy* (Kalamazoo, Upjohn Institute, 1996) 65.

[20] ibid.

The drug trade numbers from international organisations are equally suspect. In the 1990s the United Nations Drug Control Program (UNDCP) often reported the global annual value of the illicit drug trade to be US$500 billion. This number was picked up in the press and recycled through so many stories that it took on a life of its own, becoming a widely accepted figure. Some scholars perpetuated the problem by using this number in their own work, which was then reused by other scholars, repeating and further extending the recycling pattern found in the media.[21] RT Naylor describes his encounter with a senior UN anti-drug official who used the $500 billion figure at an international conference:

> I diplomatically suggested to him that to get such a number, he and his colleagues must have not only included the value of every donkey owned by every campesino in the Andes but priced those donkeys as if they cost as much as a pickup truck. His response was to huff away. But he returned a while later, perhaps mellowed by cocktails, to suggest that although there were problems with the number, it was great for catching public attention.[22]

The UNDCP later lowered the estimate to $400 billion, reporting that it represented approximately 8 per cent of international trade. Yet closer scrutiny reveals that this number is not actually a trade estimate but rather an estimate of retail-level expenditures (sale price on the street) – which, as Reuter notes, are considerably higher given the value-added in consumer countries. The estimate is further inflated because it relies on US drug prices, which are typically higher than elsewhere.[23]

In one case, illicit trade numbers that failed to sufficiently impress were discarded. In the late 1990s, the Financial Action Task Force (FATF), the leading international institution responsible for combating criminal finance, began an effort to determine the size of the illicit global economy, in particular the illicit drug trade. Francisco Thoumi, an economist and former UNDCP consultant, writes that:

> The resulting study is probably the most serious attempt to ascertain the size of the world illegal drug market and resulted in an estimated range between $45 and $280 billion. Unfortunately, after an internal debate at FATF it was apparently decided not to publish the study because some country members expected a larger figure.[24]

Inflated statistics on illicit trade contribute to the construction of a dominant narrative about transnational crime as an enormous and rapidly growing global threat. As Deborah Stone reminds us, 'numbers are commonly used to tell a story. Most obviously, they are the premier language for stories of decline and decay.

[21] Some scholars continued to use this inflated number many years after it had been challenged and revised downward. See, eg L Shelley, 'The Rise and Diversification of Human Smuggling and Trafficking into the United States' in Thachuck (ed), *Transnational Threats* (n 11) 194.

[22] RT Naylor, *Wages of Crime* (Ithaca, Cornell University Press, 2002) xxi.

[23] P Reuter and V Greenfield, 'Measuring Global Drug Markets: How Good are the Numbers and Why Should We Care About Them?' (2001) 2 *World Economics* 160.

[24] FE Thoumi, 'The Numbers Game: Let's All Guess the Size of the Illegal Drug Industry!' (2005) 35 *Journal of Drug Issues* 191.

Figures are invoked to show that a problem is getting bigger and worse. . .'[25] Nowhere is this more strikingly evident than in the use of 'scary numbers' about illicit flows.[26] Indeed, such numbers have helped fuel a cottage industry of 'global crime' books since the early 1990s. These popular accounts both depend on and further legitimise dubious statistics about the size and growth rates of various illicit flows. They all have the same basic storyline: global crime is booming, unprecedented and a grave threat.

One of the most influential books in this genre is Moises Naim's, *Illicit: How Smugglers, Traffickers and Copycats are Hijacking the Global Economy.*[27] The numbers used support the underlying message of the book: illicit global markets are an unprecedented threat to the global economy and growing at a startling rate. If these numbers were not available, Naim would not have been able to write the same book and tell the same story. This is evident in his depiction of the counterfeiting business:

> Since the early 1990s, according to INTERPOL, trade in counterfeits has grown *eight times* the speed of legitimate trade. Twenty years ago, commercial losses around the world due to counterfeiting were estimated in the $5 billion range; today they are around $500 billion. That puts the cost of counterfeiting between 5 and 10 percent of the total value of world trade, on a par with, say, the GDP of Australia.[28]

Even more eye-catching are the statistics Naim uses regarding money laundering:

> The rule of thumb to estimate the scope of money laundering today is between two and five percent of world GDP, or $800 billion to $2 trillion. Some estimates run as high as 10 percent of global GDP.[29]

Naim, who does not question these statistical claims, explains: 'All of the numbers in this book come from the most reliable sources possible – usually international organisations and governments or non-governmental organisations whose work is generally deemed to be serious and reliable.'[30] None of the reviews of Naim's book raise an eyebrow regarding his uncritical use of official numbers.[31]

Even the titles of some popular books in this genre use head-turning numerical claims. One book on international money laundering is titled, *The Laundrymen: Inside the World's Third Largest Business.*[32] The title of a book about counterfeiting is equally provocative and rarely cites the sources of numbers used: *Knockoff: The Deadly Trade in Counterfeit Goods: The True Story of the World's Fastest Growing*

---

[25] D Stone, *Policy Paradox: The Art of Political Decision Making* (New York, Norton, 1997) 172.

[26] Joel Best devotes a chapter to the phenomena of 'scary numbers' in *More Damned Lies and Statistics* (Berkeley, University of California Press, 2004).

[27] Naim, *Illicit*, above n 9.

[28] ibid, 112 (emphasis in original).

[29] ibid, 137.

[30] ibid, 11.

[31] The only exception I found is the review by RT Naylor in *London Review of Books* (22 March 2007).

[32] J Robinson, *The Laundrymen: Inside the World's Third Largest Business* (New York, Arcade Publishing, 1997).

Crime Wave.[33] The statistics presumably come from the many business and trade groups created to combat these problems (which are listed at the end of the book). As a report by the Organisation for Economic Co-operation and Development (OECD) on intellectual property crime observes: 'Many of the anti-counterfeiting organisations are lobby groups and have an incentive to present exaggerated figures that may bias the true picture.'[34]

The Triumph of the (Illicit) Market and a Borderless World?

Regardless of the specific numbers used, the dominant story of illicit globalisation is one of markets trumping states: state controls are flaunted and circumvented with growing ease by geographically nimble clandestine economic actors meeting a growing market demand for illicit goods, labour and services.[35] Yet states, at the most basic level, define what economic activities are illicit in the first place: laws precede and define criminality. Through their law making and law-enforcing authority, states set the rules of the game even if they cannot entirely control the play. States monopolise the power to determine who and what has legitimate territorial access and define the terms of such access.[36] For example, changes in tax, tariff and duty laws and enforcement policies have profound effects on the incidence and profitability of smuggling ventures.[37] Thus, rather than simply reflecting 'globalisation out of control', the prevalence of illicit global commerce reflects how limited and incomplete globalisation actually is. In other words, there would be no illicit trade in a truly 'borderless world' where free trade fully reigns in all sectors of the economy.

In understanding the relationship between states and illicit globalisation, it is important to differentiate between authority and control as distinct dimensions of state power. As Janice Thomson has explained, states claim meta-political authority: the right to decide what is political and, thus, subject to state coercion.[38] However, the authority to make the rules is not the same as the capacity to enforce them. When state actors invoke metapolitical authority to ban or restrict specific economic practices, the gap between the authority to create laws and the ability to

---

[33] T Phillips, *Knockoff: The Deadly Trade in Counterfeit Goods: The True Story of the World's Fastest Growing Crime Wave* (London, Kogan Page, 2005).

[34] OECD, *The Economic Impact of Counterfeiting* (Paris, OECD, 1998) 27.

[35] HR Friman, 'Crime and Globalisation' in Friman (ed), *Crime and the Global Political Economy*, above n 17, 9.

[36] SD Krasner, 'Power, Politics, Institutions, and Transnational Relations' in T Risse-Kappen (ed), *Bringing Transnational Relations Back In* (New York, Cambridge University Press, 1995) 268.

[37] For an insightful early account, see JI Dominguez, 'Smuggling' (1975) 20 *Foreign Policy* 87–96, 161–64.

[38] J Thomson, 'State Sovereignty in International Relations' (1995) 39 *International Studies Quarterly* 213.

enforce such laws is where illicit globalisation operates. Put differently, illicit globalisation is defined by and depends on the state's exercising its metapolitical authority to impose restrictions and prohibitions without the full capacity or willingness to enforce its laws. Thus, paradoxically, illicit global market actors are pursued by the state but are also kept in business by the state.

The power of the state to define the content of illicit globalisation should not be overlooked or discounted. New laws turn once legal transnational activities into criminal activities, resulting in sudden and sometimes dramatic overall increases in transnational crime. Indeed, a century ago, much of what today is considered transnational crime (most notably drug trafficking) was not even criminalised by most states – and by definition was not a crime problem. In fact, some of today's illicit economic activities were only criminalised a few decades ago, including trade prohibitions on toxic waste, CFCs, antiquities, endangered species and money laundering. Illicit globalisation is thus not only about more expansive transnational crime but also about more ambitious global prohibitions.[39] At the same time, we should recall that some of today's legitimate economic activities were previously criminalised and considered a serious transnational crime threat. For instance, alcohol smuggling networks linking the US to suppliers in Europe, Canada, Mexico and the Caribbean created a formidable policing challenge during the Prohibition Era – and were eliminated with the stroke of a pen with the repeal of the Volstead Act in 1933.

The effectiveness of state controls has typically depended on the nature of the smuggled commodity, the ease of production, concealment and transport, the availability of legal substitutes, and the nature and levels of consumer demand.[40] Policing efforts often fail to eliminate the targeted activity, but nevertheless function as a form of market regulation: the method, intensity, and focus of law enforcement can profoundly shape the location and form of smuggling, the size and structure of the smuggling organisations, and the cost and profitability of smuggling. Transnational crimes such as drug trafficking and migrant smuggling are so profitable precisely because states impose and enforce prohibitions. In this regard, prohibitions function as price supports – which in turn help to attract new market entrants regardless of the occupational hazards.

Corruption can also be viewed as an informal type of market regulation. Illicit market participants may attempt to bully and buy off state officials, but this is primarily because they lack the capacity to fully bypass them. Corruption thus reflects state weakness, but also state power as an informal method of taxation.[41]

The dominant account of illicit globalisation also views national borders as increasingly irrelevant; yet the centrality of the state in determining transnational crime is evident, at the most basic level, in the creation and dissolution of

---

[39] Nadelmann, 'Global Prohibition Regimes', above n 14.
[40] ibid.
[41] See, eg HV der Veen, 'Taxing the Drug Trade: Coercive Exploitation and the Financing of Rule' (2003) 40 *Crime, Law and Social Change* 349.

borders.[42] The splintering of the Austro-Hungarian Empire during World War I, for example, internationalised what had previously been intra-imperial criminal activities. Similarly, the dissolution of the Ottoman Empire during roughly the same period, and of the British, French, and other Western European empires following World War II, turned domestic crime into transnational crime. Much the same happened with the fragmentation of the Soviet Union and of Yugoslavia in the early 1990s. Border shifts can also transform transnational crime into domestic crime: consider the respective consolidation of Italy, Germany and the US during the nineteenth century, and the absorption of the Baltic states by the Soviet Union during the early 1940s.

To the degree that non-state activities predating the imposition of borders persist, they are often the targets of new controls and relabelled as criminal. Previous trading relations and labour flows may be re-categorised as smuggling and illegal migration. Enduring illustrations are the ancient trade routes and migrations throughout parts of Asia and Africa that continue despite the imposition of borders, first by European colonialists and later by the states left in their wake. Finally, the imposition of borders can stimulate crime that previously had not existed in the region as either criminal or legal activity. The impetus has often come from inducements to illicit trade that are created by tariffs, duties and differences in criminal laws and enforcement on either side of the border.

As always, borders have been far more permeable than the Westphalian ideal implies. Nostalgic calls to 'regain control' of borders falsely imply that borders used to be truly 'under control'. Those who suggest that there was a 'golden age' of state control suffer from a severe case of historical amnesia.[43]

The US–Mexico border, for instance, is often given as an illustration of illicit markets overpowering the state. The first boom in migrant smuggling across the border into the US was not of Mexicans but rather Chinese migrants using the border as an entry point to the US labour market after the Chinese Exclusion Act of 1882. Looking even further back, the US–Mexico economic relationship was actually founded on smuggling – and unlike today, most of what was smuggled flowed from north to south. The first conflict over illegal immigration was over the unauthorised influx of US settlers in defiance of Mexican immigration restrictions prior to the Mexican–American war and the redrawing of the boundary. High tariffs and low enforcement capacity also meant that much of Mexico's cross-border trade after independence from Spain in 1821 was contraband. This contraband trade has now been largely eliminated since the signing of NAFTA, which dismantled trade barriers between the two countries.[44]

---

[42] See G Gavrilis, *The Dynamics of Interstate Boundaries* (Cambridge, Cambridge University Press, 2008).

[43] JE Thomson and SD Krasner, 'Global Transactions and the Consolidation of Sovereignty' in E Czempiel and JN Rosenau (eds), *Global Changes and Theoretical Challenges: Approaches to World Politics for the 1990s* (Lexington, Lexington Books, 1989) 198.

[44] See LS Sadler, 'The Historic Dynamics of Smuggling in the US–Mexican Border Region, 1550–998', in J Bailey and R Godson (eds), *Organised Crime and Democratic Governability* (Pittsburgh, University of Pittsburgh Press, 2000).

The fact that 'trade barriers' for labour and drugs have not also been eliminated (and indeed have been strengthened) is the reason they now dominate efforts to combat smuggling across the US–Mexico border. Ironically, trade barriers against marijuana imports – the bulkiest and therefore the easiest drug to interdict – have inadvertently provided a form of protectionism for domestic marijuana producers.[45] The border also profoundly shapes cocaine shipments: the value of a kilo of cocaine increases approximately 600 per cent once it crosses the border into the US.[46] With the tightening of state controls, migrant smuggling has become a much more sophisticated and organised business since the early 1990s. The border remains highly porous, but is far more difficult for migrants to cross than ever before. The fact that migrants keep crossing in the face of more formidable border barriers has less to do with the power of smuggling organisations than with the unwillingness of the state to target domestic employers (the demand for cheap migrant labour).[47]

State capacities to detect, deter and detain transnational crime have, if anything, substantially increased since the heyday of smuggling several centuries ago. The number of safe havens for criminals across the world has shrunk dramatically over time as the law enforcement reach of the state has expanded domestically and internationally.[48] It should be remembered that some key control tools, such as the universal adoption of the passport, did not arrive until the early twentieth century.[49] Importantly, while difficult to measure, it is also clear that across much of the world, societal norms have shifted to the advantage of state controls. In the eighteenth-century Atlantic world, for example, smuggling in defiance of the authorities was widely viewed as acceptable, 'normal' economic and social behaviour. Today, large-scale and highly organised illicit trade continues but is more likely to be viewed as deviant and to carry a social stigma.

The Technology Factor

A common theme in conventional accounts of illicit globalisation is the role of new and inexpensive technologies, such as the Internet, in facilitating and enabling illicit transnational economic activities. This is no doubt true, but it is also simply the latest chapter in an old story. For centuries, law enforcement officials have bemoaned the crime-enabling effects of new technologies – and have

---

[45] RR Clayton, *Marijuana in the 'Third World': Appalachia, USA* (Boulder, Lynne Rienner, 1995).

[46] Williams, 'Transnational Organised Crime and the State', above n 3.

[47] For a more detailed analysis, see P Andreas, *Border Games: Policing the US–Mexico Divide* (Ithaca, Cornell University Press, 2009).

[48] P Andreas and E Nadelmann, *Policing the Globe: Criminalization and Crime Control in International Relations* (New York, Oxford University Press, 2006).

[49] J Torpey, *The Invention of the Passport: Surveillance, Citizenship, and the State* (New York, Cambridge University Press, 2000).

successfully used this as a rationale to further expand their policing reach.[50] However, the impact of such innovations may be equal to, or considerably less than, in earlier eras. Consider, for instance, the profound effect of the steamship, the railway, the telegraph, the telephone, the automobile and the airplane in enhancing (legal and illegal) cross-border mobility and communication.[51]

Moreover, technology is double-edged, not just challenging but also aiding the state. Consider, for example, how the development of photography and finger-printing has revolutionised criminal investigations and long-distance police cooperation.[52] Technological innovations have long played a key role in the development of government-issued travel documents.[53] The invention of the steamship in the nineteenth century played an important role in largely wiping out maritime piracy[54] (a problem that is making a comeback these days, but is so far geographically isolated). Innovations in printing technology over time have made it possible for governments to maintain a technological lead (however tenuous) over currency counterfeiters. Currency counterfeiting remains a worldwide problem – and probably always will be, especially if state-sponsored (as in the case of North Korea) – but the magnitude of the problem today pales in comparison to the extent of counterfeiting in earlier centuries. The banking system in nineteenth-century America, for example, was plagued by counterfeit currency, prompting the creation of the Secret Service and a major crackdown by the end of the century.[55]

The role of new technologies in facilitating law enforcement has, if anything, been growing. For instance, even as new information technologies enable cross-border crime, these technological advances also greatly increase tracking and surveillance capacities, well beyond traditional wiretapping.[56] Technology has also dramatically lowered the costs and increased the intensity and frequency of trans-governmental law enforcement networks.[57] In short, many of the same technological transformations that facilitate the globalisation of crime also facilitate the globalisation of crime control.[58]

---

[50] See especially, M Deflem, 'Technology and the Internationalization of Policing: A Comparative Historical Perspective' (2002) 19 *Justice Quarterly* 453.

[51] Naylor, *Wages of Crime*, above n 22, 5.

[52] See SA Cole, *Suspect Identities: A History of Fingerprinting and Criminal Investigation* (Cambridge, MA, Harvard University Press, 2001).

[53] See J Kaplan and J Torpey (eds), *Documenting Individual Identity: State Practices in the Modern World* (Princeton, Princeton University Press, 2001).

[54] Nadelmann, 'Global Prohibition Regimes', above n 14.

[55] See especially, S Mihm, A Nation of Counterfeiters: Capitalists, Con Men, and the Making of the United States (Cambridge, MA, Harvard University Press, 2007).

[56] W Diffie and S Landau, *Privacy on the Line: The Politics of Wiretapping and Encryption* (Cambridge, MA, MIT Press, 2007).

[57] On the role of technology in enhancing trans-governmental networks, see K Raustiala, 'The Architecture of International Cooperation: Transgovernmental Networks and the Future of International Law' (2002) 43 *Virginia Journal of International Law* 21.

[58] For a review, see B Bowling, 'Transnational Policing: The Globalisation Thesis, a Typology and a Research Agenda' (2009) 3 Policing 149.

New technologies will continue to enhance the ability of states to police the cross-border flow of cargo, money and people. For example, the 'virtual borders' currently promoted by US law enforcement strategists are essentially electronic borders.[59] This digitisation has ranged from the use of more expansive and sophisticated databases for 'data mining' and computer tracking systems to the creation of more tamper resistant travel documents and 'smart' IDs with biometric identifiers (such as digital fingerprints and facial and retinal scans). Cutting-edge technologies enabling future crimes such as DNA theft and illicit cloning will, no doubt, have equally significant policing applications, including new types of DNA mapping and testing and other forms of identification.

Some illicit uses of new technologies, such as electronic banking, leave digital fingerprints that state authorities can detect and trace.[60] This is one reason why the use of informal banking mechanisms (such as *hawalas*) are often preferred over the formal banking system, and why concerns about digital eavesdropping sometimes make transnational law evaders wary of using various forms of electronic communication. Similarly, illicit online commercial transactions are often constrained by the need to use credit cards, which leave a record. This is partly the reason why so many illicit activities on the Internet – whether they be the circulation of pirated music or child pornography – involve a barter exchange economy based on file sharing rather than financial transactions.

Governments are also increasingly enlisting the private sector to electronically monitor and police illicit transnational flows. Shipping companies and airlines are being compelled to track and screen cargo and passengers more carefully. The same is true for banks and other financial institutions in monitoring and reporting suspicious monetary transactions. These and other mechanisms make it possible to 'monitor, surveil, or analyse data and behaviors beyond the reach or capacity of traditional state surveillance or monitoring power'.[61]

State-promoted Illicit Globalisation

Too often glossed over in conventional accounts of illicit globalisation is that some clandestine economic flows are state-promoted. This is readily apparent, for instance, in the case of sanctions busting.[62] Prominent cases of large-scale evasion

[59] On the turn to new technologies, see SE Flynn, 'The False Conundrum: Continental Integration Versus Homeland Security' in P Andreas and T Biersteker (eds), *The Rebordering of North America: Integration and Exclusion in a New Security Context* (New York, Routledge, 2003); and R Koslowski, 'International Migration and Border Control in the Information Age' Rutgers University-Newark (12 April 2002).

[60] In the case of electronic finance, see E Helleiner, 'Electronic Money: A Challenge to the Sovereign State?' (1998) 51 *Journal of International Affairs* 387.

[61] KA Taipale, 'Transnational Intelligence and Surveillance: Security Envelopes, Trusted Systems, and the Panoptic Global Security State' (Beyond Terror Conference, Brown University, June 2005).

[62] RT Naylor, *Patriots and Profiteers: On Economic Warfare, Embargo Busting, and State Sponsored Crime* (Toronto, Mclelland and Stewart, 1999).

of economic sanctions via illicit trade and financial networks include Iraq and Yugoslavia in the 1990s. In both cases, state leaders strategically co-opted and collaborated with the criminal underworld to undermine external controls, much like Napoleon did with the British during the Napoleonic Wars.[63]

State-sponsored illicit trade is not restricted to a handful of 'rogue states' such as Iraq under Hussein, Serbia under Milosevic, or Myanmar (Burma) and North Korea in more recent years.[64] Political leaders in many developing and developed countries, for example, routinely disperse the benefits of illicit trade as part of the larger system of patronage politics.[65] Bank secrecy laws reflect another form of state sponsorship and long predate the contemporary era of financial globalisation.[66] Switzerland's stubborn refusal to relax its strict bank secrecy laws in the face of intense US pressure is based on the long-standing practice of facilitating tax evasion.[67]

Illicit technology transfer also often involves state complicity – nowhere more evident than in nuclear smuggling. As is now well known, Pakistan not only illicitly acquired nuclear technology but then became a leading player in the global black market through the clandestine networks developed by its nuclear scientist and national hero, Abdul Qadeer Khan.[68] This technological acquisition enhanced the power and prestige of Pakistan, despite exacerbating regional insecurity.

Illicit finance and the arms trade have also long been closely tied to covert government operations. The Cold War, not globalisation, provided the most important impetus: the intelligence services of the US and the Soviet Union exploited illicit networks for a variety of purposes, including funding and supplying insurgents across the globe. In the realm of illicit finance, the scandal involving the Bank of Credit and Commerce International (BCCI) revealed that this major international bank was not only favoured by money-launderers but also by a number of governments and their intelligence services for covert financial transactions.[69] In the post-Cold War era, no arms dealer gained more notoriety than the transportation specialist Victor Bout. Often overlooked, was that his list of clients included many governments such as the US government, which contracted Bout's cargo planes for airlift operations after the US invasion of Iraq.[70]

---

[63] P Andreas, 'The Criminalizing Consequences of Sanctions: Embargo Busting and its Legacy' (2005) 49 *International Studies Quarterly* 335.

[64] S Chestnut, 'Illicit Activity and Proliferation: North Korean Smuggling Networks' (2007) 32 *International Security* 80.

[65] See W Reno, 'Illicit Commerce and Peripheral States' in Friman (ed), *Crime and the Global Political Economy*, above n 18.

[66] See especially, R Palan, 'Tax Havens and the Commercialization of State Sovereignty' (2002) 56 *International Organization* 151.

[67] D Jolly, 'Swiss Vow to Block UBS from Providing Data to US' *New York Times* (New York, 8 July 2009).

[68] See G Correra, *Shopping for Bombs: Nuclear Proliferation, Global Insecurity, and the Rise and Fall of the AQ Kahn Network* (New York, Oxford University Press, 2006).

[69] N Passas, 'The Mirror of Global Evils: A Review Essay on the BCCI Affair' (1995) 12 *Justice Quarterly* 801.

[70] D Farah and S Braun, *Merchant of Death: Money, Guns, Planes and the Man Who Makes War Possible* (New York, Wiley, 2008) 214–30.

Of course, in the murky world of covert operations, the distinction between state actors and non-state illicit actors can become blurry.[71] A 'non-state actor' involved in smuggling may be a former intelligence agent or an active informant on the government payroll. State actors may subcontract out covert tasks to private third parties to maximise plausible deniability. The arms trade is most notorious for this collaboration.

Some illicit cross-border economic activities need not involve state sponsorship to serve state objectives. Clandestine migration, for instance, can provide an important 'safety valve' helping labour-exporting countries to cope with their unemployment problems and reap the benefits of remittances sent home. Mexico is an obvious case, but others include Ecuador, El Salvador, Guatemala Honduras and Morocco. Moreover, some countries, such as Malaysia, even actively recruit unauthorised migrants for political reasons.[72] While the international community generally discourages clandestine migration, the remittances send home by migrants is often encouraged and viewed as a vital source of revenue.[73]

Similarly, the large-scale production of counterfeit goods in China can be viewed as indirectly serving state interests. Although impossible to measure with any accuracy, it is clear that the Chinese counterfeiting industry is a major employer on which the country relies. This explains why the Chinese government has been so resistant to external pressure to crack down more aggressively on piracy and counterfeiting. It is simply not in its interests to close the large gap between its formal international obligations and actual domestic enforcement on the ground.[74]

Again, historical comparison is illuminating. In today's intellectual property protection debates the fact that the US government tolerated and even encouraged intellectual piracy and technology smuggling during the country's initial industrialisation process, especially in the textile industry, is typically ignored. These legal oversights ultimately enabled Samuel Slater, the father of the American industrial revolution, to illegally leave England to work on and perfect smuggled machinery in the US.[75] Only later, once it was a leading industrial power, did the US become a forceful advocate of intellectual property protection. In other words, the US message to China and other countries today is, 'do as I say, not as I did'.

Intellectual piracy in nineteenth-century America extended beyond illicit technology transfers. American authors and filmmakers today, as in the nineteenth

---

[71] For a general discussion of the 'covert world', see R Cox, *Political Economy of a Plural World: Reflections on Power, Morals, and Civilization* (London, Routledge, 2002) 118–38.

[72] K Sadiq, 'When States Prefer Non-Citizens over Citizens: Conflict over Illegal Immigration into Malaysia' (2005) 49 *International Studies Quarterly* 101.

[73] For an especially celebratory account, see D Kapur and J McHale, 'Migration's New Payoff' (2003) *Foreign Policy* 48.

[74] A Mertha, *The Politics of Piracy: Intellectual Property in Contemporary China* (Ithaca, Cornell University Press, 2005).

[75] DS Ben-Atar, *Trade Secrets: Intellectual Piracy and the Origins of American Industrial Power* (New Haven, Yale University Press, 2004).

century, are understandably upset that bootleg copies of their books and films immediately enter the black market.

Violence, 'New Wars' and Illicit Globalisation

According to the standard story of illicit globalisation, as criminal enterprise has become global, so too has the violence associated with it. This violence comes in two forms: first, violence as an inherent attribute of illicit business transactions; and second, illicit business as an economic motivator and/or enabler of contemporary internal wars – also called 'new wars'.[76]

Regarding the first claim, it is certainly the case that illicit markets are more prone to violence than legal markets, given that illicit market actors do not have recourse to the law to enforce contracts or to protect or punish depredations by participants or outsiders. Lacking the protections of the law, illicit market actors must rely on forms of informal social control, such as violence, to resolve their disputes and deter those who might otherwise interfere. However, actors in the illicit global economy are defined more by stealth than violence.[77]

Part of the reason that organised violence and illicit markets are so conventionally linked is that episodes of violence draw the most attention and provoke the most concern. Thus, the analysis is distorted by selection bias, which privileges the most violent sectors of the illicit economy – most notably the illicit drug trade (though even drug markets are less violent than is commonly perceived[78]).

Moreover, within the drug trade there is a privileging of attention to hard drugs such as cocaine and heroin (relatively high levels of violence) over soft drugs such as marijuana and MDMA (much lower levels of violence). Within the trade in hard drugs there is selection bias that favours attention to the most violent places and actors, such as Colombia, rather than less violent places such as Bolivia. Similarly, the relatively high violence in domestic US drug markets overshadows the strikingly low levels of violence in domestic European and Japanese drug markets.[79]

Selection bias is also evident in accounts of violence related to other illicit economic activities. Consider, for instance, the organisation of migrant smuggling. Most of the stories that generate media and political attention are of extreme cases of death and abuse with smugglers blamed for abandoning migrants, robbing and deceiving them, and sometimes even throwing them overboard. As tragic as these

---

[76] See especially, M Kaldor, *New and Old Wars: Organised Violence in a Global Era* (Stanford, Stanford University Press, 1999) 95–119.

[77] For a more detailed discussion, see the special issue of *Crime, Law and Social Change* focusing on the relationship between illicit markets and violence (September 2009).

[78] See P Reuter, 'Systemic Violence in Drug Markets' (2009) 52 *Crime, Law and Social Change* 275.

[79] HR Friman, 'Drug Markets and the Selective use of Violence' (2009) *Crime, Law and Social Change* 285–95.

cases are, they are relatively rare given the high volume of illicit cross-border pop-ulation flows.[80]

Violent confrontations between migrant smugglers and the state are also extraordinarily rare. The business of migrant smuggling typically seeks to evade (or pay off) state authorities rather than violently challenge them. Here, government corruption can have a pacifying effect, since it reflects informal accommo-dation. Indeed, the breakdown of this arrangement in Mexico has contributed to the upsurge in violence since 2006.[81]

It should be stressed that violence in the illicit global economy is typically selec-tive and instrumental rather than random and gratuitous. Victims tend to be other market participants rather than state actors or the general public (and some state actors are targeted because they are market participants). The targeting of state actors generates the most attention and reinforces assumptions about the highly violent nature of illicit markets. Excessive violence (regardless of the target) can be bad for business, since it is disruptive and invites unwanted police and media scrutiny. High-profile police crackdowns, meanwhile, can unintentionally fuel more market-related violence – as some illicit actors are removed, new ones emerge to fill the void and claim market share through violent competition. Mexico is the most dramatic contemporary case of this phenomenon.[82]

Illicit global trade has also been increasingly blamed for fueling armed con-flicts, and vice versa, a defining attribute of so-called 'new wars'.[83] The economic incentives and opportunities presented by illicit trade are also an important part of the 'greed and grievance' debate in the literature on contemporary civil wars.[84] Prominent cases include drug production and trafficking (Colombia and Afghanistan); export of 'blood diamonds' (West Africa); and embargo busting and theft and diversion of humanitarian aid (the Balkans). New transportation and communication technologies also clearly facilitate long-distance diaspora mobilisation and funding of conflicts, as evident in the Balkans and elsewhere.[85]

Illicit trade and conflict are clearly connected and international interventions of various sorts (delivering humanitarian aid, deploying peacekeepers, and

---

[80] See, especially, D Kyle and R Koslowski (eds), *Global Human Smuggling* (Baltimore, Johns Hopkins University Press, 2001). See also D Kyle and M Scarcelli, 'Migrant Smuggling and the Violence Question: Evolving Illicit Migration Markets for Cuban and Haitian Refugees' (2009) *Crime, Law and Social Change* 297.

[81] M Serrano, 'Drug Trafficking and the State in Mexico' in Friman (ed), *Crime and the Global Political Economy*, above n 17.

[82] ibid. See also R Snyder and A Duran-Martinez, 'Does Illegality breed Violence? Drug Trafficking and State-sponsored Protection Rackets' (2009) 52 *Crime, Law and Social Change* 253.

[83] See M Kaldor, *New and Old Wars: Organised Violence in a Global Era* (Stanford, Stanford University Press, 1999).

[84] See M Berdal and D Malone, *Greed and Grievance: Economic Agendas in Civil Wars* (Boulder, Lynne Rienner, 2000) and K Ballentine and J Sherman (eds), *The Political Economy of Armed Conflict: Beyond Greed and Grievance* (Boulder, Lynne Rienner, 2003).

[85] F Adamson, 'Globalisation, Transnational Political Mobilization, and Networks of Violence' (2005) 18 Cambridge Review of International Affairs 35. For a more general discussion of the links between migration and conflict, see F Adamson, 'Crossing Borders: International Migration and National Security' (2006) 31 International Security 165.

imposing economic sanctions and arms embargoes) can unintentionally exacerbate this connection.[86] However, this connection is too easily overstated and oversimplified. Take the case of the illicit drug trade, a business depicted to be connected to armed conflict.[87] There is nothing automatic and predetermined about this connection, which is readily apparent by the fact that many drug producing and transit areas are not war zones, and that many war zones are not drug producing and transit areas. In Mexico (a major heroin, marijuana and methamphetamine producer and the main transshipment point for US-bound cocaine), the country's large drug trade and small and isolated insurgency have been strikingly disconnected. Similarly, Bolivia has long been a major coca producer and has gone through many bouts of political instability without armed conflict. In Colombia, the drugs trade has been a key factor in extending the armed conflict amongst left-wing guerillas and right-wing paramilitaries, but it should be noted that the conflict long predates the rise of the Colombia drug trade.[88]

Armed conflict can certainly be good for illicit business, but it can also be bad for business. Consider the traditional 'Balkan route' for heroin smuggling into Western Europe, which was suddenly cut off during the violent conflicts in the region in the 1990s. The heroin transshipment route shifted westward, away from the violence; since the end of the wars, the smuggling economy has flourished.[89] Apparently, many illicit economic actors – like their legal counterparts – prefer a more stable and predictable business environment. Rather than simply being obstructionist peace spoilers, illicit economic actors can also be stakeholders in the post-war order (transcending ethnic divisions through illicit trade while simultaneously using it to fund nationalistic political projects).[90]

Illicit trade is often blamed for impeding and complicating post-war reconstruction in newly independent states such as Bosnia and Kosovo[91] but this was equally true for the US in the aftermath of the Revolutionary War. The very smuggling practices that aided the War of Independence became an obstacle for the newborn American state. The powerful legacy of colonial smuggling contributed to merchant resistance to centralised state authority and regulation of commerce.[92] This was a particularly serious problem for the nascent federal government given that virtually all of its revenue derived from trade duties. In this

[86] In the case of international intervention in Bosnia, see, eg P Andreas, *Blue Helmets and Black Markets: The Business of Survival in the Siege of Sarajevo* (Ithaca, Cornell University Press, 2008).
[87] See, eg PR Kan, *Drugs and Contemporary Warfare* (Washington, Potomac Books, 2009).
[88] M Chernick, 'Economic Resources and Internal Armed Conflicts: Lessons from the Colombian Case' in C Arnson and W Zartman (eds), *Rethinking the Economics of War: The Intersection of Need, Creed, and Greed* (Baltimore, Johns Hopkins University Press, 2005).
[89] For the case of human trafficking, see HR Friman and S Reich (eds), *Human Trafficking, Human Security, and the Balkans* (Pittsburgh, University of Pittsburgh Press, 2007).
[90] See the special issue of *Problems of Post-Communism* focusing on transnational crime and conflict in the Western Balkans (May–June 2004).
[91] ibid.
[92] JM Smith, *Borderland Smuggling: Patriots, Loyalists, and Illicit Trade in the Northeast, 1783–1820* (Gainesville, University Press of Florida, 2006).

regard, smuggling was a more serious problem for the newly independent American state than it is for many new states today.

Illicit trade was thus a major challenge to initial American state building – just as it is for state building efforts across the globe today. Indeed, this was a key – though often overlooked – part of America's 'strong society, weak state' profile. At the same time, concerns about smuggling stimulated early government expansion and border management activities, notably the creation of the US Customs Service and its revenue cutters as one of the first components of the federal bureaucracy. Efforts to combat maritime piracy, smuggling, and embargo busting also stimulated the early development of the navy.[93] Thus illicit trade and related activities were double-edged, both challenging and building up the new American state. The same is true today, suggesting far more continuity with the past than is typically recognised.

Conclusion

In this paper I have critically examined the central claims in the standard account of illicit globalisation and have argued that these claims are based on questionable assertions about the size, nature and novelty of this 'new' transnational threat. I have provided a corrective to the common public perception that states are 'losing control' in the face of illicit economic globalisation. This illicit sphere of the global economy is indeed a serious concern, but sweeping claims of unprecedented transnational crime threats need to be tempered. As I have emphasised, far from being a new threat, illicit globalisation is in many ways an old story. What has changed over time are the particular clandestine trading activities, their organisation and methods of transport, laws and the intensity of their enforcement, the degree of political and societal tolerance, and consumer demand. Illicit globalisation has long been a challenge to the state but it has not been exclusively an antagonistic relationship. Across time, place and smuggling activity, state engagement with illicit economic flows has ranged from condemnation and discouragement to toleration and complicity.

In today's era of illicit globalisation, there is clearly a substantial gap between stated policing goals and actual results. There are certainly inherent limits to how much states can deter and forbid illegal cross-border economic activities, especially if they wish to maintain open borders and societies.[94] But the popular 'sky is falling' story of illicit globalisation, which continues to dominate the public debate, does not hold up very well under close critical scrutiny.

---

[93] G Daughan, *If By Sea: The Forging of the American Navy From the Revolution to the War of 1812* (New York, Basic Books, 2008).

[94] More generally, as Herbert Packer long ago argued, there are inherent limits to what criminal sanctions can accomplish. HL Packer, *The Limits of the Criminal Sanction* (Stanford, Stanford University Press, 1968).

Unfortunately, this standard, misguided account of illicit economic globalisation can lead to counterproductive policy prescriptions. Urgent calls to 'do something' about the illicit side of globalisation can provide ammunition for politicians and bureaucrats to justify costly high profile and politically popular crackdowns that ultimately fail. It can also contribute to growing calls to further securitise and militarise policing efforts regardless of their effectiveness. This is especially evident in the case of drug control, which has had an exceptionally poor track record. Simplistically blaming globalisation can fuel calls for much tougher border enforcement that would do more to impede legitimate trade and travel than deter transnational crime. This is not meant to suggest that illegal cross-border flows are not a serious concern – far from it. It is precisely for this reason that we need more dispassionate, nuanced and historically grounded analysis.

Alarmist accounts of illicit economic globalisation in many ways echo the familiar arguments in globalisation literature about the withering away of the state in the face of increasingly globalised markets, but in this case the market actors and forces are considered to be threatening and sinister. In this narrative, global crime groups, not global corporations, are the threats. Commenting on the globalisation debate, Daniel Drezner has noted that: 'Scholarly work in this area is necessary because the popular discourse on the subject has been dreadful.'[95] This observation applies even more forcefully to the illicit globalisation debate, where anxieties about globalisation are especially pronounced and the tone of the discourse is particularly shrill. More scholarly attention should be devoted to this important but often misunderstood realm of economic globalisation. Hyperbolic condemnations and eye-catching statistical claims draw attention to the problem, but are too often a substitute for sound analysis.

---

[95] D Drezner, *All Politics is Local: Explaining International Regulatory Regimes* (Princeton, Princeton University Press, 2007) 7.

4

Political Economy and Policing:
A Tale of Two Freudian Slips

ROBERT REINER

Political economy and the 'science of police' were the progenitors of criminology *avant la lettre*. Both were occluded by the birth of *soi-disant* 'criminology' in the late nineteenth century, appearing only fitfully in criminology thereafter. There has been a recent resuscitation of political economy in the analysis of punishment, but not in the study of policing. A political economy of policing has been occluded by the bifurcation of policing studies in recent decades between cultural grand theory and 'what works' policy concerns.

This chapter will probe this double 'forgetting': of policing by political economy; and of political economy by policing studies. Both forgettings are Freudian slips, not mere oversights but driven – albeit subconsciously – by deeper processes. It will be argued that despite this repression, a political economy perspective is needed to illuminate policing.

The chapter will begin by exploring what is 'political economy'? It will then demonstrate that criminology in general, and the study of policing in particular, were rooted in eighteenth-century political economy and 'police science'. An exodus followed this genesis. As 'criminology' became a distinct discipline in the later nineteenth century political economy was largely ousted from its repertoire, until a brief flourishing with the radical criminologies of the 1960s and 1970s. Despite the emergence in the last decade of a new political economy of punishment, as yet there has been little sign of this in the analysis of policing, as will be shown by a review of the evolution of policing studies. The chapter concludes with an argument for the centrality of political economy for understanding policing.

What is Political Economy?

'Political economy' is usually distinguished from 'economics',[1] the academic discipline that flourishes in contemporary universities around the world (despite
what might be seen as a discrediting of its prevailing models since the crunching
of credit in 2007 and the subsequent economic malaise in the Western world). At
its inception in the eighteenth and early nineteenth centuries, 'political economy',
in the hands of Adam Smith, Ricardo, Mill, Marx and other pioneers, was insepa-
rable from moral philosophy and from other aspects of social life that have come
to be the province of separate disciplines. The 'economic' was seen as inter-related
with the 'political', 'moral' and 'social'.

'Economics' now signifies a powerful, institutionalised academic discipline that
purports to offer 'value-free', apolitical, 'scientific' analysis of economic processes
(but increasingly also a host of other phenomena). It primarily deploys mathemati-
cal modelling techniques based on highly abstract *a priori* assumptions about
human motivation, cognition, and social organisation. In spite of criticism of the
neo-classical approach within the profession,[2] it remains the dominant perspective.

Despite some variations, the most common usage of the term 'political economy' connotes a holistic attempt to synthesise different dimensions of explanation and interpretation, aimed at analysing both differences between times and
places of whole societies and of specific institutions, policies and actions within
them. Political economy allows a role for ideal as well as material factors, micro,
meso and macro levels, postulating a dialectic of structure/action, autonomy/
determinism.

Political Economy and the Development of Criminology

Pre-criminologies

The genesis of the modern study of crime, criminal justice, and police lie in
eighteenth-century political economy, in Beccaria's classical approach to penality
and in the science of police. These are criminologies *avant la lettre* as the term
criminology itself was not coined until the 1870s. Both pre-criminologies embodied political economy in their conceptual structures. 'Classicism' presupposed the

---

[1] Somewhat confusingly they are also occasionally used as synonyms. The house journal of the
Chicago School, a bastion of the dominant neo-classical economics framework, is called the *Journal of
Political Economy*. 'Political economy' is also sometimes used to refer to the application of economics
models to analysis of political institutions.

[2] For example, the 'post autistic economics' network, www.paecon.net, and the New Economics
Foundation www.neweconomics.org.

same rational economic person model of human action as political economy.[3] The 'science of police' was more explicitly an aspect of political economy.

The 'science of police' was a vast body of work that flourished in the eighteenth and early nineteenth centuries, but has been overlooked by criminologists until recently.[4] The term 'police' was essentially synonymous with the internal policies of governments. In his 1763 *Lectures on Justice, Police, Revenue and Arms* Adam Smith defined 'police' as 'the second general division of jurisprudence. The name . . . originally derived from the Greek "politeia" which properly signified the policy of civil government'.[5]

In England the leading exponent of the 'science of police' was the magistrate Patrick Colquhoun, most commonly remembered as an architect of the modern British police in the narrow post-1829 sense. However, he also wrote extensively on political economy, crime and criminal justice. 'Colquhoun's starting point is the insecurity of property.'[6] Wealth depended on labour, but incentives to labour required that the working class remained poor, creating a perennial problem of order.[7] The task of police 'is to prevent the poverty-stricken class from becoming a criminalised and pauperised rabble'.[8] To achieve this, police had to be both tough (and smart) on crime, *and* on the (multi-layered) causes of crime.

To Colquhoun, crime and criminal justice were not independent phenomena that could be considered in isolation from broader issues of social and economic structure. Colquhoun located the ultimate causes of crime in the overall structure of economy and society, but he was concerned to trace down the social and cultural mediations generating criminality and conformity. Crime was 'the constant and never-failing attendant on the accumulation of wealth', providing the opportunities and temptations for misappropriation.[9]

The task of police was to minimise indigence — the inability or unwillingness of some to labour in order to relieve poverty. Indigence arose for both structural and cultural reasons. Structural factors included variations in the opportunities for training available to different ethnic groups, and downturns in the economic cycle. But cultural and informal moral controls (such as religion, and the promotion of uplifting rather than 'bawdy' forms of popular pastimes) were also important to encourage manners that were 'virtuous' rather than 'depraved'.

---

[3] P Beirne, *Inventing Criminology* (New York, State University of New York Press, 1993) ch 2.

[4] The main exception is Radzinowicz, who discussed it extensively in L Radzinowicz, *A History of English Criminal Law and its Administration from 1750*, Vol III (London, Stevens and Sons, 1956). Originally rediscovered by M Foucault in *Discipline and Punish* (London, Penguin, 1977) and some of his followers such as P Pasquino in 'Theatrum Politicum: The Genealogy of Capital – Police and the State of Prosperity' (1978) 4 *Ideology and Consciousness* 41, it has been increasingly influential in recent years, above all in Foucauldian discussions of 'governmentality'.

[5] Cited in Radzinowicz, *A History of the English Criminal Law*, above n 4, 421.

[6] M Neocleous, *The Fabrication of Social Order: A Critical Theory of Police Power* (London, Pluto Press, 2000) 49.

[7] P Colquhoun, *Treatise on Indigence* (London, J Hatchard, 1806) 7–8.

[8] ibid.

[9] P Colquhoun, *Treatise on the Commerce and Police of the River Thames* (London, J Mowman, 1800) 155–56.

The reform of formal policing arrangements for which Colquhoun is best known was only a relatively minor aspect of the policies required to prevent crime. The beneficial effects of police patrol were more to encourage moral discipline than to deter or catch perpetrators. Its terrain was to be

> upon the broad scale of General Prevention – mild in its operations – effective in its results; having justice and humanity for its basis, and the general security of the State and Individuals for its ultimate object.[10]

Overall, the analysis advanced by Colquhoun and the 'science of police' was more sensitive to the interplay of politics, law and justice with criminality than the later nineteenth-century 'science of the criminal'. As with the contemporaneous displacement of political economy by economics, the apparent gain in 'scientific' rigour was bought at a high price in terms of the obscuring of the political, economic and ethical dimensions of crime and welfare.

The Partial Eclipse of Political Economy by 'Criminology'

The origin of the term 'criminology' was associated with a positivist attempt to explain crime by the individual biological characteristics of the criminal, bracketing out political economy and sociology. Paul Topinard, a French doctor and physical anthropologist, coined the word 'criminology' as the label for the 'science of the criminal' pioneered by Lombroso's 1876 book *Criminal Man*. 'Criminology' has been dominated by positivist approaches for most of its history since the 1870s, originally largely biological and psychological, but with an admixture of sociological analyses especially after the 1930s.

Political Economy in Sociological Criminology

Political economy played a role in the sociology of deviance and crime, especially in anomie theory. Durkheim's analysis of anomic suicide related it to economic development and cycles, arguing that both downturns and upturns disrupted the regulation of aspirations.[11] Merton's subsequent elaboration of the concept argued that crime varied between societies, being higher if the political economy was more conducive to anomie because of a materialistic culture and an unequal social structure.[12]

Outside mainstream academic criminology, the Marxist tradition developed various analyses of crime and punishment in terms of political economy. Marx himself in Chapter 10 of *Capital* analysed the emergence of the Factory Acts primarily as a response to a structural survival requirement of capitalism needed to

---

[10] ibid at 38.

[11] E Durkheim, *Suicide* (London, Routledge, 1897/1951).

[12] R Merton, 'Social Structure and Anomie' (1957) 3 *American Sociological Review* 672. Revised in R Merton, *Social Theory and Social Structure* (London, Free Press, 1957).

mitigate the consequences of extreme competitive pressures, but mediated by human actions and conflicts that translated economic exigencies into legislative and enforcement practices.[13] In the early twentieth century, the Dutch criminologist Bonger argued that capitalism generates an egoistic culture that was conducive to crime (amongst both the proletariat and the powerful). The law and its enforcement reflected economic power, but also the general social interest in order.[14] In the 1930s Rusche and Kirchheimer constructed a political economy of punishment, relating the intensity of penal measures to the labour market.[15]

The 'realisms' of both the Right and Left after the 1970s aimed to divert analysis from macro causes, including political economy, in favour of what works in immediate control terms but both allowed a role for economic factors. Associated with Right realism was a revived neoclassical economic analysis of crime and punishment.[16] Left Realism included the Mertonian cousin of anomie, relative deprivation, in its aetiology of crime and disorder, whilst also emphasising the notion of an aetiological crisis of economic explanations.[17]

A Revived Political Economy of Punishment – But Not Policing

Since the turn of the millennium there has been a vigorous resuscitation of the political economy of punishment and control, with some forays into the analysis of broad crime patterns.[18] This has not been echoed in studies of policing, even

[13] K Marx, *Capital* Vol 1 (London, Penguin, 1867/1976).

[14] W Bonger, *Criminality and Economic Conditions* (Bloomington, Indiana University Press, 1916/1969).

[15] G Rusche and O Kircheimer, *Punishment and Social Structure* (New Jersey, Transaction, 1939/2003).

[16] G Becker, 'Crime and Punishment: An Economic Approach' (1968) 76 *Journal of Political Economy* 175; I Ehrlich, 'Participation in Illegal Activities: A Theoretical and Empirical Investigation' (1973) 81 *Journal of Political Economy* 521.

[17] J Lea and J Young, *What Is To Be Done About Law and Order?* (Harmondsworth, Penguin, 1984) ch 3; J Young, 'The Failure of Criminology: The Need for a Radical Realism' in R Matthews and J Young (eds), *Confronting Crime* (London, Sage, 1986).

[18] I Taylor, *Crime in Context* (Cambridge, Polity Press, 1999); J Young, *The Exclusive Society* (London, Sage, 1999); D Garland, *The Culture of Control* (Oxford, Oxford University Press, 2001); C Beckett and B Western, 'Governing Social Marginality: Welfare, Incarceration and the Transformation of State Policy' (2001) 3 *Punishment and Society* 43; JR Sutton, 'The Political Economy of Imprisonment in Affluent Western Democracies, 1960–1990' (2004) 69 *American Sociological Review* 170; J Pratt, J Brown, D Brown, S Hallsworth and W Morrison (eds), *The New Punitiveness: Trends, Theories, Perspectives* (Cullompton, Willan, 2005); D Downes and K Hansen, 'Welfare and Punishment in Comparative Perspective' in S Armstrong and L McAra (eds), *Perspectives on Punishment* (Oxford, Oxford University Press, 2006); B Western, *Punishment and Inequality in America* (New York, Sage, 2006); A di Giorgi, *Rethinking the Political Economy of Punishment* (Aldershot, Ashgate, 2006); M Cavadino and J Dignan, *Penal Systems: A Comparative Approach* (London, Sage, 2006); J Pratt, *Penal Populism* (London, Routledge, 2006); L Cheliotis, 'How Iron is the Iron Cage of New Penology? The Role of Human Agency in the Implementation of Criminal Justice Policy' (2006) 8 *Punishment and Society* 313; R Reiner, *Law and Order: An Honest Citizen's Guide to Crime and Control* (Cambridge, Polity, 2007); J Simon, *Governing Through Crime* (New York, Oxford University Press, 2007); N Lacey, *The Prisoners' Dilemma: Political Economy and Punishment in Contemporary Democracies* (Cambridge, Cambridge University Press, 2008); L Wacquant *Punishing the Poor: The Neoliberal Government of*

though the 'science of police' had been a crucible for the emergence of criminology.

The virtually complete absence of the police from the broad theorisations of crime control change is something of a mystery. It is only possible to speculate about why legal and criminological theory have played down policing, as compared to penal policy, even though the former touches far more lives than the latter, and is at least equally fundamental to the understanding of state power.

Perhaps a clue lies in the very concept of police as originated by eighteenth-century political economy. Adam Smith defined 'police' as the 'regulation of the *inferior* parts of government, cleanliness, security, and cheapness or plenty'. The personnel of the police (unlike the politicians and lawyers who shape penality) have always and everywhere been drawn largely from the relatively disadvantaged, and not educated to anything like the standards of 'professionals' – and this is true a fortiori of the burgeoning ranks of private security. Moreover, their clientele (both those who call upon the police and those who are targeted by them as suspects) have been even lower in the hierarchies of power and privilege, drawn from the most disadvantaged groups that have been aptly called 'police property'.

Apart from a few very high-profile exceptions (which disproportionately figure in popular culture accounts) policing is dirty work, processing perceived threats to the propriety of public space by a calibrated manipulation of the threat of force. They may be called 'The Law' (amongst some more derogatory epithets) but the police are mainly moral street sweepers. Their daily practices are largely below the radar of respectable culture and intellectual analysis.

Studies of Policing:
Whatever Happened to the Material Base?

The police research which emerged in the late 1950s and early 1960s, the zenith of social democratic sensibility, produced a picture of policing that contrasted with the common sense of popular and police culture. The increasing hegemony of neoliberalism since the early 1970s has brought with it a politics of law and order that fundamentally changed the subject of police studies and reinstated the common-sense folklore of policing, with an associated shift in the agenda of research. There has been a displacement of larger scale sociological analyses by pragmatic problem-solving.

Paradoxically, at the same time as the majority of studies of policing have become narrowly policy-focused (in a sociological style that CW Mills long ago dubbed 'Abstracted Empiricism'), there have also emerged some new (even more 'abstracted') 'Grand Theories' (again borrowing Mills' labels) of policing (Mills

Social Insecurity (Durham, Duke University Press, 2009); E Bell, *Criminal Justice and Neoliberalism* (London, Sage, 2011).

1957[19]). The two main strands are the 'nodal security' perspective,[20] and the 'new police science'.[21] Both are intellectually sophisticated, scholarly and in many ways inspirational works, rooted above all in Foucault's ideas about governmentality. Both play down, almost ignoring altogether, the public police. Both foreground cultural analysis rather than political economy (in which the 'old' police science was rooted). Above all, both share a rejection of 'mainstream criminological discourse', said to be 'still preoccupied with issues relating to the administration of security and justice by states'.[22] Similarly, the 'new police science' castigates 'the trap of twentieth century criminology, which tries to think of policing in isolation from other practices of power'.[23]

In an otherwise sophisticated scholarly analysis of the 'Theoretical Foundations of the "New Police Science"', Neocleous starts from a caricature of research on policing that is echoed in much of the new theoretical literature. He speaks of:

> the backwater of a very narrowly conceived 'police studies' . . . Reduced to the study of crime and law enforcement . . . most research on the police eschewed any attempt to make sense of the concept itself or to explore the possible diversity of police powers in terms of either their historical origins or political diversity.[24]

The main thrust of his essay is to relocate the idea of police within a framework of political economy and broader issues of governance, harking back to the eighteenth-century 'police science' that preceded the coming of the modern police. I am entirely in sympathy with the call for a political economy of policing – but I will suggest this grows out of the mainstream of the sociology of the police, *pace* Neocleous' dismissal of this as a 'backwater'. Much more turns on this than a dispute over past scholarship, however, because in their wholesale dismissal of the importance of the empirical sociological research on policing the new theories have thrown out the baby with the 'backwater'.

Policing Studies: A Critical History

Empirical research on policing emerged in the early 1960s, in both the United States and the United Kingdom.[25] What is striking compared to more recent work is that the research of the 1960s and 1970s was mainly research *on* rather than *for* the police. Although many researchers were interested in policy issues (above all civil libertarian concern about police violations of the rule of law), their work was

---

[19] CW Mills, *The Sociological Imagination* (Oxford, Oxford University Press, 1959).

[20] L Johnston and C Shearing, *Governing Security* (London, Routledge, 2003).

[21] M Dubber and M Valverde (eds), *The New Police Science* (Stanford, Stanford University Press, 2006).

[22] Johnston and Shearing, *Governing Security*, above n 19, 10.

[23] M Neocleous, 'Theoretical Foundations of the "New Police Science"' in M Dubber and M Valverde (eds), *The New Police Science* (Stanford, Stanford University Press, 2006) 19.

[24] ibid at 17.

[25] R Reiner and T Newburn, 'Police Research' in R King and E Wincup (eds), *Doing Research on Crime and Justice* (Oxford, Oxford University Press, 2006).

primarily aimed at understanding the nature, dynamics, sources and impact of policing through 'thick' ethnographic description and theoretical analysis.[26]

The original emergence of policing research itself reflected the epistemological break in criminology in the 1960s marked by the advent of the 'labelling' perspective. This rendered intellectually problematic the practices of criminal justice, and the social construction of categories of deviance and crime. Another remarkable feature of the early classic fieldwork studies is the high proportion that originated as doctorates and other 'lone scholar' studies, with minimal external funding. In the 1970s, more radical frameworks supplanted the predominantly liberal political and theoretical perspectives of the researchers in the 1960s. These drew on Marxism above all, reflecting the broader dominance of radical criminology in this period, with feminism and Foucault becoming more influential in the late 1970s.

During the 1970s and early 1980s academic research on policing began to be increasingly joined by official research undertaken by the police themselves, by government agencies responsible for policing, and by specialist think tanks (for example, the American government's National Institute of Justice, the British Home Office, the American and British Police Foundations). This was driven, but not dictated, by policy concerns. Official research could often be sharply critical of policing, noteworthy examples being the negative assessments of the effectiveness of crime control of traditional policing strategies by Ron Clarke, Mike Hough and others for the British Home Office, following the seminal 1974 Kansas City Preventive Patrol Experiment.[27] Academic research was also increasingly commissioned and financed by official bodies and was becoming more policy-oriented.[28]

Following the emergence of a new consensus on tough law and order in the early 1990s, the police mandate was specified in narrow crime control terms, and was to be delivered by a businesslike management regime of targets, performance measurement and financial sanctions. These policing changes reflected the broader domination of public services in general by the 'New Public Management' model.[29]

The criminal justice and policing developments are related to fundamental shifts in political economy and culture, above all the triumph of neo-liberalism. During the 1980s (the Reagan/Thatcher era), neo-liberalism became dominant in the West, but was nonetheless continuously challenged. Its triumph was particularly marked in the early 1990s when the social democratic parties of the Western world accepted the neo-liberal economic framework as both inevitable and broadly desirable in the new era of globalisation, symbolised by their espousal of 'third way' politics.

---

[26] For contemporary collections of papers illustrating this, see P Manning and J van Maanen (eds), *Policing: The View From the Streets* (Santa Monica, Goodyear, 1978) and S Holdaway (ed), *The British Police* (London, Arnold, 1979).

[27] R Clarke and M Hough, *Crime and Police Effectiveness* (London, Home Office, 1984).

[28] R Rumbaut and E Bittner, 'Changing Conceptions of the Police Role: A Socio-logical Review' (1979) 1 *Crime and Justice* 239 and M Weatheritt (ed), *Police Research* (Aldershot, Avebury, 1979).

[29] E McLaughlin, *The New Policing* (London, Sage, 2007) 96–99, 182–87.

This expelled from the political agenda any discussion of social democratic policies to tackle the root causes of crime at a macro-level – such as the Mertonian anomie theory fuelled by the rapid increase in inequality simultaneously with the spread of consumer culture. New Labour did seek to alleviate the poverty and exclusion that it associated with crime and antisocial behaviour, and encouraged partnership between police, other criminal justice agencies and local authorities, in particular in its flagship 1998 Crime and Disorder Act and the subsequent Crime Reduction Programme. Over time, however, the evidence-led and partner-ship approaches intended to be 'tough on the causes of crime' were subordinated to the perceived need to be 'tough on crime' in the wake of criticism from the tabloid press. (For a critical evaluation of the Crime Reduction Programme see the special issue of *Criminal Justice* 4/3 2004, and in particular the essays by Mike Maguire, Mike Hough and Tim Hope.[30]) Crime had to be controlled primarily by policing and criminal justice, albeit with help from private security and responsi-ble citizens.

Consequently, the police were expected to deliver what they had always sym-bolised but in reality had little to do with: effective protection of the public against crime. Most policing research now consists of 'abstracted empiricism', narrowly focused evaluations of specific policy issues and initiatives. At the same time, there have been some ambitious 'grand theory' attempts to analyse the new con-stellation of policing. However, both have neglected the results of earlier empiri-cal research and theorisation.

The classics of early research on policing in the 1960s and 1970s had built up a core set of results that implicitly call into question more recent policies. These can be summarised as the following seven findings:

(i)   *Police Are Marginal to Social Order, Not Sovereign:* 'The police are only one among many agencies of social control'.[31] This was the first line of the first British book reporting empirical research on policing. Pace the extensive discussions of the contemporary transformation of policing by pluralisa-tion, ending the supposed sovereign state and police monopoly of crime control,[32] it has always been recognised by most social theorists that order is created and reproduced by a diverse array of processes to which the formal machinery of 'codes, courts and constables' are marginal.[33]

(ii)   *The Police Role is Not Primarily Law Enforcement or Crime Control:* Empirical research on calls for police help, and on how officers react to calls, showed that most police work did not involve law enforcement or crime control.

---

[30] Mike Maguire, 'The Crime Reduction Programme in England and Wales: Reflections on the vision and the reality' (2004) 4 *Criminal Justice* 213–37; Tim Hope, 'Pretend it works: Evidence and governance in the evaluation of the Reducing Burglary Initiative' (2004) 4 *Criminal Justice* 287–308; Mike Hough, 'Modernization, scientific rationalism and the Crime Reduction Programme' (2004) 4 *Criminal Justice* 239–53.

[31] M Banton, *The Policeman in the Community* (London, Tavistock, 1964) 1.

[32] D Bayley and C Shearing, 'The Future of Policing' (1996) 30 *Law and Society Review* 586.

[33] T Jones and T Newburn, 'The Transformation of Policing? Understanding Current Trends in Policing Systems' (2002) 42 *British Journal of Criminology* 129.

Different studies agreed on that, but expressed what the police did do in somewhat different (although related) terms: peace-keeping,[34] acting as 'philosopher, guide and friend' to the troubled,[35] order maintenance,[36] 'secret' social service,[37] and discretionary deployment of legitimate force to control 'something-that-ought-not-to-be-happening-and-about-which-someone-had-better-do-something-now!'[38]

As research became more influenced by radical perspectives, these characterisations of the police role were challenged as obfuscatory and bland – the police were really servants of power, repressing challenges to ruling class dominance. Alternatively, in more sophisticated formulations they reproduced both general and specific order – 'Parking Tickets and Class Repression'.[39] What first-wave research agreed upon from all points on the political spectrum was that policing had little to do with crime, the antithesis of popular and police mythology.

(iii) *The Police Exercise Considerable Discretion*: A key finding of early empirical work was the extent of police discretion, the routine under-enforcement of law. Police discretion, whether prohibited by law or not, was not only normal practice, but inevitable. What was problematic about the routine exercise of police discretion was that it appeared to deviate from the principles of due process of law, for example because police powers were more frequently used against the less powerful, including ethnic minorities. Much empirical work and analysis was directed at this problem of the gap between the 'law in action' and the 'law in the books', the routine deviation of policing from the principles of legality.[40]

(iv) *Police Work is Shaped by Cultural/Situational rather than Legal Factors*: Police operations have 'low visibility'[41] because they are physically dispersed and their targets are weak in the politics of credibility.[42] They are thus only formally accountable to law and management. Police work is primarily influenced by police sub-culture(s) and situational factors (such as the social characteristics, location and demeanour of those encountered), not legal considerations. Legal powers were resources for police action, shaping after-the-event accounts to protect officers from sanctioning.[43]

---

[34] Banton, *The Policeman in the Community*, above n 29.

[35] E Cumming, L Cumming and L Edell, 'The Policeman as Philosopher, Guide and Friend' (1965) 12 *Social Problems* 276.

[36] JQ Wilson, *Varieties of Police Behavior* (Cambridge, MA, Harvard University Press, 1978).

[37] M Punch, 'The Secret Social Service' in Holdaway (ed), *The British Police*, above n 25.

[38] E Bittner, 'Florence Nightingale in Pursuit of Willie Sutton: A Theory of the Police' in H Jacob (ed), *The Potential for Reform of Criminal Justice* (California, Sage, 1974).

[39] O Marenin, 'Parking Tickets and Class Repression' (1983) 6 *Contemporary Crises* 241.

[40] J Skolnick, *Justice without Trial* (New York, Wiley, 1966); D McBarnet, 'Arrest' in Holdaway, above n 25.

[41] J Goldstein, 'Police Discretion Not to Invoke the Criminal Process: Low Visibility Decisions in the Administration of Justice' (1960) 69 *Yale Law Journal* 543.

[42] S Box and K Russell, 'The Politics of Discreditability' (1975) 23 *Sociological Review* 315.

[43] M Chatterton, 'The Supervision of Patrol Work under the Fixed Points System' in Holdaway, above n 25.

(v)   *Policing Mainly Targets the Powerless:* From early on, research on policing indicated that the use of police powers was directed primarily at groups who were low in the structure of power and advantage. Young, black, economically marginal men were (and remain) disproportionately subject to stop and search, arrest, detention, charge and prosecution (and, ultimately, incarceration or even execution). There has been extensive debate about how far this is the result of police bias and discrimination as distinct from differential offending rates or other legally relevant factors.[44] Underlying differential policing and offending patterns are deeper structural processes that shape both, such as economic and educational disadvantage and discrimination. The basic institutions of privacy and property make the economically disadvantaged more vulnerable to police attention.[45] Altogether, groups weak in social power and credibility become 'police property'.[46]

(vi) *Traditional Policing has Little Crime Control Effectiveness:* During the 1970s, empirical research showed not only that crime was relatively marginal to policing, but also that traditional policing tactics ('preventive' uniform patrol and after-the-event investigation by detectives) had little impact on crime levels.[47] This was not because of a lack of policing skills or effort, but was intrinsic to policing and the nature of crime. Preventive patrol at any feasible level of resourcing is simply too stretched in relation to the vast number of potential perpetrators and targets of crime to handle more than a tiny proportion.[48] Successful detection of offenders by investigators is heavily dependent on the quality and quantity of initial information at the scene, which is negligible for most routine crimes.[49] This pessimistic conclusion of studies of traditional methods has prompted the development of a variety of innovative methods, predicated primarily on more meticulous analysis of risk patterns in victimisation and offending, leading to smarter, 'intelligence-led' prevention, investigation and 'problem-solving'.[50] Coupled with a widespread trend towards lower crime rates in

---

[44] C Phillips and B Bowling, 'Ethnicities, Racism, Crime, and Criminal Justice' in M Maguire, R Morgan and R Reiner (eds), *The Oxford Handbook of Criminology* (Oxford, Oxford University Press, 2012).

[45] A Stinchcombe, 'Institutions of Privacy in the Determination of Police Administrative Practice' (1963) 69 *American Journal of Sociology* 150.

[46] JA Lee, 'Some Structural Aspects of Police Deviance in Relations with Minority Groups' in C Shearing (ed), *Organizational Police Deviance* (Toronto, Butterworth, 1981).

[47] R Reiner, *The Politics of the Police* (Oxford, Oxford University Press, 2010).

[48] Clarke and Hough, *Crime and Police Effectiveness*, above n 26; Audit Commission, *Streetwise: Effective Police Patrol* (London, HMSO, 1996).

[49] M Innes, *Investigating Murder: Detective Work and the Police Response to Criminal Homicide* (Oxford, Oxford University Press, 2003).

[50] LW Sherman, *Policing Domestic Violence: Experiments and Dilemmas* (New York, Free Press, 1992); A Braga and D Weisburd, *Policing Problem Places* (Oxford, Oxford University Press, 2010); M Levi and M Maguire, 'Something Old, Something New, Something Not Entirely Blue: Uneven and Shifting Modes of Crime Control' in J Peay and T Newburn (eds), *Policing: Politics, Culture and Control* (Oxford, Hart Publishing, 2012).

many countries during the 1990s, these have stimulated a new 'can-do' confidence about the potential for crime reduction by effective policing.

(vii) *Policing has Symbolic rather than Instrumental Impact*. The implications of the early empirical research on policing debunked much popular and police mythology. Crime, law and policing were marginal to each other. Policing involved a combination of mundane peacekeeping and the reproduction of unequal structures of power and advantage. This did not mean that the police were not of general and fundamental social value. They were of practical help to people who called them in a variety of small-scale troubles and conflicts. More broadly, they have dramaturgical and symbolic significance. They represent the promise of security through the rule of law – however little they may actually contribute to it in practice because the fundamental sources of order or deviance lie in social, economic and cultural processes beyond the reach of policing.[51]

As argued above, since the early 1990s there has been a major change in the politics of law and order in the UK (paralleling similar changes in the US), reflecting the broader triumph of neo-liberalism through its incorporation by the parties of the centre left, notably New Labour. The new consensus in law and order politics is the need and the possibility of crime control through 'tough' and/or 'smart' criminal justice. This is related to an eclipse of faith in the existence of 'root causes' of crime, or at any rate in the possibility of affecting them by rehabilitation or social reform. Concerns about discrimination, the rule of law and human rights remain politically potent, although their salience relative to fears about security varies with the latest crisis. These issues now focus at least as much on inequalities in protection from criminal victimisation as on the disproportionate targeting of particular groups as suspects, as the Stephen Lawrence case illustrated most clearly.

In this era, policing research has become increasingly policy-oriented and managerialist, focusing on evaluations of specific initiatives, strategies and developments, or emerging special areas of interest. Many are extremely valuable, and indeed continue the critical agenda of earlier work, for example, the Home Office and Metropolitan Police studies of stop and search arising out of the Macpherson Report on the Stephen Lawrence murder,[52] the Met-sponsored partial replication of the seminal 1983 Policy Studies Institute (PSI) study,[53] and the evaluation of the impact of the Macpherson Report sponsored by the Home Office.[54]

---

[51] P Manning, *Police Work* (Cambridge, MA, MIT Press, 1977); I Loader and A Mulcahy, *Policing and the Condition of England* (Oxford, Oxford University Press, 2003).

[52] M Fitzgerald, *Searches in London under Section 1 of the Police and Criminal Evidence Act* (London, Metropolitan Police, 1999); J Miller, N Bland and P Quinton, *The Impact of Stops and Searches on Crime and the Community* (Research Paper 127) (London, Home Office, 2000); P Quinton, N Bland and J Miller, *Police Stops, Decision-making and Practice* (Research Paper 130) (London, Home Office, 2000).

[53] DJ Smith, S Small and J Gray, *Police and People in London: the PSI Report* (London, Policy Studies Institute, 1983); M Fitzgerald, M Hough, I Joseph and T Quereshi, *Policing for London* (Cullompton, Willan, 2002); A Henry and D Smith (eds), *Transformations of Policing* (Aldershot, Ashgate, 2007).

[54] J Foster, T Newburn and A Souhami, *Assessing the Impact of the Stephen Lawrence Enquiry* (London, Home Office, 2005).

Some are informed by mid-range theoretical work, even though they are directed at assessing very specific policy initiatives, for example, the reassurance policing studies inspired by the concept of 'signal crimes'[55] and the research sponsored by the Nuffield Foundation on plural policing.[56] These are all valuable and rigorous studies of particular issues, and there are many other examples. However, they are focused on limited aspects of policing: specialised units, practices and initiatives. Unlike the earlier ethnographic studies, they cannot tell us much about routine policing practice or culture(s).

Co-existing with this proliferation of specific policy-oriented studies are a number of 'grand theory' analyses of trends in policing.[57] These involve a partial return to the issues raised by the radical and Marxist analyses of the 1970s and 1980s,[58] a level and form of analysis addressing questions that are still pertinent, transcending the specific politics of Marxism. They focus on the overall nature and function of the police and policing in reproducing social order, and their place in fundamental structures of power and (in)justice. They probe how policing simultaneously reproduces order in general (the conditions of existence of social order per se), and 'specific' order (particular structures of power, domination, advantage and inequality). This inextricably Janus-faced function of policing is what makes analysis and policy so complex and essentially contested, rendering the current dominant concerns with crime control, risk and security one-dimensional.

The fundamental source of this change is probably a sense of hopelessness about fundamental social transformation since the political triumph of neo-liberalism in the early 1990s. This expelled 'root cause' analyses of crime from practical politics, as conservative criminologists such as James Q Wilson had sought to do since the 1970s. For both conservative and liberal criminologists, rescue arrived at just the right time in the form of the widespread fall in crime rates after the early 1990s. There was a widespread tendency to attribute this to criminal justice and especially policing changes.[59] More conservative voices emphasised the 'tough' dimensions of these changes ('zero-tolerance' policing and harsher sentencing), liberals the 'smart' aspects (intelligence-led crime analysis, more effective targeting of prevention, problem-solving policing and punishment). The contribution of

---

[55] M Innes and N Fielding, 'From Community to Communication Policing: "Signal Crimes" and the Problem of Public Reassurance' (2002) 7 *Sociological Research Online*.

[56] A Crawford, S Lister, S Blackburn and J Burnett, *Plural Policing: The Mixed Economy of Visible Patrols in England and Wales* (Bristol, Policy Press, 2005).

[57] See, eg Bayley and Shearing, 'The Future of Policing', above n 30; Johnston and Shearing, above n 19; JP Brodeur, *The Policing Web* (New York, Oxford University Press, 2010); B Hoggenboom, *The Governance of Policing and Security* (London, Palgrave, 2010); P Manning, *Democratic Policing in a Changing World* (Boulder, Paradigm, 2011); B Bowling and J Sheptycki, *Global Policing* (London, Sage, 2012); M Brogden and G Ellison, *Policing in an Age of Austerity: A Postcolonial Perspective* (London, Routledge, 2012).

[58] M Brogden, *The Police: Autonomy and Consent* (London, Academic Press, 1982); R Grimshaw and T Jefferson, *Interpreting Policework* (London, Unwin, 1987).

[59] F Zimring offers the most comprehensive account in *The Great American Crime Decline* (New York, Oxford University Press, 2007).

policing to the crime drop has been challenged, in particular because there does not seem to be any clear relationship between the timing and location of the crime fall throughout the Western world, and the adoption of particular police tactics.[60]

The new 'can-do' optimism of the police and their cheerleaders in the 1990s is reflected in a paler form in the theoretical analyses of transformation, forgetting the lessons of the past. Bayley and Shearing, for example, explicitly argue that a combination of 'the profit motive' generating more private security and 'smarter enforcement tactics . . . community policing with a hard edge' can make policing 'more effective in truly preventing crime'.[61] The combination of market-based reforms of private and public policing is explicitly turned to because of a perceived impossibility of wider 'root cause' changes. The prospects of market-based solutions to disorder, however, are like the attempts of the sharks in *Finding Nemo* to become vegetarian. Markets are effective means of allocating private consumer goods efficiently and of generating innovation and overall growth. However, they also have fundamental pathologies that have long been identified above all, but not only, by socialists of all varieties.

Most crucially for criminological purposes, unfettered markets remorselessly generate inequality and encourage egoistic and anomic cultures, feeding crime at all levels.[62]

For a Political Economy of Policing

The elements of a political economy of crime and control were spelled out in the 'fully social theory of deviance' model of *The New Criminology*.[63] This was explicitly intended as 'a political economy of criminal action, and of the reaction it excites', aiming 'to move criminology out of its imprisonment in artificially segregated specifics . . . to bring the parts together again in order to form the whole'. Specifically, it was argued, this required analysis of: (1) the wider origins of the deviant act – *a political economy of crime*; (2) immediate origins of the deviant act – a *social psychology of crime*; (3) the actual act (4) immediate origins of social reaction – a *social psychology of social reaction*; (5) wider origins of social reaction – a *political economy of social reaction*; (6) the outcome of the social reaction on deviant's further action; and (7) the nature of the deviant process as a whole.

The closest attempt to incorporate all these elements into the study of one specific phenomenon was the magisterial study of mugging and the reaction to it,

---

[60] B Bowling, 'The Rise and Fall of New York Murder' (1999) 39 *British Journal of Criminology* 531; A Karmen, *New York Murder Mystery* (New York, New York University Press, 2000); J Eck and E Maguire, 'Have Changes in Policing Reduced Violent Crime?' in A Bloomstein and J Wallman (eds), *The Crime Drop in America* (Cambridge, Cambridge University Press, 2000); M Punch, *Zero Tolerance Policing* (Bristol, Policy Press, 2007); A Tseloni, J Mailley, G Farrell and N Tilley, 'Exploring the International Decline in Crime Rates' (2010) 7 *European Journal of Criminology* 375.

[61] Bayley and Shearing, above n 30, 268–80.

[62] Reiner, *Law and Order*, above n 18; S Hall, S Winlow and C Ancrum, *Criminal Identities and Consumer Culture: Crime, Exclusion and the New Culture of Narcissism* (Cullompton, Willan, 2008).

[63] I Taylor, P Walton and J Young, *The New Criminology* (London, Routledge, 1973).

Policing the Crisis.[64] Starting from a particular robbery in Birmingham, and the sentencing of its perpetrators, the book analysed mass media construction of a 'moral panic' about 'mugging', and police responses to this ('actual act', 'immediate origins of social reaction'). It then proceeded to a wide-ranging account of British economic, political, social, and cultural history since World War II, to excavate the deeper concerns that 'mugging' condensed ('Wider origins of social reaction'). Later chapters analysed the impact of transformations in the political economy on black young men in particular ('wider origins of deviant act'), and how this structured the formation of specific subcultures in which robbery was more likely to be perpetrated ('immediate origins of deviant act'). Policing the Crisis remains a uniquely ambitious attempt to synthesise macro-, middle-range and micro-analysis of a particular offence and the reaction to it, embodying all the facets of political economy as 'fully social theory'. It was not just an analysis of structural forces: cultural meanings were interpreted in dialectic interaction with structural developments (for example, the meaning of mugging as symbol of decline and the acculturation of second generation children of immigrants to British aspirations).

Most research studies inevitably focus on a narrower range of phenomena or policy issues, using more limited methodological tools and explanatory variables. The checklist of elements for a 'fully social theory' serves as a constant reminder of the wider contexts in which particular aspects of deviance and control are embedded, and their mediations and interrelationships. Since the 1970s the pincer pressures of the realist and interpretive turns have squeezed out recognition of the significance of political economy for understanding crime and control. Re-emphasising the importance of political economy is not intended to encourage a reverse one-sided accentuation, but to show that holistic sensibility of political economy is needed to explain patterns and trends in crime and control, including policing.

Political Economy and the Politics of the Police

In my attempts to synthesise the empirical findings of historical, sociological, socio-legal research on policing and to understand contemporary policy transformations I have used political economy as the tacit framework for the successive editions of my book *The Politics of the Police*. I am going to trace the use of political economy in the book, not to suggest that it is in any way the ideal way forward, but to illustrate its use in understanding the principal elements of policing. Political economy is most explicit in the first three, largely macro-historical, chapters. The first analyses the concepts of 'police' and 'policing', tracing their evolution through human history. 'Policing' is a universal phenomenon, 'police' an essentially modern development of specialised policing institutions. The emer-

---

[64] S Hall, C Critcher, T Jefferson, J Clarke and B Roberts, *Policing the Crisis* (London, Macmillan, 1978).

gence of specialised police institutions is related to social differentiation and inequality. The specifically modern form of police is the condensation in specialised institutions of the state's (contingent and potentially contestable) dominance of legitimate force, as suggested most influentially by Weber,[65] and in the analysis of policing by Bittner and Brodeur.[66]

The development of modern specialist state police in Britain in the early nineteenth century is analysed in Chapter 2 again in terms of an explicit political economy framework. It charts the political conflicts about policing, related to differing class interests. The birth of the Peelian police was facilitated by the shift of power from the landed gentry to the industrial and commercial urban bourgeoisie. These 'wider origins' of 'social reaction' also underpinned the changing conceptualisations and patterns of 'disorder' and 'crime'. The actual 'Acts' by which police development was accomplished are mediated by intermediary chains of 'immediate origins' and interactional dynamics, as are the specific riots, protests, quotidien disorders and crimes which police are mandated to prevent and control.

Chapter 3 analyses the fluctuating legitimation of the police in Britain, in the face of the wide and deep opposition to their creation, a process that reached its apogee in the post-World War II decades. Eight dimensions of police policy contributed to the eventually celebrated model of 'policing by consent', including internal discipline, accountability to law and popular sentiment, minimum force, primacy of prevention and public service. The success of this strategy was fundamentally dependent on wider transformations in political economy: the growing inclusion of all into a common status of civil, political and socio-economic citizenship. De-legitimation became increasingly pronounced after the late 1960s, primarily because of the unintended consequence of shifts in political economy: inequality, exclusion and conflict surged as neo-liberalism ousted social democracy, creating multiple lines of conflict and tension. A fragile and ambiguous re-legitimation since early 1990s has occurred as adjustments (with varying degrees of enthusiasm) to the hegemony of neo-liberalism and the politics of law and order became a brittle new consensus, at any rate until the 2007–2008 economic crash.

The macro-level political economy processes that historically generated policing organisations continue to shape their functioning, although the myriad small-scale studies of culture and operations that are surveyed in Chapters 4 and 5 are mainly informed by pragmatic concerns, and concentrate on immediate or middle-level factors that are more readily amenable to policy intervention. A key aspect of how policing has developed in liberal capitalist societies is their relative autonomy from policy or managerial regulation. Their main role as missionaries

---

[65] M Weber 'Politics as A Vocation' in M Weber (ed), *The Vocation Lectures* (Indianopoli, Hackett, 2004).

[66] E Bittner, 'Florence Nightingale in Pursuit of Willie Sutton: A Theory of the Police' in H Jacob (ed), *The Potential for Reform of Criminal Justice* (Beverly Hills, Sage, 1974); J-P. Brodeur, *The Policing Web* (Oxford, Oxford University Press, 2010)

of established order in public spaces means their street-level operational deployment has what socio-legal scholars in the 1960s called 'low visibility' from the point of view of organisational managers, and political and social elites. The targets of their powers are the low status 'police property' people whose lives are lived out predominantly in public space, which makes them more 'available' to the police in the aseptic jargon of Home Office analysis. Meanwhile, the work, leisure and residence areas of the more privileged are protected from surveillance and intrusion by the legal barriers of 'privacy'. This isn't just a matter of sheer physical observability. The controversial actions of police are all too visible to their 'property'. But these low status groups are high in the 'politics of discreditability' in a clash of conflicting accounts, making the police version of events more likely to be accepted as authoritative. This gives rank-and-file police the de facto high discretion (even if the law purported to deny it) that was observed with surprise by the first generation researchers. This is not natural or inevitable, but a result of the police mission being primarily to surveille and control public places on behalf of elites who are implicitly content for them to operate 'permissive' powers.

It is this socially constructed discretionary space that makes the informal culture of police as 'street-corner politicians' so significant as the immediate source of practice. The plethora of studies of police culture do not only identify modal or core features antithetical to the rule of law and resilient to reform initiatives. They also exhibit a variety of tactics for presentationally packaging improper practices into the requirements of due process legality. The research further shows that cop culture is informed by a social mapping that renders the relatively powerless as objects of suspicion. Although variations of emphasis around these traits can be observed, structured by the organisational division of labour, demographic differences, and wider environmental and cultural influences, the fundamental patterns of police culture are generated by the basics of their role in liberal capitalist societies. Thus cop culture is ultimately structured by the political economy, shaping the role, pressures, constraints and incentives which affect policing. These can only be changed by deep social transformation, not by the reforms of selection, training and formal law and discipline that scandals normally produce.

Key features of policing practice are also structured by political economy. What people call the police for, and how officers react to these calls, differs from abstract popular conceptions. Law enforcement is only a small part of police work, apart from specialist units (which are proliferating locally, nationally and transnationally). Police are called to a miscellany of emergencies united only by a perceived potential need for legitimate force to sort them out. The order that police seek to guard ranges from universally necessary prerequisites of social co-existence to partisan propping up of social injustice: 'Parking Tickets and Class Repression'. The balance between these varies according to the structure of the political economy. Comparing social democracies with more neo-liberal political economies suggests the former enjoy greater police legitimacy, presumably because fewer encounters are along the 'class repression' end of the spectrum.

Huge disproportionalities and discrimination in police handling of suspects and victims in terms of race, gender, class, age and sexuality have been demonstrated by studies across a wide range of time and space. These reflect wider structural inequalities, mediated by differential victimisation, 'availability' of suspects, and the institution of 'privacy'.

Policing has limited effectiveness in crime control because deterrence and detection are limited by the huge gap between the vast sea of problems facing the police and any conceivable level of resourcing. New methods, in particular 'intelligence-led' targeting tactics such as 'hot spots' and problem-oriented policing designed to 'take the oil to the squeak', and evidence-based deployment of situational and physical security, 'work' to reduce victimisation and account for much of the drop in crime throughout the Western world since the mid 1990s. Nevertheless, political economy and cultural trends are probably exacerbating 'criminality', the tendency of our society to generate crime, even if the pressure is prevented from translating into criminal acts by preventive security. The big question is how long and how generally can 'liddism' (the suppression of symptoms leaving causes intact) work?

Media representations of policing are crucial in framing the politics of law and order. They predominantly reproduce a perspective that can be called 'police fetishism', depicting the police as the essential prerequisite of social order and security. The media picture of policing has become less monolithic over time, but despite more negative stories police fetishism is still the predominant mode. This is structured by the political economy of the media (mainly large corporations), and the exigencies of production (police are crucial sources of stories, thus becoming 'primary definers'). There is some contestation of images according to differences in the demographics and the political position of the particular markets aimed at (contrast *The Guardian* and *The Sun*), and with the spread of citizen recording devices permitting some 'sousveillance' to balance traditional one-way 'surveillance' (synopticon v panopticon), but the playing field remains far from level.

The political economy of 'guarding the guards', regulating police powers and accountability, is discussed in Chapter 7. In the last half-century the powers of the police have been hugely expanded by case law and by statute (especially since the 1984 Police and Criminal Evidence Act (PACE)). This was legitimated politically as a response to rising crime, which was rooted in the increasing social divisions and desubordination produced by neo-liberalism. The traditional legitimation of the British police as merely 'citizens in uniform' was dead but it was replaced in the struggles over PACE by a new myth: 'fundamental balance' between necessary powers and safeguards for suspects. The strategy has been aptly labeled 'authorise and regulate': new powers were authorised but were hopefully subject to appropriate regulation. [67] During the first decade of PACE law and order was still

---

[67] D Dixon, 'Authorise and Regulate: A Comparative Perspective on the Rise and Fall of a Regulatory Strategy' in E Cape and R Young (eds), *Regulating Policing* (Oxford, Hart Publishing, 2008).

contested fiercely as was neo-liberalism more broadly. Whether a fundamental balance had indeed been struck was reflexively monitored by a plethora of research.

Following the hegemony of the politics of tough law and order in the early 1990s, and the ensuing redefinition by governments of the policing role as crime control in the narrowest sense, the concern moved away from achieving balance between powers and safeguards. From the 1994 Criminal Justice and Public Order Act onwards there has been a stream of legislation that expands police powers, accompanied by a watering down of safeguards. These have been legitimated mainly by a rhetoric of exceptional powers being the lesser evil in a new climate of insecurity and emergency, especially since the terrorist attacks in the early 2000s. Reflecting the new tough consensus there has been almost no research evaluating powers and safeguards since the late 1990s.

Traditionally, debates about police governance have been between two polarised models: The dominant 'explanatory and cooperative' mode (enshrined by the 1964 Police Act) stressed a strong doctrine of 'constabulary independence' keeping policing out of politics, but was challenged by the 'subordinate and obedient' mode that would subject policing policy to elected local authorities (as advocated in the 1980s by several radical 'Old' Labour councils). Both were supplanted in the early 1990s by a new 'calculative and contractual' model, beginning with the 1994 Police and Magistrates' Court Act, and reinforced by several New Labour measures, notably the 2002 Police Reform Act. These embodied the neo-liberal New Public Management (NPM) strategy being adopted across the public sector, seeking to apply private enterprise 'businesslike' methods to managing public services. Nominally, the legal doctrine of 'constabulary independence' remained intact, but the aim and effect was to structure its operation by market sanctions nudging decisions towards efficient and effective, but above all, economic choices. The Coalition's revolutionary steps towards enhanced local control through elected Police and Crime Commissioners (PCCs) continues the calculative and contractual crime control model, albeit with a veneer of local democracy or at any rate populism. There is huge debate about these changes, but the one certainty is that the law of unintended consequences will prevail, upsetting the predictions of both supporters and critics.[68]

Conclusion: For Social Democratic Policing

All commentators agree that policing, like the wider political economy, has undergone fundamental change, but there is debate about its sources, nature and consequences. The most influential position is the basically optimistic so-called

---

[68] T Jones, T Newburn and D Smith, 'Democracy and Police and Crime Commissioners' in J Peay and T Newburn (eds), *Policing: Politics, Culture and Control* (Oxford, Hart Publishing, 2012).

'transformation thesis', which argues that: 'Future generations will look back on our era as a time when one system of policing ended and another took its place.'[69] The claim has two elements:

A. *Pluralisation*: that 'policing is no longer monopolised by the public police' (begging the question whether it ever was).
B. 'Public police are going through an identity crisis' because of A: they are adopting new 'businesslike' approaches modelled on private enterprise models: NPM, 'risk' prevention rather than post-hoc law enforcement. These are indeed embodied in the governance changes of the last 20 years, as seen above.

A + B results in a new policing paradigm: 'governance of security' on a nodal or networked rather than centralised pattern.[70]

The transformation theorists view this optimistically: pluralised security can be more effective, humane and accountable. They assume we can counter the inherent dynamic towards greater inequality built into neo-liberalism so as to avert the 'new feudalism' that their initial interpretations of pluralisation feared.[71] On this model, private security is more humane because it lacks coercive special police powers, but also more 'efficient' because more exposed to market pressures. An alternative analysis would suggest that the greater success private security has in achieving order in mass private property spaces is not due to efficiency but to deploying exclusionary property powers (preventing entry to or ejecting 'undesirables', stop and search at will and so on) with a selective mandate of protecting limited spaces.

The transformation thesis neglects the increasingly apparent dysfunctions of neo-liberalism. In the absence of countervailing state regulation, markets lead to ever greater inequality, wealth trickles up not down, pollution and exploitation abound, and plutocracy corrupts politics, with the ugly symbiosis of more crime/ disorder and a stronger, tougher state.

The literature contains many valuable analyses of legal, constitutional, procedural and organisational requirements for democratic and legitimate policing. The above sketch of the political economy of policing suggests a further ingredient is needed: social as well as liberal democracy. The organisational elements of police legitimation only succeeded because of the wider social transformation of society culminating in the post-war Keynesian welfare state settlement, incorporating all sections of society into a common status of citizenship. The political triumph of neo-liberalism since the 1970s and the ensuing 'death of the social' eroded the conditions of peace, security and 'policing by consent'. The dire consequences of this in the economic arena have become manifest with the return of depression on a scale without precedent since the 1930s. The holes in the neo-

---

[69] Bayley and Shearing, above n 30.
[70] Johnston and Shearing, above n 19.
[71] C Shearing and P Stenning, 'Private Security: Implications for Social Control' (1983) 30 *Social Problems* 493.

liberal model are widely acknowledged now even by erstwhile neo-liberal economists and policy-makers. 'Risk society' and neo-liberal 'responsibilisation', were euphemisms for a massive 'risk shift' from government and corporations to the mass of the population who could not carry the burden. In the absence of economic stability and justice batons, handcuffs and handguns cannot secure peace beyond temporary suppression.

5

The Failures of Police Legitimacy: Attacks from Within

MARGARET E BEARE

A vast body of literature from the late 1960s onwards has looked at the organisational needs of policing in Western countries in gaining and maintaining legitimacy and community support. Those needs and that precariousness remain but the domestic and international policing environments have changed radically. While polls still claim fairly high approval for the Canadian police, scandals have reduced the 'general' rankings and have created significant pockets of disapproval of the police – even, or perhaps particularly, the iconic Royal Canadian Mounted Police (RCMP) in Canada. Jean-Paul Brodeur argues that the British bobby is as much a part of the British identity as the RCMP is in Canada, and those approval rates in Britain as well as in Canada have dropped dramatically.[1] This chapter looks at how police in Canada have adapted to changes that have been 'inflicted' on their working environment. While questions of maintaining legitimacy have traditionally focused on the relationship of the police to their communities, we look here at the possible impact on the organisations themselves and on the responses of individual officers.

While appreciating the existence of an 'enacted environment' as conceived by Peter Manning, Richard Ericson and others in their discussions about the ability of the police to make/define – or at least influence – their working environment, some external changes require more conscious adaptations. The literature tells us that the police have used various key strategies for gaining and maintaining legitimacy to counter the various contradictions and tensions within their mandate: control of the media's message; the use of crime-fighting and crime control rhetoric; the creation and profiling of elite units; the identification of a 'dangerous class'; the ideology of law and professionalism; and the rhetoric focused on the 'community' aspect of a proactive police presence.[2] Current responses of the police to some extent follow these 'tried and true' selling techniques, but with some new strategies that will be examined in this chapter.

---

[1] JP Brodeur, *The Policing Web* (Oxford, Oxford University Press, 2010) 350.
[2] M Beare, *Selling Policing in Metropolitan Toronto: A Sociological Analysis of Police Rhetoric 1957–1984* (DPhil Thesis, Columbia University, 1987).

International influences have increasingly impacted policing strategies. At least one aspect of globalisation is the sharing of policing practices and the proselytising of policing models from one country to another. Police are active entrepreneurs, selling their 'way of policing' to less-developed or civil-war-torn nations – often as part of a country's aid to development initiatives. Concepts of democracy and the rule of law are advocated as being the essential foundation for the establishment of new policing structures in these nations. However, we might argue that this confidence in the promotion of Canadian (or US, UK or Australian) policing abroad is not necessarily supported by the record of our own compliance with some of these ideals. David Bayley outlined the required components for 'change' abroad in his 2001 publication entitled *Democratizing the Police Abroad: What to Do and How to Do It*[3]. He makes no mention of the failure of policing in the United States to alter significantly their own operations in response to the numerous recommendations made by various inquiries. More recently, an industry has developed that examines and advises on the 'best practices' in policing protests, and again some of these enthusiastically shared strategies are less democratically inclined than one might hope. We import and we export – 'kettling' came to Canada during our 2010 G20 meetings, possibly from the experiences in the United Kingdom and Miami. When the RCMP discovered a new 'extreme' form of undercover work that removed them from various forms of accountability, Australia was seen as fertile ground in which to spread these 'Mr Big' methods. These are some of the areas of policing that this paper examines.

Exposing Policing to Scrutiny

Over the past 50 years the 'secret' world of policing has been invaded by academics – 'older' academics including Skolnick, Bordua and Reiss, Brodeur, Wilson, Bittner, Manning, Ericson, Punch, Rubinstein and Reiner, and a bevy of newer scholars. Much of what we are concerned about when we look at the police hinges on issues that arise from the discretionary decisions that the police make.[4] Once it was obvious that the police make hundreds of conceivably significant discretionary decisions every day, it became important to examine how those decisions were made. This interest led criminologists to make use of research methodologies such as participant observation. Criminologists rode with various police officers from various police services, sat in courts, analysed police reports, listened to their

---

[3] Report prepared for the US Department of Justice, office of Justice Programs. June 2001. http://observatoriodeseguranca.org/files/bayley.pdf.

[4] An awareness of these discretionary powers and the decision-making that results were only a subject for research and theorising from the 1960s in publications such as: J Goldstein, 'Discretion Not to Invoke the Criminal Process: Low-Visibility Decisions in the Administration of Justice' (1960) 29 *The Yale Law Journal* 543; WR LaFave, *Arrest: The Decision to Take a Suspect into Custody* (Boston, Little Brown, 1965); and KC Davis, *Discretionary Justice* (Westport, Greenwood Press, 1969).

conversations, and in extreme cases became police officers.[5] Academic research has been supplemented by media coverage. The police have moved from a position where their actions were rarely reported by the media to being scrutinised daily and in some cases being the subject of an intensive series of investigative reports. As often noted, the TV police drama dominates the public stations. These various methods of gathering previously protected information pertaining to police work, revealed much – but continued to hide much, since the exposure gained by researchers and journalists was often prescribed by the police services and limited by time and resources.

The major difference came relatively slowly as incident after incident was captured on street surveillance cameras, video tape or wire-tapes, and with the current presence of personal phone cameras in every street and every public or private facility. In addition to the ever-present technology, the media is there to enthusiastically show the captured incident to the wider public – wider than a mere domestic audience – to 'entertain' internationally. Video surveillance, access to information, leaked information, and perhaps a less compliant public has resulted in the police being challenged in unfamiliar ways. The requirements mandated by exclusionary rules, and in the case of Canada, the *Canadian Charter of Rights and Freedoms*, provide the arena by which police actions receive further exposure, with a seemingly increased number of cases resulting in evidence being deemed inadmissible.[6]

During the past six years, our historically 'untouchable' policing icon, the RCMP, has been seen to stumble from one public relations disaster to another. To use the Queen's words, the RCMP has had not one but a series of '*Anni Horribiles*' that have resulted in descriptions of the force as being 'broken' and 'tarnished', with a 'ripped culture', allegations of fraud, nepotism, bullying and intimidation, lying, and perhaps most damagingly, incompetence. Two Commissioners in a row (Zack Zaccardelli and William Elliot) were accused of bullying and intimidating the members of the force – one was offered the chance to resign for having mislead (lied to) the House of Commons committee about the Maher Arar national security/torture case, and the other was dismissed after losing the confidence of his senior officers. From the command positions, to the officers on the

---

[5] See R Ericson, *Making Crime: A Study of Detective Work* (Toronto, Butterworths, 1981); R Ericson, 'Rules for Police Deviance' in C Shearing (ed), *Organisational Police Deviance* (Toronto, Butterworths, 1981) 83–110; and R Ericson, *Reproducing Order: A Study of Police Patrol Work* (Toronto, Toronto University Press, 1982). D McBarnet, 'Arrest: The Legal Context of Policing' in S Holdaway (ed), *The British Police* (Sheffield, Edward Arnold Ltd, 1979); and D McBarnet, *Conviction: Law, the State and the Construction of Justice* (London, Macmillan, 1981). M Punch, *Fout is fout: Gesprekken met de politie in de binnenstad van Amsterdam* (Amsterdam, Boom, 1976); Punch, *Policing the Inner-City* (London, Macmillan, 1979); M Punch, *Control in the Police Organisation* (Cambridge, MA, MIT Press, 1983); WK Muir, *Police: Streetcorner Politicians* (Chicago, University of Chicago Press, 1977).

[6] In the UK the Police and Criminal Evidence Act 1984 created the rule that evidence would be excluded if its admission would have such an adverse effect on the fairness of the proceedings that the court ought not to admit it. The Australian High Court in *Bunning v Cross* (1978) HCA 22, (1978) 141 CLR 54 ruled that trial judges have the discretion to reject illegally or unfairly obtained evidence after considering various competing public policy requirements and weighing them against each other.

ground, to the accountability mechanisms, the appearance has been of a force out of control.

While Canadians remain on the whole uncritical of the police, scattered across Canada among our various police services publicity has been given to a number of police performances that have shocked citizens who had previously had little access to the visual evidence of deception, arrogance and violence. The exposure, while arguably required in order to improve the operation of the police by holding them to greater account, has not been accomplished without impacting the police in perhaps unanticipated ways with results that may run counter to the desired objectives. This paper looks at 'external' organisational responses and 'internal' organisational responses. While no direct causal relationship can be claimed between the exposure to scandal and these responses, together they paint a picture of policing in near crisis. It goes without saying – but should be said repeatedly – that the majority of police officers join for the very best of reasons and serve honourably throughout their careers. These are the officers who may be the most affected when 'their' organisation is criticised. While police officers will seldom report a colleague for disreputable behaviour, the rogues or criminals in the ranks are not highly regarded.

'External' Organisational Responses: Lies and Denial

Along with greater exposure of their practices came police denial and lies. Ironically, one way to avoid being found to have lied is to continue lying and commit perjury. While we may worry about the police control over general facts, this control becomes particularly dangerous when it involves the control of the evidentiary facts as presented in courts. While we are all aware that convictions of the police even for major offenses are rare and expensive to attempt, what is less rare are the debates in court as to the appropriateness, constitutional acceptance or actual criminality of some police actions. Scott Sundby makes the argument that in the US the suppression hearings themselves, regardless of their outcome, act much like a 'morality play for police officers, judges, prosecutors, and defense attorneys' by instructing everyone involved both about the Fourth Amendment's rules and why those rules are of a constitutional significance mandating honour and respect.[7]

By the mid 1990s police perjury was acknowledged to be widespread, and to a certain degree ingrained within police culture as made evident by the findings of

---

[7] SE Sundby, '*Mapp v Ohio's* Unsung Hero: The Suppression Hearing as Morality Play' (2010) 85 *Chicago-Kent Law Review* 255. The article draws our attention to a summary of arguments for and against the exclusionary rule as a deterrent. See 'Report to the Attorney General on the Search and Seizure Exclusionary Rule' (1989) 22 *University of Michigan Journal of Law Reform* 573.

the Knapp and Mollen Commissions into police misconduct within the New York Police Department (NYPD), the Christopher Commission related to instances of corruption and brutality within the Los Angeles Police Department (LAPD), and the Fitzgerald and the Wood Commissions in Australia.[8] All of these inquiries, and many others, revealed that the practice of police perjury was virtually commonplace and normalised and 'formally' acknowledged with a distinct term for the practice which was known as 'testilying'.[9] When lies are revealed following acknowledged wrongful convictions it is clear the police have 'gone too far'. Dianne Martin has maintained, however, that more disturbing than out-and-out lies, is the notion that for the police 'defining "truth" to achieve a police goal is as much a tool of the job as understanding the law, or knowing how to use a stick and a gun'.[10] The policing work environment is one where officers skate between necessary lying such as undercover work, questionable lying during aggressive interrogations, and criminal lying in court.

According to Joseph McNamara, former police chief of San Jose and Kansas City, police perjury in criminal cases, particularly in the context of searches and other exclusionary rule issues, is so pervasive that 'hundreds of thousands of law-enforcement officers commit felony perjury every year testifying about drug arrests' alone.[11] Alan M Dershowitz quotes a 1949 source who perhaps jokingly claimed that cases were often decided 'according to the preponderance of perjury'.[12] Cynically, in his book, *The Best Defense*, Dershowitz identified 13 'key rules' that apply to perjury[13] – rules that support the pronouncement of 'Mickey Haller' that:

Everybody lies.

Cops lie. Lawyers lie. Witnesses lie. The victims lie.

---

[8] Knapp Commission, *Report to the Commission to Investigate Allegations of Police Corruption and the City's Anti-Corruption Procedures* (New York, Knapp Commission, 1972); (Warren) Christopher Commission, *Report of the Independent Commission on the Los Angeles Police Department* (Los Angeles, Christopher Commission, 1991); Mollen Commission, *Report of the Commission to Investigate Allegations of Police Corruption and the Anti-Corruption Procedures of the Police Department* (New York, City of New York Police Department, 1994); Commission of Inquiry Pursuant to Orders in Council, *The Fitzgerald Inquiry into Possible Illegal Activities and Associated Police Misconduct* (1987–1989) (Brisbane, Commission of Inquiry Pursuant to Orders in Council, 1989); Wood Commission, *Report of the Royal Commission into the New South Wales Police Service* (Sydney, Royal Commission into the New South Wales Police Service, 1997).

[9] L Cunningham, 'Taking on Testifying: The Prosecutor's Response to In-Court Police Deception' (1999) 18 *Criminal Justice Ethics* 26. See also, M Cloud, 'Judges, Testifying and the Constitution' (1996) 69 *Southern California Law Review* 1341.

[10] D Martin, 'Police Lies, Tricks and Omissions: the Construction of Criminality' (CALT meetings, Quebec, 29 May 2001).

[11] JD McNamara, 'Has the Drug War Created an Officer Liars' Club?' *Los Angeles Times* (Los Angeles, 11 February 1996) M1.

[12] J Frank, 'Courts on Trial' (1949) 85. Quoted in the testimony of AM Dershowitz, 'Testimony' (House of Representatives Judiciary Committee, 1 December 1998) available at www.constitution.org/lrev/dershowitz_test_981201.html.

[13] AM Dershowitz, *The Best Defense* Vintage (May 12 1983) xxi–xxii. Quoted by MD Wilson, 'Judging Police Lies – An Empirical Perspective' (January 2010) http://works.bepress.com/cgi/view content.cgi?article=1002&context=melanie_wilson.

A trial is a contest of lies. And everybody in the courtroom knows this. The judge knows this. Even the jury knows this. They come into the building knowing that they will be lied to. They take their seats in the box and agree to be lied to.[14]

While everyone may lie, we are here most concerned with police lies. Looking to law to hold the police accountably proves to be potentially counter-productive. Over 30 years ago, Doreen McBarnet,[15] in a study of arrests, identified the degree to which sociologists of policing assume that rules of law are irrelevant to controlling police behaviour – research shows that the police will work around or through those rules.[16] John Kleinig, a professor at John Jay College of Criminal Justice, noted that following *Mapp v Ohio*, studies had showed that the number of annual drug arrests in the US had not greatly changed but there was a sharp increase in officers claiming that suspects had dropped drugs on the ground: 'Either drug users were suddenly dropping bags all over the place or the cops were still frisking but saying the guy dropped the drugs.'[17] In response to these police lies, rather than bolstering the exclusionary provisions, the opposite appears to be happening. In 2009 a Supreme Court 5 to 4 ruling in *Herring v US*[18] held that evidence obtained from certain unlawful arrests may nevertheless be used against a criminal defendant.[19]

It is not necessarily the exclusion of the information so much as the exposure of the policing actions that has become the greatest concern. Over time, it has contributed to an awareness that police actions are not sacrosanct but require examination and challenge. The greatest threat to the legitimacy of the police may come when the 'norm' becomes to question the truthfulness of police statements not just by defence lawyers in court, but also on the front pages of our newspapers and when it is examined in detail in various inquiries.

---

[14] M Connelly, *The Brass Verdict* (London, Orion Books Ltd, 2009) 1, with cynical defence attorney Mickey Haller.

[15] D McBarnet, 'Arrest: The Legal Context of Policing' in S Holdaway (ed), *The British Police* (Sheffield, Edward Arnold Ltd, 1979);

[16] MW Orfield, 'Exclusionary Rule and Deterrence: An Empirical Study of Chicago Narcotics Officers' (1987) 54 *University of Chicago Law Review* 1016. In keeping with McBarnet's findings, the 'exclusionary rule' legal powers that were designed to ensure proper police practices appear to have had the opposite effect. Since its application to individual US states in 1961, the 'exclusionary rule' has been 'one of the most controversial and divisive issues in American Constitutional Law', with regard to its purpose and effectiveness.

[17] A Efrati, 'Legal System Struggles With How to React When Police Officers Lie' *The Wall Street Journal* (New York, 29 January 2009).

[18] *Herring v US* 555 US 135, 129 SCt 695, 172 LEd2d 496, 77 BNA USLW 4047, Fed S 582, US, 14 January 2009 (NO 07-513) 492 F3d 1212, affirmed. Holding: 'The United States Supreme Court, Chief Justice Roberts, held that "In analysing the applicability of the exclusionary rule for Fourth Amendment violations, the Court must consider the actions of all the police officers involved. USCA. When police act under a warrant that is invalid for lack of probable cause, the exclusionary rule does not apply if the police acted in objectively reasonable reliance on the subsequently invalidated search warrant". USCA Constitutional Amendment 4 at [8].

[19] Efrati, 'Legal System Struggles', above n 16.

External Responses to Exposure within the Canadian Policing Environment

'Deny Deny Lie'

The Toronto Star headlines for an entire week in April 2012 catalogued for the outrage of the reading public an array of scenarios where police had been found to have been lying. Headlines screamed the words judges had used to describe the police evidence and testimony:

> Untruthful. Deliberate state misconduct. Absurd. Patently absurd. Inconsistent and Inaccurate. Lie. Nonsensical. Deliberately mislead. Fabricate. Evasive. Ridiculous. Subversive. Disturbing. Pure fiction.[20]

Following the nearly week-long series on police lying, the responses from the various bodies with responsibilities for the conduct of the Toronto police, reminded one of Captain Louis Renault's famous lines from *Casablanca* on finding out that gambling may be taking place in Rick's cafe: 'Shocked, Shocked'. There was a rebuttal from the head of the police association but no public word from individual police officers who were 'tarred with the same brush' as their colleagues.

Whether there is more police perjury is an important question which I cannot answer. We do know that in contrast to the days of Lord Denning and his infamous support for the execution of the Birmingham Six, rather than accepting the 'unfathomable notion' that the police might have lied, police lying is no longer unfathomable.[21] In Boston, in 2010 Police Commissioner Edward F Davis initiated a policy to terminate officers who lie in court, to investigators or in department reports.[22] When the new policy was first proposed, Peter Manning called Davis' plan to fire police officers for lying 'very unusual but admirable' and questioned whether a union-dominated police culture that shuns internal written rules would allow the change to take place. Manning said: 'It's worthwhile exploring it, but I think it's highly unlikely that something will go forward from it.'[23] In

---

[20] D Bruser and J McLean, 'Testimony from Police "Pure Fiction"' *Toronto Star* (Toronto, 29 April 2012) A1 and A8–9.

[21] '[I]f it were proved that the confessions had been obtained by violence and threats, the Six might have to be pardoned; and this was such an appalling vista that every sensible person in the land would say it would not be right for the action to proceed.' available at www.mojuk.org.uk/Portia/archive%2010/ludovic.html. In the Canadian context, the threat of prosecution for public mischief made by a prosecutor to Mrs LeBourdais following the release of her book, *The Trial of Steven Truscott* (Philadelphia, JB Lippincott, 1966) for questioning the investigation by the police and the errors made by the court, we no longer find deliberate police lies to be 'unfathomable'.

[22] J Ellement, 'Officers Who Lie Will Face Dismissal' *The Boston Globe* (Boston, 21 January 2010) available at www.boston.com/news/local/massachusetts/articles/2010/01/21/officers_who_lie_will_face_dismissal.

[23] J Fargen and P Gelzinis, 'Mass Officers Caught Lying on Duty Will be Fired' *Boston Herald* (Boston, 28 September 2009) available at www.policeone.com/chiefs-sheriffs/articles/1915693-Mass-officers-caught-lying-on-duty-will-be-fired.

January 2012, the first officer was dismissed under this policy.[24] Dismissing police in Canada is almost impossible and this is one of the concerns of the newly appointed RCMP Commissioner. In May 2012 RCMP Commissioner Robert Paulson appealed for changes to the Police Act so he could dismiss the 'bad apples' that disgrace the force – he did this via an open letter to the public. The laborious process of dismissing or even suspending Mounties without pay after serious misconduct was referred to as 'absolute madness' by the officer in charge of RCMP in British Columbia.[25] In response, Federal Public Safety Minister Vic Toews promised new legislation to deal with RCMP discipline.[26] Bill C-42 was the response and as of January 2013 is working its way through the law-making process.[27]

British Columbia supplies us with several prime examples of a force out of control. In 2005, controversy surrounded the shooting to death of Ian Bush, a 22 year-old mill-worker who had been taken into custody for having given a false name to the police while drinking beer outside a local hockey game. This death was the subject of four investigations by the RCMP and external agencies. He was shot in the back of his head while in police custody and left dead in the RCMP detachment for two days before being taken to the morgue. The police officer produced his statement three weeks after the event and the forensic pathologist allowed (or encouraged) two RCMP officers to be present and offer 'scenarios' during the autopsy. Given that the officer was alone with Bush when the shooting occurred, all of the investigations accepted the police officer's version and exonerated the police.[28]

However, no explanation of the shooting could justify the performance of the police following the shooting. The public relations officer within the RCMP, in responding to the numerous calls from the public for information, declared 'we don't have to tell the public anything' and no adequate explanation for the delays with the body and with the internal investigations was ever offered. In another incident, in response to a critical report by the British Colombia Civil Liberties Association which contained allegations of systemic rights violations against youth, aboriginal people and the homeless by the RCMP, the RCMP public relations officer Tim Shields said that the RCMP was 'dismissing the report and any changes in policy that could be drawn from it'.[29] After a degree of media concern

---

[24] E Mason and T Mashberg, 'Boston Officer Fired for Using Excessive Force, Lying to Officials' *The Boston Globe* (Boston, 19 January 2012).

[25] CTV News, 'Top RCMP Officer: Firing Process Is "Absolute Madness"' *CTV News* (Toronto, 17 April 2012) available at www.ctvnews.ca/top-rcmp-officer-firing-process-is-absolute-madness-1.797158#ixzz2HKLyjPCc.

[26] CBC News, 'New RCMP Discipline Legislation to be Introduced: Government Promises to Help RCMP Deal with Problem Officers' *CBC News* (Toronto, 29 May 2012) available at www.cbc.ca/news/canada/british-columbia/story/2012/05/29/bc-rcmp-discipline-law.html.

[27] BILL C-42 Act to Amend the Royal Canadian Mounted Police Act and to Make Releated and Consequential Amendments to other Acts available at www.parl.gc.ca/HousePublications/Publication.aspx?Language=E&Mode=1&DocId=5818050&File=39.

[28] Despite the testimony of a blood spatter police expert that in his opinion the shooting could not have happened as the officer claimed.

[29] D Eby, 'Small Town Justice: A Report on the RCMP in Northern and Rural British Columbia' (Vancouver, BCCLA, 2011) available at www.bccla.org/pressreleases/11RCMP_newtune.html.

over yet another example of RCMP's cavalier attitude, senior management reconsidered and the RCMP announced that they will be taking the report seriously and investigating trends and allegations in the report.

The RCMP, and apparently their Ottawa political masters, do not appreciate receiving critical reports. Following the incident involving the death by tasering of Robert Dziekanski – now called 'Canada's Rodney King moment' – the notes and testimony of the police officers were shown to be false. A widely-viewed amateur video by a member of the public (Paul Pritchard) captured Dziekanski's agonising final moments. Brodeur's calculations found that in 2009 there were 888 YouTube videos related to Dziekanski's death.[30] Two separate extensive reports – the *Braidwood Commission of Inquiry* and a report by the Chairman of the Commission for Public Complaints against the RCMP, investigated the death of Dziekanski. Both reports were highly critical of the RCMP.[31] While Commissioner Braidwood could not be sanctioned, the Chair of the Commission for Public Complaints against the RCMP, Paul Kennedy, was dismissed from his position following the release of his critical evaluation of the police performance.

What was particularly amazing in the Dziekanski case was the refusal of the RCMP officers to change their stories even after the video was made public. As stated by Braidwood:

> I am satisfied that these were deliberate misstatements of Mr Dziekanski's actions and behaviours, made for the purpose of justifying his deployment of the weapon. But for the Pritchard video, this revisionist account of the incident would have lived on.[32]

The public watched the televised *Inquiry* proceedings as officer after officer rose to swear that what could not possibly have been true, was true. The Commission of Inquiry noted that the RCMP is an iconic institution in Canada but the 'less-than-forthright' accounting for the conduct of the four officers has had repercussions that extend beyond this one incident: 'Mr Dziekanski's death appears to have galvanised public antipathy for the Force and its members . . . the most important weapon in the arsenal of the police is public support.'[33]

Not every report with allegations of police misconduct can be ignored, and not every author of those reports can be dismissed – but intimidation might be successful. Following a critical report of the way the RCMP had handled the 'Picton' investigation – where over 50 women were missing from the streets of Downtown

Responses to the report are available at http://bccla.org/wp-content/uploads/2012/03/2011-BCCLA-Report-Small-Town-Justice.pdf

[30] Brodeur, *The Policing Web*, above n 1, 338.

[31] P Kennedy, *Report Following a Public Interest Investigation into a Chair-Initiated Complaint Respecting the Death in RCMP Custody of Mr Robert Dziekanski* (Vancouver, Commission for Public Complaints Against the RCMP, 2009). See also, P Kennedy, 'A Crisis in RCMP Accountability' (Speech, National Press Club of Canada, 9 May 2007). Kennedy had served from May 2005 until his dismissal January 2010.

[32] Braidwood Commission on the Death of Robert Dziekanski, *Why? The Robert Dziekanski Tragedy* (Vancouver, Braidwood Commission on the Death of Robert Dziekanski, 2010) 267 available at www.braidwoodinquiry.ca/report/.

[33] ibid at 269.

Eastside of Vancouver, British Columbia with eventual evidence proving that many of them had been murdered by Robert Picton – the Deputy Commissioner, Gary Bass, Officer in Charge of BC, sent an email to Professor Robert Gordon at Simon Fraser University stating:

> The ongoing bias you display against the RCMP in articles such as this have caused many to ask why we would want to continue to be in that partnership [financial support to the criminology department] given this apparent lack of support from the head of the department.

Bass copied his email to about 25 other people, including senior RCMP officials, municipal police chiefs and the president of Simon Fraser University Later that week, again only after critics had referred to the Bass email as a 'thinly veiled threat', Bass said his comments were in no way intended as a threat to pull financial support for the Institute. 'There's no intention to muzzle him!'[34] Bass has now left the RCMP but the RCMP members must now live with the highly critical 2012 *Missing Women Commission of Inquiry* report. Much publicity upon the release of this report focused on the numerous failures of the police. According to the *Commissioner Oppal Inquiry* report, those failures included 'discrimination, a lack of leadership, outdated policing approaches, and a fragmented police structure'.[35]

Increasingly Aggressive Policing against the Most Vulnerable

While the missing, mainly marginalised, Aboriginal women – a seemingly invisible population – receive inadequate policing, other marginalised groups receive an excess! Three policing strategies could be argued to reduce the accountability of the police: unique policing strategies that appear to be Carter protected; the targeting of vulnerable communities; and employing 'security' rhetoric. These might be seen as 'safe harbours' with lower accountability. In many situations the police remain able to either define a situation to avoid any challenge, or successfully justify any action, or successfully deny and perhaps eventually lie their way clear of sanction. Alternatively, there are certain policing initiatives that allow the police to operate with far less exposure and hence less likelihood of being held to account. In this section I shall examine three less vulnerable policing strategies: Gangs'n Guns policing of 'priority' neighbourhoods; 'Mr Big' undercover work; and finally 'national security' policing. I suggest that these strategies are gaining in popularity with the police in part as a result of the pummeling from the criticism they are receiving while carrying out more traditional police work and the fact

---

[34] K DeRos, '"Veiled Threat" to Pull Funding angers Critic' *Winnipeg Free Press* (Winnipeg, 9 April 2010)

[35] CBC News, 'Pickton Inquiry Slams "Blatant Failures" by Police' *CBC News* (Toronto, 17 December 2012) available at www.cbc.ca/news/canada/british-columbia/story/2012/12/17/bc-pickton-missing-women-report.html. The report contained 63 recommendations including striking an independent expert committee to develop a model and implementation plan for a new police force. Missing Women Commission, *Report to the Missing Women Commission of Inquiry* (Victoria, Missing Women Commission, 2012) available at www.missingwomeninquiry.ca/obtain-report/.

that lies and denial do not always work. The idea is to select your policing strategy, select your targets, and if possible evoke the notion that whatever you are doing is the result of 'security' requirements. In addition to protection of the police from criticism, each of these strategies reveals a disregard for the 'letter of the law' even if the law is, at that time, legitimising the strategies. Individuals or groups who are most vulnerable have become the target for aggressive police actions as if to reconfirm or even widen, the 'we vs they' divide that three decades of community policing were intended to bridge.

From Pukers and Assholes to 'Priority Communities'

Police researchers have acknowledged those populations within any city that the police 'police' rather than 'provide policing to'. Richard Ericson found that the police referred to 'pukers'. John Van Maanen found that the police referred to 'assholes' – and the list goes on[36]. In most cases these were troublesome individuals within an urban city. In Toronto, rather than – or in addition to – the troublesome policed individuals, the government has supplied the police with officially designated 'high priority areas' that critics might claim have become 'free-zones' for unchecked invisible policing. The policing is not undercover nor in disguise but is unseen in the sense that the targeted population is without a voice. The stigma of being recognised as a gang-related jurisdiction places the population – both gang and non-gang – outside the 'rights' protections afforded to other areas of the city.

By 2014 there were 31 specifically identified at-risk neighbourhoods that have become the areas that are targeted by Toronto Anti-Violence Intervention Strategy (TAVIS) units and receive what is called the 'Neighbourhood TAVIS Initiative' (NTI). These communities are thereby officially 'branded'. TAVIS, together with the Rapid Response Teams officers, saturate these communities. TAVIS serves as the Gangs'n Guns Task Force 'on the ground' presence in these specific neighbourhoods, which can then become the target of the 'gangs'n guns sweeps'.[37] While police presence is perhaps a good strategy against gang violence, some of the law-abiding citizens who live in those neighbourhoods find the constant surveillance to be closer to police harassment and detrimental to the safety of their streets. Particularly intrusive was the police practice of stopping and questioning individuals – most notably black youths – in situations unrelated to any incident, and the filling out of what are called '208' cards (index-sized-cards used as a 'field information reports'). It is estimated that on one regular shift TAVIS

---

[36] See Richard Ericson, *Reproducing order: A study of Police Patrol Work* (Toronto, University of Toronto Press, 1982); John Van Maanen, 'The Asshole' in PK Manning and J Van Maanen (eds), *Policing: A View from the Street* (Santa Monica, Goodyear, 1978).

[37] In 2007 TAVIS was expanded beyond the Toronto borders with the creation of a Provincial Task Force into 15 PAVIS communities. By 2012, PAVIS was in 22 communities and the Ontario Provincial Government announced that the funding would be made 'permanent' (or as permanent as any funding can be guaranteed under a change in government).

officers will stop and identify 50 to 75 people culminating in over 250,000 cards filled out each year.[38] Data from these mainly non-criminal encounters are fed into a massive database. Police Chief Blair explained that this is all part of 'getting to know the neighbourhood'. He acknowledged that these are often 'racialised' areas and hence he is 'getting to know' a disproportionate number of black males. In addition to the main person 'carded' during each stop, the 208 card requires information on 'associates' including information on parents.

The number of black men between 15 and 24 who were 'carded' between 2008 and 2011 was 3.4 times greater than the actual number of black men who live in those areas giving rise to the concern that all black men are being carded numerous times. Black people account for 8.3 per cent of Toronto's population and 23.4 per cent of the 1.25 million contact cards filled by the Toronto police.[39] This 'getting to know' practice can obviously be counter-productive. Canadian Civil Liberties Association general counsel, Nathalie Des Rosiers, argues that the questioning and carding practice, regardless of intention, can be intimidating and coercive:

> When perceived as excessive or discriminatory, it can create distrust in law enforcement, undermine public faith in police, and, ultimately, weaken efforts to root out and punish crime.[40]

Chief Blair admits there are issues with this approach:

> 'nine out of 10 youths stopped and documented on a street corner may be perfectly good kids, and the encounter might leave them "pissed at us" . . . Those relationships are the toughest things,' says Blair. He expects his officers to be sensitive to how the youth feel and explain themselves. Even then, he acknowledges, the encounters may not go well.[41]

A focus group was held on 24 September 2010 with high school students from Malvern (one of the priority areas with populations including Jamaican, Tamil and Indian youth).[42] These non-gang member youth were living near or among two Toronto street gangs – the *Malvern Crew* and the *Galloway Boys*. There was an overwhelming negative response when asked about their overall impression of the

---

[38] M Welsh, 'Elite Toronto Police Squad Goes Looking for Trouble' *Toronto Star* (Toronto, 8 March 2012) available at www.thestar.com/specialsections/raceandcrime/article/761310--elite-toronto-police-squad-goes-looking-for-trouble.

[39] J Rankin and P Winsa, 'Known to Police' *Toronto Star* (Toronto, 10 March 2012) IN4.

[40] J Rankin, 'Race Matters: Blacks Documented by Police at High Rate' *Toronto Star* (Toronto, 6 February 2010) available at www.thestar.com/specialsections/raceandcrime/article/761343--race-matters-blacks-documented-by-police-at-high-rate.

[41] ibid.

[42] The group was organised and run by Kelvin Ramchand. An unpublished report was completed for Margaret Beare as part of ongoing police research, Nathanson Centre, York University. The majority of the youth were highly sceptical as to whether this relationship can be improved or repaired because they feel that the police are reluctant to change. Overall, they felt that the police really need to 'treat us the way they would want to be treated', emphasising that officers need to respect youth when they come in contact with them. This would mean having calm conversations without giving the youth any 'attitude' or talking to them too 'harshly'.

police. The youth were adamant that they are unable to trust the police. Specifically, they felt the police: often speak disrespectfully and unnecessarily harshly to youth; misrepresent the statements made by youth in order to criminalise them; never believe what the youth say; and harass and search youth without reason thereby abusing their powers. A manager with the Community Action Resource Centre in one of the priority areas stated that there was a significant difference between the attitude and approach of the community policing officers and tat of the TAVIS officers. He claimed that TAVIS officers 'see the youth as criminals before seeing them as anybody else'.[43]

Canada is obviously not unique in these police practices. *New York Times* reported on the 'World of the Summons Court' in New York where black and Latino people dominate the courts for an array of petty offenses including drinking in public, bicycling on the pavement and talking back to the police, which apparently becomes disorderly conduct.[44] In January 2013, a NYC programme in the Bronx, similar to the Toronto carding initiative, was declared unconstitutional. Judge Scheindlin stated:

> For those of us who do not fear being stopped as we approach or leave our homes or those of our friends and families, it is difficult to believe that residents of one of our boroughs live under such a threat.[45]

Critics claim, and statistics document, that minority communities are targeted for both the summons and the related 'stop-and-frisk' programme. As in Canada, these programmes are sold as 'quality of life', supposedly a community policing initiatives – with lots of weaponry! The gang and guns label, the drama, the seemingly unlimited resources, the specially built, secretly located 'Operations Centre' in central Toronto, all speak to an elite crime-fighting unit.[46] All that was needed was the right to operate with near impunity. The priority area designations and the mandate to sweep away the gangs provided that immunity. As criticism mounts, there are hints at efforts being made to bring some transparency and conceivably greater accountability to the policing of these zones. Demands have been made for the police to hand out receipts to those who they 'card'. Further demandshave been made that the 208 form should specify a specific crime that the police were actively investigating with some explanation of why the individual was stopped in relation to that crime. Some form of receipt process will happen – it remains unlikely that the police will restrict their carding to only 'crime'

---

[43] J Rankin and P Winsa, 'Known to Police' *Toronto Star* (Toronto, 10 March 2012) IN 1, 3, 4, 5.

[44] B Staples, 'Inside the Warped World of Summons Court' *New York Times* (New York, 17 June 2012) 10. While at least 20% are thrown out of court, the danger lies in what happens if the person fails to appear at the summons court on the assigned day and time. A warrant is issued (170,000 in 2011) which can begin the process of the defendant being handcuffed, fingerprinted, and taken to prison to await an appearance before a criminal court judge.

[45] J Goldstein, 'Police Stop-and-frisk Program in Bronx is Ruled Unconstitutional' *New York Times* (New York, 9 January 2013) A17.

[46] A budget that covered 450 new police officers in 2005; 150 new TAVIS officers and $5m in 2008 and a $26 Operations centre for the Anti-Guns and Gangs Task Force out-resources by far any prevention initiatives.

related stops however that was the new policy that was finally agreed to by the Toronto Police Services Board on April 2014—after much media and public controversy over what was widely viewed a racially biased practice. The new policy eliminates the actual 'cards'. However the information – now referred to as 'Community Contacts' – is still recorded and retained on computer. Tighter guidelines have been introduced but the city awaits how the policies will be put into operation.

From 'Peel's Bobby' to 'Mr Big': Made-in-Canada Policing

The initial approval of the new professional police in England in 1829 was in part due to the dictate that the police would be unlike the French gendarmerie in that they would wear distinctive uniforms and be a physical presence. The British pointy hats, the RCMP brilliant red serge, the badges and array of ceremonial attire all have come to represent the visible presence of the police in our midst. Some police work, however, requires a more discrete approach and plainclothes detectives were seen to be the answer.[47] Wearing a uniform and being visible has been proven to have its drawbacks. Members of the public photograph actions of the police and attempt to hold them to account in court. This visibility can be reduced via undercover work – but not just any undercover work. Beyond sting operations, and further still beyond reverse sting operations, the RCMP in Canada has discovered 'Mr Big' operations.

While we sometimes believe that traditional Canadian policing is becoming 'Americanised' (a word which does not usually have a positive meaning), in this case Mr Big operations are a strictly Canadian invention – 'the Canadian technique'.[48] These operations are believed to have been first used by the RCMP in Vancouver, and have since been taken to Australia where the RCMP have trained the Australian police in this method. They were originally used in 'cold-

---

[47] Ericson, above n 4, See R Ericson, *Making Crime: A Study of Detective Work* (Toronto, Butterworths, 1981); 1. Ericson states that the first references to detective work in London were in the late 1830s with the first actual detective branch established in 1842. Coincidentally, in May 2012 Sussex Constabulary were discussing a proposal under which over 700 UK officers would switch back into uniforms – with the only exceptions being those detectives working undercover or carrying out surveillance. See S Wright, 'Detectives prepare to hang up their plain clothes' *Mail Online* (London, 2 May 2012) available at www.dailymail.co.uk/news/article-68846/Detectives-prepare-hang-plain-clothes. Described as being 'fiercely opposed' by the rank and file, plain-clothes detective work is seen as a mark of status. According to the Home Office, at any given time only 68% of the country's 125,000 police are in uniform. More than 22,000 are routinely on plainclothes duty. The main reasons for returning the officers to uniform are: the public is demanding greater visibility of the police; a saving in costs since officers get an allowance to buy plain clothes; a desire to eliminate the cultural stigma of being in uniform; and the perceived status differences within the force – these are, of course, also the reasons why the officers want to remain in plain clothes.

[48] B Hutchinson, 'US Appeal Court Allows RCMP Sting to Stand Despite Use of Controversial Technique' *National Post* (Toronto, 20 June 2012) available at http://fullcomment.nationalpost.com/2012/06/20/brian-hutchinson-brought-down-by-mr-big. Although Mr Big strategies are not allowed in the US, the US Appeal Court has allowed a Mr Big confession obtained by the RCMP in the case of two Canadians accused of killing a parent and sister living in Washington State.

case' homicide cases where a confession was desired and no other evidence was available.[49] However, their popularity has since extended beyond these confines. These police-led operations can be carried out for a seemingly indefinite period of time with the aim of getting a confession. As Timothy Moore states 'while it is not unusual for the police to attempt to obtain incriminating evidence by infiltrating a criminal organisation, in the Mr Big situation the police create the criminal organisation'.[50] In a typical sting operation the crime is facilitated under controlled conditions. In the Mr Big cases the officers are deeply immersed not only in the criminal activity, but in every aspect of the lives of the participants. Any sense of an external oversight is diluted and could be seen to be unnecessary given the exclusion of these cases from Charter protections.

Most, if not all, of the 'protections' that come back to haunt the police in court following 'normal' police work do not apply to the behaviour of the police while performing their 'Mr Big' roles. From the police perspective not only are they able to take on various roles as big-time mobsters, throw large amounts of money around, work almost totally without supervision – but Charter protections do not apply because the courts have concluded that the police are not acting in their official capacity. According to the former President of the Law Institute of Victoria, Christopher Dale: 'The technique undermines a number of fundamental legal principles including the right to remain silent, the right to a lawyer and the right to receive formal warnings during interviews with police.'[51]

In Canada, the Supreme Court and several appellate courts have held on many occasions that confessions obtained as a result of the crime boss technique are admissible at common law. Canadian courts have also held that, since the suspect in a Mr Big operation is not 'detained' when making the confessional statements, the right to silence guaranteed by section 7 of the Canadian Charter of Rights and Freedoms ('Canadian Charter') is not violated.[52] According to Justice McLaughlin, in these undercover operations the individual is not under the control of the State and therefore there is no need to protect that person from the greater power of the State.[53] The *voluntariness* requirement is equally problematic. While the enticement might be great and while there might be intimidation from the 'mobsters', the rule appears to be that the voluntariness condition only applies if the person is aware that they are dealing with someone in legal authority. The result, as Moore

---

[49] S Rodrick, 'Open Justice and Suppressing Evidence of Police Methods: The Positions in Canada and Australia – Part Two' (2007) 31 *Melbourne University Law Journal* 171. See also, S Smith, V Stinson and M Patry, 'Literature Review: Confession Evidence in Canada: Psychological Issues and Legal Landscapes' (2010) *Psychology, Crime & Law* 1.

[50] TE Moore, 'Lying for the Truth: Do "Mr Big" Tactics Generate Reliable Admissions?' (Professional Development Series on Wrongful Convictions and Unmerited Acquittals. Good Science, Bad Evidence? New Perspectives on the Reliability of Evidence in Criminal Proceedings) (Toronto, Osgoode Hall Law School, 5 December 2009).

[51] I Munro, 'Lawyers Warn against Police Stings' *The Age* (Melbourne, 9 September 2004) 3.

[52] See, eg *R v Hebert* [1990] 2 SCR 151; *R v McIntyre* [1994] 2 SCR 480; *R v Osmar* 217 CCC (3d) 174 (2007).

[53] *R v Unger* (1993) 85 ManR (2d) 284, 83 CCC (3d) 228, 20 WCB (2d) 395, MJNo 363 (Man CA) (QL) at 76.

suggests, is a double bind for the accused. The Mr Big operations skirt both constitutional protections and common law protections. They operate deceptively but without detention, and they offer inducements and/or coercion but without the suspect knowing that he or she was dealing with a person in authority. As described by Moore:

> If the target had no friends, he does now. If he has low self-esteem, they bolster it. If he has no money, they supply it . . . If he is naive and uncomfortable around women, an appreciative female friend appears . . . They also 'create an atmosphere of apprehension' by conveying to the suspect that they will use violence against those who betray the gang.[54]

As Moore observes, the suspect is far worse off than if they were being 'controlled' by the State and yet they receive none of the State protections.[55]

According to the RCMP, the Mr Big method is a 'tried, tested and true technique' and charges are 'always supported with corroborating physical evidence and/or compelling circumstantial evidence'. While the police claim that they are seeking information that 'only the killer would have known', the problem arises that during the course of many months of this form of undercover work, the police themselves could relay this 'protected' information to the suspect.[56] A prime example is the case of Kyle Unger, who served 14 years of a sentence for murder before being released on bail in 2005 and eventually acquitted in 2009. The judge described the confession as 'fraught with serious weaknesses'[57] but the confession was still allowed. It was noted that the police accepted a description from Unger as to where he had committed the murder – a location under a bridge that in fact had not existed at the time of the offence. The acquittal rested on the fact that the only other evidence (of hair) was discredited. Unger was denied compensation by the Manitoba Justice Minister with the explanation: 'Without his confession, he would not have been charged. Without the confession, he would not have been convicted.'[58] Police are the main actors in these performances – but they are not alone.[59] The desire for a conviction in these high profile serious cases

[54] Timothy E. Moore, unpublished presentation about 'Mr Big' undercover sting operations at an international conference of law enforcement investigators and academics in Toronto. Quoted in 'Innocent at Risk in "Mr Big" Stings, Professor Says' *National Post* (Toronto, 24 May 2012).

[55] See also, Timothy E Moore, Peter Copeland and Regina Schuller, 'Deceit, Betrayal and the Search for Truth: Legal and Psychological Perspectives on the "Mr Big" Strategy' (2009) 53 *Criminal Law Quarterly* 349. Quoted by L Vartanian, 'Supervised Research Paper: Policing Injustice in Wrongful Convictions' (unpublished law paper, Osgoode Hall, 2012).

[56] D Quan, 'Lying for Justice: RCMP "Mr Big" Stings Effective, but Risky, Says Academic' *Postmedia News* (23 May 2012) available at http://www2.canada.com/edmontonjournal/news/story.html?id= d6b48956-b825-41a6-92a2-af37fd30a2ac. Kouri Keenan, a PhD criminology student at Simon Fraser University, analysed 81 Mr Big cases and found that 23 cases lacked substantial corroborating evidence – obviously making the cases vulnerable to wrongful confessions and wrongful convictions.

[57] *Unger v Canada* (MJ), 2005 MBQB 238, [2005] 196 ManR (2d) 280, 67 WCB (2d) 853, MJ No 396 (MBQB) (QL).

[58] CBC News, 'Unger Won't Get Compensation: Minister' *CBC News* (Toronto, 23 October 2009) available at www.cbc.ca/news/canada/manitoba/story/2009/10/23/mb-compensation-unger-chomiak-manitoba.

[59] Crown Prosecutor George Dangerfield in the *Unger* case and the prosecutor in several high-profile wrongful conviction cases, including *Thomas Sophonow and James Driskell and the Association*

runs throughout the justice system and hence the Mr Big strategies have an appeal that extends beyond the police. However, the game is played by the police and the police hide both in their undercover disguises and they hide behind the protections that these strategies carry.

The question must be asked why this strategy has become increasingly popular with the RCMP who must see it 'from the inside' as being in basic violation of due process – whether or not the court has allowed it to date. The exploitation of marginalised people, carried out at great expense places a much greater emphasis on achieving the conviction than on enacting justice. However, this policing strategy may eventually fall under the weight of the growing controversy. In September 2012, the Newfoundland Court of Appeal reversed a murder conviction on the grounds that:

> The Mr Big strategy is built on lies and deceit . . .The strategy uses inducements and implied threats, strong social and psychological control over the subject, manipulation and exploitation of the suspect's motives and often – certainly in Mr Hart's case – involves persistent reinforcement of the advantages of complying with the fictitious culture that has been created.[60]

The majority agreed that the State abused its power by employing considerable resources to gain control over a weak and vulnerable person – creating a situation where 'rejecting Mr Big was impossible given Mr Hart's circumstances'.[61] If future courts continue to strike down this policing strategy, the RCMP will have to return to the more transparent investigative practices that have previously brought them into disrepute. In 2014 the Supreme Court of Canada (*R v Hart* 2014 SCC 52) called into question the reliability of confessions obtained during so-called Mr Big sting operations – calling those confessions 'presumptively inadmissible' and that the onus is now placed on the crown to prove the admissibility of such confessions.[62]

High Policing for Global 'Security'

The final form of diminished accountability is the explosion of 'national security directed policing'. This is not policing in the face of an actual national security threat, but a potential scenario. Moreover, it is not policing by the security forces, but rather by the police who are typically seen as responsible for criminal code

---

in *Defence of the Wrongfully Convicted,* have filed an appeal in a further case involving Stanley Ostrowski.

[60] *R v Hart* 2012 NLCA 61 (CanLII) (Supreme Court of Newfoundland and Labrador Court of Appeal).

[61] K Makin, 'Police's Mr Big Technique Falls under Scrutiny' *The Globe and Mail* (Toronto, 18 September 2012).

[62] CBC News. August 1, 2014. 'Mr. Big' ruling a "game changer" for those convicted in sting operations: Up to 2008, the tactic has been used at least 350 times to try to solve cold murder cases', by Mark Gollom, http://www.cbc.ca/news/politics/mr-big-ruling-a-game-changer-for-those-convicted-in-sting-operations-1.2724310.

violations. While policing tactics can be hidden through lies, or can fall outside the Charter in Mr Big tactics, or are excused in Gangs'n Guns situations – nowhere are they less restrained while being either extremely visible with fantastic displays of force and might, or guiding the activity by extensive undercover operations and the activities of agents provocateurs, while clothed in the secrecy of national security rhetoric.

'Security' becomes the licence for policing autonomy. The two prime Canadian examples are the policing of the G20 meetings in Toronto and the role of the RCMP (and the Canadian Security Intelligence Service (CSIS)) in the case involving the rendition and torture of Mahar Arar. In both cases various inquiries *belatedly* exposed the activities of the police that were deemed to have fallen outside the bounds of acceptable policing, and in both cases, even after the numerous inquiries, beyond the simple 'facts' of the cases, much remains hidden.[63] This paper looks specifically at the policing of G20 – a traditional police service responsibility that took on security service dimensions.

One month before the June 2010 meetings were held, Chief Blair gave a formal dinner talk where he stated clearly that during the G20 summit, 'the number one responsibility of the Toronto Police Service is the protection of the protestors'.[64] The RCMP would be inside the protected area with the international dignitaries but outside that perimeter the Toronto municipal police, together with officers from other jurisdictions including a few RCMP and Ontario Provincial Police members, would ensure the safety of the protestors while policing any protestor violence. Using Brodeur's terminology, the dominant characteristics of this role therefore 'sounds' like low/criminal code focused policing. As Jean-Paul Brodeur explained: 'As part of the criminal justice system, low policing share its aim of protecting society. In contrast, the protection of the political regime is the raison d'être of high policing.'[65]

How then did the policing of the G20 summit move so sharply and quickly from a low policing role of protection of the citizenry into the realms of a mixture of low and high policing where abuses to the citizens were justified on the basis that none of the leaders were threatened and in the process no-one was actually killed? The eleven inquiries and reports plus numerous investigations into this event serve to illustrate Brodeur's argument that low and high policing lie side by side and rather than two distinct agencies or distinct incidents, the concepts may refer to policing practices that blend – combining the traditional violence of low policing with the deception and covertness of high policing.[66] These international meetings are an excellent arena in which to see the priority assigned to the protec-

---

[63] Following 9/11 the RCMP police found themselves back into the national security territory from which they had been partially removed in 1984 with the creation of CSIS – and one might say, 'removed for cause'. Mr Arar, among others, suffered as a result. See the Arar Commission, *Report to the Commission of Inquiry into the Actions of Canadian Officials in Relation to Maher Arar* (Ottowa, Arar Commission, 2006).

[64] Mid-May 2010, one month before the G20 summit at Bistro 990.

[65] Brodeur, above n 1, 226.

[66] ibid at 252.

tion of the State rather than its citizenry. Policing such events does not happen at borders or in response to articulated threats, but rather within communities, and everyone is indiscriminately involved in the security measures. As one example, a man objected to being stopped and searched far from any of the international protected areas. He stated that he was in Canada and therefore had civil rights. A police officer responded: 'This ain't Canada right now.' Another officer chimed in, 'You're in G20 land.' The first officer continued: 'There's no civil rights here in this area. How many times you gotta be told that?'[67]

Brodeur comments about the concept of 'self-regulated lawlessness' being pushed to the limits in high policing.[68] During Saturday night and Sunday the Toronto police were operating within this 'lawless' zone and even the notion of self-regulation appeared to be absent given the lack of coordination, communication failures, and the 'missing' senior officers. Over 1,105 arrests, the largest number of arrests in Canadian history, followed the kettling, violence, and general round-up of seemingly anyone present in central Toronto.[69] All efforts to instigate a compellable formal Commission of Inquiry were refused by both the federal and provincial governments and instead at least nine 'little' examinations were held – illustrating that the holding of inquiries can itself become a political issue.[70] In this case, while the formal police and government response was that the event was a policing success, separate inquiries revealed: a chaotic leadership structure; poor to non-existent communication from the control centre to the officers on the ground; indiscriminate rounding up of everyone in certain areas – including other plainclothes police officers, a TTC driver, a man with one leg, civil liberties monitors, tourists and children; physical violence; racist and sexist taunts by the police; and various declaration that all Charter rights were suspended during the policing of that event.[71]

---

[67] Torstar Network, 'Police Won't Lay Charges Against Officer' *Torstar Network* (Orlando, 6 June 2012). The Office of the Independent Review Director (OIPRD) substantiated three allegations of misconduct against Sgt Charlebois, including that he acted discreditably and exercised unlawful or unnecessary force. York Region's police chief had to ask the board's permission to place the charges since the allegations were made after a six-month deadline. He was refused.

[68] Brodeur, above n 1, 339.

[69] Ombudsman (A Marin), *Caught in the Act: Investigation into The Ministry of Community Safety and Correctional Services' Conduct in Relation to Ontario Regulation 233/10 under the Public Works Protection Act* (Ontario, Ombudsman, 2010) 25. Just under 700 people were eventually released without charge, other charges were stayed or withdrawn dropped leaving 99 cases that went to court.

[70] Following the previous 1997 APEC Summit the *Hughes* Inquiry reported on the RCMP handling of the protest. However, following the policing of the 2010 G8 and G20 protests, the government resisted demands for a similar wider-mandated Inquiry. In British Columbia in advance of the APEC meetings, the Federal government decided to show the international leaders how beautiful Vancouver is from the heights of the BC University campus. Holding such a meeting on or near a university campus resulted in what should have been predictable consequences. In 2010, the federal government gave the law enforcement six months, instead of on average two years to prepare for not one but both the G8 and the G20 meetings in Ontario – with the decision that the G20 summit would be located in central Toronto.

[71] The inquiries were:

• Special Investigations Unit probe into six allegations of police brutality (SIU); A review by the civilian-run Toronto Police Services Board focusing on policy, oversight and governance (Morden

Questions that might have been answered via a Commission of Inquiry with subpoena powers remained unanswered. The reports did not address what appeared to critics to be examples of provocation by the police: disabled cruisers left in the midst of the protest area as if 'asking' to be burned; vandalism by the 'black box' that appeared to be exempt from police action; and little explanation when it was later revealed that a number of undercover police officers had infiltrated two activist communities in southern Ontario and rather than monitor and report on their planning activities in advance of the meeting, they played key roles in planning the G20 protests – going so far as identifying targets for mayhem. *The Globe and Mail* reported that 'one officer helped develop a list of locations for protesters to congregate at or vandalise and another was such a prominent presence in pre-G20 marches that his face was twice featured in newspapers alongside the activists he was spying on'.[72]

While national security was discussed before, during, and after the policing of the G20 summit, the policing was still seen to fall to the traditional policing services lead by the Toronto Police Service, with criminal code charges decreed for violators. High policing techniques, however, dominated the policing of this event: the use of infiltration and police informants; what Brodeur calls the 'conflation of executive, judicial, and legislative powers', in this case the hastily and near-secretly passed Regulation 233/10 which as the Marin Ombudsman noted 'changed the rules of the game';[73] and finally, what Brodeur calls the 'concrete hallmark of high policing', the resort to preventive detention.[74] The massive arrests would attest to that final point. Undercover work and surveillance was also a key aspect of the G20 policing, claimed in fact to be the 'largest ever' spy operation by the RCMP.[75]

Review); the Office of the Independent Police Review Director (G McNeilly, 'Policing the Right to Protest'); the Toronto Police Service's Summit Management After Action Review Team (Blair); RCMP G8 & G20 Summits After Action Report;the Ontario Ombudsman (Marin, *Caught in the Act*); Ontario Chief Justice Roy McMurtry (into Public Works Protection Act: Regulation 233/10); The Federal House of Commons Standing Committee on Public Safety is holding several days of hearings looking into G20 security matters; The Office of the Commissioner for Public Complaints against the RCMP, *Public Interest Investigation into RCMP Member Conduct Related to the 2010 G8 and G20 Summits* (McPhail Report); Canadian Civil Liberties Association, *Breach of the Peace*; Office of the Auditor General of Canada, *Chapter 1 – Expenditures for the 2010 G8 and G20 Summits* (9 June 2011).

[72] K Mackrael and A Morrow, 'Undercover Officers Knew of Plans for Downtown Mayhem during G20' *The Globe and Mail* (Toronto, 24 November 2011) available at http://theglobeandmail.com/news/national/toronto/undercover-officers-knew-of-plans-for-downtown-mayhem-during-g20/article2245680.

[73] Brodeur, above n 1, 347. See Ombudsman, *Caught in the Act*, above n 66, 5.

[74] Brodeur, above n 1, 358.

[75] T Groves and Z Dubinsky, 'G20 Case Reveals "Largest Ever" Police Spy Operation: RCMP Collaborated with Provincial and Local Police to Monitor Activists' *CBC News* (Toronto, 22 November 2011) available at http://www.cbc.ca/news/canada/g20-case-reveals-largest-ever-police-spy-operation-1.1054582 The operation might have been the largest but was definitely the one with the least sense of humour! A 'white' member of a protest group where all the members were white except one, jokingly said 'Kill Whitey' during discussions as to whether the group should lend support to the First Nations Rally. Later in court when the undercover officer was asked what he thought that meant, he said he thought it meant that they were going to 'kill a white person'.

This paper was focusing on policing strategies and types of policing that are seen to be less vulnerable to exposure. Clearly the nine inquiries plus various reports did expose the policing of the G20. The police force clearly did not expect this result in part because they failed to acknowledge the target of their violence.[76] The population that was targeted were from every age, ethnicity and social class. However, the crowds also included educated, white, English-speaking, citizens of varying degrees of influence. Visible minorities in certain 'priority' areas of Toronto may have been far less shocked by the policing of this event, holding a different view 'normal' policing based on their experience. With any other population there would have been less focus on the actions of the police and much more focus on the actions of the protesters – although even here the evidence against the police was successfully gathered only after two-and-half years when all of the reports were finally published – and nothing guarantees that another 'security' oriented event would not produce the same policing behaviour.

'Internal' Responses: Kicking and Whining toward Culture Change?

The evidence of increasing aggression toward the population appears to be coupled with increasing aggression within the police force. The outward hostility that has been demonstrated may be less consequential than the internal loss of legitimacy. With a focus on the RCMP, we look here at three issues that appear to indicate stress within the police force: dissension within the policing ranks; grievances and harassment charges; and post-traumatic stress disorders. As the protective concealing facade over policing cracks, fingers are being pointed in all directions to identify or lay blame on the culprit(s) who are responsible for the humiliations. Old rules of respect for rank, line of command, and protecting the 'family secrets' are replaced by a rush to the media. The introduction of change into any organisation is usually fraught with some difficulty – introducing even much needed change into a troubled organisation may be even harder.

Publicised Dissension within the Policing Ranks

The RCMP is a military-structured hierarchical organisation with strict rules of command. It is unprecedented to violate the rigid reporting relationships by going above or around one's immediate boss. That is what has been happening. A revolt by senior officers under Commissioner Elliott resulted in a layer of officers, including two Deputy Commissioners, complaining to the highest levels of the

---

[76] R Demanno, 'Hands Tied, Blair Says' *Toronto Star* (Toronto, 9 December 2010). M Beare, N DesRosiers and A Deshman, *Putting the State on Trial: The Policing of Protest during the G20 Summit* contains chapters examining a wide range of issues pertaining to protest policing and the G20 in Toronto. University of British Columbia Press, BC, December 2014.

federal government about what they termed Elliott's 'verbally abusive, closed-minded, arrogant and insulting behaviour'.[77] This led to several of these officers being asked to resign and others resigning. The media covered each of these developments. Elliott was eventually replaced with an internal candidate, Bob Paulson, but the complaints have not ceased.

With a build-up of unfavourable media and tension within the force that began in earnest under Commissioner Zaccardelli and continued under Elliott, Commissioner Paulson's task was to restore confidence – internal confidence in his management ability, and external confidence in the abilities of the RCMP. In an open letter to the members, government officials and the public, Commissioner Paulson outlined the difficulties with trying to run the RCMP with a 25-year-old disciplinary system that essentially meant that no-one could be dismissed for substandard work. Referring to 'weeding out bad apples' from the force, Paulson stated: 'I know that legislation alone is not enough to keep your trust ... but we will create a modern and even stronger organisation that continues to make you proud.' The response to this was not uniformly positive. A group calling themselves the Re-Sergance Alliance sent anonymous emails to the media warning senior officers that the rot was not merely at the bottom but also at the top and 'threatened to expose certain 'investigative files' and compromising pictures of members of upper management. . . . Basically, both RCMP upper management and some officers are threatening to expose the other side's dirty secrets.'[78] One cannot imagine this happening before the leadership of Zack Zaccardelli. Protecting the integrity of the force was a main mission of the members.

Gender-based Harassment Complaints

Claims of sexual harassment of women in the RCMP have existed for a long time and in this section does not challenge the validity of their complaints. However, in a manner similar to the disgruntled officers referred to above, hundreds of women are now filing and publicising formal grievances for a wide array of complaints, from actual sexual assault and intimidation to lesser complaints, against their male colleagues. Notably, Corporal Catherine Galliford, the 'face of the RCMP' as their spokesperson, filed a 115-page internal complaint that she then shared with CBC News. As at November 2012, 150 women have applied to be part of a class-

[77] CBC News, 'Top RCMP Officers Forced Out or Quitting: Commissioner Elliott's Leadership Style Blamed for Turmoil' *CBC News* (Toronto, 18 October 2010).

[78] C Nardi, 'If Cleaning up the RCMP, Do It from Top to Bottom' *National* Post (Toronto, 21 August 2012) available at fullcomment.nationalpost.com/2012/08/21/chris-nardi-if-cleaning-up-the-rcmp-do-it-from-top-to-bottom. Criticism was heightened when it became known – and spread through the media – that an officer had been quietly transferred to British Columbia after an internal disciplinary process in Edmonton demoted him for drinking and having sex, while on duty, with a woman under his command. Critics referred to BC becoming the 'dumping ground' for misbehaving Mounties. This action was coupled with the resignation before the RCMP could act to fire Monty Robinson who had received full salary for four years while being suspended from duty for obstruction of justice following a fatal car accident where he left the scene and then drank alcohol to invalidate the breathalyser (he was also one of the officers involved in the tasering of Dziekanski), and of Constable MacLeod who received full salary for seven years before being forced out over a sexual assault charge.

action lawsuit against the RCMP filed by a former Nanaimo, BC officer, Janet Merlo.[79] A consulting police psychologist (whose services have since been terminated) stated: 'Senior executives for decades have been accountable to no one and they've created a toxic work environment, high levels of employee stress and a culture of fear.'[80]

Sexual harassment in the RCMP is not new.[81] In 1993, the RCMP as an organisation was sued for failing to protect a female officer from the harassment of her co-workers. In 1994 Alice Clark was awarded $93,000 plus costs.[82] This case was particularly significant because it implicated not one or two officers but the entire RCMP as so many levels of the organisation were involved. Court testimony spoke of a 'gang mentality' with a group of the men who remained firm against having women in policing. Galliford, Merlo and the more than 100 other women – and many others who have not come forward – would probably agree that not much has changed. What is new is the seeming desire to bring all of the complaints directly to the media for public exposure at the cost of a further sullying of the RCMP's reputation.

Post-traumatic Stress

Galliford joined more than 225 British Columbian RCMP officers who are taking sick leave suffering post-traumatic stress disorder (PTSD) – which is apparently referred to by some of the membership as 'off-work-mad'. Like the above recognition of the increased filing of gender grievances, the intention is not to judge the merit of these PTSD claims and one imagines that they fall along a continuum from serious and largely ignored by the police services for decades, to the less serious conditions. The increase in statistics may reveal the changes in the acceptance of, and awareness regarding, PTSD symptoms as well as an increase in actual cases. Statistics provided by Veterans Affairs to *The Globe and Mail* show that the number of Mounties receiving PTSD pensions was 1,239 in 2009, 1,437 in 2010 and 1,711 by early 2011.[83]

---

[79] CBC News, 'RCMP says Force is Changing after Sexual Harassment Allegations: Reforms Underway, but Scepticism and Fear Remain for Whistleblowers' *CBC News* (Toronto, 8 November 2012) available at http://www.cbc.ca/news/canada/british-columbia/rcmp-says-force-is-changing-after-sexual-harassment-allegations-1.1270973

[80] CBC News, 'BC Mountie Alleges Years of Sexual Harassment' *CBC News* (Toronto, 7 November 2011) available at http://www.cbc.ca/news/canada/british-columbia/b-c-mountie-alleges-years-of-sexual-harassment-1.1034369

[81] See M Beare, 'The Few among the Many: Women and Policing' in M Beare (ed), *Honouring Social Justice: Honouring Dianne Martin* (Toronto, University of Toronto Press, 2008).

[82] Clark v Canada (TD), [1994] 3 FC 323, April 26, 1994, Docket: T-648-89. Available at http://reports.fja-cmf.gc.ca/eng/1994/1994fca0302.html.

[83] C Freeze, 'Hike in Stress – Disorder Claims by Mounties Raises Questions for Policy Makers' *The Globe and Mail* (Toronto, 8 August 2011) available at http://www.theglobeandmail.com/news/national/hike-in-stress-disorder-claims-by-mounties-raises-questions-for-policy-makers/article590947/. Receiving the PTSD benefits does not prevent the person from working since it is payment 'for past suffering' and there is no time limit for members to apply. See also, CBC News, 'Stress Disorder on Rise in RCMP' *CBC News* (Toronto, 27 October 2009) available at www.cbc.ca/news/canada/story/2009/10/27/rcmp-stress-leave.

The duties of all police forces are not identical. The Ontario Provincial Police (OPP) police the major highways within the province in addition to more traditional policing of communities and some of these OPP officers have witnessed the carnage of horrendous car crashes. A 2012 report by the Ombudsman, Rene Marin, was highly critical of the OPP for not recognizing how significant the PTSD problem is and he recommended to the Ministry that the government 'implement a province-wide confidential survey and other means to identify how many Ontario police officers, active and retired, are suffering or have suffered from PTSD'.[84] Marin called the current state of neglect of the officers a 'Bureaucratic brush-off' with five OPP suicides within an 18-month period. OPP Commissioner Chris Lewis revealed his own crises when early in his career he witnessed a fellow officer mistakenly shoot a fellow technical officer: 'We did nothing as an organisation to support me, and I was afraid to say anything . . . we're trying to change that.'[85] Different policing services – different potential for PTSD claims. What is new is the increased awareness, increased claims based on a wider range of causes – and increased publicity regarding PTSD from the officers.

Conclusion

> I think Canadians expect that we'll make mistakes. And when we do, as long as they're sort of good-hearted mistakes, people are patient . . . Dark-hearted behaviour has no place in police work. And Canadians are right to expect that the higher standard of conduct comes from their police officers. And so we're going to take some very simple but decisive steps in the first little while to try and get that back on track. (Commissioner Paulson, upon taking over as head of RCMP)[86]

Paulson is probably right in his assumption that people forgive mistakes that are acknowledged and that would be a valuable lesson for the police. Cameras are everywhere and any account of an incident must take into account that there may well be a technologically produced 'version' of what happened. In terms of main legitimising actions by the police, the general strategies have not changed much. However, the success of these strategies has changed. The police still attempt to control the media presentations of the 'facts' of any encounter, but public and

---

[84] A Marin, *In the Line of Duty: Ontario Ombudsman Report on PTSD* (Ontario, Ombudsman, 2012). See also, C Rush, 'Ombudsman Slams OPP or Lack of Action on PTSD among Police' *Toronto Star* (Toronto, 24 October 2012) available at www.thestar.com/news/canada/politics/article/1276556-
-ombudsman-slams-opp-and-government-for-lack-of-action-on-ptsd-among-officers.

[85] C Rush, 'OPP Chief Open to New Ideas for Officers in Trauma' *Toronto Star* (Toronto, 24 August 2012). By October, Lewis was less willing to concede all of the points raised by Marin. See C Rush, 'OPP Chief Fights Back after Ombudsman's Report: Marin too "Theatrical"' *Toronto Star* (Toronto, 29 October 2012) available at www.thestar.com/news/canada/article/1278958--opp-chief-fights-back-after-ombudsman-s-report-marin-too-theatrical.

[86] CTV News, 'New RCMP Boss Says He'll Fire Serious Wrong-doers' *CTV News* (Toronto, 6 December 2013) available at www.ctvnews.ca/new-rcmp-boss-says-he-ll-fire-serious-wrongdoers-1.736312.

social media have done an extraordinary job of exposing policing abuses and the 'normalised' degree of police perjury. At any one time the police identify and target their most aggressive tactics upon a 'dangerous class' and today those targets are the marginalised neighbourhoods in which gangs may be found. There have traditionally been elite units within police forces that are seen to be doing the 'real policing' – in the past units such as homicide or drugs. Today that honour goes to the 'Gangs'n Guns' units. Secrecy has always been an operating tool and this paper argues that the police attempt to reduce exposure to accountability. Denying and lying, targeting the priority neighbourhoods, engaging in the deep undercover Mr Big scenarios, and claims to national security in the policing of protests (especially with their badges removed), are some of the ways they attempt to achieve this anonymity.

What is unique, and may be linked to the humiliations experienced by the members of the RCMP, is the undermining of the legitimacy by the members themselves through bringing every grievance into the public domain. Internal complaints are aimed at the Commissioners – two eliminated and one currently under scrutiny. The Commissioner in an open letter addressed the problems of 'bad apples' among his officers with the result that the rank and file send public emails complaining of senior management. Women contact the media to complain about sexual harassment from the men – and in the process helped to destroy at least one candidate's chance to become commissioner. Like a prisoner's dilemma, it looks as if once the cracks formed to let some light get in everyone wants to be behind a complaint and not the target of it. Selling the force to the public is no longer the focus. Selling the force to the members will be the real challenge.

6

Seeing Like a Small State: Globalisation and the Politics of Immigration Detention in the Margins of Europe

LEONIDAS K CHELIOTIS*

This chapter addresses an important but little studied juncture between two phenomena that are both in themselves closely associated with globalisation; namely, with the greater mobility of capital and the rise of vital international interconnections between nation states as the latter are incorporated into the global economy and informational cyberspace.[1]

The first phenomenon is irregular migration. To the extent that globalisation requires the flow of labour across borders, it has been a strong force behind the rise of international immigration over recent decades, although governments of receiving countries have increasingly, if variably, engaged in what John Muncie calls 'de-globalisation';[2] that is, they have recently sought to limit the number of immigrants on their soil according to contingent market needs and dominant political interests. Such efforts have primarily targeted irregular migrants and have typically spanned the militarisation of national borders in order to prevent new clandestine entries, as well as the deployment of aggressive policing and administrative detention with the eventual aim of deportation for those who have already crossed the borders without documentation.

The second phenomenon concerns the ever-increasing prominence of international judicial, inspectorate and non-governmental bodies that share the general principles and aims of what is now commonly referred to as 'global justice', each of them working in their diverse capacities to ensure that international human rights legislation is observed inside the borders of individual nation states. This

---

* This chapter is an updated and extended version of LK Cheliotis, 'Behind the Veil of Philoxenia: The Politics of Immigration Detention in Greece' (2013) 10 *European Journal of Criminology* 725.

[1] On defining 'globalisation', see further, D Nelken, 'Afterword: Studying Criminal Justice in Globalising Times' in D Nelken (ed), *Comparative Criminal Justice and Globalisation* (Ashgate, Aldershot, 2011).

[2] J Muncie, 'On Globalisation and Exceptionalism' in D Nelken (ed), *Comparative Criminal Justice and Globalisation*, above n 1.

second phenomenon can be viewed as a positive counterweight to the first, at least insofar as it comprises efforts to pre-empt, stop or redress policies and practices of immigration control that stand in violation of human rights treaties.

The specific focus of this chapter is on the use and conditions of administrative detention of irregular migrants inside national borders, particularly as they may be reprimanded and punished by international actors whose mission is to promote and protect the human rights of detainees. With the aim of adding further nuance to the findings of pertinent scholarship, the chapter proceeds to problematise the effectiveness of such external interventions by exploring in detail the reactions of a multiply censured and fined European Union Member State: Greece. Although one might expect states occupying a peripheral position in the international arena to respond positively to pressures from prominent or otherwise powerful actors abroad, the case of Greece illustrates that being a small power may actually be associated with a reduced degree of effectiveness of foreign pressures.

Irregular Migration and Immigration Detention in Contemporary Greece: Some Preliminary Remarks

Despite variation in the ways in which so-called 'host' countries in Europe have responded to migration flows over recent decades, there is no doubt that immigration is a hot political issue across the continent, both within individual nation states and at the EU level, particularly with reference to irregular migrants. But few, if any, countries in Europe have concerned themselves with immigration and have found themselves at the epicentre of pertinent international attention as much as Greece. In good part, this has been due to the fact that Greece's extensive coastal and mainland borders with Turkey are the main point of entry for irregular migration in the EU, hence also the exceptionally large numbers of migrants entering the country clandestinely. Indeed, although irregular migration into the EU as a whole has dropped in recent years, entries into Greece have grown to constitute the large majority of detected illegal border crossings in the continent.[3] Additionally, however, immigration in Greece has increasingly been debated in terms of how immigrants are treated in the country, with several domestic and especially international actors levelling heavy and sustained criticism against the Greek state for what they commonly describe as its unjust, inhumane and degrading policies and practices towards immigrant populations. Central to this debate have been the excessive use and harsh conditions of administrative detention of irregular migrants in Greece.

---

[3] FRONTEX, *Extract from the Annual Risk Analysis 2010* (Warsaw, FRONTEX, 2010).

Bringing together material from a range of sources in both Greek and English, from official documentation by government and independent actors to media reports and scholarly research, this chapter sets out to offer a systematic summary of the policies, practices and experiences of immigration detention in Greece, as well as outlining how they have been critiqued domestically and internationally. Against this background, the chapter proceeds to shift the focus to the ways in which the Greek state has reacted to criticisms and pressures for reform, especially from abroad. State reactions to such interventions have received relatively little attention to date, whether in relation to Greece or other jurisdictions. Scholarly research has been mainly preoccupied either with the scope and validity of criticisms as such or the specific structure and operations of the institutions that raise them (for example, inspectorate and judicial bodies). Much less is known about the nature of reactions from the states concerned, the forces that determine them, and their respective influence on the effectiveness of censures.[4] Greece readily lends itself as a case study through which to advance understanding of these issues, given both the variety and intensity of criticisms the country has recently received.

The chapter finds that neither domestic nor international pressure have succeeded in bringing about substantive progressive change in the Greek immigration detention system. As is shown, Greek state authorities have systematically neutralised criticisms by employing an array of rhetorical techniques, most notably through evocation of national heritage in the form of both direct and indirect claims that Greeks are the philoxenos people *par excellence*, descended directly from the ancient Hellenes of the days of Xenios Zeus, the god of hospitality to foreigners and strangers more generally. In addition to highlighting the dubious and paradoxical dimensions of the rhetorical defences deployed by the state in Greece, particularly of concern is its discourse of philoxenia, the chapter goes on to briefly address the main socio-political functions that have subtly been served inside the country's borders through maintenance of unjust and inhumane policies and practices of immigration detention. These functions have ranged from facilitating the sustenance of a vast exploitable labour pool, in line with what is referred to in pertinent Anglophone literature as the 'less eligibility' principle, to allowing for the symbolic management of a variety of discontents amongst average Greek citizens, including by compensating for their spreading pains of downward mobility and falling living standards since the financial crisis hit Greece in

---

[4] For partial exceptions, see G Cornelisse, *Immigration Detention and Human Rights: Rethinking Territorial Sovereignty* (Leiden and Boston, Martinus Nijhoff Publishers, 2010); N De Genova and N Peutz (eds), *The Deportation Regime: Sovereignty, Space and the Freedom of Movement* (Durham and London, Duke University Press, 2010); D Wilsher, *Immigration Detention: Law, History, Politics* (Cambridge, Cambridge University Press, 2012). Information on the ways in which states react to external pressures for reform of their conventional prison systems, can be found, amongst others, in A Cassese, *Inhuman States: Imprisonment, Detention and Torture in Europe Today* (Cambridge, Polity Press, 1996); MD Evans and R Morgan, *Preventing Torture: A Study of the European Convention for the Prevention of Torture and Inhuman or Degrading Treatment of Punishment* (Oxford, Oxford University Press, 1998); R Morgan and MD Evans (eds), *Protecting Prisoners: The Standards of the European Committee for the Prevention of Torture in Context* (Oxford, Oxford University Press, 1999).

2009, in accordance with what this chapter terms the 'more eligibility' principle. Once one begins to grasp these functions, one has already gone a long way towards explaining why the Greek state stubbornly persists in making use of rhetoric that is blatantly indefensible and bound to attract further disapprobation. The irony is that these functions both reflect and help to reproduce Greece's weak position in the international arena.

Irregular Migration in Contemporary Greece

Greece first became a country of net immigration in the 1990s, following the fall of communist regimes in Eastern Europe and the Balkans. Despite variations in terms of size and composition over the years, the population of migrants entering Greece irregularly has grown to constitute a large part of the total population of immigrants in the country. In 2011, for example, out of an estimated total of 887,658 immigrants in Greece (itself amounting to around 8 per cent of the country's total population), close to half are believed to have been unregistered, with a substantial decrease recorded in the proportion of irregular migrants from Albania and a concomitant increase in the proportion of Asians and Africans.[5]

What has made Greece such a common destination for irregular migrants is, on one hand, her extensive land and coastal borders with several migrant source countries (for example, Turkey and Albania), which renders her the main gateway for irregular migration to the EU, and, on the other hand, her large informal labour market (including agriculture, the construction industry and domestic services), which in practical terms has readily absorbed unskilled and semi-skilled workers without papers.[6] Opportunities for long-term settlement in Greece, however, are few and far between, not least due to state reluctance to recognise the status and address the needs of asylum seekers and irregular migrants. For example, although the volume of asylum applications to Greece has grown to be amongst the highest in Europe, the country has maintained one of the lowest rates of asylum recognition in the continent, having long avoided putting in place an efficient and effective system for processing applications.[7] Similarly, whilst irregular migrants are over-

[5] See A Triandafyllidou, *Greece: How a State in Crisis Manages its Migration Crisis?* (Paris and Brussels, Institut français des relations internationals, 2012); also T Maroukis, 'Update Report Greece: The Number of Irregular Migrants in Greece at the End of 2010 and 2011' (2012) Clandestino Project Database on Irregular Migration, available at irregular-migration.net; T Maroukis, 'Migration and the Crisis in Greek Society: The Parameters of a Coordinated Departure' ELIAMEP Briefing Note 08, available at www.eliamep.gr/wp-content/uploads/2012/01/thanos.pdf.

[6] See, further, C Lawrence, 'Re-Bordering the Nation: Neoliberalism and Racism in Rural Greece' (2005) 29 *Dialectical Anthropology* 315; A Papadopoulou-Kourkoula, *Transit Migration: The Missing Link between Emigration and Settlement* (Basingstoke, Palgrave Macmillan, 2008).

[7] European Committee for the Prevention of Torture and Inhuman or Degrading Treatment or Punishment (CPT), 'Public Statement Concerning Greece' (Strasbourg, Council of Europe, 2011); L Karamanidou and L Schuster, 'Realising One's Rights under the 1951 Convention 60 Years On: A Review of Practical Constraints on Accessing Protection in Europe' (2011) 25 *Journal of Refugee Studies* 169.

represented in Greece amongst the poorest and most vulnerable, there is no clear legal basis for them to submit claims for emergency social assistance.[8]

Immigrants' prospects for integration in Greek society are further undermined by the treatment they receive by the police. Immigrant communities in Greece are systematically subject to over-policing, including a greater likelihood of being stopped and searched and so-called 'sweep' or 'cleaning operations' launched in the name of fighting illegal immigration, drug-related criminality and prostitution.[9] Practices of police violence against immigrants have also been reported with notable regularity, from the unwarranted use of force and the deliberate destruction of residence permits during routine identity checks, to physical maltreatment in police stations.[10] Police authorities have shown remarkable restraint, on the other hand, in cases where members of the neo-fascistic party Chrysi Avyi ('Golden Dawn') have perpetrated open attacks on immigrants and their property,[11] and where they have issued threats against activist organisations that offer assistance to immigrants in need.[12] More generally, according to data provided by Greek and international NGOs, racist violence has been a serious and rapidly growing issue in the country.[13] It comes as no surprise that the number of immigrants who wish to leave Greece has reportedly been on the rise (although this has also been due to the contraction of employment opportunities in key sectors of the informal labour market, such as the construction industry, amidst conditions of financial crisis since 2009).[14]

An accumulating throng of reports from domestic and especially international media and organisations have strongly condemned Greece for the unjust and harsh treatment immigrants receive in the country, as well as for the continuing failure of the Greek state to tackle the issue.[15] This criticism, described by segments of the

[8] European Committee of Social Rights, *European Social Charter: Conclusions XIX-2 (2009) (Greece): Articles 3, 11, 12, 13, 14 and Article 4 of the Additional Protocol of the Charter* (Strasbourg, Council of Europe, 2011). See further, LK Cheliotis and S Xenakis, 'What's Neoliberalism Got to Do With It? Towards a Political Economy of Punishment in Greece' (2010) 10 *Criminology and Criminal Justice* 353.

[9] See, further, LK Cheliotis and S Xenakis, 'Crime, Fear of Crime and Punitiveness' in LK Cheliotis and S Xenakis (eds), *Crime and Punishment in Contemporary Greece: International Comparative Perspectives* (Bern, Peter Lang AG, 2011).

[10] See, eg Amnesty International, *Police Violence in Greece: Not Just Isolated Incidents* (London, Amnesty International, 2012).

[11] S Xenakis, 'A New Dawn? Change and Continuity in Political Violence in Greece' (2012) 24 *Terrorism and Political Violence* 437.

[12] See Editorial, 'Doctors of the World: Complaint over Intimidation by Chrysi Avyi' *Eleftherotypia* (Athens, 8 February 2013) (in Greek).

[13] S Xenakis and LK Cheliotis, 'Spaces of Contestation: Challenges, Actors and Expertise in the Management of Urban Security in Greece' (2013) 10 *European Journal of Criminology* 297.

[14] Editorial, 'Migrants in Greece "Have Had Enough"' *BBC* (London, 17 April 2011) available at www.bbc.co.uk/news/world-europe-13108642; Editorial, 'Immigrants in Greece "want to go home" as conditions worsen' *BBC* (20 February 2012) available at www.bbc.co.uk/news/world-europe-17094303.

[15] See, eg Amnesty International, *Police Violence in Greece*; United Nations High Commissioner for Refugees (UNHCHR), 'UN Special Rapporteur on the Human Rights of Migrants Concludes the Fourth and Last Country Visit in His Regional Study on the Human Rights of Migrants at the Borders of the European Union: Greece' (Geneva, 3 December 2012) available at www.ohchr.org/EN/NewsEvents/Pages/DisplayNews.aspx?NewsID=12858&LangID=E; Human Rights Watch, *World Report 2013: Photo Essays* (New York, Human Rights Watch, 2013).

Greek press in such terms as 'international ridicule'[16] and 'repeated slaps',[17] has not yet brought about substantial remedial action on the part of the Greek state and its authorities, who have rather chosen to erect walls of denial.

In March 2013, the Greek government reportedly tried to exert diplomatic pressure on the US State Department to exclude critical reference to Greece from the introduction to its annual human rights report.[18] When criticisms come to light, as they increasingly do, they are typically dealt with by the Greek state, whether directly or indirectly, through various rhetorical defences: from rationalising the type of treatment immigrants experience in Greece by emphasising the criminal and other dangers their presence allegedly creates (a technique aptly captured in the all-too-common phrase 'I am not a racist, but . . .'); to explaining away failure to address the problem by reference to the exceptionally large number of irregular migrants in Greece and a lack of financial resources, especially since the onset of the financial crisis in the country;[19] to undermining the extent of the problem[20] or even denying the very possibility that racism can manifest itself amongst Greek people. As the Greek prime minister himself put the latter point in a highly publicised speech he gave in March 2013, Greeks have been against racism 'from the depths of centuries', because they are both culturally and biologically predisposed to oppose it; because 'their tradition does not allow them [to do otherwise]' and because 'there are very powerful antibodies in our DNA, in our gene, which fight that "virus"'.[21]

It is little wonder that harsh state policies towards immigrants have not only continued unabated, but have also intensified and expanded in recent months and years. In 2012, for instance, a barbed-wire fence was constructed along a section (12.5 kilometres) of Greece's mainland borders with Turkey in the prefecture of Evros in a bid to prevent irregular immigration. Similar developments have taken place inside Greece, although often under the familiar banner of Greek philoxenia. Most notably, an unprecedentedly large police operation to capture irregular migrants was launched around the country in 2012, during which several thousands of suspects were temporarily detained and many of them, including tourists, were also allegedly subjected to physical abuse by officers.[22] The operation was named after the Ancient Greek god of hospitality, 'Xenios Zeus',

[16] Editorial, 'International Ridicule for Greece, which has become a Cradle of Racism' *To Vima* (Athens, 20 July 2012) (in Greek).
[17] Editorial, 'Repeated Slaps due to Racist Violence' *Kyriakatiki Eleftherotypia* (London, 3 March 2013) (in Greek).
[18] Editorial, 'New Democracy's Far-right Paths' *To Vima* (Athens, 16 March 2013) (in Greek).
[19] See, eg Editorial, 'Nikos Dendias: The University Asylum Law Will be Enforced' *To Vima* (Athens, 19 November 2012) (in Greek).
[20] See, eg Editorial, 'Annette Groth: If Greece Was Germany, the Immigration Issue Would Have Been Resolved' *To Vima* (Athens, 23 January 2013) (in Greek).
[21] Prime Minister's Press Office, 'Address by Prime Minister Mr Antonis Samaras at the Commemorative Event for the Seventieth Anniversary of the Displacement of Greek Jews in Thessaloniki' (Athens, 17 March 2013) (in Greek) available at www.primeminister.gov.gr/2013/03/17/10133.
[22] Editorial, 'The Tourists Held by Greek Police as Illegal Immigrants' *BBC* (London, 10 January 2013) available at www.bbc.co.uk/news/magazine-20958353.

and has been portrayed by the Minister of Public Order and Citizen Protection, Nikos Dendias, as an effort to restore the human rights of illegal immigrants,[23] if also, ironically, as part of a broader strategy of deterrence, aimed to turn Greece into an 'unfriendly destination' for those considering entering or staying in the country clandestinely.[24]

The most controversial developments, however, have occurred on the front of immigration detention, even though Greek state authorities have once more responded with denial to criticism from inside the country and abroad.

Immigration Detention in Contemporary Greece

Greek law formally provides for the administrative detention of irregular migrants from non-EU (or 'third') countries as part of a process whereby their deportation can be organised. As of April 2014, based on a controversial opinion by the Legal Council of the Greek State, irregular migrants may be detained in Greece indefinitely so long as their eventual deportation has not yet been made possible. Previously, following a series of extensions of the legal maximum duration of administrative detention, irregular migrants could be detained in the country for a period of up to 18 months. Similar to pertinent international legislation, Greek law stipulates that administrative detention pending deportation should be used only when there is a risk that the migrant in question might abscond or pose a danger to public safety. In practice, however, Greek authorities enforce detention as a matter of course, automatically and indiscriminately, which raises issues of arbitrariness.[25] As far as asylum seekers are concerned, they must remain in detention until a decision is reached on their application. Yet procedural delays are typically so excessive that asylum seekers whose deportation is deemed unfeasible are often essentially forced to withdraw their application in order to expedite their release,[26] whilst the long legal maximum duration of detention for asylum seekers, also previously raised to 18 months for those who lodged an asylum application

---

[23] Editorial, 'N Dendias on Immigration' *SKAI* (Athens, 6 August 2012) (in Greek).

[24] Editorial, 'Autopsy' *SKAI* (Athens, 4 October 2012) (in Greek). The scope of the Ministry's operations may thus be reflected more accurately in the Ministry's name itself, at least insofar as the latter implies that ministerial provision of protection extends only to those already granted citizenship, to the exclusion of non-citizens such as asylum seekers and irregular migrants.

[25] ICJ and ECRE, 'Second Joint Submission of the International Commission of Jurists (ICJ) and of the European Council on Refugees and Exiles (ECRE) to the Committee of Ministers of the Council of Europe in the case of *MSS v Belgium and Greece* (Application no 30696/09) and Related Cases' (The Hague, 6 February 2013) available at www.ecre.org/component/downloads/downloads/707.html. See also, Médecins Sans Frontières, *Migrants in Detention: Lives on Hold – Greece June 2010* (Athens, Médecins Sans Frontières, 2010); Amnesty International, *Greece: The End of the Road for Refugees, Asylum-Seekers and Migrants* (London, Amnesty International, 2012); UNHCHR, 'Working Group on Arbitrary Detention Statement upon the Conclusion of its Mission to Greece' (21–31 January 2013) (Geneva, 31 January 2013) available at www.ohchr.org/EN/NewsEvents/Pages/DisplayNews.aspx?NewsID=12962&LangID=E.

[26] See further, Médecins Sans Frontières, *Migrants in Detention*, above n 25.

once detained, has been perceived by many as a means of dissuading them from seeking international protection in the first instance.[27]

Upon arrest, irregular migrants are routinely subject to a temporary detention order that is issued by local police authorities and does not need to be approved by a judge. Temporary detention may last up to three days, during which time an administrative deportation order must be issued in order for detention to continue further without contravening pertinent legislation. Indeed, the deportation order is usually accompanied by an order for the continuation of detention. Most detention orders only briefly state that the individual concerned is considered to be at risk of absconding or poses a danger to public safety, but they provide no evidence or additional details in either of these respects. Although practices may vary from one locality to another, but also according to the nationality of the apprehended migrant, the vast majority of migrants are held in detention beyond the initial three-day period. Not all remain in detention until the legal maximum duration is reached because, for example, preparations for deportation are completed, or, conversely, because deportation is deemed unfeasible and the migrant has to be released. Detainees who have applied for asylum and whose applications are still pending at the time of release, are usually issued a deportation order and a note to leave the country within 30 days, as if they had never lodged an asylum application.[28]

The administrative detention infrastructure in Greece includes two main types of facilities: first, police and border guard stations, which are meant to be used for the purposes of short-term detention and screening of apprehended migrants; and second, detention centres, which are controversially referred to in official discourse as 'philoxenia centres' and are meant to hold foreign nationals awaiting deportation. Due largely to reasons of overcrowding, these distinctions are hardly observed in practice, in that police and border guard stations are commonly used to detain migrants for extended periods of time.[29] There were six detention centres in place at the time of writing, their combined operational capacity being officially around 5,000, with plans seemingly under way to add new centres and construct extra accommodation at existing sites so as to quadruple the system's overall capacity.[30] These plans are not surprising given, on one hand, the repeated extensions to the legal maximum duration of immigration detention in Greece, and, on the other hand, various reports indicating that the population of immi-

---

[27] UNHCHR, 'Working Group on Arbitrary Detention Statement upon the Conclusion of its Mission to Greece' 21–31 January 2013. See also, Amnesty International, *Greece: Irregular Migrants and Asylum-Seekers Routinely Detained in Substandard Conditions* (London, Amnesty International, 2010).

[28] See, further, Amnesty International, *Greece: Irregular Migrants and Asylum-Seekers Routinely Detained in Substandard Conditions*; Amnesty International, *Greece: The End of the Road for Refugees*, above n 26; European Union Agency for Fundamental Rights (FRA), *Coping with a Fundamental Rights Emergency: The Situation of Persons Crossing the Greek Land Border in an Irregular Manner* (Vienna, FRA, 2011); Pro Asyl, *Walls of Shame: Accounts from the Inside: The Detention Centres of Evros* (Frankfurt, Pro Asyl, 2012).

[29] See, eg Pro Asyl, *Walls of Shame*, above n 28.

[30] 'The "Non-friendly" Country Greece: Behind the Fences of Concentration Camps' *Ios* (Athens, 9 December 2012) (in Greek).

grant detainees in the country has undergone a rapid rise over recent years and that the total annual numbers of irregular migrants held in particular detention centres (and especially in the centre of Fylakio in Northern Greece) are already well above the official operational capacity of the Greek immigration detention system as a whole.[31] The vast majority of detainees are kept in the centres of Fylakio, Amygdaleza and Corinth, but further relevant information from official sources has long been unavailable or unreliable.

It should be noted here that irregular migrants may also be held in conventional prisons. Over the last two decades, non-Greeks have grown to outnumber Greeks behind bars (amounting, for example, to 7,875, or 60 per cent, out of a total of 12,912 pre-trial and convicted prisoners on 1 January 2013) with a significant and increasing proportion of non-Greeks – half of them by 2012, for example – being imprisoned in connection with illegal entry into, departure from, or stay in the country. Albeit a crucial aspect of the broader phenomenon of punitiveness against irregular migrants in Greece, their detention in conventional prisons is not elaborated in this chapter for reasons of space.[32]

Conditions of Immigration Detention[33]

Unlike with trends in the use of immigration detention as such, abundant solid evidence has been publicly revealed, if not by the Greek state itself, on the conditions under which irregular migrants are detained in Greece.

A wealth of reports both by domestic and international mass media and organisations, and also a growing body of pertinent scholarship, have demonstrated that

---

[31] See, eg Pro Asyl (ed), '*The Truth May Be Bitter, But It Must Be Told': the Situation of Refugees in the Aegean and the Practices of the Greek Coast Guard* (Frankfurt, Pro Asyl, 2007); Government of Greece 'Response of the Government of Greece to the Report of the European Committee for the Prevention of Torture and Inhuman or Degrading Treatment of Punishment (CPT) on Its Visit to Greece from 20 to 27 January 2011' (Strasbourg, Council of Europe, 2012).

[32] But see LK Cheliotis, 'Immigrants and the Penal State: Punitiveness in the Margins of Europe' (forthcoming); LK Cheliotis, 'Order through Honour: Masculinity and the Use of Temporary Release in a Greek Prison' (2014) 113 *South Atlantic Quarterly* 529. The use of imprisonment in Greece has risen dramatically over the last three decades or so (see LK Cheliotis, 'Prisons and Parole' in LK Cheliotis and S Xenakis (eds), *Crime and Punishment in Contemporary Greece: International Comparative Perspectives* (Bern, Peter Lang AG, 2011)), and has been exacerbated further since the onset of the financial crisis in 2009 (see M Aebi and N Delgrande, *Council of Europe Annual Penal Statistics, SPACE I, Survey 2010* (Strasbourg, Council of Europe, 2012) available at www3.unil.ch/wpmu/space/files/2011/02/SPACE-1_2010_English1.pdf.

[33] Due to space restrictions, the focus in this section is specifically on border guard stations and detention centres, although similar conditions are found in all other sites where irregular migrants may be detained in Greece, including very often in conventional prisons (on which see LK Cheliotis, 'Suffering at the Hands of the State: Conditions of Imprisonment and Prisoner Health in Contemporary Greece' (2012) 9 *European Journal of Criminology* 3; also Cheliotis, 'Order through Honour', above n 32). Detention conditions in the police station on the coast of Igoumenitsa in Nortwestern Greece are, in fact, known to have been so deplorable that a local court, in an unprecedented and as yet unrepeated decision reached in October 2012, cited them as reasons justifying the escape of 15 irregular migrants from police detention earlier in that year. See, further, Cheliotis, 'Immigrants and the Penal State', above n 32.

immigration detention in the country entails lengthy exposure to conditions that amount to inhuman and degrading treatment. Immigration detention, moreover, extends to particularly vulnerable groups such as pregnant women, seriously ill and elderly individuals, and children. Indeed, the very detention of minors, whether they are held with their families or unaccompanied, stands in violation of the UN Convention of the Rights of the Child, of which Greece is a signatory.[34]

More specifically, irregular migrants are usually detained in facilities that are neither purpose-built (for example, former military bases and storage facilities, or border guard station cells designed only for short periods of detention) nor meet basic standards of quality.[35] Meanwhile, the rising number of detainees in itself has combined with repeated increases in the legal maximum duration of immigration detention to far outstrip the official operational capacity of the immigration detention system in Greece. Snapshot measurements of the population of immigrant detainees in specific border guard stations and detention centres around the country have shown, for example, that the number of detained persons is typically several times greater than the sites in question can properly accommodate.[36] Overcrowding is so high that detainees often have to share beds and sleep in shifts, or otherwise simply use the floor, lying at best on mattresses or sleeping bags provided by NGOs and at worst on cardboard and blankets. At their most extreme, overcrowded conditions render sleeping possible only in a sitting position, or force detainees to lie down next to garbage and in the sewage of toilets.[37] There have also been reports of men, women and unaccompanied children being held together in the same detention space, but also, conversely, of close family members being separated from one another.[38]

Other commonly reported problems include lack of ventilation, limited sanitation, unsuitable room temperature and poor hygiene. As regards temperature in cells, it is often overly cold in the winter due to problems with the provision of heating (for example, limited supply of petrol) and a lack of weather-proofed windows and doors, just as it tends to be excessively hot in the summer due to faulty or non-existent air conditioning. As for hygiene, access to functioning

---

[34] See further, Pro Asyl, *The Truth May Be Bitter*, above n 31; Pro Asyl, above n 28; CPT, 'Report to the Government of Greece on the Visit to Greece carried out by the European Committee for the Prevention of Torture and Inhuman or Degrading Treatment of Punishment (CPT) from 23 to 29 September 2008' (Council of Europe, Strasbourg, 2009); CPT, 'Report to the Government of Greece on the Visit to Greece carried out by the European Committee for the Prevention of Torture and Inhuman or Degrading Treatment of Punishment (CPT) from 17 to 29 September 2009' (Strasbourg, Council of Europe, 2010); CPT, 'Report to the Government of Greece on the Visit to Greece carried out by the European Committee for the Prevention of Torture and Inhuman or Degrading Treatment of Punishment (CPT) from 19 to 27 January 2011' (Strasbourg, Council of Europe, 2012); Human Rights Watch, *The EU's Dirty Hands: Frontex Involvement in Ill-Treatment of Migrant Detainees in Greece* (New York, Human Rights Watch, 2011); J Lauth Bacas, 'Not a Safe Haven: The Reception of Irregular Boat Migrants in Greece' (2010) 14 *Ethnologia Balkanica* 147.

[35] Pro Asyl, above n 31; Pro Asyl, above n 28.

[36] See, eg Pro Asyl, above n 31; Pro Asyl, above n 28; FRA, *Coping with a Fundamental Rights Emergency*, above n 28.

[37] See, eg *Human Rights Watch, The EU's Dirty Hands* above n 34; Pro Asyl, above n 28.

[38] Pro Asyl, above n 31; Médecins Sans Frontières, above n 25.

latrines has frequently been found to be severely limited, with dozens or even hundreds of detainees having to share a single toilet that may offer no privacy. When there are no latrines in operation, detainees are driven to urinate in bottles or through the bars outside their cells, and are escorted by guards to nearby fields where they can defecate. Serious problems have also come to light with regard to access to functioning showers and hot water, whilst provision of basic material necessities, from clothing, toilet paper, soap and shampoo to toothbrushes, toothpaste and towels, is typically extremely deficient.[39]

Meals are reportedly eaten inside cells, where tables or chairs are generally unavailable. In the absence of cleaning services, moreover, detainees are themselves responsible for keeping their cells clean but are given no or insufficient products to this effect, and garbage may be retained in cells until detainees are allowed at the discretion of guards to dispose of it outside.[40] Finally, there have been reports of dysfunctional sewage systems, as a result of which urine and faecal matter spread out over the cell floor, their smell combining with body and garbage odours to create a suffocating and deeply unhealthy atmosphere for detainees (but also for guards, at least some of whom have been found to wear surgical masks as a protective measure).[41]

According to various reports, food provision is usually substandard both in terms of quality and quantity, and drinking water is often dirty and only available from latrines and showers.[42] Medical provision, meanwhile, has been minimal due to a lack of specialist staff, medication and proper facilities, and guards may sometimes actively discourage or otherwise hinder detainees from seeking medical care. Even health screening of new detainees upon their reception tends to be either insufficient or entirely absent, and medical NGOs such as Doctors of the World are largely relied upon to fill the gaps. This is despite the fact that the majority of immigrant detainees in Greece are known to be suffering from such health problems as respiratory tract infections, diarrhoea, skin diseases or depression, which are linked, directly or indirectly, to the long duration of their detainment under deplorable conditions.[43]

[39] See further, FRA, above n 28; Human Rights Watch, above n 34; CPT, 'Report to the Government of Greece on the Visit to Greece from 23 to 29 September 2008'; CPT, 'Report to the Government of Greece on the Visit to Greece from 17 to 29 September 2009'; CPT, 'Report to the Government of Greece on the Visit to Greece from 19 to 27 January 2011'; Pro Asyl, above n 29; ICJ and ECRE, 'Second Joint Submission', above n 25.

[40] Pro Asyl, above n 28.

[41] See further, FRA, above n 28; Human Rights Watch, above n 34.

[42] Pro Asyl, above n 31; Pro Asyl, above n 28; Médecins Sans Frontières, above n 25; Amnesty International, above n 25; Ios, The "Non-friendly" Country Greece, above n 30.

[43] See, further, Médecins Sans Frontières, above n 25; Médecins Sans Frontières, *The Impact of Detention on Migrants' Health: Briefing Paper* (Brussels, Médecins Sans Frontières, 2010); CPT, 'Report to the Government of Greece on the Visit to Greece from 23 to 29 September 2008'; CPT, 'Report to the Government of Greece on the Visit to Greece from 17 to 29 September 2009'; CPT, 'Report to the Government of Greece on the Visit to Greece from 19 to 27 January 2011'; Pro Asyl, above n 28; ICJ and ECRE, above n 25. In the general population of Greece, meanwhile, there is an oversupply of medical specialists, dentists, and pharmacists (indeed, an oversupply that is impressive by European standards) (K Davaki and E Mossialos, 'Financing and Delivering Health Care' in M Petmesidou and E Mossialos (eds), *Social Policy Developments in Greece* (Aldershot, Ashgate, 2006).

To a significant extent, detainees are trapped and secluded in those conditions. Outdoor access has been found to be a rare occurrence in various centres, whilst centre yards, when they exist at all, tend to be too small and unprotected from harsh weather conditions. More broadly, communication with the outside world is particularly difficult for detainees. At times, this is partly because detention centres are geographically isolated, as in the case of the centre in Fylakio, half an hour's drive outside the city of Orestiada. Geographical considerations aside, however, entry into detention centres may be restricted or otherwise obstructed by the authorities for lawyers and representatives of NGOs, and basic means of communication, such as card-phones, are regularly unavailable for detainees or simply impossible to use (for example, phones are often not working and detainees lack the financial means purchase cards with which to make calls). At the same time, detainees are faced with serious difficulties in terms of lodging asylum applications, ranging from a lack of knowledge of pertinent requirements, to an inability to read relevant legal documentation, to a lack of professional translators and interpreters, to insufficient financial means necessary for hiring a lawyer, to excessive bureaucratic delays and even denial of access to the procedure itself.[44]

The plight of immigrant detainees is further exacerbated by the violent treatment to which members of detention staff may reportedly subject them on a frequent basis. Such violence can range from racist verbal abuse, to destruction of detainees' religious symbols, to aggressive body searches and direct physical assaults (for example, slaps, punches, kicks and beatings with clubs). Indeed, assaults by guards are known to have caused serious injuries, at times so serious that victims were in need of hospitalisation. In the absence of a credible complaints procedure and a well-resourced and independent inspectorate, staff violence appears to be treated with impunity hence it may even take place in front of witnesses such as NGO workers.[45] There have also been allegations of sexual harassment of detainees by guards, and revelations of severe ill-treatment amounting to torture, which may also go unpunished, at least by the domestic authorities. In the most well-known case, a guard aided by colleagues raped a male Turkish detainee with a truncheon, and the victim was subsequently denied access to medical care. An internal administrative inquiry found no guilt based on evidence that had been blatantly falsified, and when the case eventually reached the national courts, the prison sentences imposed in the first instance upon the perpetrator and some of his accomplishes became suspended sentences and were commuted to fines at the appeal stage.[46]

[44] See, further, Pro Asyl, above n 31; Pro Asyl, above n 28; Médecins Sans Frontières, above n 25; Médecins Sans Frontières, *The Impact of Detention on Migrants' Health*, above n 43; Human Rights Watch, above n 34; Ios, above n 30; *SKAI*, 'Autopsy' (n 24).

[45] See further, Pro Asyl (n 31); Pro Asyl, above n 28; Médecins Sans Frontières, above n 25; FRA, above n 28; Human Rights Watch, above n 34; Amnesty International, above n 25; SKAI (n 24).

[46] See, further, ECHR (European Court of Human Rights), 'European Court Finds an Illegal Migrant Was Tortured by one of the Greek Coastguard Officers Supervising Him' (Press Release) (Strasbourg, 17 January 2012) available at www.redress.org/downloads/Chamber%20judgment%20 Zontul%20v.%20Greece%2017.01.2012.pdf; also Pro Asyl, above n 28.

It comes as no surprise that detainees frequently describe the conditions of their detention by using terms such as 'grave' and even 'hell', going so far as to draw unfavourable comparisons with previous experiences of warzones that they may have had and managed to escape.[47] Indeed, these conditions of detention are conducive not only to health problems, as mentioned earlier, but also to violent tensions amongst detainees themselves. For example, fights are quick to erupt over access to sleeping space or the toilet, and such instances are also known to have triggered indiscriminate physical violence against detainees on the part of guards in order to discipline them.[48] Additionally, lengthy periods of detention under deplorable conditions commonly drive detainees to engage in various forms of protest, some of which ironically entail direct infliction of further pain upon detainees' own bodies, and may equally be met with violent reactions by the authorities in charge.

Long and exhaustive hunger strikes, for example, are highly prevalent in detention centres throughout Greece, with some detainees even stitching their lips together. In April 2013, around 1,800 detainees went on hunger strike in all detention facilities around the country, protesting against the length and conditions of their detention.[49] As with periods of relative normality, moreover, self-harm and suicide attempts are likely to occur during times of protest.[50] There have been reports of staff employing violence in response to detainee protests, but also of riot police having been called in and intervening aggressively (to suppress violence by protestors, according to controversial claims by the riot police themselves), including using water cannon, tear gas and stun grenades, and making arrests that eventually resulted in detention in conventional prisons.[51]

Criticisms of the Greek State

A number of domestic actors, from humanitarian NGOs to political parties and media outlets on the left of the political spectrum, have expressed urgent concerns about the excessive use and deplorable conditions of immigration detention in Greece, contesting the state discourse of philoxenia with such suggestive expressions as 'barbarism', 'concentration camps' and 'Greek Guantanamo'.[52] On the

[47] See, eg Human Rights Watch, above n 34; Pro Asyl, above n 28.

[48] SKAI (n 24).

[49] Editorial, 'Thousands of Migrants Started a Hunger Strike in Detention Centres' *To Vima* (Athens, 8 April 2013) (in Greek); Editorial, '1,800 Immigrants on Hunger Strike' *Eleftherotypia* (Athens, 9 April 2013) (in Greek).

[50] See further, Médecins Sans Frontières, above n 25; Pro Asyl, above n 28; 'Two Hunger Strikers Attempted Suicide in Amygdaleza' *To Vima* (Athens, 7 April 2013) (in Greek).

[51] See further, Human Rights Watch, above n 34; Pro Asyl, above n 28; Editorial, 'Disturbances at the Detention Centre of Komotini' *To Vima* (Athens, 23 November 2012) (in Greek); Ios, above n 30; Editorial, 'With Chemicals against Immigrant Detainees in Corinth' *Eleftherotypia* (Athens, 11 April 2013) (in Greek).

[52] See, eg Ios, above n 30; Editorial, 'Barbarism Should Stop at Last' *Rizospastis* (Athens, 12 April 2013) (in Greek); *Eleftherotypia*, '1,800 Immigrants on Hunger Strike', above n 50.

international level, too, Greece has regularly been subject to harsh criticism, not just by inspectorate bodies, NGOs and other activist groups, but also politicians from various political parties, some of whom have themselves participated in inspection visits to Greek immigration detention centres.

For example, following a series of visits to Greek immigration detention centres in her capacity as a member of a delegation of the Council of Europe, German left-wing parliamentarian, Annette Groth, said that

> the situation [in Greece] resembles nothing like the human rights we talk about in Europe, this policy of mass detention in deplorable conditions of all incoming migrants and refugees. For the latter, it is equivalent to denying them the right to asylum any longer.[53]

Groth has also argued that the term 'detention centre' is a euphemism in the Greek context, and that what in Greece are called detention centres are, in fact, conventional prisons.[54] John Dalhuisen, Amnesty International's Director for Europe and Central Asia, has similarly described irregular migrants' treatment in Greece, including the conditions of their administrative detention, as being embarrassingly un-European, 'totally unworthy of the Nobel Peace Prize-winning European Union, and so far below international human rights standards as to make a mockery of them'.[55]

In a growing number of cases, meanwhile, the European Court of Human Rights has ordered Greece to pay damages to irregular migrants who had been held in administrative detention in the country under inhumane and degrading conditions, in contravention of international human rights treaties of which Greece is a signatory. In January 2011, moreover, the Court issued the more general ruling that detention practices in Greece violated Article 3 of the European Convention on Human Rights, which prohibits torture and inhuman and degrading treatment, and ordered that other EU Member States cease transferring migrants to Greece under the Dublin-II agreement, or they would be knowingly exposing them to conditions of detention that amount to degrading treatment, thus violating their own international obligations.[56] For commentators such as British Conservative MEP Timothy Kirkhope, however, Europe should adopt an even more punitive stance towards Greece. 'If the UK or France had such inadequate systems and poor asylum conditions as Greece', Kirkhope has argued, 'then I have no doubt the Commission would come down on us like a ton of bricks.'[57]

Neither domestic and international criticism, nor judicial intervention and calls for more punitive action against Greece at the European level, have so far

---

[53] Editorial, 'European Commission Bankrolls Anti-immigrant Policies' *Inter Press Service (IPS)* (17 March 2013).

[54] *To Vima*, above n 21.

[55] Amnesty International, 'Asylum-seekers and Migrants in Greece Hounded by Police Operations and Right-Wing Extremists' (London, Amnesty International, Press Release, 20 December 2012).

[56] See further, Human Rights Watch, above n 34; Pro Asyl, above n 28.

[57] Editorial, 'EU Court Says Asylum Seekers Can Stay' *Daily Express* (London, 22 December 2011).

succeeded in bringing about fundamental changes in the use and conditions of administrative detention in the country. A number of reports have come to light over the years, including notably an 'exceptional' public statement by the European Committee for the Prevention of Torture and Inhuman or Degrading Treatment or Punishment (CPT) in March 2011, emphasising the continuing failure of the Greek state to follow pertinent recommendations and improve the situation.[58] In January 2013, Vladimir Tochilovsky, member of the United Nations Working Group on Arbitrary Detention that had just concluded a fact-finding mission in Greece, told a press conference that the Greek state had made some progress in terms of legislative provisions (eg, setting safeguards for the fair and efficient examination of application for asylum). But then, Tochilovsky swiftly added, 'you take off your 3D glasses and find yourself in a different world', where any positive legislative amendments are practically ignored, administrative detention conditions may be worse than those found in conventional prisons, and human rights violations continue unabated.[59]

The Greek State's Reactions to Criticisms

Overall, the Greek state has reacted to domestic and international pressures by employing an array of rhetorical defence mechanisms, some of which substantively contradict one another.

In their direct official responses to CPT reports, for example, Greek state authorities have essentially denied critical findings by stating that: unaccompanied children are systematically detained separately from adults (yet with the important proviso of space availability); immigrant detainees are given unrestricted access to functioning toilets and showers, as well as to hot water; they are regularly provided with sufficient food and hygiene products (even though partly from contributions by NGOs); and they have available to them legal aid and medical services (if again in part through NGOs). Greek state authorities have additionally tried to absolve themselves of responsibility for any recurrent or remaining problems by pointing to the excessively high numbers of detainees and the high ratio of detainees to staff, which allegedly render the situation inside detention centres particularly difficult to manage, although it is emphasised that 'formidable' and 'enormous' efforts are made to this effect.[60] The Greek state has also blamed poor detention conditions on detainees themselves and their protests, for instance by claiming that:

---

[58] CPT, 'Public Statement Concerning Greece', above n 7. See also, 'Warehouses of Immigrant Detainees or Centres of Philoxenia' *To Vima* (Athens, 10 April 2013) (in Greek); CPT, 'Report to the Government of Greece on the Visit to Greece from 19 to 27 January 2011'; Pro Asyl, above n 28; Editorial, 'Greek Treatment of Illegal Migrants Criticised' *Financial Times* (London, 15 March 2011).

[59] Associated Press, 'UN Official Concerned at Greek Prison Conditions' *Associated Press* (31 January 2013); IPS (n 53). See also, UNHCHR (n 27).

[60] Government of Greece (n 31).

> The detained, in their effort to 'blackmail' their immediate release, destroy the [hygienic] installations, break the fountains, stuff the drainages with towels, shoes, etc., the result of which is the dirty water to flow in the toilets and the other spaces.[61]

Albeit without necessarily addressing critics in a direct manner, Greek state authorities have defended their immigration detention policies and practices through various other rhetorical techniques. Much relevant material can be drawn from a televised interview which took place at the detention centre in Amygdaleza in late 2012 with none other than the then Minister of Public Order and Citizen, Nikos Dendias. During the interview, for example, Dendias explained in no uncertain terms that administrative detention pending deportation forms part of a wider strategy of deterrence that seeks to make Greece an 'unfriendly destination' for those considering entering or staying in the country without papers. The Minister elaborated this point by drawing a comparison between human trafficking and the tourist industry, a comparison in which he gave Greece anything but its familiar role of the archetypically philoxenous country. The Minister's dialogue with his interviewer is revealing:

> Minister: The trafficker is, quote, unquote, like a tourist office. He has to persuade the client . . . If it is known that Greece is a country that is not at all easy to enter, where if at any rate you enter, the most likely outcome is that they will arrest you and put you in a centre, and you will stay there until you go back, then there will be no clientele for Greece. The trafficker, then, may want to sell his product, but there will be no public to sell it to.

> Interviewer: Let's hope so, given that at least over the last decade, [Greece] was for tourist offices, as you mean them, the best destination . . . The Seychelles of illegal immigration.

> Minister: It's exactly as you put it.[62]

As with the very fact of administrative detention, Minister Dendias also attributed a deterrent potential to the specific conditions under which irregular migrants are held in Greece. An immigration detention centre, he stated, 'is not a space where one can have a party' or a 'hotel'. Conditions in Greek immigration detention centres, he went on to say, stand at the 'lowest acceptable civilised minimum', as they, too, may contribute to the goal of discouraging illegal immigration by sending a message that the country is 'unfriendly' to it. Indeed, Dendias suggested, the deterrent effect of administrative detention as such is inversely proportional to the particular quality of detention conditions.[63]

In the same interview, the Minister also made the assertion that Greece respects and observes the standards set by the EU. This assertion not only indirectly denied the mass of independent reports attesting to the contrary nor did it just imply that conditions in Greek immigration detention centres are as good or no worse than elsewhere in the continent, it also paved the way to the claim that responsibility

---

[61] ibid at 9. See further Cheliotis, above n 32.
[62] SKAI (n 24).
[63] ibid.

for at least some of the centres' most controversial aspects (for example, the use of containers to house detainees) rests beyond the Greek state itself.[64] Similarly, the very reliance on immigration detention pending deportation was described by the Minister as an unavoidable choice according to international experience; as 'the internationally accepted and sole mechanism of confronting migratory flows'. This was despite the fact that many different domestic and foreign groups and organisations, including formal European authorities, have long been calling upon the Greek state to seriously consider alternatives to administrative detention of migrants, especially for vulnerable groups such as unaccompanied children and pregnant women.[65]

Greek state authorities have also evoked financial difficulties in an effort to explain away responsibility for the conditions in immigration detention centres across the country, particularly since the financial crisis hit Greece in 2009.[66] Although here it is recognised, at least implicitly, that action should be taken to improve conditions of detention, Greece's failure to take such action has, in fact, been due to how funding is administered, rather than it being a matter of limited financial resources. To take one example relating to the administration of domestic funding, in 2011, two years into the financial crisis, the Greek state chose to pay €1.38 million towards the renovation and conversion into a museum of the Nebojsa Tower in Belgrade, in order to honour a hero of the struggle for Greek independence who was imprisoned and put to death there in 1798 by Ottoman Turkish authorities.[67] That sum was close to one-third of the total annual funds the Greek state allocated at the time to the operation of detention and reception centres for irregular migrants (for example, to cover costs for food, medication, hygiene, clothing and transportation). It would have also been singly sufficient to support for a year the running of detention and reception centres in at least nine out of the 12 prefectures of the country involved.[68]

Greece has additionally had access to substantial EU funding for immigration and asylum management, at least some of which could have been used to ease pressures on immigration detention centres (for example, through supporting NGOs that operate shelters for asylum seekers). Yet the Greek state has long made particularly limited use of such funding possibilities,[69] not to mention that it has typically also failed to explore cost-effective alternatives (for example, using empty hospitals to house vulnerable irregular migrants).[70] In 2012, EU funding was made available specifically for supporting infrastructure projects (that is, renovation, refurbishment or construction of facilities) and running costs relating to

---

[64] ibid.
[65] See, eg UNHCHR (n 27); ICJ and ECRE, above n 25; Amnesty International (n 27); Pro Asyl, above n 28.
[66] Cheliotis, above n 32.
[67] 'Papoulias to Open Nebojsa Tower' *Athens News* (Athens, 28 April 2011).
[68] See further, Editorial, 'Greek Public Sector: Hundreds of Millions for Immigrants' *Epikaira* (Athens, 3 February 2011) (in Greek).
[69] UNHCHR (n 15).
[70] See, eg FRA, above n 28.

detention centres, so as to help Member States 'improve the reception conditions in detention facilities'.[71] To what extent, and in what ways, these funds will be utilised by the Greek state may be somewhat early to judge, yet the first signs are far from encouraging. At the same time that independent reports about persistently substandard detention conditions continue to be published, Greek authorities appear to have given priority to the expansion, through construction work, of the number of centres around the country, which cannot in itself suffice to guarantee better conditions of detention. Indeed, insofar as their official classification might provide an indication of what new centres will be like on the ground, it is important to note that the majority of them have clearly been referred to in government documentation as places of detention rather than reception,[72] although there is no plan in sight to drop the term 'philoxenia' from the formal name of centres categorised as detention sites.

At least as far as the new reception centres are concerned, ministerial authorities have stated that those to be located on the islands of Samos and Chios (in spaces that have previously been used for holding irregular migrants) are in the process of being 'perfected',[73] whist the centre scheduled to operate in Orestiada 'will be the most modern in the whole of Europe'.[74] It is not clear, however, how the concepts of 'perfect' and 'modern' will turn out to be interpreted and applied in practice, and whether they will be treated as loosely and perversely as the notion of philoxenia has been treated to date. Nor, equally, can one be sure that Greek authorities will objectively evaluate detention conditions according to commonly accepted European understandings and standards, or that they will allow themselves to perceive and engage with possible external criticism on its own terms and merits.

As well as repudiating condemnations as such, the Greek state is also known to have denied negative assessment by twisting it into approval. In late 2012, Greece submitted an official report to the Secretariat of the Committee of Ministers of the Council of Europe regarding the 'living conditions of illegal migrants [o]n the border of Evros and in Athens', where it was stated that the detention centre in Amygdaleza had recently been found by the UN High Commission for Refugees (UNHCR) to be 'exemplary as regards accommodation and security'. Yet as the International Commission of Jurists and the European Council on Refugees and Exiles stressed in a subsequent joint report of their own, 'in reality, the UNHCR has expressed reservations regarding the centre. UNHCR's only positive assessment of the centre was that it was in better condition than others in Greece, a comparative estimate that does not qualify as "exemplary"'.[75]

---

[71] IPS, above n 53.

[72] ICJ and ECRE, above n 25.

[73] SKAI, above n 24.

[74] Editorial, 'The New Migrant Reception Centre at the Border Guard Station of Orestiada Will Be Ready in June' *Proto Thema* (Athens, 12 April 2013) (in Greek).

[75] ICJ and ECRE, above n 25 at 8.

What Lies Behind the Veil of Philoxenia?

To date, the Greek state has essentially rebutted or otherwise circumvented domestic and international pressures to effectuate substantive progressive changes to its treatment of immigrants. In so doing, Greek state authorities have deployed a range of dubious rhetorical defences against criticism, the most blatant being the evocation of philoxenia as an innate and constant national trait. But to show, as this chapter has done so far, that immigrants in general, and irregular migrants in particular, are hardly accorded philoxenia in Greece today, is by no means to imply a call for restoring philoxenia in the country. Such a call would at best be superficial, and at worst play into the hands of those whose policies practically deny philoxenia even as they lay claim to it rhetorically. The philoxenia deficit, if the term can be used at all, is not merely a matter of exclusion or insufficient inclusion of immigrants. It is ultimately a matter of domination, given that immigrants' exclusion, and indeed certain forms of their inclusion, have long served to reproduce asymmetrical relations of power in the Greek context.

In this account, the discourse of philoxenia is an ideological veil that supports the reproduction of power imbalances, whether by denying them altogether on the deterministic premise that unconditional openness is the only attitude Greeks are naturally inclined to adopt towards outsiders, or by helping to legitimate injustices against immigrants through connoting the established superiority of the host community and the inherently conditional nature of its hospitality to newcomers. *As Derrida argues, conceptions of hospitality that do not necessarily or fully extend to uninvited strangers are essentially marks of sovereignty.*[76] Minister Dendias himself brought this point home during the interview he gave at the detention centre in Amygdaleza in 2012, when he defended the choice of naming the then newly launched police operation to capture irregular migrants around Greece so as to deport them after the ancient Greek god of hospitality:

> The country, the society, reserves to itself the right to host those whom it wishes itself to host. This is the semiology of the name ['Xenios Zeus']. We do not have the obligation to host whomever judges that they wish to cross the borders clandestinely. . . . We are an organised society, we want to show everyone that we are not a fenceless vineyard, that not everyone who crosses our borders has the right to stay here; it's not like that, it can no longer be like that.[77]

---

[76] See, further, G Borradori, *Philosophy in a Time of Terror: Dialogues with Jürgen Habermas and Jacques Derrida* (Chicago, University of Chicago Press, 2003); also M Herzfeld, *The Social Production of Indifference; Exploring the Symbolic Roots of Western Bureaucracy* (Chicago, The University of Chicago Press, Chicago, 1992); LK Cheliotis, 'The Sociospatial Mechanics of Domination: Transcending the "Exclusion/Inclusion" Dualism' 21 (2010) *Law & Critique* 131; K Rozakou, 'The Biopolitics of Hospitality in Greece: Humanitarianism and the Management of Refugees' (2012) 39 *American Ethnologist* 562.

[77] SKAI, above n 24.

And yet, although the conditions under which irregular migrants find themselves in Greece, be it in society at large or inside detention centres, are anything but philoxenous in the conventional sense of the word, the Greek state has practically shown much less determination to reduce the number of irregular migrants in the country than Minister Dendias' statement suggests. In fact, whether by commission or omission, the Greek state appears to have played a key role in the maintenance of what it portrays, more often than not in apocalyptic terms, as the excessive size of the irregular migrant population in the country.

The long barbed-wire fence in the region of Evros, for example, was constructed with a delay inversely proportional to the urgency ascribed to it in dominant political discourse as a means of preventing irregular immigration into Greece from her mainland borders with Turkey. Stringent policies and infamously protracted bureaucratic procedures, meanwhile, have long limited the chances of regularisation for those entering Greece, as attested by the stubbornly low rates of refugee recognition and the vast numbers of migrants facing difficulties in acquiring or renewing stay permits for work purposes.[78] The case of policing is not dissimilar: whilst no substantial changes appear to have occurred in recent years in the size of the irregular migrant population resident in Greece,[79] the annual volume of apprehensions of irregular migrants in the country nearly halved between 2008 and 2012.[80] Moreover, the legal maximum duration of immigration detention has undergone repeated extensions since 2009, at the same time that a significant overall downward trend has been recorded in the volume of deportations actually carried out (although this is to some extent due to a lack of cooperation on the part of Turkey in terms of readmitting irregular migrants of Asian and African descent).[81]

Given, on one hand, that Greece has been subject to international criticism for its continuing failure to curb irregular migration and its inefficient asylum system, and, on the other hand, that irregular migrants themselves have reportedly grown increasingly willing to leave Greece, it is a paradox of no small proportion that the Greek state has largely subverted or otherwise thwarted its very own proclamations about the need to constrain the number of irregular migrants in the country. In the last analysis, the reproduction of power imbalances that is achieved in Greece through policies and practices disguised behind the veil of philoxenia needs to be understood primarily as a process of deliberate if qualified inclusion, rather than a question of designed but often failed exclusion.[82]

---

[78] S Xenakis, 'Organised Crime and Political Violence' in LK Cheliotis and S Xenakis (eds), *Crime and Punishment in Contemporary Greece: International Comparative Perspectives* (Bern, Peter Lang AG, 2011); H Cabot, 'The Governance of Things: Documenting Limbo in the Greek Asylum Procedure' (2012) 35 *Political and Legal Anthropology Review* 11.

[79] Maroukis, 'Update Report Greece' (n 5); Maroukis, 'Migration and the Crisis in Greek Society' (n 5).

[80] See, further, Cheliotis, above n 32.

[81] See, further, A Triandafyllidou and M Ambrosini, 'Irregular Immigration Control in Italy and Greece: Strong Fencing and Weak Gate-keeping Serving the Labour Market' (2011) 13 *European Journal of Migration and Law* 251.

[82] For similar arguments, see D Bigo, 'Security and Immigration: Toward a Critique of the Governmentality of Unease' (2006) 27 *Alternatives* 63; D Melossi, '"In a Peaceful Life": Migration and

Since the late 1980s, for instance, the irregular or precarious legal status of large swathes of migrants, their poverty, and the limited social rights meted out to them have combined with the looming prospect of imprisonment, and increasingly of administrative detention, to render them exploitable in the Greek labour market.[83] Indeed, the fact that standards of living inside prisons and immigration detention centres in Greece have been kept so low has functioned to threaten the most marginalised fractions of the population into accepting any available condition of work in the free community, in accordance with what has come to be known in pertinent Anglophone literature as the 'less eligibility' principle, arguably much more than to deter irregular migration into the country.[84]

More recently, and especially since the financial crisis hit Greece in 2009, the widely publicised intensification in the use of penal and particularly administrative detention against migrants has been deployed by governing parties as a convenient cathartic remedy for a range of discontents amongst the Greek public, from heightened socio-economic anxieties, to increased anger with political elites, to a spreading sense of national humiliation before foreign audiences.[85] In this case, the notoriously harsh conditions of conventional imprisonment and immigration detention may be said to have helped alleviate the pains of downward mobility and falling living standards for the average Greek citizen, providing him or her with reassurance that they continue to enjoy material advantages over those on the margins of society (and even over some foreign population). The point here is not so much that immigrants are detained under conditions that remain inferior to those found in free society, as the principle of 'less eligibility' stipulates, but rather that free society itself tends to interpret the substandard conditions of imprisonment and immigration detention in terms of personal and in-group superiority – as a form of 'more eligibility'.[86]

One should nevertheless take care not to conclude that responsibility for the ways in which immigrants are treated on Greek soil resides exclusively within Greece itself, or even that the case of Greece has no parallels elsewhere in Europe, although neither of these caveats could provide a plausible excuse for immigrants' plight at the hands of the Greek state. The European Commission, for example, has offered both rhetorical and financial support to Greek state authorities in order for them to strengthen the policing of national borders and territory as an

the Crime of Modernity in Europe/Italy' (2003) 5 *Punishment & Society* 371; K Calavita, *Immigrants at the Margins: Law, Race, and Exclusion in Southern Europe* (Cambridge University Press, Cambridge, 2005); A De Giorgi, 'Immigration Control, Post-Fordism, and Less Eligibility: A Materialist Critique of the Criminalisation of Immigration Across Europe' (2010) 12 *Punishment & Society* 147.

[83] See, further, Cheliotis and Xenakis, 'What's Neoliberalism Got to Do With It?', above n 8.

[84] Cheliotis, above n 32. On the 'less eligibility' principle, see further, De Giorgi, 'Immigration Control', above n 83.

[85] Cheliotis and Xenakis, above n 8; Cheliotis and Xenakis, above n 9; S Xenakis and LK Cheliotis, 'Crime and Economic Downturn: The Complexity of Crime and Crime Politics in Greece since 2009' (2013) 53 *British Journal of Criminology* 719; S Xenakis and LK Cheliotis, 'Anger Management and the Politics of Crime in the Greek Crisis', in G Karyotis and R Gerodimos (eds), *Greece beyond the Crisis: The Politics of Extreme Austerity* (Basingstoke, Palgrave Macmillan, 2014).

[86] See further, Cheliotis, above n 33.

'imperative' for the protection of immigrants' human rights,[87] whilst Italy has continued to summarily return unaccompanied migrant children and adult asylum seekers to Greece in violation of international law, thereby adding further pressure on an already overcrowded system.[88]

At the same time, other EU Member States have not been immune to the cruel repressive policies and practices adopted against immigrants in Greece, and one can also find occasions where the notion of hospitality is similarly perverted by Greece's European counterparts so as to justify their own treatment of immigrants and consolidate underlying power hierarchies.[89] That Greece has been particularly likely to face international disapprobation is no doubt reflective of the exceptional degree to which the country has fallen below, and has even challenged, the very standards of the all-inclusive philoxenia she purports to archetypically embody. Arguably, however, the likelihood of disapprobation would not be as strong were it not for Greece's own marginal political position within Europe.[90]

This brings us full circle back to the social functionality and consequent political expediency of the discourse of philoxenia as applied to the treatment of immigrants and especially immigration detention in contemporary Greece. The country's peripheral role in the international arena and the adverse conditions that go along with it – a comparatively weak domestic economy, an increased propensity of national governments to accept relations of economic dependency vis-à-vis external powers, a heightened sensitivity to criticism from abroad, and the greater likelihood of foreign disapprobation in itself – raise the susceptibility of the Greek public to self-flattering discourses, particularly when such discourses can licence exploitation of weaker others as labourers and authorise activities against them through which to act out aggravated anxieties, angers and complexes amidst conditions of financial crisis.[91] This helps to explain the apparent paradox that the Greek state persists in employing a discourse that is so openly at odds with reality in the eyes of external observers as to risk, indeed invite, criticism afresh.

---

[87] IPS, above n 54; see also, Human Rights Watch, above n 34; Pro Asyl, above n 28.
[88] Human Rights Watch, *Turned Away: Summary Returns of Unaccompanied Migrant Children and Adult Asylum Seekers from Italy to Greece. New York: Human Rights Watch* (New York, Human Rights Watch, 2013).
[89] See, further, Borradori, *Philosophy in a Time of Terror*, above n 77; A Hall, *Border Watch: Cultures of Immigration, Detention and Control* (London, Pluto Press, 2012).
[90] See, further, Herzfeld (n 77).
[91] ibid; Cheliotis, above n 33.

7

The UK and EU Criminal Law: Should we be Leading, Following or Abstaining?

JOHN R SPENCER

EU Criminal Law: What is it?

In an episode of the popular Danish TV political drama *Borgen*, a journalist tells her editor that she would like to write an article about the EU. In turning her idea down, the editor said: 'No – the EU isn't sexy, and it's all too complicated for our readers to understand. No stories on the EU in my paper – unless they're about overpaid officials or corruption.' The subtext of this episode was public ignorance and apathy in Denmark about the institutions of the EU. As UK lawyers working in this area are all too well aware, this problem is not limited to Denmark; and of no aspect of the EU is ignorance greater than that of EU and criminal law. So the first task in this chapter must be to explain what EU criminal law is actually about.

Contrary to what is sometimes wrongly thought, 'EU criminal law' is not remotely like Federal criminal law in the USA. US Federal criminal law comprises a set of criminal offences directly applicable in all the States of the Union, where it is directly enforced by Federal officials, using Federal criminal courts, which operate according to a Federal code of criminal procedure, the rules of which also are directly applicable in every State. As far as the EU is concerned there is none of this, nor is there any immediate prospect of a structure of this sort coming into being. After various preliminary studies,[1] in the summer of 2013 the Commission published a proposal for a Council Decision creating a European Public Prosecutor's Office, with responsibility for the prosecution, in the criminal courts of the various Member States, of frauds on the EU budget;[2] and this proposal – the future of which is still uncertain – is now working its way through the EU

[1] The proposal originally came from the *Corpus* Juris project, discussed later in this chapter. Between 2010 and 2012 the Commission funded a further project, run by the University of Luxembourg, to develop this idea. For further details, see the project website: www.eppo-project.eu/. The tangible product is a two-volume study, Katalin Ligeti (ed), *Towards a Prosecutor for the European Union* (Oxford, Hart Publishing, 2013) the first volume of which appeared in 2013.

[2] Proposal for a Council Regulation on the establishment of the European Public Prosecutor's Office; Brussels, 17.7.2013; COM (2013) 534 final, 2013/0255 (APP)

legislative process. But that proposal is, at present, as far as things have gone towards the creation of a Federal criminal law according to the US model.

At present, EU criminal law consists of five collections of legal instruments, each concerned with different issues.

First, there is a body of law regulating the three EU institutions which have been created in order to fight crime at EU level. Two of these, Europol and Eurojust, are coordinating bodies, designed to help the criminal justice agencies of the various Member States fight trans-border criminality more effectively. Europol, the European Police Office,[3] is a collegiate body, run by a Director and a Management board with representatives from each Member State, the basic task of which is to collect, store, analyse and exchange information about criminals and crimes. Unlike the Federal Bureau of Investigation (FBI) in the USA it is not itself involved in operational policing; though its staff may participate in 'joint investigation teams' created by national police forces, and it also has the right to request a Member State to take action in a particular case. Eurojust is a similar body, designed to coordinate and support the activities of the national public prosecutors of the different Member States.[4] The third institution is OLAF, the European Anti-Fraud Office.[5] This, unlike Europol and Eurojust, is body that does the job itself, as against coordinating the work of others. Using its own officials, it conducts administrative investigations into suspected fraud, corruption and other illegal activity related to EU finances, and to this end enjoys wide inquisitorial powers. However, once it has completed an investigation and (as it believes) uncovered a criminal offence, it has no power to prosecute, and if it wants the authors of the offence to be prosecuted it has to forward the file to the prosecuting authorities of the Member State or States concerned, in the hope that they will pursue the matter. The reluctance of the national prosecutors of the Member States, or some of them, to take action in these cases has been a source of deep frustration within OLAF – and is one of the reasons why the Commission would like to see the creation of a European Public Prosecutor.

Secondly, there is a collection of EU legal instruments under which the police and other law enforcement agencies of the different Member States are obliged to help each other – or in some cases, though not obliged, are facilitated in doing so. Of these there are many. An important one is the instrument creating a legal framework within which the police forces of different Member States can set up joint investigation teams.[6] Another is the instrument, often called the 'Swedish

---

[3] See Art 88 TFEU, and Council Decision 2009/371/JHA of 6 April 2009 establishing the European Police Office (Europol) [2009] OJ L121/37. A proposal for a replacement instrument was published in March 2013.

[4] See Art 85 TFEU; Council Decision 2002/187/JHA of 28 February 2002 setting up Eurojust with a view to reinforcing the fight against serious crime; and Council Decision 2003/659/JHA of 18 June 2003 amending the Eurojust Decision [2002] OJ L63/1. A proposal for a new instrument was published in July 2013.

[5] Reg (EC) No 1073/1999 of the European Parliament and of the Council of 25 May 1999 concerning investigations conducted by the European Anti-Fraud Office (OLAF) [1999] OJ L136.

[6] Council Framework Decision 2002/465/JHA of 13 June 2002 on joint investigation teams [2002] OJ L162/1.

Framework Decision', which sets up a formal system whereby the police forces of the various Member States can have speedy access to each others' information systems.[7] Another is the Schengen Information System, a central database of information relating to a range of matters, which the law enforcement agencies of the different Member States can directly access.

Thirdly, there are 'mutual recognition' instruments whereby the decisions and rulings of the courts and other competent authorities in one Member State are accepted by the courts and competent authorities of the other Member States and enforced on the same terms as their own. Mutual recognition has two forms, one passive and one active. In a passive sense, the mutual recognition principle means that the decision or ruling of a criminal court in one Member State must be given the same legal weight as would be given to an equivalent decision of the national court. An example is the Framework Decision of 2008 requiring Member States to give, in later criminal proceedings, the same legal force to previous convictions emanating from the courts of other Member States as they would give to previous convictions from their own.[8] In an active sense, mutual recognition means that the courts of Member States also where necessary take positive steps to enforce these decisions. Of these, the most obvious instrument to mention is the Framework Decision that created the European Arrest Warrant.[9]

Fourthly, there are instruments designed to ensure that the criminal justice systems of the different Member States adopt a broadly similar line when dealing with certain types of antisocial behaviour. These 'harmonising' instruments require all Member States to ensure that their codes of criminal law prohibit certain activities and also provide maximum penalties that are sufficiently dissuasive. They include instruments on terrorism,[10] drug-dealing,[11] cybercrime,[12] bribery,[13] money-laundering,[14] people-smuggling[15] and frauds in relation to electronic

[7] Council Framework Decision 2006/960/JHA of 18 December 2006 on simplifying the exchange of information and intelligence between law enforcement authorities of the Member States of the European Union [2006] OJ L386/89.

[8] Council Framework Decision 2008/675/JHA of 24 July 2008 on taking account of convictions in the Member States of the European Union in the course of new criminal proceedings [2008] OJ L220/32.

[9] Council Framework Decision 2002/584/JHA of 13 June 2002 on the European arrest warrant and the surrender procedures between Member States [2002] OJ L190/1.

[10] Council Framework Decision 2002/475/JHA of 13 June 2002 on combating terrorism [2002] OJ L164/3.

[11] Council Framework Decision 2004/757JHA of 25 October 2004 laying down minimum provisions on the constituent elements of criminal acts and penalties in the field of drug trafficking [2004] OJ L335/8.

[12] Council Framework Decision 2005/222/JHA of 25 February 2005 on attacks against information systems [2005] OJ L69/67; Directive 2013/40/EU of the European Parliament and of the Council of 12 August 2013 on attacks against information systems and replacing Council Framework Decision 2005/222/JHA.

[13] Council Framework Decision 2003/568/JHA of 22 July 2003 on combating corruption in the private sector [2003] OJ L192/54.

[14] Council Framework Decision 2001/500/JHA of 26 June 2001 on money laundering, the identification, tracing, freezing, seizing and confiscation of instrumentalities and the proceeds of crime (repealing Arts 1, 3, 5(1) and 8(2) of Joint Action 98/699/JHA) [2001] OJ L182/1.

[15] Council Framework Decision 2002/946/JHA of 28 November 2002 on the strengthening of the

payments.[16] With the interests of the EU itself in mind, they also include instruments requiring Member States to make it a criminal offence to counterfeit the euro,[17] and to punish frauds against the EU budget.[18]

Fifthly, there are instruments which require Member States to ensure that certain common rules and principles are applied within their national systems of criminal procedure. In this category are instruments designed to ensure that victims of crimes are shown a certain minimum measure of respect,[19] and a group of instruments which require all Member States to provide certain minimum levels of help and protection to defendants.[20]

The Legal Basis for EU Criminal Law Pre-Lisbon; and the UK's Role, Pre-Lisbon, in Creating EU Criminal Law

In essence, the EU criminal law prior to the Lisbon Treaty stemmed from two sources: one major and one subsidiary. The major source was the 'Third Pillar' – the constitutional arrangements whereby the 'old-style' EU was empowered to make rules on police and criminal justice matters by Title VI of the 'old' Treaty of European Union concluded at Maastricht in 1992. To the initial range of rather feeble instruments provided for by the Maastricht Treaty the Amsterdam Treaty in 1997 added a new and more powerful one – the Framework Decision. Like Directives adopted under First Pillar, Framework Decisions enabled legal obligations to be imposed on Member States, requiring them to ensure that their legal systems operated in certain stated ways; though unlike with Directives, their adoption required the unanimous vote of all Member States; and unlike the position with Directives, if a Member State failed to implement one, it could not be subjected to enforcement proceedings before the ECJ. Once available, Framework Decisions quickly became the EU's instrument of choice. The minor source of EU criminal law was the Schengen Convention. This was originally adopted in 1990

penal framework to prevent the facilitation of unauthorised entry, transit and residence [2002] OJ L328/1.

[16] Council Framework Decision 2001/413/JHA of 28 May 2001 combating fraud and counterfeiting of non-cash means of payment [2001] OJ L149/1.

[17] Council Framework Decision 2000/383/JHA of European Commission 29 May 2000 on increasing protection by criminal penalties and other sanctions against counterfeiting in connection with the introduction of the euro [2000] OJ L440/1, and subsequent instruments amending it.

[18] Council Act of 26 July 1995 drawing up the Convention on the protection of the European Communities' financial interests [1995] OJ C316/48.

[19] Directive 2012/29 of the EU and of the European Parliament and of the Council of 25 October 2012 establishing minimum standards on the rights, support and protection of victims of crime, and replacing Council Framework Decision 2001/220/JHA [2012] OJ L315/57.

[20] Directive 2010/64 EU of the European Parliament and of the Council of 20 October 2010 on the right to interpretation and translation in criminal proceedings [2010] OJ L280/1; Directive 2012/13/EU of the European Parliament and of the Council of 22 May 2012 on the right to information in criminal proceedings [2012] OJ L142/1.

outside the framework of the European Community (EC) (as it then was) by a group of Member States impatient with the want of progress at EC level, but then incorporated into the EU framework by the Treaty of Amsterdam.

The body of EU criminal law that was described in of this chapter was mainly created under the constitutional structure that existed before the Treaty of Lisbon. And though Eurosceptics seem to believe that 'Brussels' forced it all upon a reluctant United Kingdom that was anxious to have none of it, the truth is that the UK cooperated fully in the making of it. Insofar as EU criminal law was made by instruments adopted under the Third Pillar this is obviously the case, because the adoption of these instruments required a unanimous vote of all the Member States, and if the UK had objected to any of them, it could easily have blocked them. Insofar as parts of EU criminal law derive from the Schengen Convention, a goodly portion of these bind the UK, which asked to be allowed to accede to them.

To some readers this last fact may come as a surprise, because to most citizens of this country 'Schengen' is an arrangement under which the participating countries have reciprocally abolished border controls, an arrangement which the UK has emphatically refused to join. However, to compensate for the fact that the abolition of border controls would make it easier for criminals to move around, the Schengen Convention provided for closer police cooperation between the contracting States, so that mobile criminals could still be caught if they took advantage of the enhanced freedom of movement which the Convention gave them. And though it never joined the part of the Schengen scheme that involves opening borders, the UK did eventually accede to most of the police cooperation measures created to deal with the problems resulting from them. In 1999 the UK made an official request to the Council to accede to certain parts of the Schengen Convention and in 2004 the Council issued a Decision providing that a slice of the provisions of the Convention 'shall be put into effect for the United Kingdom as from 1 January 2005'.[21] Of the 142 Articles of which the Schengen Convention is composed, the UK thereby subscribed, in whole or in part, to some 28 of them. These include some of the measures on tightening border controls with non-Schengen countries, plus nearly all the measures on enhanced police cooperation, plus nearly all the measures designed to achieve speedier and more efficient mutual legal assistance between the criminal justice systems of the contracting parties once criminal proceedings have begun.

In the creation of EU criminal law the influence of the UK can be traced in at least two significant respects. The first is that the UK took the lead in promoting 'mutual recognition'. That it did so is, in a roundabout way, a result of the *Corpus Juris* project – of which more will be said later. As most readers will remember, the *Corpus Juris* project was a scheme devised to make it easier to prosecute for frauds on the EU budget – which were thought to pose difficulties for the criminal

---

[21] Council Decision 2004/926/EC of 22 December 2004 on the putting into effect of parts of the Schengen *acquis* by the United Kingdom of Great Britain and Northern Ireland [2004] OJ L395/70.

justice systems of the Member States for various reasons, one being that these frauds frequently cross national borders. To deal with this, the authors of the *Corpus Juris* proposed a 'vertical' solution involving a single code of budgetary fraud offences applicable in all Member States, enforced by a central European Public Prosecutor, with authority to prosecute offences against this code in the criminal courts of all the Member States. This proposal caused serious disquiet in the UK, where – as will be explained later – it was misrepresented by the Eurosceptic press as an attempt by 'Brussels' to force the UK to abandon the common law. Not liking the 'vertical' solution contained in the *Corpus Juris* project, but recognising that the problems it was designed to deal with were real ones, the British government put forward, as an alternative way of facing up to them, a 'horizontal' solution: the idea that the criminal courts of the different Member States should move to a system under which they gave automatic recognition to each others' rulings and orders – as had long been done by the courts of the three different criminal justice systems which exist in the three parts of the UK.[22]

The second respect in which the influence of the UK can be detected in the creation of EU criminal law pre-Lisbon is a negative one. In the mid 2000s the UK used its influence to frustrate a move by the EU to adopt a Framework Decision requiring all Member States to provide certain minimum guarantees for defendants during police enquiries and during the early stages of a prosecution. The idea behind this proposal was that such a measure was a necessary counterpart to the movement towards 'mutual recognition' – and in particular, the European Arrest Warrant. Mutual recognition, it was said, depends on 'mutual trust'. Mutual trust, it was further said, implies the willingness of the courts of all Member States to accept that the criminal courts of the other Member States whose orders they are now required to implement can be trusted to deliver an acceptable quality of justice – in particular, by ensuring a decent standard of treatment for defendants. The courts in Member States whose criminal procedure provides good safeguards against the mistreatment of suspects and defendants, and against the risk of wrongfully convicting the innocent, would (so it was thought) be unwilling to execute European Arrest Warrants, and orders made under other 'mutual recognition' instruments, if they suspected that these safeguards are absent in the Member State whose order they are expected to enforce. In the light of this, the EU should take measures to raise standards.

Moves in this direction began in 2003, shortly after the creation of the European Arrest Warrant.[23] Three years later, however, progress towards a new Framework

---

[22] See the evidence of K Hoey, Under-Secretary of State at the Home Office, to House of Lords Select Committee on the European Communities, Session 1998–99, 9th Report, 'Prosecuting fraud on the Communities' finances – the Corpus Juris' HL Paper 62, App 4, §297: 'The simplest way of putting it is that we support cooperation between jurisdictions rather than creating a single jurisdiction. Particularly as I come from Northern Ireland and Lord Hope is from Scotland, a very good model for this cooperation is what we already have here, working between the separate jurisdictions within the United Kingdom...'

[23] Commission, 'Procedural Safeguards for Suspects and Defendants in Criminal Proceedings throughout the European Union' (Green Paper) COM (2003) 75 final; followed by Commission 'A

Decision on defence rights was abruptly halted when the British government, initially in favour of the proposal, used its political muscle to block it. No coherent reason was ever given for this change of mind, but it is thought to have been connected with the government's publication of a populist White Paper announcing its intention of 'rebalancing the criminal justice system in favour of the law-abiding majority', which might have lost its impact with the electorate if it had appeared alongside headlines saying 'Government lets Brussels Give Criminals Yet More Human Rights'. By the autumn of 2009 the UK government had changed its mind again, and was actively backing the Commission in its creation of a 'Roadmap' of proposed new instruments designed to ensure the protection of defendants.[24] The story of the Roadmap will be taken up again in a later section of this chapter.

The Legal Basis for EU Criminal Law after Lisbon and the UK's Role in EU Criminal Law since the Treaty came into Force

Under Chapter 4 of Title V of the Treaty on the Functioning of the European Union, the powers of the EU to make rules in relation to police and criminal justice have been radically rewritten. The European Parliament, previously marginalised, now has a formal role to play. In place of Framework Decisions, we now have Regulations and Directives. Subject to various safeguards and exceptions, these instruments are now adopted by qualified majority voting, rather than by unanimity, as before. And whereas the Court of Justice was previously excluded from this area, except to the limited extent that those Member States that chose to do so could permit their courts to make preliminary references,[25] the Court of Justice of the EU is now fully competent, even to the extent of entertaining contravention proceedings against Member States which fail to give effect to EU instruments in the area of police and justice. For good measure, the Court is also destined, in December 2014, to acquire full jurisdiction over such of the pre-Lisbon police and justice measures as are still in existence at this date.

None of these changes were welcome to the UK. It did not relish the introduction of qualified majority voting, which would have caused it to lose the power to veto legislation in this area that it previously enjoyed, in common with every other Member State, in the days when new instruments in this area had to be

---

Proposal for a Council Framework Decision on Certain Procedural Rights in Criminal Proceedings throughout the European Union' COM (2004) 328 final; S Alegre, 'EU Fair Trial Rights – Added Value or No Value?' (2004) *New Law Journal* 758.

[24] Resolution of the Council of 30 November 2009 on a Roadmap for strengthening procedural rights of suspected or accused persons in criminal proceedings [2009] OJ C295 1.

[25] TEU (old version) Art 35.

agreed by unanimity. And – despite the fact the UK has always been conscientious about implementing EU legislation – the UK did not like the idea of the Court at Luxembourg acquiring jurisdiction in this area. Accordingly, during the negotiations leading up to the Lisbon Treaty it sought to secure exemptions from these changes.

In preserving the position whereby it could not be bound by EU legislation in the police and justice area unless it had voted for it, the UK, together with the Republic of Ireland, scored a remarkable success. By Protocol 21, no new legislation enacted under Title V of Part Three TFEU applies to either country, unless it elects to opt in to it.

This time going it alone, the UK also raised objections to the proposed change under which the Court would in future acquire full jurisdiction in relation to the Third Pillar instruments. Here the argument was: 'We voted for these on the basis that the Court could not sanction us, and it is not fair that we should now have its jurisdiction foisted onto us retrospectively.' Eventually, the UK's objections were recognised by the inclusion, in Protocol 36, of Article 10. Under this provision, the UK had the right, at any time before June 2014, to opt out en bloc of all the still-remaining Third Pillar measures on police and criminal justice; though with the right then to seek readmission one by one to any of them that, on reflection, it decides it wishes to be bound by after all. If it is readmitted to a given measure in this way, the UK must then accept the jurisdiction of the Court as part of the package. (And a fortiori, the UK also accepts the jurisdiction of the Court as part of the deal where, using its right to do so under Protocol 21, it elects to opt into any new measure adopted after Lisbon.)

In May 2010, a few months after the Lisbon Treaty came into force, the UK underwent a change of government, the Labour Party losing office in favour of a Coalition of Conservatives and the Liberal Democrats, in which the Conservatives are dominant. As everybody knows, Europe is one of the areas in which these two parties have significant differences of opinion, the Liberal Democrats being basically pro-European, and the Conservatives being basically Eurosceptic – with a bloc of backbench MPs who are loudly hostile to the EU and all its works. Unsurprisingly, one of the consequences of the change of government was that the attitude of the UK towards EU criminal law became increasingly contradictory and muddled.

At the outset, the Coalition managed to produce an official policy on the subject which gave at least an appearance of coherence. In its published 'Programme for Government'[26] it said this:

> We will approach forthcoming legislation in the area of criminal justice on a case-by-case basis, with a view to maximising our country's security, protecting Britain's civil liberties and preserving the integrity of our criminal justice system. Britain will not participate in the establishment of any European Public Prosecutor.

---

[26] https://www.gov.uk/government/uploads/system/uploads/attachment_data/file/78977/coalition_programme_for_government.pdf

In pursuance of this policy, the first act of the new government was to cause Parliament to pass legislation making it practically impossible for the UK to join in any programme to create a European Public Prosecutor. The European Union Act of 2011, while it remains in force, disables the UK from acceding to any future Treaty change that would increase the powers of the EU unless this has been approved by an Act of the Westminster Parliament, preceded by a national referendum. And while it is about it, the Act also imposes a similar 'referendum lock' on the UK's future participation in a range of other measures for which the existing Treaties already provide a legal base – one of which is the European Public Prosecutor.[27]

The reason for this, as I have explained elsewhere,[28] is the negative reaction in the Eurosceptic press towards the *Corpus Juris* project – which the *Daily Telegraph* and other newspapers portrayed as a 'Brussels Plot' to force the UK to abandon its traditional common law adversarial system of criminal justice in favour of a horror its own imagining called the 'Napoleonic system', allegedly in force in Continental Europe. This misrepresentation of the *Corpus Juris* project is bizarre, as will be clear from even the most cursory examination of the original document. But this distorted view of the matter has become widely accepted, as an online search for references to 'Corpus Juris' will instantly reveal – and it now appears to be embedded in the belief systems of those who are influential in the Conservative Party. And in consequence, the European Public Prosecutor found itself, together with the euro, on the list of developments to be subjected to the 'referendum lock'.

Since the Lisbon Treaty came into force, a number of new EU instruments in the area of police and criminal justice have been proposed; and towards these, the UK has taken what might be called a 'pick and mix' approach. One of the first was a new mutual recognition instrument called the European Investigation Order. Designed to operate on the same basis as the European Arrest Warrant, the aim of this new instrument is to ensure that search warrants and other orders for the obtaining of evidence are automatically enforceable across borders – instead of being enforceable, as now, at the discretion of the requested State. In the summer of 2010 the UK government decided to opt into this: to the outrage of the *Daily Telegraph*, which reported the decision under the headline 'Britons to be Spied on by Foreign Police'.[29] After lengthy negotiations, a Directive was finally adopted in April 2014.[30]

Other post-Lisbon measures include a new Directive on people trafficking[31] and a new Directive on the rights of victims.[32] In respect of these, the UK has (in reversal of the usual order) first blown cold and then blown hot. Having initially

---

[27] European Union Act, 2011, cl 11, s 6, and in particular, s 6(5)(c).

[28] JR Spencer, 'Who's Afraid of the Big, Bad European Prosecutor?' (2012) 14 *Cambridge Yearbook of European Legal Studies* ch 14.

[29] T Whitehead and A Porter, 'Britons to be Spied on by Foreign Police' *Daily Telegraph* (London, 26 July 2010).

[30] Directive 2014/41/EU of the European Parliament and of the Council of 3 April 2014 regarding the European Investigation Order in criminal matters.

[31] Directive 2011/36/EU of the European Parliament and of the Council of 5 April 2011 on preventing and combating trafficking in human beings and protecting its victims, and replacing Council Framework Decision 2002/629/JHA [2011] OJ L101/1.

[32] See n 19.

stood aside, it eventually decided to opt into both of them after their terms had been agreed. Then in 2012 there was a proposal for a new Directive requiring all Member States to equip their justice systems with a mechanism to enable them to strip criminals of the proceeds of their crimes. In July 2012 the government announced the refusal of the UK to opt into this: to the applause of the *Daily Telegraph*, which praised the government for 'drawing a line in the sand on inter-ference from Brussels'.[33] Despite this, the UK is following the negotiations – and if the measure eventually agreed upon is acceptable, it is conceivable that the UK will opt into it retrospectively.

Earlier in this paper, mention was made of the 'Roadmap' of proposed new measures designed to improve the position of defendants in the criminal process – a scheme devised in the autumn of 2009, shortly before the Lisbon Treaty entered into force. Under the new Treaty work on this project has continued, though now within the framework of the new constitutional arrangements. In detail, the Roadmap set out a scheme containing the following six measures:

Measure A: an instrument guaranteeing, for those who need it, translation and interpretation;
Measure B: an instrument guaranteeing the provision, for suspects and defend-ants, of information about the charges against them, and their rights;
Measure C: an instrument guaranteeing the provision, within limits, of legal aid and advice;
Measure D: an instrument guaranteeing detained suspects the right to contact relatives, employers and consular officials;
Measure E: an instrument guaranteeing special safeguards for suspects or accused persons who are vulnerable; and
Measure F: a Green Paper on pre-trial detention.

In relation to this programme of work, the UK has first blown hot and then blown cold. On Measure A (translation and interpretation) and Measure B (notification of rights) the UK decided at the outset to opt in. Directives have now been adopted in respect of both of these,[34] and in each case the UK, like other Member States, is bound by them. The UK has, by contrast, so far refused to opt into the proposal for Measure C – which would guarantee suspects access to legal advice. Having followed the negotiations, indicating that it might opt into the eventual Directive if it found the eventual contents to its taste, it has not done so. Measure F, the Green Paper on pre-trial detention, was published in June 2011.[35] The UK's reac-tion to this was distinctly reserved, making it plain that, in this area, the UK would not be in favour of EU legislation.[36] And, to jump ahead in the story to other side

---

[33] *Daily Telegraph* (London, 13 June 2012).
[34] See above n 20.
[35] 'Strengthening mutual trust in the European judicial area – A Green Paper on the Application of EU Criminal Justice Legislation in the Field of Detention' COM (2011) 327 final available at http://eur-lex.europa.eu/LexUriServ/LexUriServ.do?uri=COM:2011:0327:FIN:EN:PDF.
[36] Set out in the Fifty-ninth Report of Session 2010–12 – European Scrutiny Committee available at www.publications.parliament.uk/pa/cm201012/cmselect/cmeuleg/428-liv/42804.htm.

of the events described in the paragraph that follows, on 18 March 2014 the Minister of Justice told Parliament that the UK would not opt into proposed EU Directives on the presumption of innocence, safeguards for child defendants, safeguards for vulnerable defendants, and legal aid.[37]

At the end of September 2012, everything was thrown into confusion when the Prime Minister, David Cameron, casually announced during a trade mission to Brazil that the UK Government intended to exercise its right under Article 10 of Protocol 36 to opt out of the remaining 'Third Pillar' measures. This announcement was followed by a more cautious official statement from the Home Secretary, Teresa May, who said that the Government was 'minded' to do this: in other words, that it was thinking about it, but had not yet finally made up its mind.

These announcements were greeted with enthusiasm by the Eurosceptic press, whose reaction was reflected in an exultant headline on the front page of the *Daily Express* proclaiming 'Britain's First Step to EU Exit'. But for the Liberal Democrats, the government's junior partners in the Coalition, the news was anything but pleasing, and behind the scenes (and to some extent in public[38]) they made it clear that they would not back the exercise of the opt-out unless it were accompanied by a sizeable 'wish-list' of measures the UK would seek to opt back into. In exercising this pressure they were joined by the police, who were particularly worried about the prospect of losing the European Arrest Warrant. This combined pressure had an effect. When in July 2013 the Government gave Brussels formal notice that the Protocol 36 opt-out would be used, it indicated that it would seek readmission to most of the measures that are practically important.[39] Prominent among these measures was the European Arrest Warrant: which the Tory Eurosceptics were as keen to get rid of as the police were anxious to retain. This stance raised the obvious question: 'If we are going to opt back in again to all the important measures, what is the point of opting out?'; and it attracted both the derision of the Labour Party,[40] and the anger of the Tory Eurosceptics.[41] In August 2014, as this chapter goes to press, negotiations on

---

[37] Hansard, House of Commons, 18 March 2014, col 702.

[38] See the speech by Nick Clegg, leader of the Liberal Democrats and Deputy Prime Minister, on 1 November 2012: https://www.gov.uk/government/speeches/a-vision-for-the-uk-in-europe-speech-by-the-deputy-prime-minister.

[39] Listed in the official document *Decision pursuant to Article 10 of the Treaty on the Functioning of the European Union*, Cm 8671 (July 2013). For a comment, see 'Opting out of EU criminal justice: withdrawal, or an exercise in smoke and mirrors?' [2013] 8 *Archbold news* 6.

[40] In Parliament, Yvette Cooper, the Shadow Home Secretary, said this: 'That is the historic transfer of powers that the Home Secretary boasted about – the great liberation from Europe and the great cause for celebration that she promised . . . We have the power not to do a whole series of things we plan to carry on doing anyway, the power not to follow guidance we already follow, the power not to take action we already take, the power not to meet standards we already meet, the power not to do things that everyone else has already stopped doing and the power not to do a whole series of things we want to do anyway.' (Hansard, HC, 7 April 2013, Col 36).

[41] 'Tory right wingers clash with Theresa May over European Arrest Warrant', *Daily Telegraph*, 10 July 2014, reporting a Parliamentary debate in which a Tory Eurosceptic had called the Prime Minister a 'jellyfish': http://www.telegraph.co.uk/news/politics/10960132/Tory-right-wingers-clash-with-Theresa-May-over-European-Arrest-Warrant.html.

readmission to these measures are continuing; and it seems likely that the UK will be readmitted to the measures the government is anxious for it to rejoin.[42]

What is Wrong with the UK's Current Policy towards EU Criminal Law – and the Policy it should be Following Instead

Insofar as it is possible to detect any consistent notion underlying the UK's current policy towards EU criminal law, it seems to be reticence about further involvement, tinged with an underlying desire to be shot of it altogether. I believe that this is unfortunate, and that instead of trying to avoid contact with EU criminal law for fear of contamination, the UK should be taking a leading part in the creation of it. And this particularly as concerns the 'Roadmap' and the movement to ensure that suspects and defendants are treated fairly. This is so because, in my view, these are areas in which the UK currently holds the high moral ground. There is much in the current laws and practices of the UK that the UK is entitled to be proud of, and in respect of which it is in a position to give a lead to the rest of the EU – and in particular, to those Member States in which these things are at present less well done.

The first respect in which the UK is in a position to set an example to at least some parts of Continental Europe is the provision of proper safeguards for defendants who are being detained for questioning by the police. These are most important, for two reasons. First, without them there is an obvious risk that suspects will be subjected to ill-treatment – something which is bad enough in itself. And secondly, without them there is a risk that suspects will be pressured into making confessions that are false or, if they persist in their refusal to confess, that the police will be able to falsely claim that they have confessed when they have not.

Until relatively recently, the UK's record in this area was anything but good. Until the mid 1980s, a suspect who was held for interrogation by the police in England and Wales[43] had virtually no safeguards whatsoever – a state of affairs from which some grievous miscarriages of justice occasionally resulted. Among these, there is none more famous than the unhappy case of the Birmingham Six, whose conviction in 1975 for a multiple murder arising from bomb outrage in a pub in Birmingham was founded partly on their alleged confessions to the police – key parts of which the police were shown to have invented when the defendants' convictions were finally quashed by the Court of Appeal in 1992.[44]

---

[42] A progress report is contained in the Government's second document entitled *Decision pursuant to Article 10(5) of Protocol 36 to The Treaty on the Functioning of the European Union*, Cm 8897, July 2014.

[43] In what follows, I shall not deal with the position in Scotland and in Northern Ireland.

[44] *R v McIlkenny et al* (1991) 93 Cr App R 287.

Concerns about the absence of proper safeguards were already being aired at the time the Birmingham Six were tried. This was partly as a result of the *Confait* case, a much-publicised miscarriage of justice in which three youths were wrongly convicted over a killing, largely as a result of confessions extracted from them by heavy-handed treatment from the police – as became clear in an official Report into the case by a former High Court judge, Sir Harry Fisher.[45] In 1977 a Royal Commission on Criminal Procedure was appointed which, four years later, produced a careful and well-argued report.[46] Among other things, this recommended that the law be changed to give the police an explicit power to hold suspects for questioning,[47] but that in return, a number of strong safeguards be provided for suspects who were so held. In 1984 these recommendations were carried out by the Police and Criminal Evidence Act – a piece of legislation now known universally as 'PACE'.

Under PACE, the major rules about the detention of suspects for questioning are set out in the Act itself, while the details are fleshed out in a series of official Codes, published from time to time by the Home Secretary under powers conferred on him by section 66 of the Act. In outline, the main features of the scheme are these:

— the total length of time a suspect may be held for questioning is limited;[48]
— within that period, the duration of individual interrogations is limited;[49]
— the suspect has a right to tell a person that he has been detained;[50]
— the suspect is entitled to a lawyer, both to advise him before the questioning starts and to be present with him while it is taking place;[51]
— before he is questioned the suspect must be cautioned;[52]
— the police are required to make contemporaneous notes of the interview, and to give the suspect the opportunity to verify them;[53]
— interviews must be tape-recorded.[54]

By this package of measures, I believe, this country has largely solved a problem which in a number of other Member States continues to be a worrying source of possible injustice.

---

[45] House of Commons, *Report of an Inquiry into the circumstances leading to the trial of three persons on charges arising out of the death of Maxwell Confait and the fire at 27 Doggett Road, London SE 6* (published by order of the House of Commons, 1977).

[46] *Report of the Royal Commission on Criminal Procedure (Chairman Sir Cyril Philips)* (Cmnd 8092, 1981).

[47] As the law previously stood, the police had in reality no legal power to detain suspects for questioning at all, and when they did so they were in truth acting unlawfully; a legal vacuum which explains the absence of any formal legal structure limiting the way they went about it.

[48] PACE 1984, ss 41, 42 and 43.

[49] Code C.12 (and especially C.12.8).

[50] PACE 1984, s 56.

[51] PACE 1984, s 58.

[52] Code C.10.

[53] Code C.11.

[54] PACE 1984, s 60 and Code E.

The second respect in which the UK is in a position to set an example to at least some parts of Continental Europe is the regulation of pre-trial detention. If necessary in certain cases, pre-trial detention is a necessary evil. From a theoretical standpoint, it is evil because it inevitably means that a person is deprived of his liberty by the State on account of a crime his guilt of which the State has not established. From a practical standpoint, it is an evil because the imprisonment of a person pending trial usually makes it harder for him to prepare his defence. And it is a source of obvious injustice where, at the eventual trial, the defendant is acquitted, or given a non-custodial sentence, or a custodial sentence shorter than the period he has already spent in gaol. For these reasons, it is important that pre-trial detention should be used as sparingly as possible, and where it has to be used, that it should be as short as possible.

At present, there are big differences between the EU Member States both as regards the formal rules that govern pre-trial detention, and the informal practices in applying them. This was brought out very clearly in the Green Paper which the Commission published in 2011 as part of its work in connection with the 'Roadmap', mentioned earlier. From this document we learn that: 'Some countries have no legal maximum length of pre-trial detention. In some a person can be held in pre-trial detention for up to 4 years.'[55] From this document we also learn that, as a proportion of the prison population, the number of remand prisoners varies sharply as between the different Member States. Sadly, there can be little doubt that, in certain Member States, pre-trial detention is considerably over-used. A recent paper by the NGO Fair Trials International provides some individual examples which, at least to British eyes, are truly shocking.[56] The practical injustice caused by the unnecessary use of pre-trial detention is increased where conditions of detention are poor; and in some EU Member States prisons are seriously overcrowded, with inevitable negative consequences for conditions of detention.

Once again, this is an area in which the UK sets a relatively good example. In England and Wales, the maximum period for which a defendant may normally be remanded in custody is regulated by the Custody Time Limits Regulations, a set of statutory rules of labyrinthine complexity, the overall effect of which is that the maximum period for which a person may be held in custody pending trial is limited, in principle, to around six months.[57] In exceptional circumstances judges may override the time limits and authorise remands in custody to continue longer. But case law from the higher courts firmly discourages them from doing so. In recent years the courts, like other branches of the public service, have been subjected to serious spending cuts, leading to reduced availability of judges and of courts, and consequent delays in fixing trials; but in *R (McAuley) v Coventry*

---

[55] Green Paper, above n 35, §4.1.

[56] Fair Trials International, *Justice in Europe – Detention without Trial* (London, October 2011) available at www.fairtrials.net/justice-in-europe/pre-trial-detention/.

[57] Prosecution of Offences (Custody Time limits) Regulations 1987, SI 1987/299. For the details, see *Blackstone's Criminal Practice* (Oxford, Oxford University Press, 2014), §D15.7 *et seq.*

Crown Court[58] the Divisional Court was reluctant to accept that procedural delays caused by shortage of resources were sufficient to justify holding a defendant in pre-trial custody beyond the statutory limits. In England and Wales, it is rare for defendants, even in grave cases, to be held in pre-trial detention for as long as a year, and the average period of pre-trial detention is currently eight weeks.[59] In Scotland, furthermore, the rules on pre-trial detention are even stricter, with a statute of hallowed antiquity that limits pre-trial detention to a maximum period of 110 days.[60] The sparing use of pre-trial detention is reflected in the proportion of remand prisoners in the prison population as a whole, which in the UK is significantly below the EU average.[61]

This is not to say that everything in relation to pre-trial detention in the UK is perfect. In 2012 a report by the Prison Inspectorate was critical of the conditions under which remand prisoners are held in England and Wales.[62] A more general criticism is that, unlike in many other EU Member States, a person held in pre-trial detention has no right to compensation from the State if at trial he is acquitted. But those admissions made, it can still be said with confidence that the fairness of criminal justice in Europe generally would be improved if all the Member States contrived to make as little of a mess of pre-trial detention as we do.

So what lies behind the negative attitude of our present government (or at any rate, the dominant part of it) towards EU criminal law? – apart, that is, from the openly-stated desire of some members of it to leave the EU altogether?[63] I believe it is a combination of two ideas, both of which are seriously mistaken.[64]

The first is the theory of the *moral superiority of the common law*. In essence, this is the notion that the UK, as part of its common law heritage, enjoys a type of criminal procedure known as 'the accusatorial system' (alias 'the adversarial system'), which is inherently righteous, fair and sound, whereas the countries of Continental Europe suffer under a type of criminal procedure known as 'the inquisitorial system' (alias 'the Napoleonic system') which by contrast is inherently evil, unjust and morally degenerate. Characteristic features of the adversarial system are said to be jury trial, habeas corpus, the right of silence and the presumption of innocence – all of which are said to be unknown on the other side of the English Channel, where there are no juries, where there is no division of

---

[58] *R (McAuley) v Coventry Crown Court* [2012] EWHC 680 (Admin), [2012] 1 WLR 2766.

[59] A figure from a HM Inspectorate of Prisons, 'Thematic Report – Remand Prisoners, August' (2012) §2.15 available at www.justice.gov.uk/downloads/publications/inspectorate-reports/hmipris/thematic-reports-and-research-publications/remand-thematic.pdf.

[60] Now set out in the Criminal Procedure (Scotland) Act 1995, s 65.

[61] From the figures published in the 2011 Green Paper, above n 35, the combined average for all parts of the UK is 15.7% compared to an EU average of 24.7%.

[62] See above n 61.

[63] In the *Daily Mail* of 13 October the Minister for Education, Michael Gove, was reported as telling friends that if there was a referendum on EU membership he would vote for the UK to leave – comments which were not denied.

[64] These points are discussed at greater length in Spencer, 'Who's Afraid of the Big, Bad European Prosecutor?' above n 28.

function between prosecutors and judges, where suspects can be imprisoned indefinitely without trial, and where the presumption of innocence is replaced by a presumption of guilt.

All this is utter nonsense, as is instantly obvious to anyone who knows anything about the criminal justice systems of Continental Europe in their modern form. But yet these distorted views about Continental criminal justice are widely held, and among the holders appear to be a number of our leading politicians. Indeed, when legislation was before Parliament to implement the European Arrest Warrant they were expressed in the course of the debates – the Conservatives (then in opposition) objecting to the European Arrest Warrant because it would force the UK to deliver wanted persons to the inquisitorial systems, whose justice is inferior to our own.[65]

The second misguided notion is the theory that 'Brussels' has a master plan to impose a uniform system of criminal justice throughout the whole area of the EU – a system which would be a version of the horrendous 'Napoleonic system' described in the previous paragraph – by which the existing criminal justice systems of the UK would have to be replaced. This notion, like the one mentioned in the previous paragraph, is utter nonsense, because no such plan exists, or ever has existed, or is ever likely to do so. The origin of this idea appears to be the *Corpus Juris* project and the proposal to create a European Public Prosecutor responsible for prosecuting frauds on the Community budget – which the *Daily Telegraph* and other Eurosceptic newspapers loudly misrepresented as the first step towards a 'pan-European criminal code' modelled on 'the Napoleonic system',[66] thereby creating a myth which rapidly embedded itself in the belief-systems of many of those who are opposed to the EU.

In extreme forms, this 'Brussels plot' theory can now be found on many Eurosceptic websites. One example out of many is the website of the organisation called The People's Pledge, which exists to press for a referendum on the UK's continued membership of the EU. In April 2011 this website carried an article entitled 'Corpus Juris and the end of British Common Law' which made a series of fantastic claims, among them that 'the Corpus Juris provisions include an end to the presumption of innocence so that, if accused, it will be up to you to prove yourself innocent, not the state to prove you guilty'. All this, the writer said, would spell the end of 'Britain's most ancient and hallowed liberties'. And as this plan is now afoot, he concluded, 'Could there be a better reason to vote for withdrawal from the EU?'[67] So widely accepted has this notion now become that it seems that a large number of MPs now subscribe to it. In February 2012 a group of over 100

---

[65] See, inter alia, HC Deb 9 December 2002, vol 396, col 57.

[66] *Daily Telegraph* (London, 30 November 1998).

[67] http://blog.peoplespledge.org/2011/04/21/colin-bullen-corpus-juris-and-the-end-of-british-common-law/. Similar view were expressed by Nigel Farage, leader of the UK Independence Party, in an article in The Independent on Sunday on 10 November 2013: www.independent.co.uk/voices/comment/innocent-until-proven-guilty-not-under-the-eus-justice-system-8931215.html. For an online response by the author of this chapter, see see https://www.youtube.com/watch?v=7FyQlyXGhaU&list=PLy4oXRK6xgzHukYwMI806wyHrLBoL9K0v&index=10.

Conservative MPs signed a letter to the *Daily Telegraph* calling on the government to exercise the Protocol 36 opt-out mentioned earlier in this chapter.[68] This letter began by castigating 'the EU Commission's ambitions for a pan-European code of Euro-crimes'.

In a nutshell, the government's present policy towards EU criminal law appears to be one of avoidance of contact, in order to prevent our system being contaminated, or possibly even overwhelmed, by developments in Continental Europe.

This is unfortunate, because in reality our system has nothing to fear from EU criminal law, and, indeed, has much to offer. To put it in commercial terms, we should be doing our best to sell our product to our fellow Europeans, not attempting, as it seems, to close the market.

[68] 'Repatriate Powers in Crime and Policing, Say Conservative MPs' *Daily Telegraph* (London, 6 February 2012). http://www.telegraph.co.uk/comment/letters/9062615/Repatriate-powers-on-crime-and-policing-say-Conservative-MPs.html.

8

The European Union and the Global Governance of Crime

VALSAMIS MITSILEGAS

Introduction

The end of the Cold War coincided with a profound realignment of the global security agenda, with a number of new issues emerging as perceived global security threats alongside traditional military threats and meriting state responses at the global level. One of these major post-Cold War security issues has been the fight against transnational and organised crime. The securitisation of transnational and organised crime has led to the emergence of a far-reaching regime of global governance of crime constituted from a series of state initiatives at the global level. In this context, a multi-level model of global governance has emerged. States have responded via the conclusion of traditional international multilateral treaties, and also via the conclusion of a series of major regional treaties in the field by organisations such as the Council of Europe. These traditional forms of law-making have been complemented by the emergence of powerful 'soft' law initiatives, put forward in particular by organisations such as the Financial Action Task Force (FATF). The emergence of global standards and norms in the governance of crime has been accompanied by international mechanisms aimed at targeting not states, but individuals, via the imposition of sanctions. The work of the United Nations Security Council in the field is a key example. The aim of this chapter is to analyse the role of the European Union in the emergence of this multi-level paradigm of global crime governance. The chapter will highlight both the contribution of the EU to the development of global standards and the challenges that the EU legal order has been facing with regard to the implementation of these standards. The analysis will take into account both the constitutional complexities inherent in the EU legal order, in particular as regards the constitutional and institutional evolution of internal EU action in the field of criminal law, and the substantive considerations underlying the emergence of the EU as a global actor in criminal matters. The chapter will focus on the role of the EU in four levels of global governance: governance via global multilateral treaties (looking at the relationship between the EU and the United Nations); governance via regional multilateral treaties (looking at the relationship between the EU and the Council of Europe); governance via the emergence of 'soft' law (looking at the relationship between the EU and the FATF); and governance via the emergence of 'global administrative law' (looking at the relationship between the EU and the UN Security Council).

Governing Crime via Global Multilateral Treaties: The EU and the United Nations

Legislative action at the level of the United Nations has provided the backbone for the emergence of a regime of global governance of crime. The EU has been an active participant in the negotiation of three major UN conventions in the field of criminal law: the 1988 Convention against Drug Trafficking; the 2000 Convention against Transnational Organised Crime (also known as the 'Palermo Convention'); and the 2003 Convention against Corruption. These Conventions were negotiated and concluded in various stages of European integration, and in this light the institutional aspect of EU participation varies accordingly: the 1988 Convention was concluded in the pre-Maastricht era, in the days of the single Community pillar, whereas the Conventions on organised crime and corruption were concluded in the days of the three-pillar Union structure. The state of play of relevant internal Community/Union law at the time of their adoption also varies: while the 1988 Convention was concluded at a time when no relevant legislation in the field of money laundering was in place at Community level, the other two Conventions post-dated the adoption of internal Community/Union law in the respective fields. These differences are significant for the position of the EC/EU in the negotiation of the UN Conventions, but also in order to assess the subsequent impact of the UN standards on the Community/Union legal order.

Money Laundering – the 1988 United Nations Vienna Convention and EU Law

A major step towards the globalisation of criminal law was undertaken by the United Nations in the 1980s in the form of the conclusion of the 1988 Vienna Convention against Illicit Trafficking in Narcotic Drugs and Psychotropic Substances. To a great extent prompted by the so-called US 'war on drugs', the Convention introduced a number of detailed provisions on drug trafficking, as well as – for the first time – the criminalisation of money laundering at the global level.[1] Negotiations on the Convention coincided with a growing resolve by

---

[1] For an analysis of the Vienna Convention, see WC Gilmore, *Dirty Money. The Evolution of International Measures to Counter Money Laundering and the Financing of Terrorism*, 3rd edn

Community institutions to fight drug abuse and trafficking.[2] Although no express Community competence in criminal matters existed under the Treaties at the time, the Community did conclude the Vienna Convention on the basis of its common commercial policy competence.[3] According to the Declaration of Competence annexed to the above Decision (which was adopted under Article 113 of the EEC Treaty), the European Economic Community was at the time competent for questions of commercial policy relating to the substances frequently used in the illicit manufacture of narcotic drugs and psychotropic substances, questions which are dealt with in Article 12 of the Convention.

Leaving aside the question of its conclusion by the Community, the impact of the substantive standards of the Vienna Convention for the development of internal Community law has been significant. Evading questions of Community competence in criminal matters (still in the pre-Maastricht era), the Council adopted in 1991 the first Money Laundering Directive.[4] The Directive was adopted on a dual internal market/free movement legal basis,[5] and was justified inter alia on the grounds of protecting the stability of financial institutions and confidence in the financial system as a whole.[6] It introduced a number of provisions addressing the preventive aspect of money laundering countermeasures.[7] It also introduced a definition of money laundering, and obliged Member States to 'prohibit' conduct defined as such.[8] The definition of money laundering (a concept for the first time introduced in the Community legal order) was copied almost *verbatim* from the Vienna Convention.[9] A similar choice was made as regards the definition of property constituting proceeds of crime and as regards the *mens rea* requirement for money laundering.[10] These definitions, which are very broad and have raised concerns with regard to over-criminalisation in the field,[11] have remained virtually

---

(Strasbourg, Council of Europe Press, 2004); see also, DP Stewart, 'Internationalizing the War on Drugs: the UN Convention Against Illicit Traffic in Narcotic Drugs and Psychotropic Substances' (1990) 18 *Denver Journal of International Law and Policy* 387.

[2] See, in this context, V Mitsilegas, *Money Laundering Counter-Measures in the European Union: A New Paradigm of Security Governance versus Fundamental Legal Principles* (The Hague, Kluwer Law International, 2003) 52–54.

[3] Council Decision of 22 October 1990 concerning the conclusion, on behalf of the European Economic Community, of the UN Convention against Illicit Trafficking in Narcotic Drugs and Psychotropic Substances [1990] OJ L326/56.

[4] Council Directive 91/308/EEC of 10 June 1991 on prevention of the use of the financial system for the purpose of money laundering [1991] OJ L166/77.

[5] Arts 57(2), first and third sentences, and 100a of the EEC Treaty.

[6] For a discussion, see Mitsilegas, *Money Laundering Counter-Measures in the EU*, above n 2, ch 3.

[7] See below, Governing Crime via 'Soft' Law.

[8] The reference to 'prohibition' was introduced in order to circumvent the questionable Community competence to define criminal offences and impose criminal sanctions. However, Member States annexed to the text of the Directive a statement undertaking de facto to criminalise money laundering by the end of 1992.

[9] Art 1 of the Directive. See also, Preamble, recital 9.

[10] Art 1 of the Directive.

[11] For an analysis, see Mitsilegas, above n 2, chs 3 and 4.

unchanged in the subsequent revisions of the 1991 Directive, all the way to the adoption of the third Money Laundering Directive in 2005.[12]

The main area where Community law diverged from the Vienna Convention as regards the criminalisation of money laundering involves the criminal offences considered predicate money laundering offences. While predicate money laundering offences in the Vienna Convention were limited (perhaps unsurprisingly, given the focus of that Convention) to drug trafficking, by 1991 the Community legislator had adopted a more expansive approach, allowing Member States to include in the list 'any other criminal activity'.[13] The list of predicate offences was subsequently extended – partly via references to another international law instrument, the 1990 Council of Europe Convention on money laundering – in money laundering directives.[14] Indicative of the synergy present in the development of Community and international instruments in the field, and reflecting a move from focusing on the proceeds of drug trafficking to targeting the proceeds of organised and serious crime more generally, the list of predicate offences (which was also mandated by the FATF on money laundering in the 1990s) was also extended at UN level in the criminalisation of money laundering by the 2000 Convention against Transnational Organized Crime.[15] The extension of the scope of the criminal law on money laundering via the extension of the list of predicate offences is thus a prime example of synergy and cross-fertilisation between international law, 'soft' law and European Community/Union law.[16]

---

[12] Directive 2005/60/EC of the European Parliament and of the Council on the prevention of the use of the financial system for the purpose of money laundering and terrorist financing [2005] OJ L309/15. The third Money Laundering Directive also calls on Member States to prohibit terrorist financing. The definition of the latter largely follows the wording of the 1999 UN Convention on the Suppression of the Financing of Terrorism (Art 1(4) of the 2005 Directive). See V Mitsilegas and B Gilmore, 'The EU Legislative Framework against Money Laundering and Terrorist Finance: A Critical Analysis in the Light of Evolving Global Standards' (2007) 56 *International and Comparative Law Quarterly* 119.

[13] Art 1, indent 5 of the 1991 Directive. See also, Preamble, recital 5, stating that 'Whereas for the purposes of this Directive the definition of money laundering is taken from that adopted in the Vienna Convention; whereas, however, since money laundering occurs not only in relation to the proceeds of drug-related offences but also in relation to the proceeds of other criminal activities (such as organised crime and terrorism), the Member States should, within the meaning of their legislation, extend the effects of the Directive to include the proceeds of such activities, to the extent that they are likely to result in laundering operations justifying sanctions on that basis.'

[14] The Second Money Laundering Directive called upon Member States to bring the definition of 'serious crime' in line with the definition in the then Joint Action on Confiscation ([1998] OJ L333/1). Art 1 of the Joint Action (which was formally repealed by, but in substance largely retained in, the 2001 Framework Decision on confiscation ([2001] OJ L182/1) in turn called upon Member States not to make or uphold reservations with regard to Arts 2 and 6 of the 1990 Council of Europe Money Laundering Convention, as regards offences punishable under certain thresholds. The Third Money Laundering Directive consolidated the position by including under 'serious crimes' all offences punishable by a minimum custodial sentence of one year or, as regards Member States which have a minimum threshold for offences in their legal system, all offences punishable by a minimum custodial sentence of at least six months (Art 3(5)(f)).

[15] See Art 6(2) of the Convention. Art 6(2)(a) calls upon State Parties to apply the criminalisation of money laundering 'to the widest range of predicate offences'.

[16] On recent developments with regard to the alignment of EU law predicate offences with FATF Recommendations, see below, Governing Crime via 'Soft' Law.

Transnational Organised Crime – the 2000 Palermo Convention and EU Law

Perhaps the most impressive contribution of a UN multilateral treaty towards the globalisation of criminal law has been that of the Convention against Transnational Organized Crime and its Protocols, symbolically signed in Palermo in 2000. Negotiated throughout the 1990s, and reflecting the growing securitisation of organised crime at the time, the Convention is an ambitious and comprehensive multilateral instrument aiming at combating and preventing organised crime. It contains provisions ranging from the criminalisation of participation in an organised crime group, money laundering and corruption, to provisions on judicial cooperation with regard to organised crime, police cooperation and the law of criminal procedure. The Convention is complemented by three Protocols, on human trafficking, human smuggling, and the illicit manufacturing of and trafficking in firearms.[17]

Participation of the EU in the negotiations to the Convention was marked by legal complexity. The Convention was negotiated post-Maastricht (with negotiations continuing and the final conclusion taking place after the entry into force of the Amsterdam Treaty), at a time where the Union was granted competence in criminal matters under the third pillar. However, the wide range of provisions included in the Convention and its Protocols meant that there were also matters deemed to fall within Community competence. The result was that those parts of the Convention where Community competence could be established were negotiated by the Commission, whereas matters falling under the third pillar were negotiated primarily by the Member States. It has been pointed out that the European Commission had joined the negotiations with observer status but during the negotiation process requested the Council to adopt recommendations allowing it to negotiate on behalf of the Community.[18] Ironically, transparency in terms of the negotiating mandate was greater in terms of the 'third pillar' aspects of the Convention than with those aspects related to Community law. Whereas a Joint Position (adopted before the entry into force of the Amsterdam Treaty) outlined the EU negotiating position,[19] subsequent negotiating mandates to the

---

[17] See D McClean, *Transnational Organized Crime. A Commentary on the UN Convention and its Protocols* (Oxford, Oxford University Press, 2007). For an overview of the background to and the negotiating history of the Convention, see also, D Vlassis, 'Drafting the United Nations Convention against Transnational Organized Crime' in P Williams and D Vlassis (eds), *Combating Transnational Crime: Concepts, Activities and Responses* (London and Portland, Oregon, Frank Cass, 2001) 356.

[18] C Rijken and V Kronenberger, 'The United Nations Convention against Transnational Organised Crime and the European Union' in V Kronenberger (ed), *The European Union and the International Legal Order: Discord or Harmony?* (The Hague, TMC Asser Press, 2001) 493–94. The authors argue that on the other hand, during the negotiation process, the Member States never gave full competence to the Presidency to negotiate the UN Convention on their behalf (at 493).

[19] Joint Position of 29 March 1999 defined by the Council on the basis of Art K.3 of the Treaty on European Union, on the proposed United Nations convention against organised crime [1999] OJ L87/1.

Commission can be found in an ad hoc manner in various Council Conclusions.[20] An exception to this trend has been the publication of a Common Position on the negotiation of the firearms Protocol; however, this Common Position was adopted on a third pillar legal basis,[21] with the Commission participating in negotiations (on the basis of Community competence) only subsequently.[22] Greater transparency at third pillar level may be explained by the combination of the relative lack of experience in international negotiations in the field, but also by the ambition to establish visible precedents confirming the emergence of the Union as a global actor in the field of criminal law.

The 1999 Joint Position provides important insights into both the constitutional aspects of negotiating international agreements with content related to the third pillar, and the content of the EU goals in these negotiations. Adopted under a combination of Maastricht third pillar legal bases (Articles K.3(2) and K.5 Treaty on European Union (TEU)), the Joint Position was justified as necessary in order to contribute as fully as possible to the negotiation of the proposed convention and to avoid incompatibility between the proposed convention and instruments drawn up in the Union.[23]

In this light, the Joint Position called for account to be taken of measures already adopted, or in the course of preparation or adoption in accordance with the 1997 EU Action Plan on Organised Crime.[24] Particular emphasis in this context was placed on the need for Member States to ensure consistency between the UN Convention and the 1998 EU Joint Action on the criminalisation of participation in a criminal organisation[25] as regards the definition of such participation and its criminalisation.[26] The Joint Position then went on to provide detailed

---

[20] See, eg the conclusions of the Telecommunications Council of 2 May 2000 (Council Doc 8058/00, Presse 127-G), according to which 'the Council authorised the Commission to negotiate on behalf of the Community the draft UNTOC with regard to measures against money laundering, one of the main strands of the Convention, which fall within the scope of the Community's powers, taking the provisions of the 1991 money laundering Directive as a basis'.

[21] Council Common Position of 31 January 2000 on the proposed protocol against the illicit manufacturing of and trafficking in firearms, their parts and components and ammunition [2000] OJ L37/1, adopted on the basis of the TEU, and in particular Art 34(2)(a).

[22] See the conclusions of the ECOFIN Council of 31 January 2000 (Council Doc 5565/00, Presse 19-G), according to which 'the Council adopted a decision authorising the Commission to participate, on behalf of the European Union – in the negotiation of the draft protocol to the UNTOC to combat the illegal trafficking in and the manufacture of firearms, their parts, components and ammunition'. The reference to the Commission negotiating on behalf of the European Union – rather than the European Community – is noteworthy in this context.

[23] Joint Position, above n 19, Preamble, recital 8.

[24] ibid, Preamble, recital 5. For an overview of the Action Plan, see WC Gilmore, 'The EU Action Plan to Combat Organised Crime: The Scope and Implementation of Legal Instruments' in *The Boundaries of Understanding. Essays in Honour of Malcolm Anderson* (Edinburgh, University of Edinburgh International Social Sciences Institute, 1999) 97–106.

[25] Joint Action of 21 December 1998 adopted by the Council on the basis of Article K.3 of the Treaty on European Union, on making it a criminal offence to participate in a criminal organisation in the Member States of the European Union [1998] OJ L351/1. For an analysis, see V Mitsilegas, 'Defining Organised Crime in the European Union: The Limits of European Criminal Law in an Area of Freedom, Security and Justice' (2001) 26 *European Law Review* 565.

[26] Joint Position, above n 19, Art 1(2). The Joint Position also called for consistency between the Convention and the 1998 EU Joint Action on confiscation, see Art 1(6).

guidelines on the negotiating position with regard to the scope of the Convention and the definition of organised crime, which mirrors the definition adopted at EU level.[27] Calls for consistency (and coordination) were primarily addressed to Member States (leaving a limited role for the Presidency).[28] The wording of the Joint Position has led commentators to argue that the Presidency was in fact not authorised by the Member States to negotiate on their behalf, and therefore that the UN Convention and its Protocols could not be considered as agreements in the sense of Articles 24 and 38 TEU.[29]

Instruments of signature and conclusion of the Palermo Convention and its Protocols were adopted only at Community level. As regards signature by the Community, two Decisions were adopted: one concerning the Convention itself and the Smuggling and Trafficking Protocols;[30] and another concerning the Firearms Protocol.[31] A clearer insight into the extent of Community competence is provided by the subsequent instruments on the conclusion of the Palermo Convention and its Protocols by the Community. Separate Decisions with regard to the Convention itself and the two Protocols on trafficking and smuggling have been adopted in this context. The Decision on the conclusion of the Convention[32] was adopted under Articles 47 (free movement/right of establishment), 55 (free movement of services), 95 (internal market) and 179 (development cooperation)

---

[27] Art 1(3) of the Joint Position, above n 19, states that 'insofar as the other provisions of the draft convention are concerned, it should apply as broadly as possible to the activities of criminal organisations and to international cooperation for combating such organisations. In principle, the relevant provisions of the draft convention should encompass the activities of persons, acting in concert with a view to committing serious crime, involved in any criminal organisation which has a structure and is, or has been, established for a certain period of time. They should not be limited to groups with a highly developed structure or enduring nature, such as mafia type organisations; and the organisations need not necessarily have formally defined roles for their participants or continuity of membership.'

[28] See ibid, Art 2, according to which 'in the negotiations on the proposed United Nations convention and any possible protocols, Member States shall, as far as is practicable, coordinate their positions, at the Presidency's initiative, and seek to arrive at common standpoints on all issues which have significant implications for the interests of the Union'. See also, Art 3, calling upon Member States to ensure that the provisions of the proposed United Nations convention and any possible protocols are not inconsistent with instruments drawn up between them.

[29] Rijken and Kronenberger, 'The United Nations Convention against Transnational Organised Crime and the European Union', above n 18, 494.

[30] Council Decision of 8 December 2000 on the signing, on behalf of the European Community, of the United Nations Convention against transnational organised crime and its Protocols [2001] OJ L30/44. The legal bases for the Decision were Arts 47 (free movement/right of establishment), 62(2)(a) (border controls), 63(3)(b) (illegal immigration and illegal residence), and 95 (internal market) TEC (in conjunction with Art 300(2)). The Decision confirms that 'the elements of the Convention and the two Protocols thereto which are subject to Community competence were negotiated by the Commission, with the approval of the Council, on behalf of the Community' (Preamble, recital 1).

[31] Council Decision of 16 October 2001 on the signing, on behalf of the European Community, of the United Nations Protocol on the illicit manufacturing of and trafficking in firearms [2001] OJ L280/5. The legal bases for the Decision were Arts 95 (internal market) and 133 (common commercial policy) TEC (in conjunction with Art 300(2)). As with the Decision on the signing of the Convention, above n 30, this Decision confirms the negotiation by the Commission of matters of the Protocol falling within Community competence (Preamble, recital 1).

[32] Council Decision of 29 April 2004 on the conclusion, on behalf of the European Community, of the United Nations Convention Against Transnational Organised Crime [2004] OJ L261/69.

TEC. It is worth quoting at length here the Declaration of Community Competence annexed thereto:[33]

> The Community points out that it has competence with regard to progressively establishing the internal market, comprising an area without internal frontiers in which the free movement of goods and services is ensured in accordance with the provisions of the Treaty establishing the European Community. For this purpose, the Community has adopted measures to combat money laundering. They do, however, at present not include measures concerning cooperation between Financial Intelligence Units, detection and monitoring the movement of cash across the borders between the Member States or cooperation among judicial and law enforcement authorities. The Community also has adopted measures to ensure transparency and the equal access of all candidates for the public contracts and services markets which contributes to preventing corruption. Where the Community has adopted measures, it is for the Community alone to enter into external undertakings with third States or competent international organisations which affect those measures or alter their scope. This competence relates to Articles 7,[34] 9[35] and 31(2)(c)[36] of the Convention. Moreover, Community policy in the sphere of development cooperation complements policies pursued by Member States and includes provisions to combat corruption. This competency relates to Article 30[37] of the Convention. Moreover, the Community considers itself bound by other provisions of the Convention to the extent that they are related to the application of Articles 7, 9, 30 and 31(2)(c), in particular the articles concerning its purpose and definitions and its final provisions.

Three points are noteworthy in the Decision and the Declaration of Competence. The first is that legal bases used to adopt the Decision concluding the Palermo Convention have been extended in relation to the signature Decision to include Articles 55 (free movement of services) and 179 (development cooperation) TEC. This 'extension' of competence is also reflected in the Declaration of Competence. The second point is that, contrary to the wording of the Declaration, there was now Community law on matters such as cooperation between Financial Intelligence Units and detection and monitoring the movement of cash across the borders between the Member States. While the Declaration recognises the potential development of Community law in this context,[38] it had not been amended at the time of writing to reflect these developments. The third point involves the scope of some of the provisions of the Palermo Convention included in the Declaration of Competence. According to the latter, Community competence relates to Articles 7 and 9 of the Convention (on money laundering and corruption respectively). While these provisions refer mostly to the preventive and not

---

[33] ibid, Annex II Declaration of competence in accordance to Art 36(3) of the Convention.
[34] Money laundering.
[35] Corruption.
[36] Prevention of the misuse by organised criminal groups of tender procedures conducted by public authorities and of subsidies and licences granted by public authorities for commercial activity.
[37] Implementation of the Convention through Economic Development and Technical Assistance.
[38] 'The scope and the exercise of Community competence are, by their nature, subject to continuous development and the Community will complete or amend this declaration, if necessary, in accordance with Art 36(3) of the Convention.' Declaration, above n 33, Annex II.

the criminal law aspects of money laundering and corruption law (these are dealt with in Articles 6 and 8 of the Convention respectively), they can still be seen as containing certain criminal law elements (not falling expressly within Community competence at the time).[39]

A two-pronged strategy was followed with regard to the conclusion of the Smuggling and Trafficking Protocols.[40] Two Decisions were adopted for the conclusion of each of the Protocols, reflecting the wide range of fields in which Community competence did arise: one set of Decisions was adopted on legal bases related to development cooperation and economic, financial and technical cooperation with third countries;[41] and another set of Decisions was adopted on a Title IV legal basis (related to Community immigration and borders law).[42]

The Declaration of Community Competence (found in Annex II and similar to all Decisions, with differences in terminology mainly in respect of the titles of the respective Protocols, that is trafficking/smuggling) aimed at translating the à la carte participation of Denmark, Ireland and the United Kingdom in Title IV measures, and refers to exclusive Community competence with regard to border controls and visas, immigration policy regarding conditions of entry and residence and measures to counter illegal immigration and illegal residence, including repatriation of illegal residents and cooperation between the relevant departments of the administrations of the Member States, as well as between those departments and the Commission, in the aforementioned areas.[43] It was added that Community policy in the sphere of development cooperation complemented policies pursued

---

[39] Art 9(1) of the Palermo Convention calls upon State Parties to 'adopt legislative, administrative or other effective measures to promote integrity and to prevent, detect and punish the corruption of public officials'. Art 7(4) of the Convention calls for 'global, regional, subregional and bilateral cooperation among judicial, law enforcement and financial regulatory authorities in order to combat money laundering'. To the extent that this provision refers to Financial Intelligence Units, it must be noted that relevant provisions have since appeared in the (first pillar) 2005 third Money Laundering Directive (for an analysis of the constitutional implications of this inclusion, see Mitsilegas and Gilmore, 'The EU Legislative Framework against Money Laundering and Terrorist Finance', above (n 12)).

[40] At the time of writing the EU has not yet concluded the Firearms Protocol, above n 31. This is due to the need to wait for the implementation of relevant EU legislation by Member States, see Commission 'Report on Implementation of the Hague Programme for 2007' COM (2008) 373 final.

[41] Arts 179 and 181a TEC respectively. See Council Decision of 24 July 2006 on the conclusion, on behalf of the European Community, of the Protocol to Prevent, Suppress and Punish Trafficking in Persons . . . in so far as the provisions of this Protocol fall within the scope of Arts 179 and 181a of the EC Treaty [2006] OJ L262/44; and Council Decision of 24 July 2006 on the conclusion, on behalf of the European Community, of the Protocol Against the Smuggling of Migrants . . . in so far as the provisions of this Protocol fall within the scope of Arts 179 and 181a of the EC Treaty, [2006] OJ L262/24.

[42] Council Decision of 24 July 2006 on the conclusion, on behalf of the European Community, of the Protocol to Prevent, Suppress and Punish Trafficking in Persons . . . in so far as the provisions of this Protocol fall within the scope of Part III, Title IV of the EC Treaty [2006] OJ L262/51; and Council Decision of 24 July 2006 on the conclusion, on behalf of the European Community, of the Protocol Against the Smuggling of Migrants . . . in so far as the provisions of this Protocol fall within the scope of Part III, Title IV of the EC Treaty [2006] OJ L262/34.

[43] According to the Declaration, the Community has adopted rules and regulations in these fields and, where it has done so, it is solely for the Community to enter into external undertakings with third States or competent international organisations.

by Member States and includes provisions to prevent and combat trafficking in persons. It is noteworthy that, unlike the Decision concluding the Palermo Convention, this was a rather general Declaration of Competence in that there was no reference to specific provisions of the Protocols with regard to Community competence.[44] This is notwithstanding the fact that a number of provisions in both Protocols relate to the adoption of criminal law, an area where the powers of the Community to legislate were contested at the time.[45]

The substantive provisions of the Palermo Convention as regards the criminalisation of organised crime demonstrate that the 'consistency' objective outlined in the 1999 EU Joint Position has been largely achieved. The definition of an organised crime group and the criminalisation of participation in a criminal organisation in the Convention[46] largely mirror the provisions of the EU 1998 Joint Action making it a criminal offence to participate in a criminal organisation in a Member State of the EU.[47] The Joint Action, which constituted the first major attempt at international level to provide for harmonisation of the criminal law on organised crime, contained a broad definition of an organised crime group and a 'dual' model of criminalisation, with Member States given the choice to criminalise either participation in a criminal organisation as defined in the Joint Action, or conspiracy.[48] The Convention's criminalisation of participation in a criminal organisation largely follows this approach,[49] with the Convention text adding the criminalisation of 'organising, directing, aiding, abetting, facilitating or counselling the commission of serious crime involving an organised crime group'.[50]

The Palermo Convention was in turn a benchmark for the development of subsequent EU law on organised crime. In 2005, the Commission tabled a proposal for a Framework Decision 'on the fight against organised crime', aimed at replacing the 1998 Joint Action.[51] According to the Commission, the new proposal took into account developments since 1998, including the introduction of Framework Decisions as a form of third pillar law in Amsterdam and the need to take into account subsequent legislative developments, such as the Palermo Convention

---

[44] A general clause common to all four Decisions states that they will apply in so far as the provisions of the Protocols fall within the scope of their respective legal bases (see, eg Art 2 of the Decision on the conclusion of the trafficking Protocol on a Title IV legal basis, above n 42).

[45] The Community later adopted (still in the pre-Lisbon era), a first pillar Directive including criminal law provisions in the field of Title IV (on illegal work) [2009] OJ L168/24. EU competence to adopt criminal offences and sanctions is established in Art 83(1) and (2) TFEU post-Lisbon.

[46] Arts 2 and 5 respectively.

[47] Mitsilegas, 'Defining Organised Crime in the European Union', above n 25.

[48] For a discussion, see Mitsilegas, above n 25, 571–72.

[49] See McClean, *Transnational Organized Crime*, above n 17, 67. Commenting on the implementation of Art 5, he notes that 'the statute books of the common law countries which have ratified the Convention will be searched in vain for crimes defined as set out in this Article. As has been clear from the beginning, the offences of conspiracy, soliciting, and other forms of participation in criminal conduct more than adequately cover the field described in the text of the Article.'

[50] Art 5(1)(b).

[51] Commission, 'Proposal for a Framework Decision on the fight against organised crime' COM (2005) 6 final.

and the EU Framework Decision on terrorism.[52] Negotiations have resulted in the recent adoption of a third pillar Framework Decision 'on the fight against organised crime'.[53] The Framework Decision claims to build upon the Palermo Convention[54] and repeals the 1998 Joint Action. The wording of the provisions on the definition of criminal organisation and the criminalisation of offences relating to participation therein are broadly similar to the provisions of the Palermo Convention. This is particularly the case in respect of the definition of an organised crime group and the maintenance of the option for Member States to criminalise either participation in a criminal organisation or conspiracy. Unlike the Palermo Convention, however, the Framework Decision refrained from criminalising the *direction* of an organised criminal group. On the other hand, the EU instrument goes further than the Convention by including provisions of greater detail than the latter which are common to EU third pillar law, in particular detailed provisions on penalties. In this case, the Union legislator has used international law to update the internal *acquis*, while at the same time adding Union-specific elements in the internal instrument. Here, taking into account international standards was also used to enhance the effectiveness of EU law in the field of organised crime, by justifying the transition from an EU instrument of uncertain legal force (a Joint Action) to a clearly legally-binding Framework Decision.[55]

In respect of the criminalisation of human trafficking and human smuggling, the Palermo Convention came at a time when no detailed EU legislation existed in the field.[56] A number of EU measures followed the adoption of the Convention. In 2002 the Council adopted a third pillar Framework Decision defining and criminalising trafficking in human beings.[57] It was designed not to implement, but rather to complement the work of the UN in the field.[58]

[52] See V Mitsilegas, 'The Third Wave of Third Pillar Law: Which Direction for EU Criminal Justice?' (2009) 34 *European Law Review* 523.

[53] Framework Decision 2008/841/JHA on the fight against organised crime [2008] OJ L300/42.

[54] ibid, Preamble, recital 6.

[55] See V Mitsilegas, 'The EU and the Implementation of International Norms in Criminal Matters' in M Cremona, J Monar and S Poli (eds), *The External Dimension of the Area of Freedom, Security and Justice* (Bern, Peter Lang, 2011).

[56] Note, in this context, the Maastricht Joint Action 97/154/JHA concerning action to combat trafficking in human beings and sexual exploitation of children [1997] OJ L63/2. However, the scope of the Joint Action was rather limited, with the focus being largely on trafficking for the purposes of sexual exploitation.

[57] Council Framework Decision of 19 July 2002 on combating trafficking in human beings [2002] OJ L203/1.

[58] See Preamble, recitals 4 (referring to the Palermo Protocol as 'a decisive step towards international cooperation in the field) and 6 (referring to the need for the EU to complement work done in international *fora*, in particular the UN). A similar reference, indicating awareness of, but not overt deference to, the relevant UN standards can be found in the Preamble of a 2004 first pillar Directive on residence permits for victims of trafficking who cooperate with essentially law enforcement authorities ([2004] OJ L261/19, recital 3). The Directive (adopted on a Title IV legal basis) is largely drafted from the perspective of the efficiency of State action against traffickers, with the protective spirit permeating the Palermo Trafficking Protocol (in particular Art 6 thereof) as regards victims being scarcely discernible in the EU instrument.

Having said that, the definition – and criminalisation – of human trafficking in the Framework Decision follows very closely the definition adopted in the Palermo Protocol.[59] Unlike the Protocol, the Framework Decision introduces penalty levels (including a minimum custodial sentence of eight years) when a series of aggravating circumstances applies. The criminalisation of human trafficking in those terms has also been reflected in the recent post-Lisbon Directive on human trafficking, which has also placed great emphasis on the position of the victim.[60] The year 2002 also saw the adoption of EU measures on human smuggling (or, according to EU terminology, the facilitation of unauthorised entry, transit and residence): a first pillar Directive defining 'facilitation', accompanied by a third pillar Framework Decision criminalising it.[61] Neither of these instruments contains references to the Palermo Convention. The Directive defines 'facilitation' as intentionally assisting a third country national to enter or transit an EU Member State in breach of its aliens' laws, and intentionally assisting 'for financial gain' a third country national to reside in an EU Member State irregularly. The definition goes beyond the UN Smuggling Protocol, which requires 'a financial or other material benefit' as a condition for the criminalisation of procuring of illegal entry.[62]

The Framework Decision introduces a series of criminal sanctions, including heavier penalties if the offences are committed for financial gain, or if they are committed within the framework of an organised crime group or they endanger the lives of the smuggled persons. The last two elements are also mentioned in the UN Smuggling Protocol, but the Protocol includes a further aggravating circumstance when smuggling entails inhuman or degrading treatment, including exploitation.[63]

---

[59] The offence includes trafficking for the purpose of labour exploitation. A notable omission from the EU text is trafficking for the purpose of removal of organs. A proposal tabled in 2003 by the then Greek EU Presidency to criminalise the trade in human organs has been blocked in the Council. See V Mitsilegas, *The Coherence of the Adopted Measures During the Last Years by the EU with Regard to Organised Crime and the UN Convention on Organised Crime*, Briefing Paper for the European Parliament LIBE Committee (2006). Reproduced in D Bigo and A Tsoukala (eds), *Controlling Security* (Paris, L'Harmattan, 2008) 65.

[60] Directive 2011/36/EU of the European Parliament and of the Council of 5 April 2011 on preventing and combating trafficking in human beings and protecting its victims, and replacing Council Framework Decision 2002/629/JHA [2011] OJ L101, 1.

[61] Council Directive 2002/90/EC of 8 November 2002 defining the facilitation of unauthorised entry, transit and residence [2002] OJ L328, 4, and corresponding Framework Decision, of the same OJ, 1. This 'dual' approach was adopted in order to address Member States' concerns with regard to the extent of Community competence to adopt criminal law in the field; for an overview of the constitutional debate in this context, see V Mitsilegas, *EU Criminal Law* (Oxford and Portland, Oregon, Hart Publishing, 2009) ch 2.

[62] The disassociation of the financial gain element from the facilitation offence for the purposes of entry and transit raised concerns among humanitarian NGOs, which felt that they would be prosecuted for assisting third country nationals, including asylum seekers, to enter the EU. For that reason, and after protracted negotiations, a clause was added to the Directive granting Member States the discretion not to impose sanctions where the aim of the behaviour is to provide humanitarian assistance to the person concerned. See V Mitsilegas, J Monar and W Rees, *The European Union and Internal Security* (Basingstoke, Palgrave Macmillan, 2003) 106–108.

[63] Protocol Against the Smuggling of Migrants by Land, Sea and Air, supplementing the United Nations Convention Against Transnational Organized Crime, Article 6. The UN Smuggling Protocol

Corruption: the 2003 UN Convention on Corruption and EU Law

The most recent major UN multilateral treaty in criminal matters is the 2003 UN Convention against Corruption. It aims to establish a comprehensive anticorruption framework, by focusing on both prevention and control.[64] The breadth of the Convention's scope meant that some areas covered were deemed to be related to Community competence, whereas other areas were deemed to be related to Union, third pillar powers. The approach taken with regard to the negotiations was thus broadly similar to the approach followed in the negotiations of the Palermo Convention. Transparency with regard to the various negotiating positions was limited. The eventual Council Decision on the conclusion, on behalf of the European Community, of the United Nations Convention against Corruption[65] confirmed that the elements of the Convention which were subject to Community competence were negotiated by the Commission.[66] The Community concluded the Convention on the basis of a plethora of legal bases, ranging from provisions on free movement and the internal market to development cooperation and provisions related to the functioning of the EU institutions.[67] Similarly, the Declaration annexed to the Decision established Community competence for a range of issues, starting with the prevention of corruption (including the adoption of codes of conduct and action within EU institutions), continuing with the proper functioning of the internal market (emphasising that the Community had adopted measures regarding transparency and equal access to public contracts and markets of Community relevance, appropriate accounting and auditing standards, and the prevention of money laundering) and concluding with development cooperation. This is a wide range of quite disparate fields, where Community action had not necessarily taken the form of legally-binding instruments. It reflects the many areas potentially affected by anti-corruption law, and extends to both addressing corruption at an internal, institutional level and addressing corruption externally, as conduct which is detrimental to markets, the economy and beyond.

---

also contains provisions on ensuring the safety and humane treatment of smuggled persons who are intercepted at sea, and a series of detailed provisions on prevention, elements which are absent from the EC/EU documents; see Mitsilegas, *The Coherence of the Adopted Measures During the Last Years by the EU*, above n 59.

[64] For an overview, see P Webb, 'The United Nations Convention against Corruption. Global Achievement or Missed Opportunity?' (2005) 8 *Journal of International Economic Law* 191.

[65] [2008] OJ L287/1.

[66] ibid, Preamble, recital 1.

[67] The legal bases of the Decision were: Arts 47(2) (free movement/right of establishment), 57(2) (free movement of capital), 95 (internal market), 107(5) (monetary policy, ESCB), 179 (development cooperation), 181a (economic, financial and technical cooperation with third countries), 190(5) (European Parliament), 195(4) (Ombudsman), 199 (European Parliament rules of procedure), 207(3) (Council rules of procedure), 218(2) (Commission rules of procedure), 279 (Council financial regulations), 280 (fraud against EC financial interests) and 283 (staff regulations of officials) TEC.

As regards the negotiations of the third pillar/criminal law aspects of the Convention, a series of draft negotiating common positions have now been declassified. The first of these documents refers to a draft Common Position at the initiative of the Belgian EU Presidency.[68] The draft Common Position contained detailed guidelines on the criminal law aspects of corruption to be included in the UN Convention.[69] It contained a 'red line', stating that the criminal offences and penalties shall not call into question the fundamental principles underlying Member States' legal systems, and that 'in particular, in the negotiations on "illicit enrichment", the Union should oppose any inclusion in the Convention of criminal offences so defined as to undermine those fundamental principles.[70]

The draft Common Position called for the Palermo Convention to be taken as the basis for a number of provisions in the new Convention.[71] Reflecting the growing importance of the fight against corruption in the context of the accession negotiations leading to the 2004 enlargement, candidate countries were invited to support the Common Position.[72] Member States were called upon to ensure that the provisions of the Convention did not call into question the instruments drawn up between them, 'in particular with regard to judicial assistance, extradition, combating corruption and the protection of the Community's financial interests'.[73] Last, but not least, the draft Common Position called upon Member States to 'coordinate their positions at the Presidency's initiative and seek to arrive at common standpoints on all issues which have significant implications for the interests of the European Union'.[74]

This three-fold approach, of mandating substantive negotiating guidelines (including 'red lines' in particular as regards provisions which would be deemed as threatening fundamental legal principles in Member States), safeguarding the internal *acquis* and calling for coordination in negotiations, was repeated in two subsequent draft Common Positions now publicly available. The draft second

---

[68] Initiative of the Kingdom of Belgium for the adoption by the Council of a draft Common Position defined by the Council on negotiations within the United Nations to draw up a United Nations Convention against Corruption, Council Doc 12837/2/01 REV 2 (2003). The draft Common Position was approved by the Art 36 Committee at its meeting of 12 and 13 November 2001, and Coreper was invited to recommend to the Council its adoption Council Doc 14114/01 (2001).

[69] According to Art 2 of the draft Common Position, the Convention should cover, inter alia, active and passive corruption in the private sector, and apply to corruption both of national officials and of foreign officials, and include corruption of international officials; it should also cover the criminalisation of the laundering of proceeds of corruption and seizure/confiscation matters; active and passive corruption in the private sector, trading in influence and accounting offences should also form part of the negotiations.

[70] Draft Common Position, Art 2(3).

[71] Particularly for the provisions on laundering, seizure and confiscation of the proceeds of corruption, for the provisions on sanctions, the protection of witnesses, assistance and protection of victims, the liability of legal persons and jurisdiction, and for the provisions designed to improve international cooperation in criminal matters (draft Common Position, Art 2(5)). See also, the EU Presidency Statement of 21 January 2002 on the UN Convention against corruption, in particular paras 9–12, available at www.eu-un.europa.eu/articles/en/article_1081_en.htm.

[72] Draft Common Position, Art 4.

[73] ibid, Art 5.

[74] ibid, Art 7.

Common Position[75] expressed support in principle for the inclusion of anti-money laundering measures in the Convention. However, Member States were asked to ensure that the provisions of the Convention do not call into question either the instruments drawn up between them, in particular the Council Decision concerning arrangements for cooperation between financial intelligence units of the Member States in respect of exchanging information and other measures taken in the field of money laundering, or other international instruments to which they are party.[76]

Moreover, for provisions on the identification, tracing, seizing, freezing and confiscation of funds, Member States were called to ensure that the provisions of the Convention concerning compliance with such measures do not call into question their fundamental principles, in particular in respect of evidence, or their provisions on data protection.[77]

The draft third Common Position[78] focused primarily on substantive guidelines on the criminalisation of corruption by public officials, and advocated consistency with standards adopted in the Palermo Convention and the relevant Council of Europe Convention in the field.[79] The red line here involved the inclusion of offences such as abuse of functions, unlawful enrichment, use of classified or confidential information, and improper benefits, which Member States should not support. In the event of criminalisation of such offences, Member States were called upon to ensure that these crimes did not call into question the fundamental principles underlying their legal systems.[80]

An examination of the finally adopted text of the UN Convention against Corruption in the light of the aforementioned documents demonstrates that the EU negotiating objectives with regard to criminal law have been largely met. The Convention requires State Parties to criminalise three types of conduct: bribery of national public officials,[81] bribery of foreign public officials and officials of public

---

[75] Draft second Common Position defined by the Council on the basis of Art 34(2)(a) of the Treaty on European Union on negotiations within the United Nations to draw up a United Nations Convention against Corruption, Council Doc 8897/4/02 REV 4, Brussels, 30 October 2003. The draft second Common Position was approved by the Art 36 Committee at its meeting of 20 and 21 May 2002, and Coreper was invited to recommend to the Council its adoption Council Doc 9375/02, Brussels, 29 May 2002.

[76] Draft second Common Position, Art 5.

[77] ibid, Art 6.

[78] Initiative of the Kingdom of Denmark concerning the adoption by the Council of a draft third Common Position defined by the Council on the basis of Art 34(2)(a) of the Treaty on European Union on negotiations within the United Nations to draw up a United Nations Convention against Corruption, Council Doc 12215/2/02 REV 2, Brussels, 30 October 2003. The draft third Common Position was approved after some amendments by Coreper at its meeting of 25 September 2002, and the Council was invited to adopt it Council Doc 12329/02, Brussels, 25 September 2002.

[79] See draft third Common Position, Arts 2 and 3 respectively. The same approach was followed with regard to criminalisation of money laundering (which, according to Art 8, should be compatible with Art 6 of the Palermo Convention) and corruption in the private sector (which should be compatible with Arts 7 and 8 of the Council of Europe Convention). It is noteworthy that compatibility is here requested with international – and not EU – standards in the field.

[80] Draft third Common Position, Art 6.

[81] UN Convention against Corruption, Art 15.

international organisations,[82] and embezzlement, misappropriation or other diversion of property by a public official.[83] The last type of conduct is not currently covered by EU criminal law, while the EU has legislated on the criminalisation of corruption of national and Community officials.[84] The criminalisation of bribery of national public officials in the UN Convention is worded in very similar terms to the relevant EU instruments on corruption.[85] The UN Convention also criminalises a series of further corruption-related offences (trading in influence,[86] abuse of functions,[87] illicit enrichment,[88] bribery in the private sector,[89] embezzlement of property[90]), but criminalisation here is not compulsory for State Parties, which need only *consider* going down that route. This wording seems to address EU concerns with regard to the criminalisation of illicit enrichment, which in any case would occur subject to the State Parties' constitutions and the fundamental principles of their legal system.[91] The inclusion in the Convention of the criminalisation of bribery in the private sector represents a partial victory for the EU. It has been reported that extending the Convention to cover the private sector was one of the most contentious issues during the negotiations, with the EU calling for criminalisation but the US resisting such a move.[92] The result has been a compromise, whereby the Convention includes the criminalisation of private sector corruption in very similar terms to the EU 2003 Framework Decision in the field,[93] but such criminalisation falls within the discretion of State Parties to the Convention.

The UN Convention against Corruption has introduced a number of corruption-related offences for State Parties to criminalise or to consider criminalising. The framework it puts forward is much more comprehensive when compared with the EU criminal law on corruption. The EU criminal law framework on corruption is both limited and fragmented, with Member States appearing reluctant to agree to a comprehensive anti-corruption law with teeth.[94] Criminalisation has been introduced in the form of the quite 'intergovernmental' Maastricht

---

[82]   ibid, Art 16.

[83]   ibid, Art 17.

[84]   See the Protocol to the EU Fraud Convention [1996] OJ C313/2; and the EU Convention against corruption involving officials of the European Communities or officials of the Member States of the European Union [1997] OJ C195/2.

[85]   The EU instruments refer to 'corruption', whereas the UN Convention refers to 'bribery'. The terms will be used interchangeably for the purposes of this chapter.

[86]   UN Convention against Corruption, Art 18.

[87]   ibid, Art 19.

[88]   ibid, Art 20.

[89]   ibid, Art 21.

[90]   ibid, Art 22.

[91]   Similarly, the Convention provisions on judicial cooperation in criminal matters appear to address EU concerns, as they are drafted in very general terms.

[92]   Webb, 'The United Nations Convention against Corruption' above n 64, 213–14.

[93]   Council Framework Decision 2003/568/JHA of 22 July 2003 on combating corruption in the private sector [2003] OJ L192/54.

[94]   See also, V Mitsilegas, 'The Aims and Limits of EU Anti-Corruption Law' in J Horder and P Alldridge (eds), *Modern Bribery Law: Comparative Perspectives*, (Cambridge, Cambridge University Press, 2013).

Conventions (which have not been replaced post-Amsterdam by Framework Decisions). Where a Framework Decision has eventually been adopted (on corruption in the private sector), its implementation by Member States leaves much to be desired.[95] Unlike the fields of money laundering and organised crime, there has been no EU legislative action in the field following the adoption of the 2003 UN Convention. This may signal the fact that, in the field of the criminal law of corruption, the Union has opted to pursue its agenda by promoting standards at the global level instead of developing a comprehensive framework in internal EU law.[96]

Governing Crime via Regional Multilateral Treaties: The EU and the Council of Europe

There are growing interconnections between the activities of the Council of Europe and the EU in the field of criminal law.[97] Along with geographical and membership factors, these interconnections are linked with the fast-moving legislative activity of both organisations in criminal matters. In recent years, the Council of Europe has adopted a number of comprehensive, pioneering criminal law Conventions in fields such as money laundering, corruption and terrorism. Provisions in a number of these instruments significantly influenced the development of internal Union law in these fields. Increasingly, the EU is using its negotiating strength in the Council of Europe first to introduce three new elements on criminal law and then to export these elements to Europe and beyond, in particular in cases where no global consensus can be encountered initially.[98] The regional Conventions of the Council of Europe form a laboratory for EU membership for candidate countries as regards criminal law and justice; this is also confirmed by the central place occupied by Council of Europe instruments in the assessment of States which are potentially future candidates for EU membership. Their ratification (along with the ratification of the relevant UN Conventions and the FATF Recommendations) is also a key requirement in the European Neighbourhood Policy Action Plans developed by the EU and in the EU's relations with Russia.[99]

---

[95] See Commission, 'Report on the implementation of the Framework Decision on corruption in the private sector' COM (2007) 328 final.

[96] For the emphasis on action in international *fora*, see, eg Commission, 'On a Comprehensive EU Policy Against Corruption' (Communication) COM (2003) 317 final.

[97] For details, see V Mitsilegas 'The EU and the Rest of the World: Criminal Law and Policy Interconnections' in M Evans and P Koutrakos (eds), *Beyond the Established Orders. Policy Interconnections between the EU and the Rest of the World* (Oxford, Hart Publishing, 2011).

[98] A prime example in this context is the conclusion of the Council of Europe Convention on Cybercrime, see V Mitsilegas, 'Regional Organisations and the Suppression of Transnational Crime' in N Boister and R Curry (eds), *Research Handbook on Transnational Criminal Law* (London, Routledge, forthcoming).

[99] For details, see Mitsilegas, 'The EU and the Implementation of International Norms in Criminal Matters', above n 55.

Last, but not least, standards agreed in Council of Europe Conventions are increasingly important for the globalisation of criminal law in view of the fact that a number of Council of Europe conventions are open for ratification to states outside Europe (most notably the United States).

The use of Council of Europe multilateral conventions to export Union-endorsed standards does not, however, mean that these standards necessarily limit the Union's autonomy of action when legislating internally in the field. In recent years the EU has become increasingly assertive in negotiations at Council of Europe level, especially in the light of the growth of the internal *acquis* in criminal law. An example of this EU strategy with regard to the adoption and subsequent use of Council of Europe criminal law instruments involves recent developments in the law of terrorism. At the EU level, a new Framework Decision was adopted in 2008 to amend an earlier Framework Decision on combating terrorism.[100] The Framework Decision expands the scope of the 2002 instrument to introduce in the EU legal order offences related to the prevention of terrorism. The basis for the elaboration of these offences was the Council of Europe Convention on the Prevention of Terrorism.[101] The 2008 Framework Decision does not repeal, but rather amends the 2002 Framework Decision on combating terrorism.[102] The 2008 instrument introduces three new offences: public provocation to commit a terrorist offence; recruitment for terrorism; and training for terrorism. However, for any of these acts to be punishable it is not necessary that a terrorist offence is actually committed. This clause, which has been copied *verbatim* from the Council of Europe Convention, did not exist in the 2002 EU instrument and signals a move towards the adoption of 'preventive' criminal law by the EU. However, criminalisation in the Framework Decision has its limits. In particular, it is noteworthy that for conduct to be treated as a criminal offence, a 'terrorist motivation' must exist.[103] This condition, which does not exist in the main body of the Council of Europe Convention,[104] may serve to limit criminalisation when the Framework Decision is implemented.[105]

The EU strategy with regard to the use of the Council of Europe Convention on the Prevention of Terrorism demonstrates the increasing assertiveness of the Union as a global actor in criminal matters, especially in fields where there is

[100] Framework Decision 2008/919/JHA amending the 2002 Framework Decision on combating terrorism [2008] OJ L330/21.

[101] Council of Europe Convention on the Prevention of Terrorism CETS No 196.

[102] Framework Decision 2002/475/JHA on combating terrorism [2002] OJ L164/3 (the 2002 Framework Decision).

[103] Framework Decision 2002/475/JHA Art 1(1) criminalises as terrorist offences which given their nature or context, may seriously damage a country or an international organisation where committed with the aim of: seriously intimidating a population, or unduly compelling a government or international organisation to perform or abstain from performing any act, or seriously destabilising or destroying the fundamental political, constitutional, economic or social structures of a country or an international organisation.

[104] For a discussion, see A Hunt, 'The Council of Europe Convention on the Prevention of Terrorism' (2006) 12 *European Public Law* 613.

[105] For further discussion of this Framework Decision, see Mitsilegas, 'The Third Wave of Third Pillar Law', above n 52.

already a developed Union *acquis*. The EU played an active part in the negotiations of the Council of Europe Convention by opposing the negotiation of a comprehensive Council of Europe counter-terrorism convention and arguing in favour of narrowing down the scope of the latter to cover only areas where there are gaps in pre-existing international law.[106] This lack of consensus with regard to the adoption of a comprehensive approach[107] resulted in an instrument covering specific aspects of counter-terrorism action, in particular the criminalisation of 'glorification-type' conduct and not covering aspects of the criminalisation of terrorism which had already been addressed in the 2002 EU Framework Decision. The Union then used the Convention to justify the extension of criminalisation internally, while justifying Union action externally by stressing the 'added value' of the Union legal order in terms of integration and enforcement.[108] According to the EU Justice and Home Affairs Ministers, the inclusion of the Convention offences in the Framework Decision is important, 'because it provides the advantages of the more integrated institutional framework of the EU and also because the legal regime of the Framework Decision in respect of the type and level of criminal penalties and compulsory rules on jurisdiction will be applicable to these offences'.[109]

The references to the special nature and features of Union law echo the arguments developing the concept of primacy of Community law in the context of EU constitutional law. The following two points are noteworthy in this context: that the specificity of the internal legal order – and the link with primacy – is established here with regard not to *Community*, but to *Union* law (a significant assertion in particular in the pre-Lisbon days); and that specificity and primacy come into play not only in relation to *national*, but also in relation to *international law*. The other side of the coin to these considerations (justifying the adoption of Union law notwithstanding the existence of a comprehensive Council of Europe Convention in the very same field) is the insertion of a disconnection clause by the EU in the body of the Council of Europe instrument.[110] Article 26(3) of the Convention states that

---

[106] Hunt, 'The Council of Europe Convention on the Prevention of Terrorism', above n 104, 606–607.

[107] See also, para 11 of the Explanatory Memorandum to the Convention.

[108] The Commission provided a similar justification when tabling recently a proposal to amend the EU Framework Decision on trafficking in human beings: the advantages of an EU approach were deemed to be related to the stronger bond created by the EU legal order, namely the immediate entering into force, and the monitoring and implementation, see COM (2009) 136 final, 7.

[109] Justice and Home Affairs Council, 'Conclusions of December 6–7' Council Doc 15966/07 Presse 275 (2007), 21. The integration of the Convention standards in the Union legal order has also been justified on the ground that the Framework Decision would 'trigger' the implementation of cooperation mechanisms under EU law, in particular as regards the exchange of information on terrorist offences between Member States and the transfer of such information to Europol and Eurojust. See comment by Tony McNulty, then a Home Office Minister, to the House of Commons European Scrutiny Committee, 26th Report (HC 2007–2008, 19-xxiv) para 26.3.

[110] The inclusion of disconnection clauses has been standard practice with regard to Council of Europe Conventions, in particular as regards recent Conventions in criminal matters. For an overview and typology of disconnection clauses used by the European Community/EU in Council of Europe

parties which are members of the European Union shall, in their mutual relations, apply Community and European Union rules in so far as there are Community or European Union rules governing the particular subject concerned and applicable to the specific case, without prejudice to the object and purpose of the present Convention and without prejudice to its full application with other parties.[111]

The wording of this clause tries to achieve a delicate balance between safeguarding the Community and Union *acquis*[112] (in particular as regards *the future*[113]) and preserving the autonomy and primacy of Community (and now Union) law[114] on the one hand, and alleviating concerns that such move might undermine the very regime established by the Council of Europe Convention on the other.[115] Such concerns reflect fears about the growing power of the EU, whose Member States now constitute the majority of Council of Europe members, and the impact of such power on the reach of Council of Europe rules.[116] From the point of view of

Conventions see International Law Commission 'Fragmentation of International Law: Difficulties arising from the Diversification and Expansion of International Law, Report of the Study Group of the International Law Commission (finalised by Martti Koskenniemi)' UN General Assembly Doc A/CN.4/L.682 (2006), paras 289–94.

[111] See also, the Declaration of Community competence annexed to the Convention, which reads as follows: 'The European Community/European Union and its Member States reaffirm that their objective in requesting the inclusion of a "disconnection clause" is to take account of the institutional structure of the Union when acceding to international conventions, in particular in case of transfer of sovereign powers from the Member States to the Community. This clause is not aimed at reducing the rights or increasing the obligations of a non-European Union Party vis-à-vis the European Community/EU and its Member States, inasmuch as the latter are also parties to this Convention. The disconnection clause is necessary for those parts of the Convention which fall within the competence of the Community/Union, in order to indicate that EU Member States cannot invoke and apply the rights and obligations deriving from the Convention directly among themselves (or between themselves and the European Community/EU). This does not detract from the fact that the Convention applies fully between the European Community/EU and its Member States on the one hand, and the other Parties to the Convention on the other; the Community and the EU Member States will be bound by the Convention and will apply it like any Party to the Convention, if necessary, through Community/Union legislation. They will thus guarantee the full respect of the Convention's provisions vis-à-vis non-EU Parties.

[112] For a categorisation of disconnection clauses as '*acquis*-saving clauses', see J Klabbers, 'Safeguarding the Organizational *Acquis*: The EU's External Practice' (2007) *International Organizations Law Review* 57, 70–71.

[113] See, in this context, the criticism that disconnection clauses are quite 'open' and subject to change – ILC, 'Fragmentation of International Law', above n 110, para 293. In this context, they are, however, similar to the Declarations of Community competence attached to the UN Conventions discussed above in 'Governing Crime via Global Multilateral Treaties'. However, the latter are also relevant for the determination of competence at EU level.

[114] For a discussion of disconnection clauses in the context of primacy in the first pillar, see M Cremona, 'Defending the Community Interest: the Duties of Cooperation and Compliance' in M Cremona and B de Witte (eds), *EU Foreign Relations Law. Constitutional Fundamentals* (Oxford and Portland, Oregon, Hart Publishing, 2008).

[115] See ILC, above n 110, para 294.

[116] According to the Deputy Secretary General of the Council of Europe, speaking in the context of the new EU proposals on trafficking in human beings and their relationship with the relevant Council of Europe Convention in the field (which also contains a disconnection clause): 'If EU legislation does not go as far as our Convention, for instance, as regards the 30 days recovery and reflection period, and if one applies the disconnection clause, we will find ourselves in a paradoxical situation of having two regimes applicable under the same Convention and a lower standard as compared to other parts of Europe.' Speech by M de Boer-Buquicchio, 'Who is fighting trafficking – who is not?' (Hearing on Human Trafficking, European Parliament, Brussels, 8 October 2008).

an international lawyer, the inclusion of such disconnection clauses in Council of Europe instruments is a matter of concern as it may lead to the fragmentation of international law.[117] However, from an EU law point of view, such concerns seem somewhat exaggerated: for *internal* Union law, efforts to safeguard the autonomy and primacy of the Community legal order are not something new;[118] for *EU external relations*, it is in the interests of the EU for Council of Europe standards to be enforced, as a key tool for EU policies with regard to candidate countries and its Council of Europe member neighbours.

Governing Crime via 'Soft' Law:
The EU and the Financial Action Task Force

The examination of interconnections between EU law and international law in criminal matters cannot be complete without an overview of the interconnections between Union law and global 'soft' law in the field. Nowhere are such interconnections better illustrated than by looking at the relationship between the European Community/Union and the FATF on money laundering (and now terrorist finance). The FATF is an ad hoc body, established by the G7 in 1989 within the auspices of the Organisation for Economic Co-operation and Development (OECD).[119] Its main normative output has been a series of Recommendations, evolving over time and covering a wide range of aspects of the fight against money laundering. The 40 FATF Recommendations produced in 1990 were revised in 1996, 2003 and 2012, with money laundering countermeasures being deemed necessary to counter a series of emerging and new threats, from drug trafficking to organised crime to terrorism.[120] The revisions of the FATF Recommendations have gone hand in hand with the renewal and gradual expansion of the FATF mandate to now include action against money laundering, the financing of terrorism and now proliferation.[121] In respect of its membership, the FATF can be

---

[117] See, in this context, the aforementioned Report by the International Law Commission, which examined disconnection clauses in the context of the fragmentation of international law. But see also the view of Klabbers, who notes that 'it is, indeed, no coincidence that the most ardent critics of the disconnection clause have to resort to systemic arguments (risk of increased fragmentation, undermining legal equality) rather than any concrete and enforceable legal norm'. J Klabbers, *Treaty Conflict and the European Union* (Cambridge, Cambridge University Press, 2009) 222.

[118] Although it is significant that disconnection clauses in Council of Europe instruments dealing with criminal law have perhaps been the closest we have come to safeguarding the primacy of *Union* (and not Community) law in the pre-Lisbon era.

[119] For a detailed analysis of the role and work of the FATF, see Gilmore, *Dirty Money*, above n 1, chs 4–6. Gilmore characterises the FATF as an 'ad hoc grouping of governments and others with a complex but highly focused agenda', ibid at 92.

[120] See V Mitsilegas, 'Countering the Chameleon Threat of Dirty Money: "Hard" and "Soft" Law in the Emergence of a Global Regime against Money Laundering and Terrorist Finance' in A Edwards and P Gill (eds), *Transnational Organised Crime: Perspectives on Global Security* (London, Routledge, 2003) 195–211.

[121] FATF, *Financial Action Task Force Mandate (2012–2020)* (Washington DC, FATF, 20 April 2012).

justifiably characterised as a rich countries club. This was particularly the case at its inception (it must be recalled that it was established by the G7 under the auspices of the OECD[122]), with its membership expanded since to include 'strategically important' countries and largely to reflect financial globalisation.[123] When looking at FATF membership today, it is striking that all 15 'old' EU Member States, along with the Commission, are now full FATF members. However, none of the 12 States which joined the EU in 2004 and 2007 is a FATF member (they are all members of MONEYVAL – the Committee of Experts on the Evaluation of Anti-Money Laundering Measures, established in 1997 under the auspices of the Council of Europe).[124]

The main output by the FATF in terms of normative production has been the 40 Recommendations, geared mainly towards the prevention of money laundering and first published in 1990. The Recommendations were revised in 1996 and 2003, and were complemented post-9/11 by a set of eight Special Recommendations on Terrorist Finance. Although these Recommendations are not strictly instruments of 'hard' international law, their influence on the development of EC/EU anti-money laundering law has been tremendous. Both the second and the third EC Directives in the field, adopted in 2001 and 2005 respectively, have been justified as reactions to international developments in the field. The second Money Laundering Directive[125] was justified by the Commission as necessary to implement (and go beyond) the revised FATF Recommendations of 1996.[126] Both main changes introduced by the Directive (namely the extension of the money laundering predicate offences and the extension of preventive duties to non-financial professions) were justified by reference to FATF findings and requirements: the Preamble to the Directive stated that there has been a trend in recent years towards a much wider definition of money laundering based on a broader range of predicate underlying offences, as reflected, for example, in the 1996 revision of the 40 Recommendations of the FATF, the leading international body devoted to the fight against money laundering.[127]

---

[122] Gilmore notes that in addition to the participants in the G7 summit establishing the FATF (Canada, France, Germany, Italy, Japan, the UK, the US and the Commission), eight other States (Australia, Austria, Belgium, Luxembourg, the Netherlands, Spain, Sweden and Switzerland) were invited to take part: Gilmore, above n 1, 89.

[123] The current membership criteria include, along with compliance with FATF standards, 'strategic importance': see FATF Membership Policy, available at www.fatf-gafi.org/pages/aboutus/membersandobservers/fatfmembershippolicy.html.

[124] See FATF, *FATF Members and Observers*, available at www.fatf-gafi.org/pages/aboutus/membersandobservers/.

[125] Directive 2001/97/EC of the European Parliament and of the Council of 4 December 2001 amending Council Directive 91/308/EEC on prevention of the use of the financial system for the purpose of money laundering [2001] OJ L344/76.

[126] 'Just as the 1991 Directive moved ahead of the original FATF 40 Recommendations in requiring obligatory suspicious transaction reporting, the European Union should continue to impose a high standard on its Member States, giving effect to or even going beyond the 1996 update of the FATF 40 Recommendations. In particular the EU can show the way in seeking to involve certain professions more actively in the fight against money laundering alongside the financial sector', COM (1999) 352 final, 3.

[127] Directive 2001/97/EC, above n 125, Preamble, recital 7.

It also accepted that there is a trend towards the increased use by money launderers of non-financial businesses as confirmed by the work of the FATF on money laundering techniques and typologies.[128]

On the basis of these findings, the Directive extended the list of predicate offences and the list of professions to be covered by the Directive obligations, to include, inter alia, lawyers.[129]

The third Money Laundering Directive was adopted in 2005.[130] Its aim was twofold: to extend the scope of the legislation also to cover the fight against terrorist finance, a key political priority in the post-9/11 world; and to update existing legislation in the light of international regulatory developments in the field, most notably as regards customer identification.[131] The Directive presents a major overhaul of the provisions on prevention – in particular those provisions on customer identification – in the light of the revised FATF Recommendations in the field, introducing a number of FATF-inspired concepts such as the so-called 'risk-based approach' to customer identification and more detailed provisions on beneficial ownership and 'politically exposed persons'.[132]

The influence of the FATF on the Community legal order is not limited to the successive Money Laundering Directives. The emphasis on terrorist finance this decade led to the adoption by the FATF of a series of 'Special Recommendations' on terrorist financing, reflecting the extension of the FATF mandate to cover the field. A number of Special Recommendations – which deal primarily with the surveillance of money flows – have now been implemented (quite swiftly) by the Union. These include a Regulation on controls of cash, which implements FATF Special Recommendation IX of 22 October 2004 and imposes, inter alia, requirements to declare cash over a certain threshold at the Union border;[133] a Regulation

---

[128] ibid, recital 14.

[129] Human rights concerns with regard to fair trial rights by the European Parliament have led to negotiations on the Directive being extended to the Conciliation stage – agreement was reached after the Directive was packaged as an emergency counter-terrorism measure in the weeks after 9/11. For an overview, see Mitsilegas, above n 2.

[130] Directive 2005/60/EC of the European Parliament and the Council of 26 October 2005 on the prevention of the use of the financial system for the purpose of money laundering and terrorist financing [2005] OJ L309/15.

[131] According to the Preamble, recital 5: 'Money laundering and terrorist financing are frequently carried out in an international context. Measures adopted solely at national or even Community level, without taking account of international coordination and cooperation, would have very limited effects. The measures adopted by the Community in this field should therefore be consistent with other action undertaken in other international fora. The Community action should continue to take particular account of the Recommendations of the Financial Action Task Force . . . which constitutes the foremost international body active in the fight against money laundering and terrorist financing. Since the FATF Recommendations were substantially revised and expanded in 2003, this Directive should be in line with the new international standard.'

[132] For further details and an overview of the Third Money Laundering Directive, see Mitsilegas and Gilmore, above n 12.

[133] Regulation (EC) No 1889/2005 of the European Parliament and of the Council of 26 October 2005 on controls of cash entering the Community [2005] OJ L309/9. See recitals 4 and 5 of the Preamble to the Regulation. Recital 4 states that 'Account should also be taken of complementary activities carried out in international *fora*, in particular those of the Financial Action task Force on Money Laundering . . . Special Recommendation IX of 22 October 2004 of the FATF calls on

on information on the payer accompanying wire transfers,[134] implementing FATF Special Recommendation VII on wire transfers (SR VII);[135] and a Directive on payment services in the internal market,[136] implementing FATF Special Recommendation VI on alternative remittance systems.[137] With the exception of the Special Recommendation on non-profit organisations (which has been dealt with by non legally-binding means at EU level), it can thus be seen that the 'preventive' FATF Special Recommendations have been implemented swiftly by the Union, and primarily in the form of Regulations (which are directly applicable across the EU).[138] This swift adoption is noteworthy in view of the potential conflict of some of these provisions with EU law. Along with the question of the existence of Community competence as regards the Cash Controls Regulation at the time,[139] there are also questions about the compatibility of these measures with the development of the Union as an area without internal frontiers. A number of these provisions are essentially about the surveillance of money flows, which arguably constitutes an obstacle to the free movement of capital – with the Union already having to convince the FATF about the impossibility of imposing controls of cash within the internal borders of Member States.[140]

The influence of the FATF Recommendations on the evolution of EU anti-money laundering law has continued to be strong in the latest proposals tabled by the European Commission with the aim of aligning EU law with the latest revisions of the FATF Recommendations in 2012. This influence is evident in the Commission's impact assessment accompanying the proposal for a fourth Money Laundering Directive, according to which one of the key 'problem drivers' is that the existing EU rules are inconsistent with the recently revised international anti-money laundering standards and explains that

---

governments to take measures to detect physical cash movements, including a declaration system or other disclosure obligation.'

[134] Regulation (EC) No 1781/2006 of the European Parliament and of the Council of 15 November 2006 on information on the payer accompanying transfers of funds [2006] OJ L345/1.

[135] According to the Preamble, recital 2, to the Regulation: 'In order to facilitate their criminal activities, money launderers and terrorist financiers could try to take advantage of the freedom of capital movements entailed by the integrated financial area, unless certain coordinating measures are adopted at Community level. By its scale, Community action should ensure that Special Recommendation VII on wire transfers (SR VII) of the Financial Action Task Force . . . is transposed uniformly throughout the European Union, and, in particular, that there is no discrimination between national payments within a Member State and cross-border payments between Member States.'

[136] [2007] OJ L319/1.

[137] See Council Doc 8864/1/09 REV 1 (2009).

[138] For further details and an evaluation in the light of the FATF standards, see Mitsilegas and Gilmore, above n 12, 130.

[139] ibid.

[140] According to the Report on the implementation of the revised Strategy on Terrorist Financing (Council Doc, above n 137, 2: 'After almost 2 years of discussion, a global agreement on an amended FATF methodology on FATF Special Recommendation IX on cash controls at the borders was reached at the February 2009 meeting in Paris. This agreement acknowledges the specificity of the EU as one jurisdiction and the possibility for it to be compliant with SR IX without (re)introducing controls at Member States' internal borders.'

there is a strong incentive on jurisdictions to correct inconsistencies with the international standards. Full compliance can send an important reputational signal which is vital for countries seeking to attract foreign investment. Non-compliance on the other hand is subject to an attentive follow-up process by the FATF or MONEYVAL. Persistent non-compliance can lead to inclusion in one of the FATF's Public Statements political and reputational damage.[141]

The Commission's Explanatory Note to the proposal for a fourth Money Laundering Directive argues that 'a revision of the Directive at this time is complementary to the revised FATF Recommendations, which in themselves represent a substantial strengthening of the anti-money laundering and combating terrorist financing framework'.[142] The need to align EU law to the revised FATF Recommendations is also reflected in the Preamble to the Directive.[143] A major step in this direction has been the extension of the scope of the money laundering predicate offences to include tax offences.[144]

The drive to align EU law with the revised 2102 FATF Recommendations is also evident in the Commission's proposal for a Regulation on information accompanying transfers of funds which accompanied the proposal for the fourth Money Laundering Directive.[145] The Explanatory Note to the draft Regulation acknowledges that Regulation 1781/2006 which it seeks to amend was to a large extent based on FATF Special Recommendation VII on wire transfers but that a new set of FATF Recommendations has been adopted in 2012.[146] The new Regulation is justified in a three-fold manner by the Commission: in order to align EU law with the new FATF Recommendations which the FATF 'is constantly seeking to improve';[147] in order to ensure a common approach between EU Member States in order to address the ongoing evaluation of the implementation of the FATF Recommendations on the one hand[148] and ensure the free movement of capital and non-discrimination within the EU on the other;[149] and in order to foster a coherent approach in the international context.[150] It is revealing in this context

---

[141] Commission, 'Impact Assessment accompanying the proposal for a Directive on the prevention of the use of the financial system for the purpose of money laundering including terrorist financing and the proposal for a Regulation on information accompanying transfers of funds' (Staff Working Document) SWD (2013) 21 final, 18.

[142] Commission, 'Proposal for a Directive on the prevention of the use of the financial system for the purpose of money laundering including terrorist financing' COM (2013) 45 final, 3.

[143] Recital 4 states that: 'The measures adopted by the European Union in the field should therefore be consistent with other action undertaken in other international fora. The European Union action should continue to take particular account of the FATF Recommendations the FATF constitutes the foremost international body active in the fight against money laundering' – Directives 2005/60/EC and 2006/70/EC should be aligned with the new FATF Recommendations adopted and expanded in February 2012.

[144] Art 3(4)(f) of the draft Directive. See also, Preamble, recital 9, stating specifically that it is important to align tax crimes in line with the FATF Recommendations.

[145] COM (2013) 44 final.

[146] Page 2.

[147] Preamble, recital 3.

[148] ibid.

[149] Preamble, recital 2.

[150] Preamble, recital 5.

that the Commission views the alignment of EU law with the FATF Recommendations not only necessary to ensure compliance with the FATF requirements at EU level, but also to ensure the coherence of the global anti-money laundering regime whose main elements as developed by the FATF are accepted uncritically in the EU legal order.

The influence of FATF standards on the EU legal order is noteworthy. These standards have been developed by a single agenda, ad hoc body, with selective membership and a minimum of transparency and accountability in its operations.[151] In turn, the FATF depoliticised expert orthodoxy in terms of both money laundering typologies and the necessary measures to counter the phenomenon[152] has constantly been renewed,[153] and every time uncritically adopted by the European Commission (influencing, along with a number – but not all – of EU Member States the evolution of the FATF standards, being itself an FATF member) in its proposals for Community and Union law in the field and subsequently by Member States in the Council. In this manner, a specific agenda developed by technocrats and with limited scrutiny at the global level has been legitimised, via the EC and EU decision-making process, and adopted at the Union level to bind both FATF and non-FATF members. The compliance of non-FATF EU members is ensured not only by the introduction of FATF 'soft' law in the EU legal order via clearly legally binding EU standards, but also by the membership of these states in MONEYVAL, the FATF-style regional body operating within the auspices of the

[151] For thoughts on the issues of transparency and accountability, which are relevant in the context of the FATF, see also, J Cohen and CF Sabel, 'Global Democracy?' (2004–2005) 37 *NYU Journal of International Law and Policy* 763, who note that 'to a substantial and growing extent, then, rulemaking directly affecting the freedom of action of individuals, firms, and nation states (and the making of the rules to regulate this rulemaking) is taking place, undemocratically but not entirely unaccountably, in global settings created by the world's nations but no longer under their effective control' (at 764).

[152] On various aspects of what I call the 'depoliticisation' in the development of global standards, see A Somek, 'Administration without Sovereignty' (2009) University of Iowa Legal Studies Research Paper 09-04, available at http://papers.ssrn.com/sol3/papers.cfm?abstract_id=1333282 (noting that 'where "problem-solving" serves as the preferred descriptor of an activity, ideological conflict does not enter the picture. Problem-solving is the antithesis of political struggle' at 17); J Klabbers, 'Institutional Ambivalence by Design: Soft Organizations in International Law' (2001) 70 *Nordic Journal of International Law* 403 (noting that 'the facility of doing business without being side-tracked or controlled, dovetails neatly with our late-modern (or postmodern) infatuation for management and technocracy as viable substitutes for politics' at 417); D Kennedy, 'Challenging Expert Rule: The Politics of Global Governance' (2005) 27 *Sydney Law Review* 5 (talking inter alia about 'the expert consensus'). For a more positive view, see AM Slaughter, *A New World Order* (Princeton, Princeton University Press, 2004). Slaughter views the FATF typologies as 'important opportunities for operational experts to identify and describe current money laundering trends and effective countermeasures' and stresses the benefits of professional socialisation (at 54). Slaughter promotes the advantages of what she calls 'government networks', marrying hard and soft power and using information, persuasion and socialisation (at 168 *et seq*).

[153] Kennedy notes in this context that progress narratives become policy programmes, 'both by solidifying a professional consensus and by defining what counts as progress for the international governance system as a whole' (Kennedy, 'Challenging Expert Rule', above n 152, 25). In the context of the FATF, the regular revision of both mandate and standards has been easier when compared to a more formal international organisation; see, in this context, A Boyle, 'Some Reflections on the Relationship of Treaties and Soft Law' (1999) 48 *International and Comparative Law Quarterly* 901, who notes that soft law instruments are easier to amend or replace than treaties (at 903).

Council of Europe. MONEYVAL membership consists primarily of countries from Central and Eastern Europe, both EU and non-EU members. The establishment of a specific peer review mechanism for these states serves to ensure that the FATF peer review was complemented for non-members in Europe, but also serves to ensure compliance of these states with EU standards in the field – as MONEYVAL benchmarks are not limited to Council of Europe standards but also include FATF, UN and *EU* anti-money laundering standards.[154]

Thus, in addition to the introduction of FATF standards in the EU legal order, a key factor which has ensured the implementation of the FATF model in the EU has been the emphasis on the evaluation of such implementation not only through the traditional compliance methods of EU law, but also through a process of mutual evaluation and peer review which is inherent in the work of the FATF and its regional-style bodies such as MONEYVAL, but which has also been influential in the internal EU constitutional framework.[155] The growing assertiveness of the EU in the production of multilateral standards in criminal matters in more traditional international *fora* such as the United Nations or the Council of Europe can only indirectly be confirmed in the context of the FATF, in large part owing to the lack of transparency in the production of 'soft law' in the field. At the same time, the EU has emerged as a major player in adopting in its internal legal order, via legally binding measures, the FATF standards in their constant evolution. The EU has also been instrumental in establishing a far-reaching, multilayered framework of mutual evaluation and compliance bringing together the mechanisms employed by the FATF, the Council of Europe (and in particular, the innovative compliance mechanisms under MONEYVAL) and the EU itself. In this manner, 'soft law' has perhaps proved to have harder teeth than the multilateral conventions in the field.

Governing Crime via 'Global Administrative Law': The EU and the UN Security Council

Calls for global, emergency counter-terrorism action post-9/11 have not resulted in the adoption of measures in the form of the traditional multilateral 'hard law' Conventions at the level of the United Nations. Rather, global standards have been adopted and promoted principally under the format of what legal scholars have labelled 'global administrative law'.[156] It has been noted that

---

[154] See the MONEYVAL terms of reference at www.coe.int/dghl/monitoring/moneyval/Evaluations/About_evaluation_en.asp.
[155] On the emergence of peer review mechanisms in EU law, see V Mitsilegas, 'The European Union and the Globalisation of Criminal Law' (2009–2010) 12 *Cambridge Yearbook of European Legal Studies* 337.
[156] B Kingsbury, N Krisch and RB Stewart, 'The Emergence of Global Administrative Law' (2004–2005) 68 *Law and Contemporary Problems* 15.

underlying the emergence of global administrative law is the vast increase in the reach and forms of transgovernmental regulation and administration designed to address the consequences of globalized interdependence in such fields as security . . . much in the detail and implementation of such regulation is determined by transnational adminis-trative bodies – including international organizations and informal groups of officials-that perform administrative functions but are not directly subject to control by national governments or domestic legal systems or, in the case of treaty-based regimes, the states parties to the treaty.[157]

It is contested whether all or some of the norms included under the rubric of 'global administrative law' can really be classified as 'law'.[158] However, the term is a useful analytical tool in focusing on the *process* of the adoption of norms and in this context highlighting key differences between the development of global norms in this context and the traditional adoption of multilateral legally binding treaties. The production of normative standards at the level of 'global administra-tive law' or 'government networks' differs from the adoption of multilateral, expressly legally binding standards at the multilateral level in four main respects: standards are put forward by a limited number of states without the need for a global consensus; standards are adopted with a minimum of transparency; stand-ards are adopted speedily (a factor which may explain the appeal of this form of normative production in times of perceived emergency); and standards are not explicitly legally binding rules of general application, but in reality have far-reach-ing consequences for law reform around the world.

The adoption of preventive counter-terrorism sanctions by the UN Security Council constitutes a prime example of global administrative law in this context. The production of normative standards in criminal matters by the UN Security Council has been linked to global counter-terrorism efforts as part of a two-fold strategy. The first element of this strategy has been the adoption, which began before 9/11, of a set of Resolutions specifically targeting the Taliban, Osama bin Laden, Al-Qaida and those associated with them. The first step in this direction was Resolution 1267 (1999), which imposed a series of restrictive measures against the Taliban, including an arms embargo, banning travel and the freezing of funds. In the latter context, paragraph 4(b) of the Resolution called on States to freeze funds and other financial resources, including funds derived or generated from property owned or controlled directly or indirectly by the Taliban, or by any undertaking owned or controlled by the Taliban, and to ensure that neither they nor any other funds or financial resources so designated are made available, by their nationals or by any persons within their territory, to or for the benefit of the Taliban or any undertaking owned or controlled, directly or indirectly, by the Taliban, except as may be authorised on the grounds of humanitarian need. The designation of those targeted by such measures and the consideration of excep-

---

[157] ibid, 16.
[158] See, in this context, B Kingsbury, 'The Concept of 'Law in Global Administrative Law' (2009) 20 *European Journal of International Law* 23; and A Somek, 'The Concept of 'Law' in Global Administrative Law: A Reply to Benedict Kingsbury' (2009) 20 *European Journal of International Law* 985.

tions will be made by a Sanctions Committee, established in paragraph 6 of the Resolution. Resolution 1333 (2000) extended the freezing regime expressly to individuals in the Al-Qaida organisation and requested the Sanctions Committee to maintain an up-to-date list of the individuals and entities designated as being associated with bin Laden, including those in Al-Qaida.[159] The next substantive amendment to the sanctions regime came about after 9/11, with Resolution 1390(2002).[160] The latter adjusted the content of Resolution 1267 to take into account political developments since its adoption but continued and consolidated the freezing regime established in paragraph 4(b) thereof. The Resolution urged all States to take immediate steps to enforce and strengthen through legislative enactments or administrative measures, where appropriate, the measures imposed under domestic laws or regulations against their nationals and other individuals or entities operating in their territory, to prevent and punish violations of the measures referred to in paragraph 2 of this resolution, including the freezing of funds.[161] The substantive and procedural elements of these Resolutions have been revised since, without changing fundamentally the emphasis on economic sanctions against specific individuals as a key Security Council counter-terrorism strategy.[162]

The emphasis on the adoption of legislative measures is even more prominent in the second element of the Security Council counter-terrorism strategy. Resolution 1373(2001), adopted less than three weeks after the 9/11 attacks, called upon all States in particular to prevent and suppress the financing of terrorist acts; criminalise terrorism finance; and extend the freezing regime to cover in general persons who commit or attempt to commit terrorist acts or participate in or facilitate the commission of such acts, entities owned or controlled directly or indirectly by such persons, and persons and entities acting on their behalf or direction.[163] Resolution 1373 expressly called upon all States to ensure that any person who participates in the financing, planning, preparation or perpetration of terrorist acts or in supporting terrorist acts is brought to justice, and to ensure that, in addition to any other measures against them, such terrorist acts are established as serious criminal offences in domestic laws and regulations and that the punishment duly reflects the seriousness of such terrorist acts.[164] It also called upon all States, inter alia, to become parties as soon as possible to the relevant international conventions and protocols relating to terrorism, including the International Convention for the Suppression of the Financing of Terrorism of 9 December 1999.[165]

---

[159] Para 8(c).

[160] In the meantime, Resolution 1363 (2001) had established a mechanism to monitor the implementation of Resolutions 1267 and 1333.

[161] Para 8.

[162] See, in this context, inter alia, Resolution 1452 (2002) amending the scope of sanctions of Resolutions 1267 and 1390; and Resolutions 1735 (2006) and 1822 (2008) introducing in particular changes in the procedures of the Sanctions Committee.

[163] Para 1(a) –(c).

[164] Para 2(e).

[165] Para 3(d).

In this manner, the international community witnessed the production of global normative standards in the field of counter-terrorism outside the framework of the multilateral treaty. This shift did not go unnoticed by international lawyers, who stressed the Security Council's 'legislative' role.[166] In this context, it has been pointed out that Resolution 1373 is of general and abstract character and does not name a single country, society or group of people;[167] that with Resolution 1373, together with the related efforts of its 1267 Sanctions Committee, the Council is no longer responding with discrete action directed at a particular state because of a concrete threat to peace arising from a specific incident;[168] and that Resolution 1373 imposed general obligations on all States for an indefinite period, while Resolution 1267 set up a sanctions committee with court-like powers to identify and freeze the assets of individuals, groups and corporations.[169] This production of normative standards by the Security Council has been criticised as undemocratic on the grounds of the limited transparency of Security Council negotiations,[170] of the adoption of the Resolutions (in particular 1373) speedily as emergency measures,[171] and last, but not least, on the ground of the selective membership of the Security Council. It has been forcefully pointed out that 'a patently unrepresentative and undemocratic body such as the Council is arguably unsuitable for international lawmaking' and that: 'Council practice may be criticised as contrary to the basic structure of international law as a consent-based legal order.'[172] It has also been argued that the Resolutions 'circumvent the "vehicle *par excellence* of community interest", namely the multilateral treaty', and that as such they serve to promote the interests of a limited number of State actors.[173] It must be noted in this context that the Resolutions do not only impose an extensive normative restrictive counter-terrorism framework, but also aim to ensure and accelerate the implementation of the enforcement standards adopted in a pre-existing multilateral treaty, the 1999 Convention on Terrorist Finance.[174] In a

---

[166] See, in particular, S Talmon, 'The Security Council as World Legislature' (2005) 99 *American Journal of International Law* 175; JE Alvarez, 'Hegemonic International Law Revisited' (2003) 97 *American Journal of International Law* 873.

[167] Talmon, 'The Security Council as World Legislature', above n 166, 176–77.

[168] Alvarez, 'Hegemonic International Law Revisited', above n 166, 874.

[169] I Johnstone, 'Legislation and Adjudication in the UN Security Council: Bringing Down the Deliberative Deficit' (2008) 102 *American Journal of International Law* 275, 283.

[170] See, in particular, Talmon, above n 166, 190.

[171] See ibid, 187, and the detailed analysis of Johnstone, 'Legislation and Adjudication in the UN Security Council', above n 169, 284.

[172] Talmon, above n 166, 179.

[173] Alvarez, above n 166, 874–75. Alvarez examines in detail US influence in the passage of the Security Council Resolutions. See also, Johnstone, above n 169, 300 who points out that multilateral treaty negotiations tend to balance global concerns, leading to trade-offs and bargains that account for a wider range of interests than typically come out of Security Council negotiations.

[174] See, in this context, the criticism of Alvarez, who notes that: 'In Resolution 1373 the Council selected certain provisions of the then recently concluded International Convention for the Suppression of the Financing of Terrorism, added to others, and omitted other portions of the Convention (such as the explicit deference to other requirements of international law, including the rights due to persons charged with terrorism-related offences, the rights of extradited persons, the requisites of international humanitarian law, and the provisions on judicial dispute settlement', above n 166, 875.

departure from the consensus required for the adoption of legally binding provisions in a multilateral international treaty, in the case of the UN Security Council
far-reaching norms are produced by a body operating with a limited agenda,
membership, transparency or scrutiny. What makes this departure even more
striking is that, in the counter-terrorism Resolutions, the individual (targeted by a
series of sanctions) directly enters the realm of a system primarily designed to
address inter-state relations.[175] What renders the reach of these Resolutions even
wider is that, in addition to the fact that they target individuals directly, they leave
(in particular Resolution 1267) States and international organisations such as the
EU with very limited discretion as to how to implement them. As Krisch has elo-
quently noted, insofar as Member State implementation is necessary to give measures effect, States' action is reduced to a subordinate, non-discretionary role in
the overall administrative machinery directed by the Council and its committees,
resulting in a significant reduction of the distance between national and international law in this domain and leading to an increasing enmeshment between those
layers.[176]

Implementation of the UN Security Council Resolutions by the EU

The Resolutions have been implemented at EU level via a combination of cross-
pillar legal instruments. Implementation of the first set of Resolutions, targeting
the Taliban, bin Laden and Al-Qaida and their associates, followed shortly after
the adoption of the measures by the Security Council and consisted of second pillar Common Positions combined with first pillar Regulations. Council Common
Position of 15 November 1999 concerning restrictive measures against the Taliban
(1999/727/CFSP),[177] adopted under Article 15 TEU, stated that action by the
Community is needed in order to implement the measures cited therein[178] and
called inter alia for flight bans[179] and for funds and other financial resources held
abroad by the Taliban under the conditions set out in UNSCR 1267(1999) to be
frozen.[180] The Common Position was accompanied by Council Regulation (EC)
No 337/2000 of 14 February 2000 concerning a flight ban and a freeze of funds
and other financial resources in respect of the Taliban of Afghanistan,[181] adopted
under Articles 60 and 301 EC. Counter-terrorism action under the first pillar was
justified by stating that the measures set out in paragraph 4 of Resolution 1267
(1999) fall under the scope of the Treaty and, therefore, notably with a view to

---

[175] See, especially, in this context, PC Szasz, 'The Security Council Starts Legislating' (2002) 96
American Journal of International Law 901; Johnstone, above n 169, 295.
[176] N Krisch, *Beyond Constitutionalism. The Pluralist Structure of Postnational Law* (Oxford, Oxford
University Press, 2010) 156–57.
[177] [1999] OJ L294/1.
[178] Preamble, recital 2.
[179] Art 1.
[180] Art 2.
[181] [2000] OJ L43/1.

avoiding distortion of competition, Community legislation is necessary to implement the relevant decisions of the Security Council as far as the territory of the
Community is concerned.[182] The Regulation stated inter alia that all funds and
other financial resources designated by the Taliban Sanctions Committee will be
frozen and that no funds or other financial resources designated by the Taliban
Sanctions Committee will be made available to or for the benefit of the Taliban or
any undertaking owned or controlled, directly or indirectly, by the Taliban.[183]
Thus, the Regulation, in combination with the Common Position, established a
system of sanctions at Community level by reference to the sanctions adopted at
the UN Security Council.

The same approach was adopted in order to implement Resolution 1333
(2000). A Council Common Position was adopted under Article 15 TEU,[184]
accompanied by a first pillar Regulation adopted under Articles 60 and 301 EC[185]
with Community competence and action justified in a similar manner as to the
adoption of Regulation 337/2000.[186] The measures continued the Community
sanctions regime established by reference to Security Council sanctions. The system was renewed, with some changes, at the implementation of Resolution 1390
(2002). A Council Common Position was again adopted under Article 15 TEU.[187]
However, the legal basis to the parallel first pillar Regulation was extended to
include, along with Articles 60 and 301 TEC, Article 308 TEC.[188] The addition of
Article 308 to the legal basis of Regulation 881/2002 has been attributed to the
need to take account of political developments taking place at the time. By January
2002 the Taliban regime in Afghanistan had fallen and so at the time the
Regulation was adopted, the persons and entities listed did not have a direct connection with the territory or governing regime of a third country. The initial
choice of legal bases of Articles 60 and 301 TEC, which was based on the principle
that the individuals and entities listed were in effective control of the territory of a

---

[182] Preamble, recital 3.

[183] Art 3.

[184] Council Common Position of 26 February 2001 concerning additional restrictive measures
against the Taliban and amending Common Position 96/746/CFSP (2001/154/CFSP) [2001] OJ L57/1.

[185] Council Regulation (EC) No 467/2001 of 6 March 2001 prohibiting the export of certain goods
and services to Afghanistan, strengthening the flight ban and extending the freeze of funds and other
financial resources in respect of the Taliban of Afghanistan and repealing Regulation (EC) No 337/2000
[2001] OJ L67/1.

[186] According to recital 3, Resolution 1333 (as with its predecessor 1267) fell under the scope of the
Treaty and, therefore, notably with a view to avoiding distortion of competition, Community legislation was necessary to implement the relevant decisions of the Security Council, as far as the territory
of the Community is concerned.

[187] Council Common Position of 27 May 2002 concerning restrictive measures against Osama bin
Laden, members of the Al-Qaida organisation and the Taliban and other individuals, groups, under-
takings and entities associated with them and repealing Common Positions 96/746/CFSP, 1999/727/
CFSP, 2001/154/CFSP and 2001/771/CFSP (2002/402/CFSP) [2002] OJ L139/4.

[188] Council Regulation (EC) No 881/2002 of 27 May 2002 imposing certain specific restrictive
measures directed against certain persons and entities associated with Osama bin Laden, the Al-Qaida
network and the Taliban, and repealing Council Regulation (EC) No 467/2001 [2002] OJ L139/9. As
with the earlier Regulations, the avoidance of the distortion of competition was evoked as necessitating
Community implementation of the relevant Security Council measures (Preamble, recital 4).

third country, or were associated with those in effective control and provided them with financial support was thus deemed no longer adequate to address the situation in Afghanistan.[189] Under this technique, sanctions against individuals not linked with the government or the control of a country now fall clearly under the scope of Community law,[190] with Regulation 881/2002 consolidating and expanding the sanctions regime in the light of developments in the Security Council.[191] Parallel second and first pillar measures were adopted subsequently under the same legal bases, including measures implementing the exceptions to the sanctions regime introduced by Resolution 1452(2002),[192] while the list of individuals or entities subject to the Community sanctions regime is being regularly updated by Commission Regulations introducing the amendments in the lists made by the Sanctions Committee into the Community legal order.[193]

A slightly different strategy was followed to implement Resolution 1373 in the Community and Union legal order. The contents of Resolution 1373 were split into two separate Council Common Positions: one concerning the general requirement for States to take action at the level of criminalisation, prevention and prosecution;[194] and one specifically concerning sanctions against individuals.[195] Adopted as emergency measures a few weeks after 9/11 (and the adoption of Resolution 1373), the Common Positions were adopted under a joint second and third pillar legal basis (Articles 15 and 34 TEU). The first, 'general' Common

---

[189] See M Cremona, 'EC Competence, "Smart Sanctions" and the *Kadi* Case' (2009) 28 *Yearbook of European Law* 559, 569. Cremona explains in detail the evolution of the interpretation of Arts 60(1) and 301 EC in Community legislation prior to the adoption of the Regulations in question. She notes that although neither of these provisions expressly mentions individuals, referring rather to 'economic relations with one or more third countries' the concept has been broadly interpreted, in the first place to allow for targeted sanctions against natural and legal persons who are connected to a government or regime – the aim being to put pressure on a third State by taking measures against those people or entities who are either part of the government or closely connected with it (at 567–68).

[190] It is noteworthy that the Preamble to Regulation 881/2002 also contains references to Resolution 1373, which extends the scope of economic sanctions beyond the Taliban (recital 3).

[191] See in particular, Arts 2, 4 and 6 of the Regulation.

[192] Council Common Position 2003/140/CFSP of 27 February 2003 concerning exceptions to the restrictive measures imposed by Common Position 2002/402/CFSP [2003] OJ L53/62; Council Regulation (EC) No 561/2003 of 27 March 2003 amending, as regards exceptions to the freezing of funds and economic resources, Regulation (EC) No 881/2002 [2003] OJ L82/1.

[193] The latest at the time of writing: Commission Regulation (EU) No 110/2010 of 5 February 2010 amending for the 120th time Council Regulation (EC) No 881/2002 imposing certain specific restrictive measures directed against certain persons and entities associated with Osama bin Laden, the Al-Qaida network and the Taliban [2010] OJ L36/9.

[194] Council Common Position of 27 December 2001 on combating terrorism (2001/930/CFSP) [2001] OJ L344/90. Along with general provisions on the freezing of funds and refraining from making funds available for terrorism, the Common Position calls inter alia for the criminalisation of terrorist finance (Art 1, elements of the definition being copied from Resolution 1373), the suppression of support for terrorism (Art 4), prevention (Art 5) and bringing persons who participate in the financing, planning, preparation or perpetration of terrorist acts to justice (Art 8). The Common Position further calls upon Member States to become parties as soon as possible to the relevant international conventions and protocols relating to terrorism listed in the annex to the Common Position (including the 1999 Terrorist Finance Convention – Art 14).

[195] Council Common Position of 27 December 2001 on the application of specific measures to combat terrorism (2001/931/CFSP) [2001] OJ L344/93.

Position contains both provisions on freezing and provisions related to general obligations of criminalisation and prevention, ordinarily covered at the time by the third pillar. The second, 'sanctions' Common Position included both provisions on sanctions, and a general provision on cooperation and assistance between Member States (Article 4), also deemed to fall under the then third pillar. This Common Position was again accompanied by a first pillar Regulation adopted under Articles 60, 301 and 308 TEC.[196] According to the Preamble to the Regulation, Community action was necessary in order to implement the CFSP aspects of Common Position 2001/931/CFSP.[197] The absence of a reference to the necessity of Community action to prevent distortion of competition (a model followed in the Regulations implementing the other Security Council sanctions Resolutions described above) is noteworthy in this context. Community action is here justified in order to implement the second pillar elements of the parallel Common Position. In this manner, an autonomous system of Community sanctions has been established, complementing the system where UN sanctions are copied by the Community described in the paragraphs above.[198] Listing is done at the Community level, and the relevant lists are updated on a regular basis, this time by Council (and not Commission) instruments.[199]

Judicial Review of the EU Implementation of UN Security Council Resolutions: *Kadi I*

The relationship between Union law and the emergence of international norms in criminal matters has been tested extensively in litigation involving challenges to the EC/EU implementation of UN Security Council Resolutions. The *Kadi I* litigation involved rulings by both the Court of First Instance[200] and, on appeal, the Court of Justice.[201] Along with the constitutionality of the Union legislator's choice of legal basis to implement UN Security Council Resolution 1267, which the Court has managed to accommodate,[202] the main issue at stake was the request by the applicants for the annulment of Regulation 467/2001 which, along with

---

[196] Council Regulation (EC) No 2580/2001 of 27 December 2001 on specific restrictive measures directed against certain persons and entities with a view to combating terrorism [2001] OJ L344/70.

[197] Recital 3.

[198] For a categorisation and overview of the various strands of the Community sanctions regime, see C Eckes, *EU Counter-Terrorist Policies and Fundamental Rights. The Case of Individual Sanctions* (Oxford, Oxford University Press, 2009).

[199] For the latest list, at the time of writing, see Council Decision 2009/1004/CFSP of 22 December 2009 updating the list of persons, groups and entities subject to Articles 2, 3 and 4 of Common Position 2001/931/CFSP on the application of specific measures to combat terrorism [2009] OJ L346/58.

[200] Case T-315/01 *Yassin Abdullah Kadi v Council and Commission* [2005] ECR II-3649; Case T-306/01 *Ahmed Ali Yussuf and Al Barakaat International Foundation v Council and Commission* [2005] ECR II-3533.

[201] Joined Cases C-402/05P and C-415/05P *Yassin Abdullah Kadi and Al Barakaat International Foundation v Council and Commission* [2008] ECR I-6351.

[202] For details, see Mitsilegas, 'The European Union and the Globalisation of Criminal Law', above n 155.

Common Position 2001/154/CFSP, implemented Security Council Resolution 1333(2000) on the ground of the breach of their fundamental rights.[203] The assertion of Community competence for the adoption of economic sanctions against individuals rendered the answer to the other main claim of the applicants, namely that the measures in question were in breach of fundamental rights, central in determining the relationship between Security Council norms and Union law and the position of the individual therein. At the heart of this issue is the question of the extent to which measures implementing Security Council Resolutions can be reviewed in the light of Community law. The Court of First Instance took a very narrow view, essentially ruling that it could only review the lawfulness of the norms in question with regard to *jus cogens*.[204] This ruling was rightly criticised for disregarding the autonomy of the Community legal order and for limiting the avenues for review on the grounds of fundamental rights.[205] In this context, the CFI ruling was marked by an uncritical deference to the security logic underpinning executive counter-terrorism action as embodied in this context by the Security Council measures.[206]

On appeal however, the Court of Justice responded with a remarkable departure from the CFI reasoning and outcome in a judgment linking the importance of respect for fundamental rights and the rule of law with the autonomy of the Community legal order. The Court began by stressing unequivocally that the Community is based on the rule of law,[207] adding that fundamental rights form an integral part of the general principles of law the observance of which the Court ensures,[208] that respect for human rights is a condition for the lawfulness of Community acts, and that measures incompatible with respect for human rights are not acceptable in the Community.[209] At the same time, the Court stressed the *autonomy* of the Community legal order, by stating that an international agreement could not affect the allocation of powers fixed by the Treaties or, consequently, the autonomy of the Community legal system,[210] adding that the obligations imposed by an international agreement could not have the effect of

---

[203] See above, 'Governing Crime via Regional Multilatral Treaties'. For a background to the legal framework of the case, see paras 11–45 of the *Kadi* ECJ ruling.

[204] *Kadi*, above n 200, paras 226 *et seq; Yusuf and Al Barakaat*, above n 200, paras 277 *et seq*.

[205] See, in particular, P Eeckhout, 'Community Terrorism Listings, Fundamental Rights, and UN Security Council Resolutions. In Search of the Right Fit' (2007) 3 *European Constitutional Law Review* 183.

[206] See, in this context, J Murkens, 'Countering Anti-Constitutional Argument: The Reasons for the European Court of Justice's Decision in Kadi and Al Barakaat' (2008–2009) 11 *Cambridge Yearbook of European Legal Studies* 15.

[207] Para 281.

[208] Para 283. The Court noted the special significance of the ECHR in this context referring to its ruling on the compatibility of the second Money Laundering Directive with fundamental rights – see above 'Judicial Review of the EU Implementation of UN Security Council Resolutions – *Kadi I*'.

[209] Para 284. The Court also stressed that the wording of Treaty Articles such as 297 and 307 EC cannot be understood as derogating from or challenging the principles of liberty, democracy and respect for human rights and fundamental freedoms enshrined in 6(1) TEU as a foundation of the Union, see paras 303–304.

[210] Para 282.

prejudicing the constitutional principles of the EC Treaty.[211] In this context, the Court noted that the primacy of international agreements in Community law would not extend to primary law, in particular to the general principles of which fundamental rights form part.[212] In this light, the review by the Court of the validity of any Community measure in the light of fundamental rights had to be considered the expression, in a community based on the rule of law, of a constitutional guarantee stemming from the EC Treaty as an autonomous legal system which is not to be prejudiced by an international agreement.[213]

The Court combined these two lines of reasoning to assert its power to review the measures in question. In this context, the Court was careful to specify that the review of lawfulness to be ensured by the Community judicature applies to the *Community* act intended to give effect to the international agreement at issue, and not to the latter as such.[214] The Court thus attempted to draw a distinction between review of Community measures (which it had the power to conduct), and review of UN measures (which fell outside its jurisdiction, even under *jus cogens*).[215] According to the Court, while for the purposes of the interpretation of the contested Regulation account had to be taken of the wording of Resolution 1390 (2002),[216] the UN Charter did not impose the choice of a particular model of the implementation of resolutions.[217] Moreover, the Regulation in question was not directly attributable to the UN.[218] The Court thus asserted its power for the full review, in principle, of the lawfulness of all Community acts in the light of fundamental rights.[219] It therefore found that the CFI had erred in law in this context.[220]

The Court then reviewed the Regulation and annulled it (setting aside the CFI judgment) finding that the rights of the defence, in particular the right to be heard, and the right to effective judicial review of those rights, were patently not respected,[221] and that the measures entailed an unjustified restriction of Mr Kadi's right to property.[222] However, the Court also ruled that the freezing of funds could not per se be regarded as inappropriate or disproportionate 'with reference to an objective of general interest as fundamental to the international community as the fight by all means against the threats to international peace posed by acts of terrorism'.[223]

---

[211] Para 285.

[212] Para 308.

[213] Para 316.

[214] Para 286 (emphasis added).

[215] Para 287. The Court further noted that any judgment given by the Community judicature deciding that a Community measure intended to give effect to such a resolution is contrary to a *higher rule of law in the Community legal order* would not entail any challenge to the primacy of that resolution *in international law*, see para 288 (emphasis added).

[216] Para 297.

[217] Para 298.

[218] Para 314.

[219] Para 326.

[220] Para 327.

[221] Para 334.

[222] Para 370.

[223] Para 363.

In *Kadi,* the Court sent a strong signal about the autonomy of the Community legal order in external relations in general and the emergence of the Union as a global actor in security matters in particular.[224] The assertion of the autonomy of the Community legal order was based on what the Court deemed as fundamental principles of the Community constitutional order, namely the rule of law and the respect of fundamental rights. The focus on these principles further enabled the Court to embark on a hierarchisation exercise, asserting the primacy of what it called 'a higher rule of law in the Community legal order' over international agreements. The determination of the Court to stress the autonomy and primacy of the Community legal order was criticised by certain commentators in that it showed an unwillingness to engage in a dialogue with the UN Security Council,[225] while others viewed it rightly as a move of empowerment for the EU.[226] A key factor in the Court's interpretative choice was the nature of the measures under review: rather than being norms of general application, these were sanctions addressed to and directly affecting individuals.[227] The focus on the individual rendered the articulation of a reasoning based on the protection of fundamental rights in a legal order based on the rule of law imperative. In this context, it is significant that the Court had to translate the position of the individual from the international to the Community legal order. Under international law (whose logic is premised primarily upon the state as a referent object), the individual is sidelined.[228] By contrast, in the Community legal order based on the rule of law and fundamental rights, the position of the individual is central. The differences between the international and the Community legal orders, and the special features of the Community legal order in this context left the Court with little choice but to focus on the individual when interpreting the relationship between Community law and Security Council norms.

These features of the Court's ruling in *Kadi* should not, however, be seen as signifying a complete dichotomy between Security Council norms on sanctions and Community law implementing these sanctions. The Court reiterated in *Kadi* its finding that when interpreting the Regulation account should be taken of the Security Council Resolution which the Regulation was designed to

---

[224] As Halberstam and Stein have noted, 'until *Kadi,* the story of European constitutionalism has focused largely on establishing the Community's legal order as autonomous from those of the Member States. With few exceptions, the constitutional gaze has been inward looking, that is, setting off the Union's legal order from, and integrating it with, those of the Member States.' D Halberstam and E Stein, 'The United Nations, the European Union, and the King of Sweden: Economic Sanctions and Individual Rights in a Plural World Order' (2009) 46 *Common Market Law Review* 13, 62.

[225] G de Burca, 'The European Court of Justice and the International Legal Order after *Kadi*' (2009) NYU School of Law Jean Monnet Working Paper 01/2009, 36 available at www.jeanmonnetprogram. org/papers/09/090101.html.

[226] T Tridimas, 'Terrorism and the ECJ: Empowerment and Democracy in the EC Legal Order' (2009) 34 *European Law Review,* 103.

[227] ibid at 113.

[228] See, in this context, the criticism of the CFI ruling by Guild, who points out that the structure of politics and law at the international level leaves the individual without a voice or visibility, E Guild, *EU Counter-Terrorism Action. A Fault Line Between Law and Politics?* (Brussels, CEPS, 2010) 9–10.

implement.[229] While in *Kadi* the Court's use of the wording of the Security Council Resolution as an interpretative tool did not avoid the annulment of the Regulation implementing Security Council Resolution 1390 (2002) on fundamental rights grounds, such use under a purposive interpretation was subsequently evoked by the Court in the case of *M and Others* to *promote* the Community law protection of the individual under the sanctions regime.[230]

On the other hand, a closer look at the relationship between the Community and Security Council norms and its interpretation by the Court demonstrates that the autonomy of the Community legal order, in particular as regards the respect of fundamental rights and the rule of law, is not that clear. Notwithstanding the Court's assertion that the Community has a leeway as to the method of implementation of the Security Council Resolution in question, and that the Regulation in question was not directly attributable to the UN, the fact remained that the mechanism used by the Community consists of directly importing listings by the Sanctions Committee in the Community legal order without the opportunity for the Community to modify them. The Community legal order thus accepted the verdict of a UN body operating beyond the scrutiny mechanisms of EC law resulting in highly invasive measures against individuals.

It could, of course, be observed in this context that the Court's intervention in *Kadi* emphasised the need for procedural standards in the listing procedure. It could, therefore, be viewed as part of a process linked with improvements in Security Council norms and practice as regards procedural rights.[231] However, while the Court is prepared to review the compatibility of both procedural and certain substantive aspects of the Community sanctions regime implementing Security Council Resolutions with fundamental rights, it did not question the legitimacy, binding character or method of adoption of these Resolutions by a body such as the Security Council.[232] This reluctance may be understandable in the light of the Court's choice to assert jurisdiction with regard to measures which could be considered to be executive and thus outside judicial review. However, the fact remains that the Court did not question the fundamental choice by the Community to follow the security logic of the Security Council and copy the latter's system of far-reaching sanctions against individuals as a counter-

---

[229] Para 297. See also, Case C-117/06 *Möllendorf and Möllendorf – Niehuus* [2007] ECR I-8361, para 54.

[230] Case C-340/08 *The Queen on the application of M and Others v Her Majesty's Treasury* (CJEU, 29 April 2009). The Court referred to the need to take into account of the wording and purpose of Resolution 1390 (2002) which Regulation 881/2002 (the implementation of which by the UK was the subject of a preliminary reference by the House of Lords) was designed to implement (para 45). The Court focused on the linguistic divergences in the wording of Art 2(2) of the Regulation in the different language versions and justified the need to take into account of the substance of Resolution 1390 (2002), but also of subsequent Security Council Resolutions and initiatives (paras 49–51). The Court opted for a restrictive interpretation of the scope of Art 2(2) of the Regulation.

[231] For an analysis of subsequent revisions of Security Council Resolutions in this light, in particular by Resolution 1822 (2008), see M Scheinin, 'Is the ECJ Ruling in *Kadi* Incompatible with International Law?' (2009) 28 *Yearbook of European Law* 637, 648–50.

[232] Indeed, the language of the Court in *Kadi* stressed the relationship of Community law with international agreements.

terrorism tool.[233] As far as the EU is concerned, the imposition of UN-led individual sanctions as such remains a central element of the Union's security policy.

Judicial Review of the EU Implementation of UN Security Council Resolutions: *Kadi II*

The Court of Justice was invited to revisit its case law following the lodging of a request by Mr Kadi of annulment of a revised EU asset freezing Regulation which continued to list him therein notwithstanding the Court's ruling in *Kadi I*.[234] During the *Kadi II* litigation, a number of key developments took place following the Court's ruling in *Kadi I* including, most notably, a series of revisions to the UN Security Council system of listing individuals whose assets should be frozen under Resolution 1267. Resolution 1822 (2008) introduced the requirement for listing proposals to identify those parts of the statement of case that may be publicly released, including for use by the Sanctions Committee for development of the summary described below or for the purpose of notifying or informing the listed individual or entity, and those parts which may be released upon request to interested States.'[235] The Resolution also provides that the Sanctions Committee, when it adds a name to its Consolidated List, is to make accessible on its website 'a narrative summary of reasons for listing' and that it is to make accessible on the same site, 'narrative summaries of reasons for listing' names on that list before the adoption of Resolution 1822/2008.[236] A further Security Council Resolution, 1904/2009, established an 'Office of the Ombudsperson', whose task is to assist the Sanctions Committee in the consideration of delisting requests. The person appointed to be the Ombudsperson must be an individual of high moral character, impartiality and integrity with high qualifications and experience in relevant fields, including law, human rights, counter-terrorism and sanctions.[237] A subsequent Resolution, 1989 (2011), extended the mandate and support of the Ombudsperson and included detailed provisions on listing and de-listing procedures.[238] The Security Council continues to have the ultimate decision-making power on delisting and is not obliged to follow a de-listing recommendation by the Ombudsperson.[239] Improvements in the listing procedure under Resolution 1822/2008 have been reflected in the EU legal order in EU Regulation 1286/2009.[240]

---

[233] See also, in this context, the criticism of Scheinin, who advocates the repeal of Resolution 1267 and its replacement with national or EU level terrorist listing pursuant to Resolution 1373, 'Is the ECJ Ruling in *Kadi* Incompatible with International Law?', above n 231.

[234] Regulation EC No 1190/2008 amending for the 101st time Regulation No 881/2001 [2008] OJ L322, 25.

[235] Para 12.

[236] Para 13.

[237] Para 20.

[238] Paras 12–35.

[239] Para 23.

[240] Council Regulation 1286/2009 amending Regulation No 881/2002 imposing certain specific restrictive measures directed against certain persons and entities associated with Osama bin Laden, the Al-Qaida network and the Taliban [2009] OJ L346/42.

According to the Regulation, the Commission will take a decision to list a natural or legal person for the first time only as soon as a statement of reasons is provided by the Sanctions Committee.[241] Once the listing decision has been taken, the Commission must communicate without delay the statement of reasons to the affected parties providing an opportunity to express their views on the matter.[242] The Commission must review its listing decision following the submission of observations which must be forwarded to the Sanctions Committee.[243] A similar process may apply for those listed before 3 September 2008.[244] Improvements in the UN listing system have led to hopes that the differences between UN Security Council practice and EU constitutional law as demonstrated in *Kadi I* could be bridged.[245] However, further academic analyses have highlighted the persistent rule of law and human rights shortcomings of the UN Security Council sanctions system and the limits to the mandate and powers of the Ombudsperson.[246]

In deciding on the *Kadi II* appeal, the CJEU was faced with the markedly different approaches adopted by the General Court and the Advocate General in their examination of the case. The General Court applied, albeit reluctantly, the reasoning of the Court of Justice in *Kadi I* and advocated the full review of not only to the apparent merits of the contested measure but also the evidence and information on which the findings made in that measure are based.[247] The General Court reiterated the CJEU emphasis in *Kadi I* on the need, in principle, for the full review of the contested Regulation in the light of fundamental rights[248] and went on to advocate extensive judicial review. The General Court highlighted the limits in judicial protection offered by improvements in the Security Council listing system.[249] It advocated the application in this case as regards the extent and intensity of judicial review of the principles set out by the General Court with respect to the scrutiny of the autonomous EU sanctions regime in its *OMPI* case law.[250] In particular, judicial review would include the review of the interpretation made by the competent Union institutions of the relevant facts: EU Courts must not only establish whether the evidence relied on is factually accurate, reliable and consis-

---

[241] Art 7a(1).

[242] Art 7a(2).

[243] Art 7a(3).

[244] Art 7c.

[245] See J Kokott and C Sobotta, 'The *Kadi* Case – Constitutional Core Values and International Law – Finding the Balance?' (2012) 23 *European Journal of International Law* 1015.

[246] G Sullivan and M de Goede, 'Between Law and the Exception: the UN 1267 Ombudsperson as a Hybrid Model of Legal Expertise' (2013) 26 *Leiden Journal of International Law* 833.

[247] Case T-85/09 *Kadi v Commission* [2010] ECR II-5177. For a commentary, see C Eckes, 'Controlling the Most Dangerous Branch From Afar: Multilayered Counter-Terrorist Policies and the European Judiciary' (2011) Amsterdam Law School Legal Studies Research Paper No 2011-08, 12–13, available at http://papers.ssrn.com/so13/papers.cfm?abstract_id=1865785.

[248] Para 126.

[249] Para 128.

[250] Para 139.

tent, but must also ascertain whether that evidence contains all the relevant information to be taken into account in order to assess the situation and whether it is capable of substantiating the conclusions drawn from it.[251] Secrecy is not compatible with the requirements of such level of judicial review: the General Court reiterated its findings in *PMOI II*[252] that the Council is not entitled to base its decision to freeze funds on information or material in the file communicated by a Member State, if the said Member State is not willing to authorise its communication to the Union Courts whose task is to review the lawfulness of that decision; more importantly, the refusal by the Member State and the Council to communicate, even to the Court alone, certain information on which the contested measure was based, had the consequence that the Court was unable to review the lawfulness of the contested decision.[253] The General Court supported these arguments further by emphasising the draconian nature of freezing orders for the applicant which had been in place for a long period of time[254] and putting forward the view that the measures in question are not temporary or precautionary, but actually of a criminal nature.[255] According to the General Court, the principle of full and rigorous judicial review of such measures is all the more justified given that such measures have a marked and long-lasting effect on the fundamental rights of the persons concerned.[256] In applying this standard of review, the General Court found that the rights of defence and effective judicial protection of Mr Kadi had been breached[257] and that the contested Regulation also entailed a breach of the principle of proportionality by infringing Mr Kadi's right to respect for property.[258]

In his Opinion, Advocate General Bot advocated a much narrower scope of judicial review.[259] He argued that freezing is merely a precautionary measure and does not constitute a criminal sanction nor does it imply an accusation of a

---

[251] Para 142.

[252] Case T-256/07 *People's Mojahedin Organization of Iran v Council (PMOI II)* [2008] ECR II-3019.

[253] Para 145.

[254] Para 149.

[255] Para 150: 'It might even be asked whether – given that now nearly 10 years have passed since the applicant's funds were originally frozen – it is not now time to call into question the finding of this Court, at paragraph 248 of its judgment in *Kadi*, and reiterated in substance by the Court of Justice at paragraph 358 of its own judgment in *Kadi*, according to which the freezing of funds is a temporary precautionary measure which, unlike confiscation, does not affect the very substance of the right of the persons concerned to property in their financial assets but only the use thereof. The same is true of the statement of the Security Council, repeated on a number of occasions, in particular in Resolution 1822 (2008), that the measures in question "are preventative in nature and are not reliant upon criminal standards set out under national law". In the scale of a human life, 10 years in fact represent a substantial period of time and the question of the classification of the measures in question as preventative or punitive, protective or confiscatory, civil or criminal seems now to be an open one'. The General Court also refers to the opinion of the United Nations High Commissioner for Human Rights (para 150) and to the interpretative notes to 'Special Recommendation III on Terrorist Financing' which recognises that the objectives of the recommended asset freezing measures are not only preventative but also punitive (para 163).

[256] Para 151.

[257] Paras 171–78

[258] Paras 192–95.

[259] Opinion of Advocate General Bot (delivered on 19 March 2013).

criminal nature.[260] He then stressed that listing at EU level is based on the decision of the United Nations and that such a decision is based on a summary of reasons drawn up by the Sanctions Committee on the basis of information or evidence which is provided to it by the State(s) which made the listing request, in most cases in confidence, and which is not intended to be made available to the EU institutions.[261] This deference to decision-making at UN level is coupled by the Advocate General view that listings are part of a political process which goes beyond any individual case and that the political dimension of this process in which the Union has decided to participate calls for moderation in the performance of the judicial review by the EU judicature, that is to say, it must not, in principle, substitute its own assessment for that of the competent political authorities.[262] In this manner, the Advocate General downplays the impact of the listing process on the affected individuals and treats listing as a political, rather than a legal, issue which merits limited judicial scrutiny. In addition to these arguments, the Advocate General cites the improvements in the procedure before the Sanctions Committee since 2008, which also militate in favour of a limited review of the internal lawfulness of the contested regulation by the EU judicature.[263] This view is in line with the arguments of the Commission, the UK and intervening Member States in the appeals before the Court of Justice.[264] According to the Advocate General, an effective global fight against terrorism requires confidence and collaboration between the participating international, regional and national institutions, rather than mistrust – the mutual confidence which must exist between the EU and the United Nations is justified by the fact that the values concerning respect for fundamental rights are shared by those two organisations.[265] The assertion of such mutual trust enables the Advocate General to accept that the listing and delisting procedures within the Sanctions Committee provide sufficient guarantees for the EU institutions to be able to presume that the decisions taken by that body are justified.[266] This mutual trust and the presumption of compliance of Sanctions Committee procedures with EU law, along with the emphasis on the need to privilege the choices of states operating within the UN sanctions system has led the Advocate General to limit considerably the scope of judicial scrutiny by concluding that the review performed by the EU judicature of the internal lawfulness of EU acts giving effect to decisions taken by the Sanctions Committee must not, in principle, call into question the merits of the listing, except in cases where the implementation procedure for that listing within the EU has highlighted a flagrant error in the factual finding made, in the legal classification of the facts or in the assessment of the proportionality of the measure.[267]

---

[260] Para 68.
[261] Para 75.
[262] Para 80.
[263] Para 81.
[264] Paras 82–84.
[265] Para 85.
[266] Para 87.
[267] Para 110.

The Court of Justice adopted a more extensive model of judicial review than the one proposed by the Advocate General.[268] It concurred with the General Court and the Advocate General in refusing to afford the contested Regulation immunity from jurisdiction.[269] The Court then made express reference to the need for the European judiciary to ensure the in principle full review of the lawfulness of all Union acts in the light of fundamental rights[270] and mentioned in particular the respect for the rights of the defence and the right to effective judicial protection as enshrined in Articles 41(2) and 47 of the Charter respectively.[271] Respect for these rights entails a number of obligations related to the provision of reasons for the EU listing authority.[272] As regards the extent of judicial review, the Court found that the EU judiciary must determine whether the competent EU authority has complied with the procedural safeguards the obligation to state reasons mentioned above.[273] Moreover, effective judicial review requires that, as part of the review of the lawfulness of the grounds which are the basis of the decision to list or to maintain the listing of a given person, the Courts of the EU are to ensure that that decision is taken on a sufficiently solid factual basis. Judicial review cannot be restricted to an assessment of the cogency in the abstract of the reasons relied on, but must concern whether those reasons, or, at the very least, one of those reasons, deemed sufficient in itself to support that decision, is substantiated.[274] To that end, it is for the Courts of the EU, in order to carry out that examination, to request the competent EU authority, when necessary, to produce information or evidence, confidential or not, relevant to such an examination.[275] The Court thus advocated a standard of evidence-based, detailed, substantive judicial review *in concreto* and not *in abstracto*.[276]

The Court of Justice thus put forward a standard of judicial review which consists of the substantive review of the listing based on evidence and information submitted to the European judiciary. The Court attempted to accommodate to some extent security arguments related to secrecy.[277] In order to strike a balance between the requirements attached to the right to effective judicial protection and those flowing from the security of the EU or its Member States or the conduct of their international relations, it is legitimate to consider possibilities such as the disclosure of a summary outlining the information's content or that of the evidence in question. However, irrespective of whether such possibilities are taken, *it is for the Courts of the European Union to assess* whether and to what the extent the failure to disclose confidential information or evidence to the person concerned

[268] Joined Cases C-584/10 P, C-593/10 P and C-595/10 P, *European Commission v Kadi* (CJEU, 18 July 2013).
[269] Paras 65–68.
[270] Para 97.
[271] Paras 98–100.
[272] Paras 111–16.
[273] Para 118.
[274] Para 119.
[275] Para 120.
[276] For further details, see paras 121–24.
[277] See paras 125–27.

and his consequential inability to submit his observations on them are such as to affect the probative value of the confidential evidence.[278] Having regard to the preventive nature of the restrictive measures at issue, if, in the course of its review of the lawfulness of the contested decision the Courts of the EU consider that, at the very least, one of the reasons mentioned in the summary provided by the Sanctions Committee is sufficiently detailed and specific, that it is substantiated and that it constitutes in itself sufficient basis to support that decision, the fact that the same cannot be said of other such reasons cannot justify the annulment of that decision. In the absence of one such reason, the Courts of the EU will annul the contested decision.[279]

While attempting to accommodate to some extent security considerations, the Court of Justice has adopted in *Kadi II* a rigorous, substantive test of judicial review of listing decisions by the European judiciary. The Court reiterated that such a judicial review is indispensable to ensure a fair balance between the maintenance of international peace and security and the protection of the fundamental rights and freedoms of the person concerned, *those being shared values of the UN and the EU.*[280] While the emphasis on shared values may have been included to diffuse potential tensions with regard to the conflict between EU law and UN Security Council measures, the Court did not hesitate to emphasise the need to protect human rights in the face of a UN framework providing with limited safeguards. The Court reiterated the substantial negative impact of sanctions to the affected individuals[281] and, in a marked departure from the reasoning of Attorney General Bot, went on to say that the improvements at UN level with regard to listing do not provide the guarantee of effective judicial protection to the affected individual.[282] In an example of judicial cross-fertilisation and dialogue, the Court of Justice based this finding on the ruling of the European Court of Human Rights in *Nada*.[283] The Court of Justice went on to define the essence of effective judicial protection, which is that it should enable the person concerned to obtain a declaration from a court, by means of a judgment ordering annulment whereby the contested measure is retroactively erased from the legal order and is deemed never to have existed, that the listing of his name, or the continued listing of his name, on the list concerned was vitiated by illegality, the recognition of which may re-establish the reputation of that person or constitute for him a form of reparation for the non-material harm he has suffered.[284] The Court found that, while errors of law were made by the General Court,[285] it is necessary to determine whether, notwithstanding those errors, the operative part of the judgment under appeal can be seen to be well founded on legal grounds other than those maintained by

---

[278] Paras 128–29 (emphasis added).
[279] Para 130.
[280] Para 131 (emphasis added).
[281] Para 132.
[282] Para 133.
[283] *Nada v Switzerland* (No 10593/08) [2012] *ECHR 1691.*
[284] Para 134.
[285] See, in particular, para 138.

the General Court, in which event an appeal must be dismissed.[286] The Court then went on to review the substance of the allegations against Mr Kadi[287] and, dismissing the appeals, concluded that none of the allegations presented against Mr Kadi in the summary provided by the Sanctions Committee are such as to justify the adoption, at EU level, of restrictive measures against him, either because the statement of reasons is insufficient, or because information or evidence which might substantiate the reason concerned, in the face of detailed rebuttals submitted by the party concerned, is lacking.[288]

The Court of Justice thus confirmed again, as in *Kadi I*, the autonomy of the EU legal order based on the respect for the rule of law and fundamental rights. While the Court's ruling in *Kadi I* has had a noticeable impact in improving listing procedures at the UN level, the Court of Justice in *Kadi II* sent a clear message that such improvements can by no means equate to effective judicial protection. The Court of Justice continued to remind the international community that it is the individual who should be the focus of authorities in the invasive process of the imposition of restrictive sanctions. At the same time, the Court of Justice in *Kadi II* sent a clear message with regard to the relationship between the executive and the judiciary: the executive cannot use secrecy and confidentiality to evade judicial scrutiny, especially when the protection of fundamental rights is at stake. However, the Court of Justice did not appear to be as protective with regard to substantive fundamental rights, including the right to property. While the Court emphasised the far-reaching and adverse impact that restrictive measures have on the affected individuals, it fell short of endorsing the General Court's strongly worded statement that restrictive measures can be considered to be in essence criminal sanctions. The Court of Justice seems to accept the preventive nature of sanctions, and did not engage with the argument of the General Court that procedural defects lead to a disproportionate impact of the affected individuals' right to property – with the logic and essence of restrictive measures remaining largely unquestioned. In this light, *Kadi II* should be viewed as a triumph of procedural justice, perhaps at the expense of the protection of substantive fundamental rights including the right to property.

Conclusion

The EU has been both actively involved in and influenced by the globalisation of criminal law which has been taking place for the last two decades. Notwithstanding internal constitutional and institutional complexities, the Union has emerged in one way or another as a global actor in the field. Along with attempts to influence

---

[286] Para 150.
[287] Paras 151–62.
[288] Para 163.

global (and regional) standards in criminal matters, the EU has proved itself ready to advance the globalisation of criminal law via its internal *acquis*. Union institutions have not hesitated to internalise international law and use the text of international 'hard' and 'soft' law instruments as a basis to justify, establish and develop Community/Union criminal law. This has been particularly the case in the context of the development of money laundering countermeasures, where interconnections between the EU, the regional European and the global level have resulted in the development of a brand new regime of criminalisation, prevention and enforcement. In this and other fields (most notably organised crime and terrorism), in terms of substance, convergence between EU and international law has largely led to the extension of criminalisation and the proliferation of the powers of the State. In terms of the protection of fundamental rights on the other hand, EU Member States have been using international law largely to shield enforcement action from Union law.

This is a reminder that the Union's stance in international *fora* must be viewed in the light of internal developments in both constitutional and substantive law. The furthering of European integration in criminal matters over the past decade has been coupled with a growing assertiveness by the Union in international negotiations. The EU has been actively involved in trying to shape the content of multilateral treaties in criminal matters (both at UN and Council of Europe levels), with not inconsiderable success thus far. At the same time –in particular in relation to the Council of Europe, but also as regards the UN – EU institutions, including the European Courts, have not hesitated to stress the autonomy of the Union legal order and to reserve the freedom to legislate in similar matters at Union level in the future. For those viewing the glass half empty in terms of coherence and consistency, this may lead to the fragmentation of international law in the field. Those more optimistic would point out the growing interconnections between the EU and other international organisations and bodies in the production of criminal law (albeit in certain cases with minimal debate or transparency), and the striking similarities between global and EU standards in combating serious and transnational crime. However, the need to assert the autonomy of the EU legal order in the development of a global paradigm of crime governance may prove to be more and more imperative, not least in order to ensure the full and effective protection of fundamental rights and in this manner ensuring the coherence of EU external action with the Union's internal constitutional objectives and values.

9

The Interplay of Criminal and Administrative Law in the Context of Market Regulation: The Case of Serious Competition Infringements

CHRISTOPHER HARDING

Some Big Questions about Criminal Law and Administrative Process

This discussion could open with a single big question: what do criminal law and administrative law have in common? For many, especially those nurtured within the well-established categorisations of the common law world, that might appear an odd question to pose and one leading to the answer – not very much, since they are areas of legal activity different in their objectives and their method. Criminal law is a primary model of significantly intrusive prescriptive and prohibitive rules, comprising a strong legal control of activities that injure or threaten the core interests and values of society. Administrative law, on the other hand, is constitutional and facilitative, an arm of public law that regulates the relations between public bodies and the detail of the relationship between public authority and individual citizens. Yet within a particular perspective – comprising in substance the regulation and ordering of economic, market and trading activities, and legally and politically located at transnational and international levels – the two categories of law may be seen operating alongside each other with some common purpose and method. In a comparative European context, for example, it is now meaningful to compare criminal procedure and sanctions with administrative procedure and sanctions, as parallel legal courses and to talk of the choice of one or the other as routes of legal control. In a number of contemporary legal systems there exists a legal competence to carry out investigations, to determine the breach of prohibitory rules, and impose sanctions of a penal nature, but which is not in formal terms a criminal law competence but one which is widely referred to as 'administrative'. In that sense, the distinction and choice between criminal and administrative now looms large in the contemporary legal world, yet is a subject relatively little explored, either as a matter of underlying legal theory or for its practical dynamics, in a number of quarters. Posing, by way of example, a more specific question, asking about the relationship between a European Union fine imposed upon a company and a prison term imposed under English criminal law, both in relation to the same infringement of competition rules, would reveal straightaway the need for a clearer overarching theoretical structure and for answers to more specific legal questions. The purpose of the present discussion is to provide something of the former as a basis and framework for supplying the latter.

On further reflection, a study of the interface of the 'criminal' and the 'administrative' in this context of regulatory law, gives rise to a number of big or significant questions concerning contemporary approaches to legal control and the constitutional ordering of the core values of contemporary society. Thus, it may be asked:

— What is the pattern of administrative procedures and sanctions which are now available in some legal systems but not others and how should the provenance of the preference for one approach or the other be mapped and understood?
— Is this pattern explicable as a matter of the legal and enforcement culture and traditions of these systems?
— What does the exercise of that choice signal regarding a society's view of certain conduct, its concept of crime and its policy of criminalisation?
— Are there political and practical forces that shape and determine policy (if policy on the question exists as such) and actual resort to these different types of legal process?
— What does the possibility of such a choice of legal process reveal about the nature and problems of regulation and regulatory models of legal control in contemporary society?

These then are the basic questions of provenance, legal culture, crime policy, pragmatic dimension and regulatory context, which may be used to inform a probing discussion of the subject. The 'criminal law versus administrative process' debate is thus an instructive testing ground for reflection on the role and purpose of both criminal law and regulation in present-day society, or societies, and the following discussion will test these questions around four main themes and issues: definition and vocabulary; underlying legal and political culture; issues of justice and agency; and the regulatory context of competition infringements.

Definition and Vocabulary: How to Categorise

What should be understood more exactly in using terms such as 'criminal law/ proceeding', or 'administrative process/sanction', and indeed what is the typological scope of the discussion? In particular, how does that terminology and nomenclature relate to other processes and sanctions, such as civil proceedings, civil penalties, and devolved self-regulation, all of which may figure importantly in the context of areas of regulatory activity such as competition law and policy?

Some clarity may be brought to the discussion by asking about the primary purpose of the alternative processes under discussion here. First, what do the regimes of 'criminal law', 'administrative sanctions' and 'civil penalties' have in common? The answer would appear to lie in the fact that each regime comprises prohibitive rules (thus giving rise to potential infringements or offences), coupled with the use of repressive sanctions of a punitive nature. In this way, the subject of this discussion may be distinguished from the regime of civil liability which depends on private initiative and would aim typically at compensation rather than punishment. It would be helpful then to visualise a spectrum of *repressive* regimes, each intending a regulation by means of clear and strong prohibition supported by the use of sanctions of a broadly penal character. Through that lens, it is sensible enough to refer to financial penalties, for instance, as being either 'criminal', 'administrative', or 'civil', the difference residing mainly in the strength and purpose of the prohibition, its attendant sanction, and the infrastructure of enforcement. It is easy enough to find a contemporary example in the field of competition regulation: a criminal fine may be imposed upon an individual (for instance, under the UK Enterprise Act 2002)[1] or an individual or a company (for instance, under the US Sherman Act 1890);[2] an administrative fine may be imposed upon a company (or more precisely, an 'undertaking', as under Article 101 of the TFEU as a matter of EU law),[3] and a civil fine or penalty may be imposed upon a company (for instance, under the UK Competition Act 1998).[4] Questions might be raised concerning the dovetailing of these processes of legal control, but they logically co-exist within a legal and regulatory spectrum as different processes of legal control which may in fact each be applied concurrently to the same case of infringement with broadly similar retributive and deterrent objectives.[5] In this way, each of these above processes may be theoretically grouped together and distinguished from a civil claim (in tort) in relation to the same conduct, the latter having distinctive aspects of private as opposed to public enforcement and compensatory rather than punitive objectives. Similarly, 'administrative procedure'

---

[1] Under s 188 of the Enterprise Act 2002, under the heading of 'cartel offence', an *individual* may be found guilty of an *offence* of making or implementing one or a number of listed arrangements and may be subject to fines or prison terms.

[2] Section 1 of the Sherman Act 1890 (15 USC) defines a *felony* which can be committed by a *person* (ie individual or company), and provides for both fines and prison terms.

[3] More specifically under Art 23 of Regulation 1/2003 [2003] OJ L1/1, *undertakings* may be subject to fines in respect of infringements of Arts 101 and 102 of the TFEU, which are said to be 'not of a criminal law nature' in Art 23(5).

[4] Section 36 of the Competition Act 1998: financial penalties may be imposed by the Director General of Fair Trading.

[5] A recent example of such sanctions being imposed in a number of jurisdictions in relation to the same cartel is provided by proceedings dealing with the Marine Hose cartel in 2008–2009: criminal law fines and prison terms imposed under the Sherman Act in the USA; corporate fines imposed in a number of jurisdictions (Australia, the EU, Japan and Korea), and prison terms and confiscation (for individuals) in the UK.

and 'sanctions' in this context is something distinct from 'administrative procedure' in a 'soft compliance' sense of a system of voluntary registration, examination or monitoring, and approval or not, without sanctions (for instance, the
earlier process of consensual, soft regulation employed under EC competition
law, under the original Regulation 17 of 1962).[6]

A broad typology of legal control in an area such as competition regulation
could then be presented, for example, in the following way, listing main categories
of legal process alongside their typical forms:

Table A: Typology of Legal Control: Competition Regulation

Consensual 'bureaucratic' administrative procedure	Voluntary registration, examination, approval
Private claim for compensation	Private litigation and tortious liability
'Repressive' prohibition and penalisation	Criminal procedure and penalties Administrative procedure and penalties Civil procedure and penalties

Two points of clarification emerge from this analysis. The first is to establish a
wider perspective (column 1 in the above table), as a continuum of legal control
leading to a choice of one or more approaches (bureaucratic, compensatory and
repressive), and it may be interesting to speculate, in a comparative law way,
whether there is a typical history of enforcement, in which legal systems adopt
those approaches successively in an upward (in the sense of tougher or more rigorous) progress of legal control.[7]

The second point of clarification is narrower, providing a focus upon penalisation as a generic objective (row 3, column 2 in the above table). The main question
then is how best to regulate through the method of prohibition and penalisation.
Criminalisation (admittedly a more high-profile issue) is then a sub-question,
just one of a number of penalisation options, alongside the choice of administrative procedure and sanctions or civil penalties (as the term is used for instance
under UK law).

However, it would also be helpful to note at this point that the distinction
between administrative procedure and sanctions, and civil penalties is more a
matter of nomenclature and jurisdictional categorisation, than of substance.
Historically, European Continental jurisdictions have widely embraced the concept of an administrative offence, especially to deal with regulatory and non-core

---

[6] For an account of the earlier 'notification' system, established under Council Regulation 17 of
1962, see DG Goyder (J Goyder and A Albors-Llorens), *Goyder's EC Competition Law*, 5th edn (Oxford,
Oxford University Press, 2009) ch 4 especially 46–49.
[7] See, eg the argument put forward by Harding and Joshua in C Harding and J Joshua, *Regulating
Cartels in Europe*, 2nd edn (Oxford, Oxford University Press, 2010) chs 4 and 5, presenting the matter
as an upward spiral of legal control.

criminality and offending, whereas common law jurisdictions have tended to retain the use of criminal law and procedure to deal with non-core criminality, or sometimes make use of civil (that is, non-criminal) penalties. One of the difficulties of comparative discussion is that different terminology across jurisdictions may then mask substantive similarities. Thus, for example, what are classified as *Ordnungswidrigkeiten* (administrative offences)[8] under German law, to deal with such matters as road traffic or competition violations, would be classified as criminal offences (for road traffic violations) or dealt with by civil penalties (for corporate competition violations) under UK law, although the procedures, infrastructure of enforcement and types of sanction may be similar to that found under German law. Such an observation reinforces the need to be aware of moving through a spectrum of prohibitive rules and penal sanctions.

Exploring the Provenance:
Underlying Legal and Political Cultures

At this stage of discussion it would be useful to carry out some jurisdictional mapping, tied to the question: why do some legal systems formally employ the idea of an administrative offence and sanction while others do not? This is clearly a fundamental question, yet one which has, on the whole, been swept under the comparative law carpet of systemic difference, and presented as something which is seen to come naturally to Continental Europeans yet is alien to common law systems. Thus in 2009, the Law Reform Commission of Saskatchewan announced that 'administrative penalties are a new means of enforcing compliance with regulatory legislation'.[9] That statement was true for Saskatchewan as a common law jurisdiction, but the approach is not new for a number of European national legal systems or the EC/EU system, which has resorted to the regime in a very significant way to deal with competition infringements among other matters, or for the European Court of Human Rights, which has grappled for some time with the implications of the difference between criminal law and administrative sanctions (see the discussion further below). What was happening in Saskatchewan was a formal adoption of terminology and legal infrastructure well known elsewhere to replace some less manifest and clear-cut distinctions within its existing system of criminal law.

More broadly and comparatively, it can be noted that many legal systems naturally enough have a graduated classification of prohibitions and offences. Within

---

[8] A major 'decriminalisation' reform was carried out in Germany (the former German Federal Republic) in 1968 with the enactment of the *Ordnungswidrigkeistgesetz* (OwiG, Administrative Offences Act).

[9] Law Reform Commission of Saskatchewan, 'Administrative Penalties Consultation Paper' (June 2009) 3.

systems of criminal law this has historically been expressed in terminology such as the common law descriptions of *felony* and *misdemeanour* or the French descriptors of *crime, délit* and *contravention*. During the twentieth century, many commentators began to draw a main distinction between 'core' criminality and 'regulatory' offending and this categorisation broadly speaking provides the rationale for the distinction between criminal and administrative offences and sanctions. This rationale was expressed succinctly by the European Court of Human Rights, explaining the German model of *Ordnungswidrigkeiten*:

> By means of criminal law, society endeavoured to safeguard its very foundations as well as the right and interests essential for the life of the community. The law on *Ordnungswidrigkeiten*, on the other hand, sought above all to maintain public order. As a general rule . . . commission of a 'regulatory offence' did not involve a degree of ethical unworthiness such as to merit for its perpetrator the moral value-judgment of reproach (*Unwerturteil*) that characterised penal punishment (*Strafe*). The difference between 'regulatory offences' and criminal offences found expression both in procedural terms and in relation to the attendant penalties and other legal consequences.[10]

Indeed, the European Court of Human Rights and the European Court of Justice have both had the opportunity to explore fully the rationale of the criminal/administrative distinction in this context and its legal consequences, especially regarding the matter of legal protection for defendant parties, and this rationale is now well established and well recognised in European legal discourse. In comparative law terms, the main issue is the translation of that now well-articulated European distinction to other systems which have not embraced such a vocabulary of categorisation, even though the basis for the distinction may have been recognised there and acted upon in other terms.

Origins

However, the question remains regarding the origin of this concept of administrative offence as a Continental European idea and one that has been utilised predominantly in that geographical context. The main idea of administrative offending may be traced back to the work of some German legal scholars in the earlier part of the twentieth century (Goldschmidt (1902), Wolf (1930)),[11] broadly conceived as an 'ethical neutral disobedience to executive power'.[12] Its significance was realised at a later point, when it provided the basis for an important programme of legislative decriminalisation undertaken in the German Federal Republic in the 1950s and 1960s, resulting in the enactment of a separate code of administrative infractions (*Ordnungswidrigkeiten*). The positive theoretical and

---

[10] *Oztürk v Germany* (1984) 6 EHRR 409 at para 52.
[11] J Goldschmidt, *Das Verwaltungsstrafrecht* (Berlin, J Guttentag, 1902); E Wolf, *Die Stellung der Verwaltungsdelikte in Strafrechtssystem* (Tubingen, August Hegler, 1930).
[12] J Sootak, 'The Concept of Crime and Estonian Criminal Law Reform' (1996) *Juridica International* 55.

practical aspects of this development were summarised by Langbein in the idea of a procedure which 'by decriminalising the morally neutral, enhances the distinctiveness of what is genuinely criminal. It rehabilitates the criminal sanction'.[13]

Theory: Criminal Law as a Special Domain

Thus far, the enquiry into the moral economy of the administrative offence clarifies its rationale, though not so much the willingness of European criminal jurisprudence to act upon the idea, both at a national and a supranational (EC/EU) level, compared to the common law adherence to a widely embracing and expansive idea of criminal law. It is interesting to consider the possibility that in Continental Europe there is a greater wariness about using the ultimate power of criminal law and the risk of devaluing the political and psychological force of the criminal law sanction.

A well-embedded European respect for the power and impact of criminal law would appear to reside in part in a strong consciousness of criminal law and its role in society, arising from an acknowledged recognition of two key qualities of criminal law – its employment of actual force, and its expressive role.

First, in a more concrete sense, criminal law in its modern incarnation involves a forcible authority, an exercise of compulsory and repressive power in relation to matters of investigation, trial and sanctions. This *extremity* of criminal law, its special invasiveness, invests it as a method with social, political and constitutional significance. As Turner has argued:

> By authorizing the state to use force against its citizens, criminal law represents one of the most important instruments of social control. The decision to use criminal prohibitions, as opposed to other sanctions to ensure compliance, is a fundamental political decision that defines a community[14]

This argument translates into two significant constitutional principles: first, the State's monopoly (as the authority of governance) of the legitimate use of violence, or force against the individual; and secondly, the use of criminal law as a measure of last resort, the *ultima ratio* principle.

The second main quality is related – because of its extreme character, criminal law possesses a strong expressive power, in relation to the core values, interests and distinctive identity of the society and polity in question. In its role of guaranteeing

---

[13] JH Langbein, 'Controlling Prosecutorial Discretion in Germany' (1973–74) 41 *University of Chicago Law Review* 439, 456. Langbein's account remains one of the few informative and critical discussions of this German legislation in English, although it was written only a few years after the enactment of the German law: see in particular, his discussion at 451–55. Compare, eg the cursory mention of the concept of the administrative offence model in Law Commission, *Criminal Liability in Regulatory Contexts* (Law Com No 195, 2010) 3.21–3.28.

[14] JI Turner, 'The Expressive Dimension of EU Criminal Law' (2012) 60 *American Journal of Comparative Law* 555, 578. See also, T Weigend, *Strafrecht durch internationale Vereinbarungen – Verlust an nationale Strafrechtkultur?* (1993) 105 *Zeitschrift für die Gesamte Strafrechtswissenschaft* 774, 789.

those values, criminal law necessarily identifies and confirms such values. As stated succinctly by the German *Bundesverfassungsgericht* in its *Lisbon* judgment in 2009:

> By criminal law, a legal community gives itself a code of conduct that is anchored in its values, and whose violation, according to the shared convictions on law, is regarded as so grievous and unacceptable for social co-existence in the community that it requires punishment.[15]

On such an argument, there is an essential relation between a society and its system of governance, and resort to criminal law, so conferring on criminal law a special constitutional force and significance, and a defining role in governance. Criminal law, criminal justice and its associated penalty can then be viewed as a crucial site for working out the constitutional relation between individual citizens and governing authority, and in this sense criminal law should be joined with constitutional law and human rights protection as an integrated legal ordering which also serves to characterise and identify a society and its polity. In short, criminal law possesses a strong expressive significance and to maintain that role should be reserved for the preservation of core values and interests and its intervention limited in that way.

Ultima Ratio as a European Concept

The foregoing argument may be seen as an exploration of a rationale and principle that has achieved wider parlance in European legal theory as the *ultima ratio* principle, viewing the deployment of criminal law as a measure of last resort. For the purposes of this discussion the important point, as already noted, is the degree of interest in and support for this idea in Continental Europe compared to an apparent indifference in common law jurisdictions and criminal jurisprudence. Douglas Husak, an American jurist who has recently turned his attention to this matter, has commented that, 'significantly, much more support for the last resort principle has been expressed on the European continent than among Anglo-American commentators', following his observation that: 'Anglo-American jurisdictions create offences so casually and routinely that the criminal law is just as likely to be employed as a *first* resort.'[16] It is also striking that those American and British commentators who have more recently urged a minimal and more considered resort to criminal sanctions have rarely employed the more explicit vocabulary of 'last resort' or *ultima ratio* in their argument.[17] As Husak has commented

---

[15] Case concerning the review of the compatibility of the Treaty of Lisbon with the German Basic Law BVerfG 2BvE 2/08 vom 30/6/2009 para 355.

[16] D Husak, 'Criminal Law as Last Resort' (2004) 24 *Oxford Journal of Legal Studies* 207, 207.

[17] Husak, 'Criminal Law as a Last Resort', ibid, refers to Andrew Ashworth, AP Simester and GR Sullivan in their criminal law textbook, as examples (AP Simester, JR Spenser, GR Sullivan and GJ Virgo (eds), *Simester and Sullivan's Criminal Law: Theory and Doctrine* 5th edn (Oxford, Hart Publishing, 2013)). As another instance, see the recent work by DJ Baker, *The Right Not to be Criminalized: Demarcating Criminal Law's Authority* (Aldershot, Ashgate, 2011) which is similarly indifferent to the vocabulary of *ultima ratio*.

elsewhere, the greater willingness on the part of European theorists to put forward and defend principles to limit the reach of the criminal law compared to their common law counterparts presents 'a fascinating question in comparative criminal theory'.[18] It is beyond the scope of this discussion to investigate the question further,[19] but this point of comparison should be noted as significant in this context, since it points to a theoretical tradition that informs the European resort to administrative process and penality.

Indeed, it would appear that *ultima ratio* is alive and kicking in European criminal jurisprudence,[20] and is now finding its place in emerging statements on EU criminal law. In 2011, for example, the Finnish jurist, Raimo Lahti, gave evidence to the European Parliament on the *ultima ratio* concept as a principle of criminal law,[21] and less than a year later the EU Commission issued a Communication on EU Crime Policy[22] in which *ultima ratio* was given a prominent position. As Harding and Banach-Guttierez have argued

> the Commission starts from the assumption that criminal law of this kind should be used as a measure of last resort, *ultima ratio*. It is recognised that the use of criminal law and sanctions is a very intrusive and high impact exercise of governmental competence, so that in practice other means of regulation should be considered, and even tested, before opting for that approach.[23]

The Commission's approach therefore is significantly wary of criminalisation and it is worth quoting in full the most relevant part of the Communication:

> Criminal investigations and sanctions may have a significant impact on citizens' rights and include a stigmatising effect. Therefore criminal law must always remain a measure of last resort. This is reflected in the general principle of proportionality (as embodied

[18] D Husak, 'Applying *Ultima Ratio*: A Skeptical Assessment' (2005) *Ohio State Journal of Criminal Law* 535. Husak himself, as an American commentator, having engaged with the idea of *ultima ratio*, then casts some doubt on the value of the principle in the debate on criminalisation.

[19] It may be speculated, for instance, whether the Continental European experience of totalitarian government and the use of criminal law as an instrument of such governance in the earlier half of the twentieth century, has contributed to the present legal culture of greater restraint in the deployment of criminal law sanctions.

[20] For some recent discussion, see N Jareborg, 'What Kind of Criminal Law Do We Want?' in N Jareborg (ed), *Scraps of Penal Theory* (Uppsala, Iustus Forlag, 2002) 89; N Jareborg, 'Criminalization as a Last Resort (Ultima Ratio)' (2005) *Ohio State Journal of Criminal Law* 521; E Herlin-Karnell, 'What Principles Drive (Or Should Drive) European Criminal Law ?' (2010) 11 *German Law Journal* 1115; JW Ouwerkerk, 'Criminalisation as a Last Resort: A National Principle under the Pressure of Europeanisation' (2012) 3 *New Journal of European Criminal Law* 228; O Fedosiuk, 'Criminal Liability as a Last Resort (Ultima Ratio): Theory and Reality' (2012) 19 *Jurisprudence* (a Lithuanian perspective).

[21] R Lahti, 'The Principles of *Ultima Ratio*, Subsidiarity and Proportionality in EU Criminal Law' (Hearing in the European Parliament, Brussels, 8 December 2011).

[22] Commission, 'Communication to the European Parliament, the Council, the European Economic and Social Committee and the Committee of the Regions, "Towards an EU Criminal Policy: Ensuring the effective implementation of EU policies through criminal law"' COM (2011) 573 final. For a critical overview, see A Klip, 'Editorial: European Criminal Policy' (2012) 20 *European Journal of Crime, Criminal Law and Criminal Justice* 3.

[23] C Harding and JB Banach-Guttierez, 'The Emergent EU Criminal Policy: Identifying the Species' (2012) 37 *European Law Review* 758, 764.

in [Article 5(4) of] the Treaty on European Union and, specifically for criminal penalties, in [Article 49(3) of] the EU Charter of Fundamental Rights). For criminal law
measures supporting the enforcement of EU policies [as laid down in Article 83(2)
TFEU], the Treaty explicitly requires a test of whether criminal law measures are 'essential' to achieve the goal of an effective policy implementation.

   Therefore, the legislator needs to analyse whether measures other than criminal law
measures, eg sanction regimes of administrative or civil nature, could not efficiently
ensure the policy implementation and whether criminal law could address the problems more effectively. This will require a thorough analysis in the Impact Assessments
preceding any legislative proposal, including for instance and depending on the speci-
ficities of the policy area concerned, an assessment of whether Member States' sanction
regimes achieve the desired result and difficulties faced by national authorities implementing EU law on the ground.[24]

In so far as the EU is now undertaking more of a directing and steering role in
relation to criminal law matters, it would seem to be drawing upon a particular
tradition in Continental criminal jurisprudence. This may prove significant in the
near future, lending weight to the use of the administrative model in a context
where much of the criminal law discussion will relate to regulatory matters, such
as the response to competition infringements.

Working Out the Modalities of the Distinction and Questions of Rights and Justice

The appeal of the administrative offence model is well recognised: the lack of for-
mality, greater flexibility, and an infrastructure of enforcement which avoids the
time-consuming, costly and confrontational resort to judicial process. It retains
the force of clear prohibition and repressive sanctioning, but enables speedier and
lower profile settlement of the matter. The main doubts and objections then
spring from this quality of informality – it is a less transparent and less procedur-
ally rigorous kind of process, and there may be consequent due process risks.[25]
Concerns have been expressed in particular regarding the appropriate level of
defence rights and in relation to the impact of sanctions, and these issues have
been tested in human rights protection arguments before both the European
Court of Human Rights and the EU courts. It has been mainly in that arena of
argument that the cogency and viability of the criminal/administrative distinction
has been interrogated to date, rather than at the legislative level in terms of the

---

[24] Communication, above n 22, s 2.2.1.
[25] For informative examples of critical discussion of the use of the administrative offence model
and related due process questions at the national level, see, eg Sootak, 'The Concept of Crime and
Estonian Criminal Law Reform', above n 12 (in relation to Estonia); A Blachnio-Parzych, 'The Nature
of Responsibility of an Undertaking in Antitrust Proceedings and the Concept of 'Criminal Charge'
(2012) *Yearbook of Antitrust and Regulatory Studies* 35 (in relation to Poland).

appropriate scope of criminal law and discussion of criminalisation and decriminalisation.

In fact, it might be thought in some respects that the arguments which have originated and been worked out in the domain of due process and basic rights protection have effectively destroyed the basis for a meaningful distinction between administrative and criminal law process and penality. In the European context there is now a substantial body of case law resulting from proceedings before the European Court of Human Rights applying Article 6 of the Human Rights Convention[26] to a range of procedures and sanctions at the national level,[27] and also from the EU Courts (the Court of Justice and Court of First Instance/ General Court) examining the basic rights of defending parties in the context of competition proceedings.[28] In the face of any clear legislative description of a process as non-criminal law, these Courts have been willing to brush aside such a categorisation in favour of an effective protection of individual rights. In the case of the Court of Human Rights, there has been an insistence that the legal label is not decisive, and that the matter depends upon substance, in terms of the nature of the offence and the severity of the sanction.[29] Thus, more specifically, if the process involves the application of a normative measure, instituted by a public authority in order to give effect to a public interest, and leads to a finding of infringement and liability, and then the imposition of a sanction embodying deterrent and punitive purposes, and may be described as 'criminal' in other comparable jurisdictions – then for Convention purposes, the procedure is 'criminal' and the appropriate level of defence protection is that of criminal procedure as referred to in Article 6 of the Convention. In this way, a penalty for a road traffic violation (*Ozturk v Germany*)[30] or a violation of competition rules (*Stenuit v France*)[31] is criminal in substance, whereas a disciplinary measure within a professional proceeding or a library fine would still qualify as administrative. The Court of Human Rights indicated at an early stage in its case law elaboration (in *Ozturk*) that this was not an objection to policies of decriminalisation, but a reminder that the concept of criminal offending was autonomous and that Convention objects and purposes – due process and fair trial – should prevail over the consequences of other legal classifications.[32]

Viewed in this light, there may then be inescapable tensions and conflict between the aims of decriminalisation on the one hand and those of basic rights protection on the other hand. In so far as the latter will prevail, then whatever the gains in terms of a more informal, flexible, speedy and less costly procedure, there

---

[26] As the principal 'due process' or 'fair trial' provision in the European Convention for the Protection of Human Rights, Art 6 has become a kind of European benchmark in this area.

[27] For a convenient overview, see MW Janis, RS Kay and AW Bradley, *European Human Rights Law: Text and Materials*, 3rd edn (Oxford, Oxford University Press, 2008) 720–91.

[28] See Harding and Joshua, *Regulating Cartels in Europe*, above n 7, ch 7.

[29] Case law from *Engel and Others v Netherlands* (1976) 1 EHRR 647, onwards.

[30] *Oztürk v Germany*, above n 10.

[31] *Stenuit v France* (1992) 14 EHRR 509.

[32] *Oztürk v Germany*, above n 10.

must by one means or another be appropriate due process guarantees, which may then undermine the purpose and viability of that kind of procedure. In relation to the EU competition infringement procedure, as applied to cartel cases for example, this may indeed be seen as the outcome. Such proceedings are not formally cast as criminal law, but they have necessarily evolved a rigour of procedure and due process guarantees, so that there is small scope for discretion, flexibility or the saving of resources, and it would be unrealistic not to recognise the hallmarks of the criminal law process beneath the surface (as emphasised, for example, in the Opinion of Advocate General Vesterdorf in the appeal against the Commission's decision against the *Polypropylene Cartel*).[33]

In trying to resolve this tension between decriminalisation values, as embodied in the *ultima ratio* principle, and due process values, as embodied in the primacy of Article 6 of the ECHR, two analytical points should be separated. The first is the quality of condemnation inherent in prohibitive rules. The second relates to the method of legal control, and the choice of a *repressive* procedure which establishes a liability leading to a punitive sanction. It is the choice of this latter method which appears to have led courts such as the European Court of Human Rights to insist upon due process requirements. Yet it is the quality of condemnation or level of censure, as a moral reflection on the nature of the offending behaviour, which appears to drive many arguments about criminalisation and decriminalisation. However, the route of legal classification followed by the European Courts appears to have been: a road traffic violation or breach of an economic regulation is not as morally reprehensible as an act of violence, and thus should not be regarded as criminal in nature; yet if such offences are dealt with by punitive measures, this is a serious reaction which should return the matter to the criminal law domain. In that analysis, the problematic issue is that of *penalisation*, and a sense that penalisation and criminalisation are inescapably linked in normative terms. The matter may be put another way, by posing this question: although it is acceptable to classify a process as administrative if it is consensual, non-confrontational, inspectorial and has an agreed rather than imposed outcome, can a process be administrative if it comprises a compulsory and adversarial procedure and the imposition of sanctions? Are repressive procedures necessarily part of the domain of criminal law (even if in substance rather than their form)? Or is there a convincing ground for easing the due process inspired criminal law categorisation, so as to allow some scope for repressive procedure within the administrative law domain? A solution to this conundrum may reside in a more careful examination of the quality of condemnation of prohibited conduct, relating that not only to the underlying grounds of objection, but also to the agency of the conduct in question.

---

[33] This may be regarded as a keynote opinion on the nature of the Commission's process in competition cases, emphasising the substantive similarity with criminal law proceedings: opinion in Cases T-1/89 etc, *Rhône Poulenc v Commission* [1991] ECR II-867 at 884–87.

The Province of Administrative Penality Determined: Issues of Bad Attitude and Agency

It may be useful at this point in the discussion to return briefly to a point of empirical observation. In so far as some legal systems have opted for an administrative offence model, which areas and types of conduct have typically been covered by this kind of process? As noted above, there will be a ready general answer in most of the examples – conduct which is not within the 'core' condemnation of criminal law, since it does not injure or threaten the essential values of society, conduct that is then cast as *mala prohibita* rather than *mala in se*, and in modern parlance is a matter of 'regulatory' control rather than 'traditional' criminal law, and conduct that finally is based not so much on a morally wrong mindset of an individual human actor, but may be the product of a more intellectually dispersed corporate mindset. These are interrelated points and they may be presented as two distinctive lists of the typical empirical characteristics of criminal and administrative penality (see Table B below):

Table B: Criminal and Administrative Penalty from Empirical Observation

Criminal law process and sanctions	Administrative law process and sanctions
Injury or threat to essential values of society	Injury or threat to non-essential (or historically variable) values
Inherent moral condemnation (*mala in se*)	Contingent and decreed condemnation (*mala prohibita*)
Core criminal law	Regulatory law
Individual bad mindset (methodological individualism) – bad attitude	Dispersed collective and corporate mindset – delinquent culture

The above analysis can serve as a reminder of an important qualitative test of what is often described as criminal, a test which is normative rather than consequentialist in its emphasis, and is not driven by argument relating to the nature of sanctions. Returning to the analysis put forward in earlier German legal theory, the relevant distinction resides in the level and nature of ethical condemnation, then reserving the term 'ethically neutral' for the kind of judgment being made of offending behaviour categorised as regulatory and appropriately dealt with through administrative process. Conduct covered by criminal law may in this way be seen as morally culpable or blameworthy *in a strong sense*, based on a finding of individualised, intentional disregard of societal core values. Such an approach may be described as 'normativist' in its definition of criminal, by elevating the ethically wrong mindset of the individual over the consequences of social action.

In this way an unfulfilled intention to kill is regarded as criminal,[34] whereas an unforeseen and unpredictable killing is unlikely to qualify as a criminal act. Regulatory law, on the other hand, is often concerned with serious harm or injury as an outcome, but in situations where the causal trail leading to such harm may be complex and uncertain – a mixture of externality and multiple participation, as well as internal choice and decision. This is the basis for the classical distinction between *mala in se* and *mala prohibita*. However, this clear line of argument becomes muddled when the distinction is related to the choice of sanctions as, for example, when the *Bundesverfasssungsgericht* in its *Lisbon* ruling referred to a violation so grievous and unacceptable as to require punishment. This slippage of argument then confuses strong ethical condemnation with penality, suggesting that a punitive sanction is a necessary indication of the latter. But as a method and as a sanction, punishment is not restricted to the domain of criminal law or reserved to that which is the subject of strong ethical censure, but may be used in a range of social contexts (for example, in the family or the workplace as well as in relation to legal rule-breaking) – a small financial penalty may be as much a punishment and penal in its social role as a term of life imprisonment.[35]

Two main lines of argument should then be emphasised. First, resort to a penal sanction does not imply that the conduct thereby dealt with is necessarily highly culpable in a moral sense. The penal method is pervasive, across a range of social contexts as an expression of disapproval but its impact in punitive terms may range through a spectrum, from a simple 'telling off' at one extreme to something as devastating as capital punishment or life imprisonment at the other end of the scale. Logically, then, a penal sanction could be employed equally in two distinct normative domains, such as the criminal and the administrative. Secondly, a high quantum of resulting harm or damage does not imply that the acts leading to that outcome are highly culpable in a moral sense. This will be the case particularly if the causal route to the harm is morally ambivalent in that it involves a significant element of external cause, the participation of several actors, and an element of non-human agency, so shifting the location of action from criminal law's comfortable basis in methodological individualism. To take again the convenient example of a competition infringement – such activity may be deconstructed, not so much as a simple interpersonal interaction between two human actors, but as an interaction of external market forces and human decision-making, and comprising a dispersed network of actions involving a number of human and corporate actors; in other words, a phenomenon within which a clean identification of moral blameworthiness is much more uncertain. In such a context, a qualitatively different normative approach, such as non-criminal law or administrative liability and penality, may provide a more appropriate response to the harmful outcome.

---

[34] Provided that there is evidence to locate that intention within a sufficiently proximate attempt to commit the homicide.

[35] See the argument presented by Harding and Ireland, qualifying the approach used by HLA Hart in his distinction between standard and non-standard cases of punishment: C Harding and RW Ireland, *Punishment: Rhetoric, Rule, and Practice* (London, Routledge, 1989) especially at 21–23.

The issue of agency should also be stressed in this context. Not infrequently, the defending party in instances of administrative offending will be a corporate actor, and empirically that may then result in uncertainty regarding the appropriate attribution of moral culpability in relation to the structure of corporate action and the psychology of a corporate 'mind'. Again, this is not so much a problem of applying typical criminal law sanctions to corporate persons, since they may be feasible enough with some resort to analogy and effort of imagination.[36] Rather, it is the problem of allocating responsibility when the corporate actor is different in kind from the human individual and there may be both practical and theoretical difficulty in disentangling the interaction of human and non-human action in the corporate context.

In this way, moral condemnation in a strong sense, depending not on the nature of the sanction which may be employed but on the *normative quality* of that condemnation, taking into account the nature of the act in question, how it comes about and its agency, may be put forward as a convincing basis for the legal boundary between the criminal and the administrative domains.

Explaining and Understanding Preferences: The Case of Serious Competition Infringements

Some of the foregoing discussion may be usefully brought together by focusing finally on a typical contemporary case, that of the serious competition infringement, as particularly exemplified by the 'hard core' cartel violation (price fixing, market sharing, output limitation and bid rigging), and its appropriate location as a criminal or administrative offence.

The EU Commission, in its 2011 Communication on Criminal Policy referred to above, encourages the use of 'criminalisation impact studies' in considering the appropriate resort to criminal law or alternative processes of legal control. Such impact studies would range through a number of considerations of advantage and disadvantage, from the more practical issues of resources and cost through to more philosophical arguments of criminal jurisprudence.[37] In relation to much regulatory offending, and competition infringements as a particular example, it would be useful to apply such an impact study approach to some of the basic characteristics of such activity, and consider the relative balance between mode of conduct and harmful outcome, the subjects of legal control, and enforcement confidence.

---

[36] It may be argued that the 'no soul to damn, no body to kick' argument has been overplayed in relation to corporate actors. Many legal systems have comfortably developed measures such as corporate probation, adverse publicity or 'shaming', or structural orders against companies having something of a penal quality.

[37] See C Harding, 'Hard Core Cartel Conduct as Crime: The Justification for Criminalisation' (2012) 3 *New Journal of European Criminal Law* 138 for an attempt to sketch out the broad lines of such an impact study in relation to the criminalisation of involvement in business cartels.

Conduct and Outcome

The criminalisation of involvement in anti-competitive business activity, particularly of the kind described as hard core cartel activity, has come to the forefront of the agenda in a number of jurisdictions over the last 20 years.[38] However, the basis for such criminalisation remains a matter for debate and some uncertainty.[39] At one end of the spectrum of argument there is the American position that the case for criminalisation, accepted at a much earlier historical point in the US Sherman Act of 1890, is manifest and unarguable. At the other end of the spectrum, a number of jurisdictions, especially in Europe, have considered the case in recent years and decided not to criminalise, usually preferring to continue the established approach of dealing with the matter by means of administrative offences and sanctions and dealing for the most part with corporate offenders.[40] This area of policy debate, therefore, provides a good testing ground for argument feeding into a choice between criminal and administrative penality.

As stated above, the rationale for criminalisation of cartel conduct is not easily extrapolated from a survey across jurisdictions. Certainly, there is now a well-established consensus that the economic impact of cartel activity is of such an injurious character to both markets and consumers as to justify strong legal control. However, this argument would appear to be largely motivated by concerns regarding deterrent effect and the operation of leniency programmes as a means of gaining evidence as much as if not more than retributive considerations.[41] It is much less clear to what extent criminalisation has proceeded upon and found its rationale in the nature of cartel conduct itself – issues such as the mindset and motivations of the cartelists, and the way in which cartels are set up and operated, generally what may be thought of as conduct rather than outcome factors. To the extent that strong legal control in the form of criminalisation is based on the fact of adverse market effects (a matter of outcome), with less emphasis on the normative question of the way in which the latter have been brought about, then the case

---

[38] For a useful critical overview of this development, see C Beaton-Wells and A Ezrachi (eds), *Criminalising Cartels: Critical Studies of an International Regulatory Movement* (Oxford, Hart Publishing, 2011).

[39] See Harding, 'Hard Core Cartel Conduct as Crime', above n 37.

[40] For example, Finland, Luxembourg, Sweden and Switzerland, and partial criminalisation or decriminalisation in Austria and Germany, reserving criminal prosecution for cases involving bid-rigging cartels. For more detailed discussion of some of these developments, see KJ Cseres, MP Schinkel and FOW Vogelaar (eds), *Criminalization of Competition Law Enforcement* (Cheltenham, Edward Elgar, 2006) especially, C Vollmer, 'Experience with Criminal Law Sanctions for Competition Law Infringements in Germany' (ch 14); P Lewisch, 'Enforcement of Antitrust Law: the Way from Criminal Individual Punishment to Semi-penal Sanctions in Austria' (ch 16); P Kalbfleisch, 'Criminal Competition Law Sanctions in the Netherlands' (ch 18). See also, for a critical account of a move towards criminalisation, V Brisimi and M Ioannidou, 'Criminalizing Cartels in Greece: A Tale of Hasty Developments and Shaky Grounds' (2011) 34 *World Competition* 157.

[41] See some of the contributions to Beaton-Wells and Ezrachi, *Criminalising Cartels*, above n 38. Note also some of the research into public perceptions of cartel offending, eg A Stephan, 'Survey of Public Attitudes to Price-fixing and Cartel Enforcement' (2008) 5 *Competition Law Review* 123.

for criminalisation, following the argument presented in the above section, would seem less convincing, and the case for administrative penalty more so.

The Limits of Methodological Individualism

This may be especially so in so far as companies, rather than individuals, are the target of legal control in the context of cartel infringements. As noted already, while criminal law remains largely rooted in methodological individualism, it is less easy to impute a criminal state of mind to a corporate actor as distinct from human individuals, and this again may explain an instinctive preference for administrative penalty in this context. One approach to resolving this debate may be to disaggregate corporate and human involvement in relation to competition matters by saying that companies act on markets, while individuals working for or representing companies operate on a more specific level of human interactions and the latter may be more appropriately cast as a matter of criminal responsibility by judging their human and personal conduct in the matter. Put quite simply: judge the companies on the basis of the outcomes of their actions on the market, without probing what was in their 'minds', and judge the individuals according to what was in their minds when they facilitated the cartel activity. It may then be said that an infringement of Article 101 of the TFEU, which may lead to a non-criminal law fine imposed on a company, is an administrative violation based on a concerted practice which *affects* trade between Member States and need only be shown to have an anti-competitive *effect*. On the other hand, an offence committed by an individual under the original version of section 188 of the Enterprise Act required a *dishonest* agreement to engage in one of the listed anti-competitive strategies, such as price-fixing.

This is the approach (whether or not it was conceived and planned in such terms) which is at present found under UK law (as mentioned above under Definition and Vocabulary), where companies can be dealt with by means of civil penalties under the Competition Act 1998 and individuals can be subject to criminal sanctions under the Enterprise Act 2002. In this way, criminal sanctions are more clearly located in the realm of *mens rea* while administrative penalties can be used more appropriately to deal with harmful outcomes, however they may come about. Indeed, this distribution of legal enforcement does reflect the existing practice in a significant number of European jurisdictions, evidencing a preference to deal with competition and cartel infringements by imposing administrative sanctions on corporate actors. In a number of European national legal systems it is common, at the time of writing, to find significant fines being imposed on companies, while criminal sanctions in relation to individuals may not be an option or are used only rarely.[42]

---

[42] The UK would provide a good example: so far there have been no criminal sanctions applied following a contested trial (see also the discussion below).

Enforcement Confidence: Catching Sheep is Best Left to Shepherds[43]

There is a further important point underlying what appears to be an emergent reluctance in some legal systems to move from administrative to criminal offences and sanctions in the context of competition infringements. In so far as new criminal law enforcement may be handed to specialised agencies dealing with competition matters, there may be a natural hesitation about taking on a significantly different enforcement role. Officials dealing with competition matters are unlikely to be expert in or familiar with criminal law and will no doubt also be aware of the higher level of resources necessary for purposes of bringing criminal cases. From the perspective of competition authorities, criminal law enforcement may appear as uncharted territory and perhaps a daunting prospect.[44] Such a view would only be reinforced by observation of the UK Office of Fair Trading's recent experience of grappling with criminal cases (the failed prosecution of British Airways executives in relation to the Fuel Surcharges cartel in 2011).[45] In this way, any reservations about criminalisation at the legislative level (is there a convincing justification?) may be supplemented by a more pragmatic reluctance at the level of enforcement (can it be managed?).

Certainly then, criminalisation debates and the use of impact studies in relation to such debates need to consider the possible alternative strategies of legal control, and in the context of 'regulatory' offending, such as competition violations, the possible resort to administrative offences and sanctions may appear increasingly as a convincing and viable alternative.

Conclusion

Just as the EC/EU has been very active in developing the concept of the administrative offence and sanction in relation to competition infringements, the EU is now entering the arena of policy debate regarding the content of an emergent system of EU criminal law. The Commission's Communication of September 2011, 'Towards an EU Criminal Policy',[46] does address in a direct way the need to choose carefully between criminal law and administrative procedures, the view of criminal law as *ultima ratio*, and the need to consider carefully the use of the dif-

---

[43] This expression is borrowed from the musical soundtrack by Michael Nyman for the film *The Draughtsman's Contract* (1982, dir Peter Greenaway).

[44] This view certainly emerges from informal conversation with competition authority officials from a number of jurisdictions.

[45] For an account of this, see J Joshua, 'DOA: Can the UK Cartel Offence be Resuscitated?' in C Beaton-Wells and A Ezrachi (eds), *Criminalising Cartels: Critical Studies of an International Regulatory Movement* (Oxford, Hart Publishing, 2011).

[46] Commission, above n 22.

ferent regimes in relation to different kinds of actor, human individual and cor-porate. The supranational steer on this subject is therefore becoming increasingly significant. Nevertheless, the European Courts have for some time engaged in a formative and influential discussion of issues of legal protection arising under the different kinds of repressive regime, in effect providing a judicial, *ex post facto* modelling of the 'criminal' and 'administrative' domains. Now that the other EU institutions look set to engage in further pre-legislative and legislative debate on the scope of criminal law and the need to consider alternative regimes of regula-tion, the substance of this discussion will gain in significance, and the suprana-tional provenance of this discourse will need increasingly to be borne in mind.

However, a clearer sense of the boundary and interrelation between the two types of process still needs to be thought through more fully. The discussion here has sought to clarify the lines of this quest, first by uncovering an important ten-sion between decriminalisation and due process values and objectives, but then advocating a clearer separation of the normative process of culpability from the process of selecting sanctions and a resort to penalisation. An appreciation of the wider and more pervasive role of penal sanctions, coupled with a normative dis-tinction between 'offences of conduct' and 'offences of outcome', can be used to articulate a more cogent rationale for the criminal and administrative domains while also, adopting Langbein's vocabulary from some time ago, serving to 'reha-bilitate the criminal sanction'.[47] Thereby, it may also prove easier to address those due process concerns by accommodating the case for a different kind of due pro-cess model in the domain of the non-criminal law procedures.

By way of final comment it may be said more generally that, in exploring the interface of the criminal and the administrative in contemporary systems of legal control, this discussion has brought together and sought to reconcile some appar-ently diverse and conflicting argument in the fields of criminal jurisprudence, economic regulation and basic rights protection. By setting the subject of admin-istrative offences and sanctions in the context of decriminalisation policy and of the European expression of the *ultima ratio* principle, the argument put forward here has sought to reassert the strong normative role of criminal law by emphasis-ing its function in dealing with conduct rather than outcomes. At the same time, by uncoupling what may be seen as an exclusive relationship between criminal law and penal sanctions, both the appropriate boundary between the criminal and the administrative, and due process concerns regarding the latter, may be clarified and addressed. It would appear that the administrative model is alive and kicking and likely to remain so, in which case its value, appeal and dynamic need to be understood more clearly and fully, especially in the common law world. In that case, the moral and strategic lesson regarding the criminal/administrative inter-face, would seem to be that chasing sheep is best left to shepherds who understand what kind of flock they are shepherding.

---

[47] Langbein, 'Controlling Prosecutorial Discretion in Germany', above n 13.

10

Cartel Enforcement: A Product of Globalisation

MICHAEL O'KANE

Introduction

It is in the arena of trade, commerce and business that globalisation has arguably had its greatest impact. From the earliest times, international trade was the force that brought nations and peoples together, settled our now most populous and prosperous cities, moulded government policies and drove increasing innovation in the manufacturing sector. The end of the Cold War, the creation of the EU and the increased installation of capitalist economic theory around the world have created an environment for governments to take further steps to limit barriers to trade and enhance competition.

As a consequence of these developments, global policing of anticompetitive practices has become increasingly homogenous amongst the developed nations over the last 20 years. Driven largely by the success of the United States model, many countries have introduced leniency programmes to encourage companies to confess to cartel conduct in return for immunity or a reduced penalty, whilst at the same time enhancing their enforcement capability by increasing fines and creating criminal liability.

History has demonstrated that cartel activity is most prevalent at times of economic volatility, so as many nations struggle to deal with the aftermath of the greatest economic downturn since the Great Depression, global cartel enforcement will remain a key enforcement priority for many years to come. This short paper examines the history of global cartel enforcement as a product of the increasing globalisation of commercial activity.

The United States

US Historical Enforcement

The Sherman Act 1890 was the first effectively enforced Federal statute targeted at cartels and monopolies, and today still forms the basis for most antitrust litigation by the US federal government. In the latter part of the nineteenth century, the US economy entered a period of rapid consolidation, with trusts or holding companies created to combine all the businesses in a particular industry, whether sugar, tobacco, steel or rail. These trusts became vast enterprises, wielding huge economic power, dominating their industries, and controlling supply and production. The Sherman Act was introduced to support the agricultural heartland of the US against the combined and coordinated freight pricing power of the railroads.[1]

The Clayton Antitrust Act 1914 and Federal Trade Commission Act 1914 reinforced and supplemented the Sherman Act so it became an 'integral part of the economic instruction of the United States'.[2] This progress was hindered by the Great Depression, during which antitrust enforcement was temporarily suspended, thereby allowing some US companies to engage openly in cartel conduct.[3] Although the Sherman Act contained reference to trade with foreign nations, it was the eventual victory in World War II that gave the US sufficient control and leverage in Germany and Japan to export legislation combating cartels to those jurisdictions.[4]

Federal criminal enforcement of antitrust laws in the US is the primary responsibility of the Antitrust Division of the US Department of Justice (ATD). During the first 50 years following the passing of the Sherman Act, imprisonment was relatively rare in comparison with the number of criminal prosecutions. Incarceration was imposed in only 24 out of 252 cases,[5] with the maximum one-year term being imposed only twice.[6]

The pattern of imprisonment remained inconsistent until the mid-1990s, with 201 incarcerations during the period 1980 to 1984, but only 29 between 1990 and 1993. A similarly inconsistent approach was taken with antitrust enforcement against US companies. The first fine was imposed 13 years after the Sherman Act

---

[1] M Furse, *Competition Law of the EC and UK*, 6th edn (Oxford, Oxford University Press, 2008) 3.

[2] JK Galbraith, *A History of Economics* (Harmondsworth, Penguin, 1987) 162.

[3] JK Smith, 'National Goals, Industry Structure and Corporate Strategies: Chemical Cartels between the Wars' in A Kudo and T Hara (eds), *International Cartels in Business History* (Tokyo, University of Tokyo, 1992).

[4] MC Levenstein and VY Suslow, 'International Cartels' in WD Collins (ed), *Issues in Competition Law and Policy* (Chicago, American Bar Association, Antitrust Section, 2008).

[5] LC Gallo, KG Dau-Schmidt, LL Craycraft and CJ Parker, 'Criminal Penalties under the Sherman Act: A Study of Law and Economics' (1994) 16 *Research in Law and Economics* 25, 39.

[6] ibid.

came into force, with fines up until the late 1950s representing only a small fraction of the company's capital.[7] Until the 1990s, given the limitations of international cooperation in criminal investigations, the ATD concentrated on local or national cartels.

Such limitations were highlighted in the 1994 prosecution of the General Electric Company (GEC) and the De Beers diamond mining company for alleged price-fixing in the industrial diamond market. The case collapsed with a central feature in the failure of the prosecution being the inability of the ATD to obtain and present foreign evidence, causing the then Assistant Attorney General to complain that

> with the sole exception of Canada, cooperation in the antitrust area today extends principally to providing copies of documents that are already publicly available . . . effective antitrust enforcement cannot be implemented solely, or even principally, on public information.[8]

Changes in international cooperation over the next decade eventually led to De Beers receiving a $10 million fine for its conduct.[9]

US Leniency Programme

The ATD introduced a Corporate Leniency Program in 1978. Unlike the leniency programmes of today, the 1978 programme did not reward the whistle-blowing company with automatic immunity. Immunity was left to the discretion of the ATD and, as a result, there was on average one application per year. The programme was revised in August 1993 to encourage more companies and individuals to rely on it.[10] Amnesty was made automatic as long as an investigation had not begun, and might still be available even if it had. Immunity from prosecution was extended to all cooperating officers, directors and employees and is the policy applied by the ATD today. As a direct consequence, the average number of leniency applications rose to 35 per year throughout the 1990s, leading to the revised regime being described as the 'most effective generator of international cartel cases' and 'unquestionably the greatest investigative tool available to anti-cartel enforcers'.[11]

---

[7] LC Gallo, KG Dau-Schmidt, LL Craycraft and CJ Parker, 'Criminal Penalties under the Sherman Act', above n 5, 42.

[8] AK Bingman, 'Change and Continuity in Antitrust Enforcement' (speech at Fordham Law School, New York City, 21 October 1993). See also, D Frantz, 'GE Wins in Diamond Price Case' *New York Times* (New York, 6 December 1994).

[9] A Rayner, 'Price-fixing Fine Reopens Door to US for De Beers' *The Times* (London, 14 July 2004).

[10] US Department of Justice, 'Corporate Leniency Program' (US Department of Justice, 10 August 1993) available at www.usdoj.gov/atr/public/guidelines/0091.htm.

[11] US Department of Justice, 'Status Report: An Overview of Recent Developments in the Antitrust Division's Criminal Enforcement Program' (US Department of Justice, 10 January 2005) available at www.justice.gov/atr/public/speeches/207226.htm.

Under the revised programme that still operates today, leniency will be granted to a corporation reporting illegal activity before an investigation has begun, if the following six conditions are met:

1. at the time the corporation comes forward to report the illegal activity, the ATD has not received information about the illegal activity being reported from any other source;
2. the corporation, upon its discovery of the illegal activity being reported, took prompt and effective action to terminate its part in the activity;
3. the corporation reports the wrongdoing with candour and completeness and provides full, continuing and complete cooperation to the ATD throughout the investigation;
4. the confession of wrongdoing is truly a corporate act, as opposed to isolated confessions of individual executives or officials;
5. where possible, the corporation makes restitution to injured parties; and
6. the corporation did not coerce another party to participate in the illegal activity and clearly was not the leader in, or originator of, the activity.

Leniency can also be granted to an individual reporting illegal antitrust activity before an investigation has begun, if the following three conditions are met:

1. at the time the individual comes forward to report the illegal activity, the ATD has not received information about the illegal activity being reported from any other source;
2. the individual reports the wrongdoing with candour and completeness and provides full, continuing and complete cooperation to the ATD throughout the investigation; and
3. the individual did not coerce another party to participate in the illegal activity and clearly was not the leader in, or originator of, the activity.

Criminal prosecutions are typically limited to intentional and clear violations such as when competitors fix prices or rig bids. The Sherman Act imposes criminal penalties of up to $100 million for a corporation and $1 million for an individual, together with up to 10 years imprisonment. Under federal law, the maximum fine may be increased to twice the amount the conspirators gained from the illegal acts or twice the money lost by the victims of the crime, if either of those amounts is over $100 million.

Enforcement

The ATD has continued to build on its track record of aggressive enforcement. In 2010, it filed 60 cases against 63 people and 21 companies. Whereas in the 1990s, 37 per cent of convicted individuals received a custodial sentence, by 2010 this had risen to almost 80 per cent. The length of prison sentences has also increased over this period, with 30 months being the recorded average prison term in 2010, compared to eight months in the 1990s. One key trend has been the increase in targeting of foreign nationals. In the 1990s, 'no jail' sentences were recommended for foreign nationals in order to secure convictions. This is no longer an option, with the average sentence for a foreign national now 10 months, a threefold increase from the first half of the 2000s.

In 2011, the ATD concluded its investigation into the air cargo fuel surcharge cartel and rendered almost $2 billion in fines, including more than $150 million in 2011 from Nippon Airways, Singapore Airlines and Taiwan's China Airlines. Although 2012 saw a drop in the number of cases brought, the ATD obtained a record $1.1 billion in criminal fines from 14 corporations.[12] This figure included the second-largest criminal fine in the history of the US antitrust enforcement programme, and a $470 million fine against Yazaki Corporation as part of the ATD's investigations into the automotive parts market.[13]

The United Kingdom

UK Historical Enforcement

In the UK, there have been provisions in place to protect market prices dating back to Roman times.[14] There is reference in the Doomsday Book of 1086 to commodity price enhancement, known in different forms as 'forestalling', 'ingrossing' and 'regrating', as a crime. In England, there are examples of historical anti-competitive legislation, such as the 1349 Statute of Labourers, aimed at preventing overcharging by merchants. The first recorded case concerning restraint of trade was that of John Dyer, who in 1414 failed to enforce a restrictive covenant preventing a competitor from practising dyeing in the same locality.[15] In considering such potentially anti-competitive arrangements, the balancing of the interests of those seeking to restrain trade against those of the wider public seems to have been a very early and vital judicial theme.[16] This development of the common law was enhanced with the repeal in the eighteenth and nineteenth centuries of many of the earlier statutes.[17]

---

[12] US Department of Justice, 'Criminal Enforcement Fine and Jail Charts through Fiscal Year 2013' (US Department of Justice, 2012) available at www.justice.gov/atr/public/criminal/264101.html.
[13] The case was settled by way of a plea agreement: *United States v Yazaki Corporation* (US District Court, Eastern District of Michigan, 12 January 2012) available at www.justice.gov/atr/cases/f280600/280689.pdf.
[14] R Piotrowski, *Cartels and Trusts* (London, George Allen & Unwin, 1933).
[15] *Dyer's Case* (1414) YB 2 H, 5 fol 5b.
[16] *Rogers v Parrey* (1613) 80 ER 1012 and the House of Lords in *Nordenfelt v Maxim Nordenfelt Guns and Ammunition Co Ltd* [1894] AC 535.
[17] The Repeal of Certain Laws Act 1772 13 geo 3, c71; The Forestalling, Regrating etc Act 1844 (7 & 8 vict c 24).

The development of more modern case law arguably commenced with the decision in *Jones v North*.[18] In this case, four quarry owners agreed that North, the defendant, would not tender for a contract with the Birmingham Corporation for the supply of stone, and that two of the remaining three would tender at prices above that of the plaintiff, so that the plaintiff would secure the contract. In return, the plaintiff agreed to purchase a fair share of the stone needed in the contract from his three co-conspirators. The defendant then defaulted on this agreement and won the contract at an assumed lower price than that tendered by the plaintiff. The plaintiff sought an injunction preventing the supply of stone by the defendant and when the defendant sought to have this action struck out on the grounds that it was 'against public policy . . . compelling the Corporation under the fiction of a public competition, to accept tenders not representing the real market price for the commodity', the Vice Chancellor, Sir James Bacon stated that:

> The case is very plain, and, on one side at least [the plaintiff's] a very honest one . . . It is perfectly lawful for the owners of three quarries to agree that they will sell their commodities upon terms suitable to themselves, and which they approve of. There is nothing illegal in the owners of commodities agreeing that they will sell as between themselves at a certain price, leaving one of them to make any other profit that he can.[19]

It is hard on any viewing to consider the actions of the plaintiff in this case as honest, given that he was a party to an agreement to make misrepresentative 'cover' bids to the Corporation, which would have caused it to pay a higher price, at public expense, for the stone. Far from being considered criminal in any way it seemed that such practices had the express approval of the Courts.

The first major legislative intervention targeting agreements in restraint of trade was the Restrictive Practices (Inquiry and Control) Act 1948. This Act created the Monopolies Commission, which was required to report on whether certain cartel agreements operated in the public interest. If improper agreements were found, then the Secretary of State had the power to declare them unlawful. Importantly, a breach of such a declaration could not give rise to any criminal liability.[20]

The first leaning towards criminalisation of cartel conduct came in the 1955 Cairns Committee Report, which concluded that as cartels tended to operate against the public interest, participation in a cartel should be a criminal offence.[21] The recommendation was rejected by the government in favour of civil sanction, with the prevailing view reflected in the Restrictive Trade Practices Act 1956. The Act required public registration of cartel agreements and referred agreements that they presumed were not in the public interest to the courts. The Act expressly excluded criminal sanction for any party to such an agreement.

---

[18] *Jones v North* (1875) LR 19 Eq 426.
[19] ibid.
[20] Restrictive Practices (Inquiry and Control) Act 1948, s 11.
[21] Cairns Committee, *Collective Discrimination: a Report on Exclusive Dealing, Collective Boycotts, Aggregated Rebates and Other Discriminatory Trade Practices* (Cm 9504, 1955), paras 242–47.

The Restrictive Trade Practices Act 1968 was designed to exempt certain cartel agreements from the registration process if they were of substantial importance to the UK economy, or if they could be shown to be for the promotion of greater efficiency or productive capacity.

In 1973, as a result of the UK joining the European Community, parties to cartel agreements contrary to Article 81 of the EC Treaty[22] became subject to potential civil penalties enforced by the European Commission. UK domestic legislation was then consolidated in the Restrictive Trade Practices Act 1976, with the broad registration scheme of earlier legislation for cartel agreements remaining intact. There was considerable criticism of these legislative attempts as they allowed the competition authorities no mechanism for reviewing the actual effects of agreements on competition. The Conservative government of Margaret Thatcher proposed new legislation designed to take the actual effects into account[23] but little progress was made on the proposed legislative reform.

Finally, the Competition Act 1998 came into force in 2000. This Act repealed much of the previous legislation. In its place, the Act introduced a regime under which the national competition authority enjoyed stronger powers of investigation, and the power to impose significant fines in a manner largely modelled on Article 81 of the EC Treaty.[24]

The harmonisation of the UK's approach with that of the European Community is enshrined in section 60 of the 1998 Act. This section places a dual responsibility on the UK authorities and courts to:

1. ensure that decisions are not inconsistent with the principles of the EC Treaty and the European Court;[25] and
2. have regard to any relevant decision or statement of the European Commission.[26]

Enforcement and Penalties

The Competition Act 1998 provides the Competition and Markets Authority (CMA) and the Financial Conduct Authority (FCA), which took over the duties of the Office of Fair Trading in April 2014, with extensive investigative powers, as well as creating a number of statutory criminal offences for failing to comply with requirements imposed by CMA, for destroying or falsifying documents, and for giving false or misleading information.[27] Undertakings that are found to be parties to any such agreement and do not benefit from an exemption can be fined up

---

[22] Now Art 101 TEFU.

[23] Department of Trade and Industry, *Opening Markets: New Policy on Restrictive Trade Practices* (White Paper, Cm 727, 1989).

[24] See above note 22.

[25] Competition Act 1998, s 59(1), referring to both the European Court of Justice and the Court of First Instance.

[26] Competition Act 1998, s 60(3).

[27] Competition Act 1998, ss 42 and 43.

to a maximum of 10 per cent of the turnover of that undertaking in the UK in the last three years.[28]

The CMA's current approach to fines in civil enforcement cases is set out in its 'Guidance as to the Appropriate Amount of a Penalty' a revised version of which was published in September 2012.[29] Under the revised Guidance, businesses who are found to have engaged in particularly serious anti-competitive conduct can be fined up to 30 per cent of their annual turnover.

The CMA also operates a leniency system akin to that found in other advanced competition regimes. The Guidance[30], updated by the OFT in July 2013 and adopted in full by the CMA, offers full immunity from prosecution for both the applicant and its past and present employees where that entity is the first to approach the OFT with evidence of anti-competitive conduct. Immunity or a reduced penalty is also available for subsequently cooperating parties.

Criminal Penalties

Shortly after the introduction of the Competition Act 1998, the UK government began considering the need to criminalise cartel conduct. There was a clear view by the UK government that civil penalties did not provide sufficient deterrence from the most egregious forms of hard-core anticompetitive conduct.[31] In coming to this conclusion, the UK government looked to the specific experience of the US, noting that:

> American and other experience suggests that there is a strong case for introducing criminal penalties, including custodial sentences for those who engage in cartels alongside a new civil sanction of director's disqualification.[32]

Cartel conduct was criminalised by the Enterprise Act 2002, as amended in 2013. The provisions work alongside the Competition Act 1998 and various pieces of consumer legislation, largely replacing the Fair Trading Act 1973. The Act provides that a person is guilty of an offence where he agrees with another person to:

— fix prices of a product or service;
— limit or prevent supply of a product or service;
— limit or prevent production of a product;
— divide supply of a product or service between customers; or
— bid-rig.

---

[28] Competition Act 1998, s 36 and the Competition Act 1998 (Determination of Turnover for Penalties) Order 2000 (SI 2000/209).

[29] OFT, 'OFT's Guidance as to the Appropriate Amount of a Penalty' (OFT, September 2012) available at www.oft.gov.uk/shared_oft/business_leaflets/ca98_guidelines/oft423.pdf.

[30] OFT, 'Applications for Leniency and No-action in Cartel Cases: a Supplementary Consultation on OFT Guidance' (London, OFT, October 2012) available at www.gov.uk/government/uploads/system/uploads/attachment_data/file/284417/OFT1495.pdf.

[31] Department of Trade and Industry and HM Treasury, 'Productivity in the UK: Enterprise and Regulatory Challenge' (2001).

[32] OFT, 'Proposed Criminalisation of Cartels in the UK' (London, OFT, November 2001) para 1.1.

Prosecuted by either the CMA or the Serious Fraud Office, the offence carries a maximum penalty of five years imprisonment and an unlimited fine.[33] Unlike in the US, only individuals can be liable for this offence, with the civil enforcement regime reserved for companies.[34] Since April 2014, the dishonesty requirement that had originally formed part of the offence was removed. The reforms also include new defences, where there was no intention to conceal the offence from customers or the CMA, or where reasonable steps were taken to disclose the activity to legal advisers for the purpose of obtaining advice about the nature of the arrangements before their implementation.

Recent UK Criminal Cases

The first successful prosecution under the Enterprise Act 2002 came in relation to anti-competitive conduct in the marine hose market. Three UK executives pleaded guilty in a UK court in accordance with an innovative plea agreement reached with both the ATD and OFT with sentences of 20 to 30 months being imposed.

In April 2010, the first contested prosecution of the UK cartel offence came to court when four current and former British Airways executives were prosecuted as a result of information provided by Virgin Atlantic Airways under the leniency policy of the OFT.[35] This information alleged participation by certain British Airways and Virgin employees in anti-competitive discussions to fix passenger fuel surcharges. On the basis of the information provided, Virgin obtained full (civil and criminal) immunity under the OFT's leniency programme.

During the early stages of the trial, a combination of disclosure problems and related difficulties led to the OFT offering no evidence against any of the defendants. This failure has cast doubt over the OFT's ability to launch and successfully prosecute individuals for a criminal cartel offence.[36] A subsequent review criticised the OFT's handling of the case stating that 'the case was very complex and the OFT found itself on a considerable learning curve. With the benefit of hindsight it was not ideal as the OFT's first contested criminal case'.[37]

The recent 2014 prosecution of Peter Nigel Snee marks the first successful prosecution of an individual for cartel activity in the UK since *Marine Hoses*. Mr Snee pleaded guilty to offences under s.188 of the Enterprise Act 2002 for his part in a cartel of galvanized steel tanks for water storage. The case of Mr Snee represents the first prosecution to be brought by the OFT/CMA since the collapse of the British Airways case, and seems to signify the CMA's newfound resolve to deal

---

[33] Enterprise Act 2002, s 190(1).

[34] Department of Trade and Industry, 'Consultation on Modernisation' (London, DTI, April 2003), para 10.16.

[35] *R v George* [2010] EWCA Crim 1148.

[36] See, eg A Osborne, 'OFT Attacked for Monumental Incompetence in Collapsed BA Price-fixing Trial' *The Telegraph* (London, 11 May 2010); D Milmo, 'OFT under Fire over Whistleblowers after BA Price-fixing Trial Fails' *The Guardian* (London, 11 May 2010).

[37] OFT, 'Project Condor Board Review' (London, OFT, 2010) 2.

with cartel matters through criminal sanction. As of July 2014, two others have been charged with related cartel activity,[38] and the CMA is also conducting parallel civil investigations into the cartel.

The EU Approach to Cartel Enforcement

EU Historical Approach

The long-standing approach of the US to anti-cartel enforcement via the criminal law has not been reflected in most of Europe until recent years, as the predominant European approach had been to view cartels as primarily an economic issue, best regulated via administrative measures.[39] In the interwar period, many cartels in Europe existed without prohibition and were blatantly open and even encouraged by governments. One example is the steel cartel agreement signed by the major producers in Belgium, France, Germany and Luxembourg in 1926.[40]

This attitude to cartels gradually changed in Europe in the aftermath of World War II, and formed part of the growing political will for economic, industrial and governmental harmonisation. This movement led to the creation of the European Community, the most important legal instrument of which is the Treaty on the Functioning of the European Union (TFEU).[41] Article 101 is aimed at cartel-type agreements, prohibiting any which 'may affect trade between Member States and which have as their object or effect the prevention, restriction or distortion of competition within the common market'.[42]

As well as the TFEU, European competition law also derives from secondary legislation in the form of regulations, decisions and directives.[43] In respect of cartel-type agreements, the most relevant of these are decisions made by the European Commission against undertakings. These decisions, albeit binding upon those to whom they are addressed,[44] are subject to the review of the General Court and European Court of Justice.

In the early stages of European competition law development, there was no uniformity of opinion amongst Members of the Community as to whether the

---

[38] Competition Markets Authority, 'Press Release – Two men face charges in ongoing criminal cartel investigation', (11 July 2014) available at https://www.gov.uk/government/news/two-men-face-charges-in-ongoing-criminal-cartel-investigation.

[39] C Harding and J Joshua, *Regulating Cartels in Europe: A Study of Legal Control of Corporate Delinquency* (Oxford, Oxford University Press, 2003).

[40] This established the Entente Internationale de l'Acier (EIA). See G Stocking and M Watkins, *Cartels in Action* (New York, Twentieth Century Fund, 1946) 171.

[41] Formerly known as the European Community (EC) Treaty. The EC Treaty was adopted by the original Member States in 1957 and is now acceded to by all 27 Member States. It was renamed as the TFEU following substantial amendment by the Lisbon Treaty in 2007.

[42] Art 101(1) TFEU, (formerly Art 81 EC Treaty).

[43] Art 288 TFEU, (formerly Art 249 EC Treaty).

[44] ibid.

competition provisions should be enforced by the National Competition Authorities or a centralised Community institution; a compromise system was subsequently introduced under Regulation 17/62.[45] Despite this, the European Court has held, from an early stage, that Article 101(1) is directly applicable before national courts.[46]

In respect of enforcement, this initial European system was much stronger than that in the UK at the time. The Commission had the power to conduct investigations into cartel agreements, including by dawn raids on business premises in the Member States, and to impose financial penalties of up to 10 per cent of an undertaking's annual worldwide turnover.

Leniency

The system in the EU lacked the certainty and transparency that was so successful in the US, and improvements have been gradual, with revisions in 2002 and 2006. For example, under the 1996 Commission Notice on the non-imposition or reduction of fines in cartel cases,[47] the Commission had discretion to fix the reduction of the fine from between 75 per cent and 100 per cent and the applicant had to wait until the end of the investigation in order to discover if their application for immunity had been successful.

The basic principle set out in the latest Commission Notice is that any party to an illegal cartel agreement may benefit from partial or total reduction in any fine by cooperation with the Commission to the required extent.[48]

In 2006, new Guidelines on setting fines were introduced stating that the basic amount of the fine is a proportion of 30 per cent of the value of sales, with horizontal price-fixing and market-sharing agreements at the higher end of that scale. In addition, in such instances, a further sum of between 15 per cent and 25 per cent would be added in order to act as a deterrent.[49] For those undertakings not benefitting from full immunity, significant fine reductions are available to those in a position to provide the Commission with evidence that offers 'added value with respect to the evidence already in the Commission's possession'.[50]

The most significant reform to date has been Regulation 1/2003 (the Modernisation Regulation) which arose from the accession of ten new Member States in 2004. Designed to make the Treaty work more effectively amongst a much larger group of nations, the major changes it brought were the abolition of the system of notification of agreements to the European Commission and the

---

[45] [1962] OJ 204/62 (Special Edition 1959–62) 57.
[46] Case 127/73 *BRT v SABAM* [1974] ECR 51. This case concerned Art 101's predecessor under the EC Treaty, Art 81.
[47] [1996] OJ C207, 4–6.
[48] Commission notice on immunity from fines and reduction of fines in cartel cases [2006] OJ C298, para 17.
[49] ibid at para 25.
[50] ibid at para 24.

empowerment of the National Competition Authorities and national courts to apply what was Article 81[51] within a European Competition Network.[52] For the Commission, the decentralisation of many of its powers in relation to certain aspects of competition law was intended to allow it to focus more of its resources on hard-core cartel conduct. As a result, the number of cartel cases dealt with rapidly increased, as did the fines that were imposed.

EU Civil Enforcement

Under Article 101, the European Commission may impose civil fines against undertakings. The penalties for a violation of Article 101/102 can be up to 10 per cent of the annual turnover of the corporation involved. There is no fine at the EU level for individuals, although they are in place in many Member States along with criminal sanctions, particularly for bid-rigging. The new Commission Guidelines on the method for setting fines imposed pursuant to Article 23(2)(a) of Regulation (EC) No 1/2003 has resulted in a tendency for higher fines in the last decade.

In 2000 to 2004, the European Commission imposed fines totalling almost €2.5 billion across 30 separate cases. However, in 2005 to 2009, the amount of fines imposed in 33 separate cases was €9.7 billion. In 2008, the EU imposed its highest ever cartel fines of more than €1.3 billion on four companies for fixing the price of glass used in cars. The four companies were said to control 90 per cent of the glass used in European cars, a market worth €2 billion in 2003. EU Competition Commissioner Neelie Kroes said that the fines announced for Asahi, Pilkington, Saint-Gobain and Soliver were high because European industry had to 'learn the lessons the hard way'.[53] In December 2012, the Commission imposed a record fine of some €1.47 billion against established electronics firms including Samsung, Philips and Panasonic, in relation to two distinct cartels centred on the production of cathode ray tubes used in colour television sets and computer monitors.[54] In December 2013, the EC fined six banks a record €1.71 billion for their participation in a benchmark interest rate rigging cartel.[55]

The EU also supports parental liability, and the Commission's policy is to hold a group parent automatically responsible for cartel violations committed by its wholly owned subsidiaries. The parent's awareness of the violation is irrelevant, and the acid test is whether they constitute one and the same undertaking. Central to this idea legal is a presumption, devised and refined by the courts, that a parent exercises 'decisive influence' over subsidiaries in which it has a direct or indirect

---

[51] Now Art 101 TFEU.

[52] Art 1 of Reg 1/2003.

[53] N Kroes (EU Competition Commissioner), 'Car Glass Cartel' (Opening remarks at press conference, Brussels, 12 November 2008).

[54] FY Chee, 'EU Imposes Record $1.9 Billion Cartel Fine on Philips, Five Others' *Reuters* (5 December 2012).

[55] European Commission Press Release, 'Antitrust: Commission fines banks € 1.71 billion for participating in cartels in the interest rate derivatives industry' *European Commission* (4 December 2013).

100 per cent holding. This policy helps to ensure better enforceability by pursuing a potentially more stable and adequately liquid entity, and helps increase the deterrent effect, as fines are increased if the parent company is financially strong. For example, Akzo Nobel was fined €40.6 million for certain Akzo Nobel subsidiaries that directly participated in a cartel that fixed prices for heat stabilisers.

EU Leniency Programme

The EU leniency programme and its cartel settlement procedure, established in 2006 and 2008 respectively, seem to follow the US lead. The EU programme covers 'undertakings' as opposed to individuals. Companies that provide information about a cartel in which they participated might receive full or partial immunity from fines, as the leniency policy offers companies involved in a cartel which self-report and hand over evidence either total immunity from fines or a reduction of fines which the Commission would have otherwise imposed on them.

In order to obtain total immunity, a company must be the first to inform the Commission of an undetected cartel by providing sufficient information to allow the Commission to launch an investigation. If the Commission is already in possession of enough information to launch an investigation, or an investigation has already begun, the company must provide evidence that enables the Commission to prove the cartel infringement. The company must also cooperate fully with the Commission throughout its procedure.

Companies which do not qualify for immunity may benefit from a reduction of fines if they provide evidence that represents 'significant added value' to the Commission and have terminated their participation in the cartel. This evidence must reinforce the Commission's ability to prove the infringement. The first company to meet these conditions is granted a 30 to 50 per cent reduction, the second a 20 to 30 per cent reduction and subsequent companies up to a 20 per cent reduction.

Global Criminalisation

Participation in cartels has become a criminal offence in numerous countries over the past 10 years. The pressure to criminalise has come from competition networks, fellow trade partners, and a recognition that the threat of criminal prosecution and potential imprisonment is a greater deterrent than fines and other economic repercussions. As part of the global trend to stiffen penalties for cartel conduct, individuals now face potential imprisonment for cartel activity in Australia, Brazil, Canada, Iceland, Indonesia, Israel, Japan, Korea, Norway, Russia, Thailand and Zambia, as well as the US and a majority of EU Member

States. Many members of the Organisation for Economic Co-operation and Development (OECD) (in addition to the US and EU Member States) have stiffened penalties for engaging in cartel activities, which vary in their civil/administrative or criminal law nature.

For example, Canada's Competition Act 1985 was amended in 2010 to substantially change the criminal enforcement regime for cartel offences by raising the maximum penalty from five to 14 years in prison and the maximum fine from CAD\$10 to \$25 million. Australia recently increased maximum fines to the greater of AUS\$10 million or three times the value of the benefit derived from the cartel. Where value cannot be determined, the law provides for a fine of 10 per cent of annual turnover. In 2009, the Australian Parliament criminalised various cartel offences, providing for up to 10 years in prison and a fine of AUS\$220,000.

In the summer of 2009, Japan increased criminal sanctions for cartel offences, changing its maximum prison sentence for cartel conduct or bid rigging from three to five years. Japan also raised the statute of limitations from three to five years, and restructured its new leniency programme.[56] In 2005, Korea also revised its competition laws to increase fines against cartel participants from a maximum of 5 per cent to a maximum of 10 per cent of sales in related goods or services, and to facilitate use of a leniency programme.[57] Most recently, in 2011, Mexico's Congress approved a new law introducing criminal sanctions of up to 10 years in prison for collusion, as well as the ability to engage in surprise inspections, known as 'dawn raids'.[58] Even Switzerland, 'where cartels were "endemic" to the economy', has recently passed a law providing for administrative fines of up to 10 per cent of a firm's total combined revenue for the preceding three years.[59]

The German anti-cartel legislation is enshrined in the Act against Restrictions of Competition (in force since 2005), but it does not include criminal liability. Since 2007, the relevant cartel provisions of the German Act against Restraints of Competition (ARC) have been aligned with Article 101 TFEU. The Federal Cartel Office recently announced that cartel enforcement will continue to be on top of its agenda and the number of cartel enforcement units will be increased from two to three in order to reflect their policy.

New Zealand is looking to use Australian legislation as a model on which to build a criminal cartel regime as 'there are some concerns regarding whether or not our current civil penalty regime is effective at deterring cartel behaviour'.[60] Draft legislation, the Commerce (Cartels and Other Matters) Amendment Bill is

---

[56] GR Spratling and DJ Arp, 'International Cartel Investigations: Evaluating Options and Managing Risk in Multi-Jurisdictional Criminal Antitrust Investigations' (2010) 1788 PLI/Corp *Antitrust Counseling & Compliance* 229, 252, 309–10.

[57] ibid at 243, 311.

[58] 'Monopolies in Mexico: Compete – or Else' *The Economist* (London, 7 May 2011) 41 available at www.economist.com/node/18651364.

[59] JA Chavez, 'International Cartel Enforcement: Creating a Fear of Detection' in *Corporate Law and Practice Handbook*, 1811 Practising Law Institute's Corporate Law and Practice Course Handbook Series (Practising Law Institute, 2010) 943.

[60] Ministry of Economic Development, 'Cartel Criminalisation Discussion Paper' (Wellington, January 2010).

currently being considered by the New Zealand Parliament, and is awaiting second reading.

According to a report from the New Zealand Ministry of Economic Development there is a lack of detection of domestic cartels in New Zealand and most international cartels operating in New Zealand are discovered as a result of enforcement activity or leniency applications in other jurisdictions. Following the introduction of criminal penalties in Australia, the Australian Competition and Consumer Commission (ACCC) has reported an increase in leniency applications, and notably a number of their key trade and investment partners, including Australia, Canada, Japan, Korea, the UK, and the US, have criminalised cartel activity, and it therefore makes sense for them to follow.

Although many nations can now impose prison sentences, they have been used sparingly. In the UK, the *Marine Hose* case has been the only case in which prison sentences have been imposed since the commencement of the Enterprise Act 2002. In Ireland, between October 2005 and December 2009, the Irish Competition Authority secured 33 criminal convictions for cartel participants, although no-one has been imprisoned. In Canada, from 1998 to 2008, 11 individuals were convicted of cartel offences, of these, nine received fines and two received suspended prison sentences. In Japan, prison sentences were imposed on five executives in 2007 for bid rigging.

International Cooperation

There are several tools that can aid both formal and informal cooperation. Formal cooperation encompasses bilateral agreements, mutual legal assistance treaties, extradition treaties, and provision in national laws. Mutual Legal Assistance Treaties (MLATs) are bilateral treaties creating reciprocal international obligations between the signatories, allowing efficient cooperation between law enforcement agencies in criminal and regulatory matters. Although they are not specific to competition investigations, they can allow the signatories to request assistance including the sharing of confidential information. However, MLATs are typically confined to criminal matters, and require the offence to be a crime in at least the requesting country's jurisdiction and may also require dual criminality – that is, that during all material times the relevant conduct consisted of a criminal offence in both the requesting and responding jurisdictions. They therefore often go unused in cartel investigations due to the absence of a criminal offence in the requested state.

Extradition treaties suffer from the same impediment as MLATs, in that dual criminality is always required in order for it to be invoked. For example, in the case of *Norris v USA*,[61] Norris, a British national, became the first overseas executive whose extradition was ordered by the US in a cartel case. This was over-

---

[61] *Norris v Government of the United States of America and Others* [2008] UKHL 16.

turned by the UK House of Lords on the basis that his alleged offence of price fixing was not a criminal offence in the UK at the time it was committed, and it was therefore not an extraditable offence.

Informal cooperation refers to all cooperations between competition authorities that do not include sharing confidential information. This tool is more commonly used and includes conferences, bilateral meetings and other exchanges which spread both expertise and mutual understanding. This is often facilitated by participation in competition networks, which encourages 'pick up the phone' relationships and gives each authority a better understanding of the other competition authorities with which they work. Although informal cooperation can be a useful tool, it cannot provide for confidential information sharing, and the investigation of cartels can be greatly constrained by the inability of competition authorities to formally exchange confidential information.

Confidential information sharing under domestic law is often prohibited, as is the use of an authority's compulsory gathering powers on the behalf of a foreign competition authority. There is a common fear that shared confidential information is more likely to reach the public domain, particularly in nations where private actions can be taken in order to be awarded damages. Often, nations find that this restriction can lead to a collapse in investigations, for example Turkey found that the absence of a formal cooperation mechanism with the European Commission limited its ability to investigate cartels. In one case, Turkey investigated suspected cartel activity in the gas-insulated switchgear industry, which appeared to operate outside Turkey but affected the Turkish market. The same suspected cartel was also being investigated by the European Commission, but despite Turkey's request for cooperation, the Commission was unable to exchange any confidential information, due to the absence of any formal instrument authorising the exchange. This significantly reduced Turkey's ability to investigate the cartel.[62]

There are several benefits to international cooperation. Having a large number of prosecuting jurisdictions can increase the exposure of cartel participants to greater penalties, which in turn acts as an enhanced deterrent. International cooperation is also crucial to controlling cartels where the companies involved have foreign offices. Coordination of surprise investigations can greatly assist authorities in avoiding potential evidence destruction, tampering or removal.

Competition networks greatly assist cooperation. The US has worked through a number of these organisations in order to aid international cooperation efforts. It has worked particularly through the OECD, the International Competition Network (ICN), bilateral treaties, and informal relations, and the EU, along with its Member States, have increasingly played an important role.

The OECD sponsors meetings of national authorities and publishes policy outlines and booklets designed to encourage certain enforcement tools such as the use of leniency programmes. It also compiles information on sanctions and lists

---

[62] OECD, 'Hard Core Cartels: Third report on the Implementation of the 1998 Council Recommendation' (2005) 32 available at www.oecd.org/competition/cartelsandanti-competitive agreements/35863307.pdf.

of best practices. The OECD's 2005 report on the implementation of their 1998 Recommendation stated that 'co-operation among authorities in investigations of cartels has reached unprecedented levels'.[63]

The ICN was created in 2001, thanks to instigation from the US, following the creation of 14 new competition authorities. It is an organisation of competition law officials and non-governmental advisers. There are around 134 national anti-trust agencies that are members of the ICN and it has become the epicentre of building consensus around competition law practices, helping to facilitate the coordination of international regulatory efforts.

Conclusion

The emergence of leniency programmes has been a major development in anti-cartel enforcement, and the general provision of immunity for the first cartelist to admit liability has created a 'race to confess'.[64] Leniency has rapidly become the more attractive option due to the increase in sanctions, particularly criminalisa-tion. Around 60 nations now have leniency programmes, and the emergence of these programmes has been described as 'the single most significant development in cartel enforcement'.[65]

However, increase in criminal enforcement across the world may discourage cartelists from making a leniency application, for fear of facing charges in other nations where their activity has transnational effects. EU Member States, in par-ticular, risk discouraging leniency applications to the European Commission, because corporate immunity granted at Community level does not automatically protect individuals from criminal prosecution in national courts.

Although there has been a significant change in attitudes, sanctions and enforcement in the area of cartels, there are still areas that need to be improved in order to achieve global homogenisation. There are also still a multitude of dis-crepancies between national legislation and leniency programmes which leads to restrictions in cooperation. As the OECD recognised:

> If an OECD 'definition' sought to capture the differences among Members' laws, it would be less a definition than a compendium, and if it did not capture those differ-ences it would have no operational utility and could be misleading.[66]

---

[63] ibid at 8.

[64] ICN Cartel Working Group, 'Anti-cartel Enforcement Manual' (2009) 2 available at www.interna-tionalcompetitionnetwork.org/uploads/library/doc341.pdf.

[65] Scott D Hammond (Deputy Assistant Attorney General for Criminal Enforcement, Antitrust Division, US Department of Justice), 'The Evolution of Criminal Antitrust Enforcement Over the Last Two Decades' (Address to the 24th National Institute on White Collar Crime, Miami, Florida, 25 February 2010) available at www.justice.gov/atr/public/speeches/255515.htm.

[66] OECD, 'Hard Core Cartels' (2000) 45 available at www.oecd.org/competition/cartelsandanti-competitiveagreements/2752129.pdf.

The US is still firmly at the forefront of anti-cartel enforcement and is continuing to push for greater cooperation and stiffer penalties across the globe.[67] The world-wide financial downturn is likely to keep a clear enforcement focus on cartel conduct. However, the lack of consensus in attitudes and enforcement priorities remains a major impediment to effective comprehensive global cartel enforcement.

---

[67] Speech by Gregory J Werden, Scott D Hammond and Belinda A Barnett, Antitrust Division, US Department of Justice, 'Deterrence and Detection of Cartels: Using all the Tools and Sanctions' (26th Annual National Institute on White Collar Crime, Miami, Florida, March 2012) available at www. justice.gov/atr/public/speeches/283738.pdf.

INDEX

abstracted empiricism 70, 73
administrative detention *see under* Greece,
    immigration detention
administrative law *see* criminal and
    administrative law in market regulation
administrative offences
    (*Ordnungswidrigkeiten*) 203, 204
Afghanistan 61
Amsterdam Treaty 138–9
anomie theory 73
anti trust laws *see* cartel enforcement
anti-social behaviour, harmonising instruments
    see under EU criminal law
Arar, Mahar, case 104
armed conflicts 61–3
asylum recognition *see under* Greece,
    immigration detention
Australia, cartel enforcement 232
Austro-Hungarian Empire 54

Balkans 61, 62
Bank of Credit and Commerce International
    (BCCI) 58
Bayley, D 78, 88
Beccaria, C 33, 66
Birmingham Six 93, 146–7
Blair, Police Chief 98
Blood diamonds 61
Bolivia 60
Bonger, W 69
Borgen (TV drama) 135
Bosnia 62
Bout, Victor 58
Braidwood, Commissioner 95
bribery 137, 167–8
Brodeur, JP 87, 104

Cameron, David 145, 167–8
Canada
    cartel enforcement 232, 233
    penal system influences 33
Canadian Charter of Rights and Freedoms 89,
    101
Canadian police legitimacy
    aggressive policing against most
        vulnerable 96–7
    background 87–8
    exclusionary rules 89
    external responses 93–7
    global security 103–7

internal responses 107–11
key issues/conclusion 87
Mr Big operations 100–3
police perjury 90–2, 93–6
police scrutiny 88–90
priority area designations 97–100
shared strategies 88
see also political economy, and policing; Royal
    Canadian Mounted Police (RCMP);
    Toronto police
Canadian Security Intelligence Service
    (CSIS) 104
Cao, J 27
cartel enforcement
    background/summary 219, 235–6
    confidential information sharing 234
    European Union
        civil enforcement 230–1
        fine-setting Guidelines 229
        historical approach 228–9
        leniency 229–30, 231
        national empowerment 230
    extradition treaties 233–4
    global criminalisation/enforcement 231–3,
        235
    international cooperation 233–5
    leniency programmes 235
    Mutual Legal Assistance Treaties
        (MLATs) 233
    prison sentences 233
    United Kingdom
        criminal cases 227–8
        criminal penalties 226–7
        enforcement/penalties 225–8
        harmonisation with EC 225
        historical enforcement 223–5
        prison sentences 233
    United States
        criminal prosecutions 222
        enforcement record 222–3
        historical enforcement 220–1
        leniency programme 221–2
cartel violation, as criminal or administrative
    offence
    conduct/outcome issues 214–15
    enforcement confidence 216
    key issues 213
    methodological individualism 215
    transnational organised crime 47
Casablanca (film) 93

Index

Cavadino, M 29, 31, 32, 33, 40
China 59
Chrysi Avyi 117
Clarke, R 72
Cold War 45, 58, 153, 219
Colquhoun, P 67–8
Columbia 60, 61, 62
common law heritage *see under* EU criminal law
Competition Act 1998 (UK) 215, 225, 226
competition infringements *see* cartel violation, as criminal or administrative offence
Competition and Markets Authority (CMA) 225–6
concepts of crime
    categories 7–8
    collective consciousness 20–1
    common social environment 18–19
    communal bonds, types of 17
    expansive concepts 18
    human rights and dignity, protection of 18, 21–2
    ICL *see* international criminal law (ICL)
    mala in se/mala prohibita distinction 8–9
    moral balance, upsetting of 18
    networks of community 17–22, 22–3
    punishment focus 11
    regulatory authority 10
    relativity of 22–3
    social harm concept 17–18
    social theory perspective 9–13, 19–21, 23
    state law focus 8–9
    transnational economic networks 19–20
    transnationalisation of crime 11–13, 20–2, 23
    two-fields approach 7, 9, 11
confidential information sharing 234
Convention against Drug Trafficking 1988 154–6
Convention against Illicit Trafficking in Narcotic Drugs and Psychotropic Substances(1988) (Vienna Convention) 154–6
Convention against Transnational Organised Crime (2000) (Palermo Convention) 154, 156, 157–64
    Community competence 159–62
    human trafficking/smuggling 163–4
    joint position 158–9
    organised crime 162–3
    subsequent law 162–4
    three Protocols 157–8
Corpus Juris project *see under* EU criminal law
corruption *see* UN Convention against Corruption (2003)
Council of Europe 169–73
    Community/Union *acquis* 172–3
    ratifications 169–70
    Union autonomy 170–1
Council of Europe Convention on the Prevention of Terrorism 170–1

counter-terrorism *see* terrorism
Court of Justice of the EU 141, 142
Crawford, A 27
crime concepts *see* concepts of crime
crime, global governance and EU
    assertiveness in negotiations 198
    background/summary 153–4, 197–8
    corruption *see* UN Convention against Corruption (2003)
    global administrative law *see* UN Security Council
    money-laundering 137, 154–6, 198
    multilateral treaties 154
    Palermo Convention *see* Convention against Transnational Organised Crime (2000)
    regional multilateral treaties *see* Council of Europe
    soft law initiatives *see* Financial Action Task Force (FATF)
    see also EU criminal law
Crime Reduction Programme 73
criminal and administrative law in market regulation
    agency issue 213
    background 199–200
    categories 200–3
    Continental/common law distinction 202–3
    criminal law as special domain 205–6
    criminal/administrative distinction 204, 208–9, 217
        penal sanctions 211–13
    graduated classification 203–4
    key issues/conclusions 200, 216–17
    legal control typology 202
    legal/political cultures 203–8
    origins of administrative offending 204–5
    as prohibitive rules 201–2
    rights and justice, distinction and questions 208–10
    serious competition infringements *see* cartel violation, as criminal or administrative offence
    ultima ratio as European concept 206–8, 210, 217
    see also EU criminal law
criminal law *see* EU criminal law
currency counterfeiting 56
cybercrime 12, 137

Daily Express 145
Daily Telegraph 143, 144
Dale, Christopher 101
Davis, Commissioner EF 93
defendant safeguards *see under* EU criminal law
Dendias, Nikos 119, 128–9
Denning, Lord 93
Derrida, J 131
Dershowitz, AM 91–2

Dignan, J 29, 31, 32, 33, 40
Doomsday Book 223
drug trade, illicit 49–50, 53, 60, 61, 62
Drug Trafficking, Convention against 1988
    154–6
drug-dealing 137
Durkheim, É 10–11, 19–21, 23, 68
Dyer, John 223
Dziekanski, R 95

Ehrlich, Eugen 22
electronic borders 57
electronic payment frauds 137–8
Enterprise Act 2002 (UK) 215, 226, 227
environmental protection 14
Ericson, R 97
EU budget, frauds against 138
EU cartel enforcement *see under* cartel
    enforcement
EU criminal law
    anti-social behaviour, harmonising
        instruments 137–8
    common law heritage 149–50
    Corpus Juris project 139–40, 143
    criminal procedures, common rules/
        principles 138
    defendant safeguards 146–7
    Framework Decisions 138–9, 140–1
    information systems, joint access 137
    institutions 136
    joint help systems 136–7
    legal instruments 136–8
    mutual recognition instruments 137
    Napoleonic system fears 149, 150–1
    post-Lisbon legal basis 141–6
    pre-Lisbon legal basis 138–41
    pre-trial detention 148–9
    qualified majority voting 141–2
    Roadmap measures 141, 144, 148
    UK areas of influence/attitudes to 139–41,
        146–9, 149–51
    US Federal criminal law, difference 135–6
    see also crime, global governance and EU;
        criminal and administrative law in
        market regulation
euro counterfeiting 138
Eurojust 136
European Anti-Fraud Office (OLAF) 136
European Arrest Warrant 140, 145
European Investigation Order 143
European Public Prosecutor 140
European Union, cartel enforcement *see under*
    cartel enforcement
Europol (European Police office) 136
extradition treaties 233–4

Financial Action Task Force (FATF) 50, 153,
    156, 173–9

influence on EU law 176–9
    Money Laundering Directives 156, 174–5
    MONEYVAL 174, 178–9
    normative output 173–4
    revised Recommendations 176–8
    Special Recommendations 174
    Special Recommendations on terrorist
        finance 175–6
Finland, penal system influences 33
First/Third Pillar decisions/measures 138–9,
    142, 145, 154
Foucault, M 72

G20 summit (Toronto) 103–7
Galliford, Catherine 108
Garland, D 29
Geneva Conventions 1949 14
Germany
    cartel enforcement 232
    Ordnungswidrigkeiten (administrative
        offences) 203, 204–5
Glenny, M 46
governance indicators, comparisons
    compliance indicators 38–9
    criminal justice management 37
    de-politicisation effect 38
    incommensurable indicators 39–40
    indicator growth, reasons for 40–1
    performative role 38, 41
    practical consequences intended 37–8
    ranking indicators 36–7
    reasons for 37–8, 41–2
    uneven quality 38–9
    see also social indicators, comparisons
Greece, immigration detention
    administrative detention 114, 119–21, 133
    asylum recognition 116–17, 124
    background 113–14
    border guard stations 120, 122
    conditions 121–5
    conventional prisons 121
    criticisms of state 125–7
    detention centres 120–1
    domestic/international criticism 117–18
    excessive use/harsh conditions 114
    food provision 123
    funding issues 129–30
    irregular migration 116–19
    key issues 114–16
    less eligibility/more eligibility principle
        115–16
    philoxenia discourse 115, 118, 120, 125,
        131–4
    police treatment/racist violence 117, 118–19
    rhetorical techniques 115, 118
    socio-political functions 115–16
    state reactions to criticisms 127–30
    temporary detention 120

Greece, immigration detention *cont.*
  violent treatment 124
Gross National Product (GNP)
      comparisons 40–1
Groth, Annette 126

Herring v US 92
Home Office 72, 73
Hough, M 72, 73
Hulsman, LHC 7, 9
human capabilities comparison 40–1
human rights discourse 18, 21–2

illicit drug trade 49–50, 53, 60, 61, 62
illicit globalisation
  armed conflicts 61–2
  background 45–6, 63
  border issues 52–5
  countries with market niches 48
  criminal finance 50–1
  dimensions 47–9
  economic flows 47–8
  electronic borders 57
  imperial collapses 54
  key issues/conclusions 46–7
  measurement 49–52
  misguided accounts 63–4
  policing agenda 48–9
  popular accounts 51–2
  power asymmetries 48
  state power 52–3
  state-promoted 57–60
  state/non-state actors 59
  technology role 55–7
  transnational organised crime 47
  violence 60–1
intellectual property protection 59–60
international community 17
International Competition Network (ICN) 234,
    235
International Crime Victimisation Surveys 33
International Criminal Court 14
international criminal law (ICL)
  addressing individuals 14
  central ideas of crime 14
  cultural legitimation 15–16
  elements 14–15
  human rights discourse 18, 21–2
  punishability 16
  states' guarantee of legitimacy 13, 15
  transnational cooperation 16–17
International Narcotics Control Strategy
    Report 49
Ireland, cartel enforcement 233
Italy
  covert police operations 35–6
  penal system influences 32–3
  punitiveness 31–2

Jones, T 34–5
Jones v North 224

Kadi I 186–92
Kadi II 191–7
Kansas City Preventive Patrol Experiment 72
Kerry, Senator J 46
Khan, Abdul Qadeer 58
Kirkhope, Timothy 126
Kleinig, J 92
Korea, cartel enforcement 232
Kosovo 62

Langbein, JH 205, 217
Larsen, N 28
Lombroso, C 33

Maastricht Treaty 138, 154
McBarnet, D 92
McNamara, JD 91
Macpherson Report 76
Maguire, M 73
Mahar Arar case 104
Manning, P 93–4
market regulation *see* criminal and
    administrative law in market regulation
Marx, K 68–9
Marxist perspectives 72, 77
Matthews, J 46
Merry, SE 37, 38, 41
Merton, R 68, 73
Mexico 54–5, 62
  cartel enforcement 232
migrant smuggling 60–1
Mills, CW 70
Money Laundering Directives 156, 174–5,
    176–7
money-laundering 137, 154–6
MONEYVAL (Committee of Experts on the
    Evaluation of Anti-Money Laundering
    Measures) 174, 178–9
Moore, TE 102
moral individualism 21
Mr Big operations 100–3
mugging, study of 78–9
Mutual Legal Assistance Treaties (MLATs) 233

Naim, M 51
Napoleonic system fears *see under* EU criminal
    law
Napoleonic Wars 58
Narcotic Drugs and Psychotropic
    Substances(1988), Vienna Convention
    against Illicit Trafficking in (1988)
    154–6
Nazi networks 22–3
neo-liberalism 40–1
  policing studies 70, 72, 76, 77

political economy, and policing 84–5
Neocleous, M 71
Netherlands, criminal justice policy
    influences 33
New Public Management model 72
new wars *see* armed conflicts
New Zealand, cartel enforcement 232–3
Newburn, T 34–5
Nolan, JL 35
nuclear smuggling 58
Nuremburg trials 15
Nussbaum, MC 40

OLAF (European Anti-Fraud Office) 136
Ontario Provincial Police (OPP) 110
Ordnungswidrigkeiten (administrative
    offences) 203, 204–5
Organisation for Economic Co-operation and
    Development (OECD) 173–4
    cartel enforcement 234–5
Ottomon Empire 54

Pakes, F 28–9
Pakistan 58
Palermo Convention *see* Convention against
    Transnational Organised Crime (2000)
Paulson, Commissioner R 94, 108, 110
penal systems comparison
    global/local variables, interplay 32–3
    neoliberalism 29–30
    prison rates 30 *Table*
people trafficking 143–4
people-smuggling 137
philoxenia discourse *see under* Greece,
    immigration detention
Picton investigation 95–6
Pillar decisions/measures 138–9, 142, 145, 154
piracy, international 19, 56
Police and Criminal Evidence Act 1985
    (PACE) 147
policing studies
    background 70–1
    core findings 73–6
    crime control effectiveness 75–6
    crime rates, fall 77–8
    cultural/situational factors 74
    discretion exercising 74
    labelling perspective 71–2
    marginality 73
    neoliberalism 70, 72, 76, 77, 84–5
    new police science 71
    non-law enforcement/crime control
        role 73–4
    official research 72
    policy-orientation 76–7
    and political economy *see* political economy,
        and policing
    powerless, targeting 75

radical/Marxist perspectives 72, 77
    symbolic impacts 76
    theoretical approach 70–1
    see also Canadian police legitimacy; Royal
        Canadian Mounted Police (RCMP);
        Toronto police
political economy
    and criminology
        eclipse by criminology 68
        elements 78–9
        pre-criminologies 66–8
        punishment and control 69–70
        science of policing 67–8
        sociological criminology 68–9
    definition 66
    and policing
        crime control effectiveness 82
        features of practice 81–2
        fluctuating legitimation 80
        governance 83
        key issues 65, 79–80
        low visibility 80–1
        media representations 82
        modern specialist state police 80
        neo-liberalism 84–5
        and policing studies *see* policing studies
        regulation 82–3
        tranformation thesis 83–4
        see also Canadian police legitimacy; Royal
            Canadian Mounted Police (RCMP);
            Toronto police
Politics of the Police, The (Reiner) 79
public official, embezzlement/misappropriation
    by 168
punitiveness 29–31, 32

qualified majority voting *see under* EU criminal
    law

refugee protection indicators 38–9
Reiman, J 18
Restrictive Practices Acts (UK) 224–5
Reuter, P 49
Ross, J 35–6
Royal Canadian Mounted Police (RCMP)
    approval rates 87
    dissension within policing ranks 107–8
    G20 summit 104, 106
    gender-based harassment complaints 108–9
    internal responses 107–11
    Mahar Arar case 104
    police perjury 94–6
    post-traumatic stress 109–10
    public relations disasters 89–90
    see also Canadian police legitimacy;
        political economy, and policing; Toronto
        police

Saskatchewan 203
Schengen Convention 138–9
Schengen Information System 137
science of policing *see under* political economy,
    and criminology, development
Scotland, criminal justice policy comparison 33
Sen, A 40
serious competition infringements *see* cartel
    violation, as criminal or administrative
    offence
Sheptychi, J 27
Sherman Act 220–1
Slater, Samuel 59
Smandych, R 28
Snee, Peter Nigel 227–8
social indicators, comparisons
    case studies 34–6
    classificatory/descriptive integration 27
    differences in approach 27–9
    different criteria 35–6
    global/local variables, interplay 32–3
    and globalisation 26–9
    governance *see* governance indicators,
        comparisons
    indicators for comparison 29
    influence 43
    international media access 33
    key issues/conclusions 25–6, 41–3
    location consequences 26–7
    moments of comparison 26, 36–7, 41
    others using comparisons 32–6
    people/organisations/entities involved 34
    punitiveness 29–31, 32
    see also penal systems comparison
Soviet Union 54
state monopoly of legitimate violence 10
Statute of Labourers 1349 223
Stephen Lawrence murder 76
Sterling, C 45–6
Stone, D 50–1
Stuntz, WJ 7, 9, 11
Sundby, SE 90
Swedish Framework Decision 136–7
Switzerland, cartel enforcement 232

terrorism 12, 13, 137
    Council of Europe Convention on the
        Prevention of Terrorism 170–1
    counter-terrorism resolutions (UN Security
        Council) 180–3
terrorist finance, FATF Special
    Recommendations on terrorist
    finance 175–6
Thomson, J 52
Thoumi, F 50
Tochilovsky, Vladimir 127
Toronto Anti-Violence Intervention Strategy
    (TAVIS) 97–8

Toronto police 93
    G20 summit 103–7
    priority area designations 97–100
    see also Canadian police legitimacy;
        Royal Canadian Mounted Police
        (RCMP)
transnational organised crime *see under*
    crime, global governance and EU;
    Convention against Transnational
    Organised Crime (2000); illicit
    globalisation
Treaty on the Functioning of the European
    Union (TFEU) 228
Turner, JI 205

ultima ratio as European concept 206–8, 210,
    217
UN Convention against Corruption (2003)
    Commission competence 165
    draft second Common Position 166–7
    draft third Common Position 167
    EU criminal law, comparison 168–9
    scope of misconduct 167–8
    third pillar/criminal law aspects 166
UN Drug Control Program (UNDCP) 50
UN High Commission for Refugees
    (UNHCR) 130
UN Security Council 153
    counter-terrorism resolutions 180–3
    global administrative law 179–81
    implementation by EU 183–6
    Kadi I (EU judicial review) 186–91
    Kadi II (EU judicial review) 191–7
    listing procedures 190–1, 197
Unger, Kyle 102
United Kingdom
    cartel enforcement *see* cartel enforcement
    Coalition Government 142–3
    EU criminal law, areas of influence/attitudes
        to 139–41, 146–9, 149–51
    penal system influences 33, 34–5
United States
    cartel enforcement *see* cartel enforcement
    cartel violation 214
    covert police operations 35–6
    Federal criminal law/EU criminal law,
        difference 135–6
    penal system influences 33
    police perjury 91–2
    post-Revolutionary War 62–3
    punitiveness 31, 39
US Department of Justice, Antitrust Division
    (ATD) 220, 221–3
US–Mexico border 54–5, 62

van Crefeld, Martin 16
Van Maanen, J 97
victim rights 143–4

Vienna Convention against Illicit Trafficking
in Narcotic Drugs and Psychotropic
Substances(1988) 154–6
violence *see under* illicit globalisation

war, as instrument of state 15–16

warfare, humanisation 14
Weber, M 9, 10, 11–12, 19, 20, 39
Williams, P 45
Wilson, JQ 77
Winterdyk, J 27

Lightning Source UK Ltd.
Milton Keynes UK
UKOW05f0803040517
300462UK00005B/96/P